上海市人民政府 国际智库咨询
发展研究中心系列报告 系列报告

SHANGHAI'S BRIDGEHEAD
ROLE IN SERVING THE BELT AND
ROAD
INITIATIVE

上海在"一带一路"建设中的桥头堡作用

2017上海国际智库咨询研究报告

Consultation Report of
Shanghai International Think Tank, 2017

上海市人民政府发展研究中心 编

EDITOR
The Development Research Center
of Shanghai Municipal People's Government

格致出版社 上海人民出版社

主　编	Chief Editor
王德忠	Dezhong Wang

副主编	Subeditor
徐　诤	Zheng Xu
周师迅	Shixun Zhou

编　辑	Editing Team
（按姓氏拼音排列）	（in alphabetical order）
陈　莉	Li Chen
潘春来	Chunlai Pan
沈　英	Ying Shen
谭　旻	Min Tan
许建红	Jianhong Xu
姚　治	Zhi Yao
曾　铮	Zheng Zeng
张明海	Minghai Zhang

论坛现场
Conference Site

论坛现场
Conference Site

上海市人民政府秘书长肖贵玉作开幕致辞

Opening Speech by Guiyu Xiao，Secretary-General of Shanghai Municipal People's Government

上海市人民政府发展研究中心主任王德忠作开幕主持

Opening Ceremony by Dezhong Wang，Director-General of the Development Research Center of Shanghai Municipal Government

埃森哲全球副总裁、大中华区副主席吴琪作主旨发言
Keynote Speech by Qi Wu，Senior Managing Director and Vice Chairman of Accenture Greater China

普华永道中国中区市场主管合伙人、上海首席合伙人黄佳作主旨发言
Keynote Speech by Elton Huang，PwC Central China Markets Leader and PwC Shanghai Senior Partner

中国欧盟商会上海分会总经理琼安娜作主旨发言

Keynote Speech by Ioana Kraft, General Manager of Shanghai Chapter, European Union Chamber of Commerce in China

麦肯锡全球董事，大中华区政府事务与基础设施业务负责人吕文博作主旨发言

Keynote Speech by Katrina Lv, Partner, Leader of Great China Public Sector and Infrastructure Practice, McKinsey & Company

德勤华东区主管合伙人刘明华作主旨发言
Keynote Speech by Minghua（Dora）Liu，Managing Partner of Eastern China，Audit Partner of Shanghai，China，Deloitte

世界银行社会、城市、农村和灾害风险管理全球发展实践局首席城市专家梅柏杰作主旨发言
Keynote Speech by Barjor Mehta，Lead Urban Specialist，Social，Rural，Urban & Resilience Global Practice，World Bank

波士顿咨询公司全球资深董事经理方寅亮作主旨发言

Keynote Speech by Thomas Fang，Senior Principal，Boston Consulting Group（BCG）

野村综研（上海）咨询有限公司副总经理天野宏欣作主旨发言

Keynote Speech by Amano Hiroyasu，Vice President of Nomura Research Institute（NRI）Shanghai Limited

毕马威中国审计合伙人杨洁作主旨发言
Keynote Speech by Tracy Yang，Audit Partner，KPMG China

安永华中区国际税务部总监张顺源作主旨发言
Keynote Speech by Shunyuan Zhang，Partner of Transaction Tax and China Tax Outbound Center，EY

美中贸易全国委员会上海首席代表欧文作主旨发言

Keynote Speech by Owen Haacke，Chief Representative，Shanghai Office，US-China Business Council

高风咨询经理陈英麟作主旨发言

Keynote Speech by Alan Chan，Associate of Gao Feng Advisory Company

波士顿咨询公司全球合伙人兼董事总经理李剑腾作总结发言
Summary Statement by Leo Li，Partner and Managing Director，Boston Consulting Group（BCG）

上海市交通委员会副主任张林作互动讨论
Roundtable Discussion by Lin Zhang，Deputy Director General of Shanghai Municipal Commission of Transportation

上海市科学技术委员会总工程师傅国庆作互动讨论
Roundtable Discussion by Guoqing Fu, Chief Engineer of Shanghai Science and Technology Committee
（STCSM）

上海社科院世界经济研究所所长权衡作互动讨论
Roundtable Discussion by Heng Quan, Director of the Institute of World Economy of Shanghai Academy
of Social Sciences（SASS）

上海市商务委员会副巡视员桑琦作互动讨论
Roundtable Discussion by Qi Sang, Deputy Inspector of Shanghai Municipal Commission of Commerce

上海出入境检验检疫局发展规划处处长赵文斌作互动讨论
Roundtable Discussion by Wenbin Zhao, Director of the Development and Planning Division of
Shanghai Entry-Exit Inspection and Quarantine Bureau

上海市农业委员会经济商务处处长王德第作互动讨论

Roundtable Discussion by Dedi Wang, Director of the Economic and Commercial Division of Shanghai Agricultural Committee

上海市金融办公室金融发展协调处副处长谢善鸿作互动讨论

Roundtable Discussion by Shanhong Xie, Deputy Director of the Development and Coordination Division of Shanghai Financial Services Office

上海市外事办公室政策研究室副处长张宇作互动讨论

Roundtable Discussion by Yu Zhang，Deputy Director of the Policy Research Office of Foreign Affair Office of Shanghai Municipal People's Government

锦江国际集团有限公司高级副总裁陈礼明作互动讨论

Roundtable Discussion by Liming Chen，Senior Vice President of Jin Jiang International（Holdings）Co.，Ltd.

上海电力股份有限公司副总经理夏梅兴作互动讨论

Roundtable Discussion by Meixing Xia, Vice General Manager of Shanghai Electric Power Company Limited

上汽集团国际业务部总经理杨晓东作互动讨论

Roundtable Discussion by Xiaodong Yang, General Manager of the International Business Department, Shanghai Automotive Industry Corporation（SAIC MOTOR）

上港集团战略研究部总经理丁嵩冰作互动讨论

Roundtable Discussion by Songbing Ding，General Manager of the Strategic Research Department，Shanghai International Port（Group）Co.，Ltd.

上海奥威科技开发有限公司董事长华黎作互动讨论

Roundtable Discussion by Li Hua，Chairman of Shanghai Aowei Technology Development Co.，Ltd.

基仕伯中国区总裁桂渐作互动讨论

Roundtable Discussion by Jian Gui，President of GCP Applied Technologies，China

西门子中国副总裁、上海和浙江公司总经理王伟国作互动讨论

Roundtable Discussion by Weiguo Wang，Vice President at Siemens Ltd. China & General Manager of Shanghai and Zhejiang

霍尼韦尔亚太区政府事务总监陈艳作互动讨论
Roundtable Discussion by Elaine Chen, Director of Government Affairs, APAC at Honeywell Corporate

罗兰贝格合伙人兼大中华区副总裁纪纲作互动讨论
Roundtable Discussion by Gang Ji, Partner and Vice President of Roland Berger Greater China

上海发展研究基金会副会长兼秘书长乔依德作互动讨论

Roundtable Discussion by Yide Qiao，Vice Chairman & Secretary General of Shanghai Development Research Foundation

嘉宾合影

Group Photo of Guests

PREFACE

序

上海国际智库高峰论坛发起于 2011 年，至今已举办 7 届。上海市人民政府发展研究中心牵头与知名国际智库共同组成上海国际智库交流中心，并商定每年围绕上海承担的国家战略或者宏观性、前瞻性、全局性重大问题，举行国际智库高峰论坛。几年来，越来越多的国际知名智库主动要求参加高峰论坛，与会国际智库由最初的 7 家核心成员增加到现在的 22 家，历届高峰论坛也受到了国内外专家学者的广泛关注。感谢国际智库和专家学者积极参与，贡献智慧！高峰论坛不仅凝聚了与会人员的广泛共识，也助推了上海国际影响力的不断提升，高峰论坛形成的成果为上海市委、市政府科学决策、民主决策提供了智力支撑，对上海建设卓越的全球城市起到了积极作用。

2017 年第七届上海国际智库高峰论坛的主题为"如何发挥上海在'一带一路'建设中的桥头堡作用"。"一带一路"建设，是习近平总书记深刻思考人类前途命运以及中国和世界发展大势，为促进全球共同繁荣、打造人类命运共同体所提出的宏伟构想和中国方案，是我国扩大对外开放的重大战略举措。把上海自贸试验区建设成为服务国家"一带一路"建设、推动市场主体走出去的桥头堡，是以习近平同志为核心的党中央站在全局高度对上海提出的新要求，有利于进一步提升上海城市综合服务功能，加快构建更高层次的开放型经济新体制，有利于推动形成我国全方位开放、东中西联动发展的新格局，更好地参与全球竞争与合作。

2017 年第七届上海国际智库高峰论坛由上海市人民政府发展研究中心主办，波士顿咨询公司、上海发展研究基金会和上海国际智库交流中心承办。本次高峰论坛吸引了来自世界银行、波士顿咨询公司、麦肯锡、埃森哲、罗兰贝格、普华永道、德勤、毕马威、安永、野村综研、高风咨询、上海美国商会、欧盟上海商会、美中贸易全国委员会、日本贸易振兴机构、印度工业联合会等国际智库，以及上海市政府部门、科研院所、企业、驻沪总领馆和新闻媒体等 200 余名专家学者，就"一带一路"建设发展趋势、企业面临的瓶颈问题和上海如何发挥桥头堡作用等问题，展开了热烈而深入的讨论交流。

在本次高峰论坛上，专家学者提出了许多有见地、有价值的对策建议。不少专家认为，目前"一带一路"建设呈现出深入发展的好势头，参与主体正从以政府部门和国企为主向社会广泛参与转变，推进领域正从单纯商品贸易和产能合作向提升服务、完善服务标准品牌技术和创新等方面拓展，投资贸易正从边境贸易向更大范围、更深层次的投资贸易演进。有专家认为，上海要成为服务"一带一路"建设的桥头堡，需要着重从加强沿线地区经济贸易和科技创新联动发展、加大金融对基础设施建设的支持力度、突破信息壁垒等方面入手，进一步发挥贸易连通枢纽作用，发挥金融中心的服务功能。有专家提出，上海要建设成为市场制度和规则制定的桥头堡、数字化的桥头堡、人才培养和人文交流的桥头堡，成为联动东中西发展、扩大对外开放的新引擎。

把专家建议推介给更多的人、起到更大的作用，是我们编辑出版本书的重要目的。本书生动再现了 2017 年论坛现场的交流盛况，翔实记录了专家学者的精彩观点。我们希望本书的出版能够对研究上海服务国家"一带一路"建设的专家学者有所裨益，从而吸引更多的国内外专家学者共同研究上海更高水平的开放型经济发展，为上海全面建设卓越的全球城市和具有世界影响力的社会主义现代化国际大都市提供决策咨询参考。

（签名）

上海市人民政府发展研究中心主任

Shanghai International Think Tank Summit has been successfully held for 7 consecutive years since it was initiated in 2011, when Development Research Centre of Shanghai Municipal People's Government established the Shanghai International Think Tank Exchange Center with well-known international think tanks and agreed to hold the Summit every year. Summit participants talk about Shanghai's role in national strategies and important issues of strategic, overall and forward-looking significance. The summit has attracted the active participation of an increasingly number of famous international think tanks and attention from domestic and foreign experts and scholars. It currently involves 22 international think tanks, up from 7 core members at the beginning, and we really appreciate the participation and contribution of wisdom of these international think tanks, experts and scholars. It has gathered broad consensus of summit participants and played an important role in increasing Shanghai's global influence, providing intellectual support for the sound and democratic decision making of Shanghai Municipal Party Committee and Government and promoting Shanghai to become a global city of excellence.

2017 Shanghai International Think Tank Summit was themed with "How to Play Shanghai's Bridgehead Role in the Belt and Road Initiative". The Belt and Road Initiative, proposed by Chinese president Xi Jinping who had a deep thinking about the shared future for mankind and a clear view of today's China and the world, represents a great vision and the Chinese solution to promote common prosperity and build a community with a shared future for humanity, as well as one of important strategies to expand China's opening-up. Faced with new requirements from the CPC Central Committee with Comrade Xi Jinping as the core in the new era, Shanghai will endeavor to play its role as a bridgehead in serving the Belt and Road Initiative and encourage more Chinese market entities to go global through taking advantage of China (Shanghai) Pilot Free Trade Zone. It will be conducive to improving Shanghai's comprehensive public service, building an open economic system at a higher level, promoting the synergetic development of the eastern, central and western regions of China and encouraging China to participate in international competition and cooperation.

2017 Shanghai International Think Tank Summit was hosted by Development Research Centre of Shanghai Municipal People's Government, and jointly organized by Boston Consulting Group, Shanghai Development Research Foundation and Shanghai International Think Tank Exchange Center on November 24, 2017. This summit has attracted participants from a variety of international think tanks, including World Bank, Boston Consulting Group, McKinsey & Company, Roland Berger, PwC China, Deloitte, KPMG, Ernst & Young, NRI Solutions Ltd, Gao Feng Advisory, AmCham Shanghai, the European Union Chamber of Commerce in China (Shanghai), Japan External Trade Organization (JETRO) and Confederation of Indian Industry Business Council (CII). More than 200 experts and scholars from various government departments and research institutes in Shanghai, officials of Consulate General of different countries in Shanghai and media representatives participated the summit. Participants have exchanged views on the trend of the development of the Belt and Road Initiative, the bottlenecks encountered by enterprises and how to play Shanghai's bridgehead role.

Experts and scholars have proposed many insightful and valuable suggestions at this summit. Some experts suggested that as the development of the Belt and Road Initiative is maintaining good momentum, the main players are shifting from government departments and state-owned enterprises to the whole of society. More efforts have been made to service-improving, Chinese brand-building and technological innovation than simple merchandise trade and collaborations on productive capacity. Broader investment and trade cooperation of higher standard than cross-border cooperation has been carried out within the framework of the Belt and Road Initiative. Some experts proposed that Shanghai, as a key trading hub and an important financial center, needs to build economic and trade relations with regions and countries along the Belt and Road, promote the synergetic development of technology and innovation, strengthen financial support for infrastructure projects and reduce information barriers with a view to better playing Shanghai's role as a bridgehead for the Belt and Road Initiative. Some experts suggested that Shanghai should endeavor to become a digital bridgehead committed to establishing rules and systems for the market, encouraging talent development and people-to-people communications and becoming a new driver for the synergetic development of the eastern, central and western regions of China and expanding China's opening-up.

The purpose of getting this book edited and published is to bring expert advice to more people and make it play a more important role. This book thoroughly records the ideas of the guests and vividly presents the grand scene of the exchange. We hope that it could benefit people who study and focus on how Shanghai play its bridgehead role in the Belt and Road Initiative, and inspire experts and scholars from home and abroad to explore and study the development of an open economy in Shanghai, as part of efforts to build Shanghai into a global city of excellence and a modern socialist metropolis of great global influence.

Dr. Dezhong Wang

Director General of the SDRC

CONTENTS

目　录

CONFERENCE REVIEW

RESEARCH PAPERS

APPENDIX

POSTSCRIPT

OPENING ADDRESS

开幕致辞

肖贵玉　Guiyu Xiao

上海市人民政府秘书长

Secretary-General of Shanghai Municipal People's Government

"一带一路"建设是我国扩大对外开放的重大战略举措，也是今后一段时期对外开放的工作重点。在各方共同努力下，"一带一路"建设逐渐从理念转化为行动，从愿景转变为现实，目前已展现初步成效。2014年至2016年，我国对"一带一路"沿线出口额达3.1万美元，占同期外贸总额的1/4以上；对沿线国家直接投资近500亿美元，占同期对外直接投资的1/10左右。截至2017年11月17日，中欧班列开行数量已突破3 000列，超过2011年至2016年开行数量的总和。在这个大背景下，上海与沿线国家的经贸合作关系也逐渐紧密，体现在以下方面。一是经贸投资增长迅速。过去三年，上海在"一带一路"沿线国家（地区）投资项目246个，实际投资额达54.9亿美元，年均增长近1.6倍；承接重大工程3 019个，累计合同额达217亿美元，年均增长9.4%；与沿线国家（地区）贸易额突破5 000亿元，占全市比重超过20%。二是上海企业"走出去"步伐加快。一批重点项目在沿线国家（地区）落地生根。比如，上海电气在"一带一路"国家（地区）承接的电站、输配电工程合同金额已达28亿美元；华谊集团在"一带一路"国家（地区）投资累计达到4.19亿美元；上海企业投资建设的印度尼西亚青山产业园被认定为国家级境外经贸合作区，园区及入园企业已完成投资总额超过30亿美元。三是经贸合作伙伴关系不断拓展。上海已与19个沿线国家（地区）建立了经贸合作伙伴关系，上海进出口商会与沿线92家商协会和企业成立了"一带一路"贸易商联盟，为企业搭建了合作平台。四是经贸规模持续增长。2017年1月—8月，上海与"一带一路"沿线国家（地区）贸易额达到4 295亿元人民币，同比增长21%；新签对外承包工程合同额19.3亿美元，占全市的比重已达到67.3%。

　　上海与"一带一路"沿线国家的经贸合作关系，顺应了上海发挥服务"一带一路"建设桥头堡作用的要求，具有非常重要的意义。一方面，桥头堡建设是深入落实国家"一带一路"倡议的重要举措。共建"一带一路"倡议是促进全球和平合作和共同发展的中国方案，也是我国在新形势下参与和引领新型全球化的重大行动。上海作为我国改革开放试验田，应当主动当好我国参与和引领新型全球化的桥头堡，为各省市参与"一带一路"建设发挥桥梁纽带作用。另一方面，桥头堡建设是上海全面深化改革开放、勇当排头兵和先行者的内在要求。当前上海已进入改革开放的更高阶段，主动对接国家"一带一路"建设，有利于进一步提升上海服务全国功能，发展更高层次的开放型经济，更好地参与全球竞争与合作。特别是在资金融通、经贸合作、航运发展等领域，上海更要主动做好服务，当好各省市对接"一带一路"的平台和跳板。

同时，上海打造服务国家"一带一路"建设的桥头堡，也具备良好的基础条件。我们拥有优越地理区位，上海位于海上丝绸之路、沿海运输大通道、长江黄金水道的交汇点，作为"一带一路"重要交汇点和东亚龙头的区位优势无可替代。我们拥有开放透明的制度环境，上海是我国开放度最高的地区，具有与国际接轨的投资、贸易、金融、政府治理制度框架。上海是上合组织发祥地和亚信峰会、APEC承办地。在沪跨国公司地区总部和功能性机构达1 321家，居全国第一。我们拥有较强的综合服务能力，上海正加快建设"四个中心"、科创中心和国际文化大都市，2016年末上海证券交易所股票市值居全球第四，上海港已与"一带一路"沿线128个主要港口建立密切联系，集装箱吞吐量连续7年居世界第一。我们拥有良好的科技创新环境，上海拥有张江国家科学中心和一批重大科研设施，留学归国人员占全国1/4，两院院士近200人，中央"千人计划"专家约500人。这些都为上海服务国家"一带一路"建设提供了坚实保障。

党的十九大对新时代推进中国特色社会主义伟大事业作出了全面部署，明确提出要以"一带一路"建设为重点，形成陆海内外联动、东西双向互济的开放格局。《上海服务国家"一带一路"建设发挥桥头堡作用行动方案》提出了下一步推进的思路和重点。我们将深入贯彻党的十九大精神，把服务国家"一带一路"建设作为上海继续当好排头兵和先行者的新载体，服务长三角、服务长江流域、服务全国的新平台，联动东中西发展、扩大对外开放的新枢纽，努力成为能集聚、能服务、能带动、能支撑、能保障的桥头堡。

上海发挥服务国家"一带一路"建设桥头堡作用，要站在国家提高开放水平的高度，以内外联动的大视野，加强与长江经济带等战略对接。要充分发挥上海优势，把服务国家"一带一路"建设与"四个中心"、具有全球影响力的科技创新中心、上海自贸试验区建设等国家战略紧密结合起来，发挥叠加效应，承接一批国家重大功能性载体，打造一批开放型合作平台，增强要素集聚和辐射能力，为上海全球城市建设注入新动力。要充分对接市场主体需求，把市场在资源配置中的决定性作用和企业的主体作用发挥出来，切实解决市场主体开展双向投资、双向经贸的发展需求。要把握远近结合、滚动推进，充分对接国家"一带一路"建设的新要求和高峰论坛成果清单，与各方共同推进，防控风险，为更长远的发展夯实基础。具体来说，将聚焦六大重点领域加快推进。

一是实施贸易投资便利化专项行动。我们将以上海自贸试验区为载体，加强与沿线国家（地区）制度和规则对接。我们将加快推进上海自由贸易港区建设，以"区港一体、一线放开、二线安全高效管住"为核心，把货物进出、国际贸易、航运物流、金融服务等相关领域改革结合起来。我们将加快促进"一带一路"服务贸易创新发展，制定上海跨境服务贸易负面清单，逐步取消或放宽对跨境交付、自然人移动等模式的服务贸易限制措施。

二是实施金融开放合作专项行动。我们将积极打造人民币跨境支付和清算中心，推动人民币在沿线国家（地区）的贸易、实业投资与金融投资中的广泛运用。我们将完善面向"一带一路"的投融资服务体系，支持沿线国家（地区）在上海发行熊猫债等人民币证券产品，支持境内外优质企业利用上海资本市场发展。我们将加强上海金融市场与沿线国家（地区）双边和多边合作，支持在沪金融市场与沿线国家（地区）交易所、登记结算机构间的双边业务和股权合作。

三是实施增强互联互通功能专项行动。我们将进一步拓展完善航线航班网络布局，加快打造高效通畅的全球集装箱海上运营网络，提升上海航空枢纽航线网络覆盖面和通达性。我们将加快构建全方位多式联运综合体系，加快海铁、空铁建设衔接，积极发展海铁联运，加强上海铁路网与中欧、中亚铁路网的衔接，以信息化提升海港、空港、铁路等交通枢纽服务能级。

四是实施科技创新合作专项行动。我们将在上海自贸试验区建设"一带一路"产权交易中心与技术转移平台，与沿线国家（地区）拓展技术转移协作网络，搭建技术转移信息平台，共建技术转移中心，促进绿色技术等转移转化。我们将与沿线国家（地区）共建联合实验室或联合研究中心，加强技术联合攻关，共建一批联合实验室、技术创新中心、工程技术研究中心。

五是实施人文合作交流专项行动。我们将依托中国上海国际艺术节，整合现有平台资源，加强与沿线国家（地区）文化交流与合作机制化发展，成立国家级"丝绸之路国际艺术节联盟"。我们将深化上海国际电影节、美术馆、博物馆、音乐创演等与沿线国家（地区）的合作机制，进一步丰富和拓展文化交流合作内容。

六是实施智库建设专项行动。我们将探索建设国家级丝路信息数据库，积极建设面向不同国家、城市和企业的国家级大型综合数据库。我们将深化完善"一带一路"智库合作联盟，为加强相关沿线国家（地区）智库资源整合、政策沟通、人才交流搭建平台。

上海国际智库高峰论坛已经走过7年的历程，在过去的高峰论坛上，各位国际智库专家围绕上海科技创新中心建设、提升国际投资贸易便利化等主题发表了许多颇有见地的意见和建议，拓宽了我们的全球视野和战略思维，有些观点和建议被市委市政府所吸收采纳。我相信，借助上海国际智库交流中心这个开放式的决策咨询研究平台，国内外智库间的交流也将迸发出新的思想火花；通过企业、智库、政府代表分享国际经验，互动对话，针对上海如何发挥在"一带一路"建设中的桥头堡作用，促进国际产能合作、探索建设自由贸易港、扩大市场渠道、加强人员交流培训、提高创新能力等方面，探索实际可行的解决思路和方案。

The Belt and Road initiative is a major strategic move for our country to expand its opening-up and is also the focus of its opening to the outside world in the coming period. With the concerted efforts of all parties, the Belt and Road initiative has gradually transformed itself from concept into action and from vision to reality. At present, initial results have been achieved. From 2014 to 2016, China's exports to the Belt and Road amounted to USD 31 000, accounting for more than 1/4 of the total foreign trade in the same period. The direct investment in the B&R countries amounted to nearly USD 50 billion, accounting for about 1/10 of the total foreign direct investment in the same period. As of November 17th, 2017, the number of dispatched Sino-European express trains has exceeded 3 000, above the sum from 2011 to 2016. In this context, closer economic and trade cooperation between Shanghai and other B&R countries has been developing, which was reflected in the following aspects. First, rapid growth in trade and investment. Over the past three years, Shanghai has undertaken 246 investment projects in the B&R countries (regions) with an actual investment of USD 5.49 billion, an average annual increase of nearly 1.6 times. It undertook 3 019 major projects with a total contract value of USD 21.7 billion, an average annual increased by 9.4%. The volume of trade with the B&R countries (regions) exceeded RMB 500 billion, accounting for over 20% of the city's total. Second, the enterprises in Shanghai have accelerated their way to "going global". A number of key projects have taken root in the B&R countries (regions). For example, the contract value of power station and power transmission and distribution projects undertaken by Shanghai Electric in the Belt and Road countries and regions has reached USD 2.8 billion; Huayi Group has invested USD 419 million in the Belt and Road countries and regions; the Indonesia

Tsingshan Park invested and built by Shanghai enterprises has been recognized as a state-level foreign economic and trade cooperation zone, in which the enterprises have invested more than USD 3 billion. Third, the economic and trade cooperation will continue to be expanded. Shanghai has established economic and trade partnership with 19 B&R countries (regions). Shanghai Chamber of Commerce for Import and Export has set up the Belt and Road merchants alliance with 92 commercial associations and enterprises in the B&R countries and regions, offering a cooperation platform for the enterprises. Fourth, the economic and trade scale has continued to grow. From January to August 2017, the trade volume between Shanghai and the B&R countries (regions) reached RMB 429.5 billion, up by 21% compared to the previous year. The contract value of newly signed foreign contracted projects was RMB 1.93 billion, accounting for 67.3% of the city's total contract value.

The economic and trade partnership between Shanghai and the B&R countries meets the requirement of playing Shanghai's bridgehead role in serving the Belt and Road initiative and is of great significance. On the one hand, building a bridgehead is an important move for the implementation of China's Belt and Road initiative. The Belt and Road initiative is China's scheme for promoting global peace and cooperation and common development. It is also a major move for China to participate in make its a new way to globalization in the new era. As a pilot area of China's reform and opening up, Shanghai should play its bridgehead role in China's endeavor to promote new-round globalization and its bridging role in involving other provinces and cities to join the Belt and Road initiative. On the other hand, bridgehead building is an inherent requirement for Shanghai to comprehensively deepen the reform and opening up and to become a vanguard and pioneer. At present, Shanghai has progressed to a higher stage of reform and opening up and actively connected itself to the development of Belt and Road initiative. That is conducive to further enhancing Shanghai's functions in serving the entire country, developing a higher-level open economy and taking a better position in global competition and cooperation. Especially in areas such as accommodation of funds, economic and trade cooperation and shipping development, Shanghai should take the initiative to provide better services and play a platform and springboard role in connecting all provinces and cities with the Belt and Road initiative.

Moreover, Shanghai has a favorable foundation for building a bridgehead that serves the Belt and Road initiative.Advantageous position: Shanghai is located at the junction of the Maritime Silk Road, the grand coast freeway and the golden waterway of Yangtze River. It is bound to be an important junction for the Belt and Road and a leader in East Asia. An open and transparent institutional environment: Shanghai is the most open area in China with an institutional framework of investment, trade, finance and government governance, which is in line with international standards. Shanghai is the birthplace of Shanghai Cooperation Organization and the place where CICA Summit and APEC are held. A total of 1 321 regional headquarters of transnational companies and functional organizations are based in Shanghai, ranking the first in China. Strong comprehensive service capabilities: Shanghai is speeding up the building of an international economic, financial, shipping and trade center, an innovation center for science and technology and an international cultural metropolis. Shanghai Stock Exchange ranked the fourth in the world in stock market value by the end of 2016. Shanghai Port has established close ties with 128 major ports along the Belt and Road, and has ranked the first in the world in terms of container throughput for the seventh consecutive year. A good environment for technological innovation: Shanghai has Zhangjiang National Science Center and a number of major research facilities, with 1/4 of the returned overseas students, nearly 200 academicians, and about 500 experts of the national "Thousand-Talent Plan". All of these provide the solid safeguard for Shanghai to serve China's Belt and Road initiative.

At the 19th National Congress of the Communist Party of China, an overall plan was proposed for advancing the great cause of socialism with Chinese characteristics in the new era, and it was clearly stated that efforts were to be focused on the Belt and Road initiative so as to form an opening scenario featuring linkage between land and sea and mutual aid from east to west. "Action Plan for Shanghai's Bridgehead Role in Serving the National Belt and Road Initiative" in which ideas and priorities for further promotion were proposed. We will uphold the spirit of the19th CPC National Congress. By regarding the service of the Belt and Road initiative as a new carrier for Shanghai to remain as a vanguard and pioneer and a new platform for serving the Yangtze River Delta, the Yangtze River area and the whole country, and a new hub for linking the development among the Eastern, the Middle and the Western regions and opening wider to the outside world, Shanghai will try to become a bridgehead that is able to gather, serve, drive, support and protect.

For Shanghai to play its bridgehead role in serving the Belt and Road initiative, it is necessary for Shanghai have a broad vision of opening wider by linking up with the outside world and enhancing strategic connections with the Yangtze River Economic Belt. Shanghai should give full play to its advantages, and closely integrate the serving of the Belt and Road initiative with the national plans of "four centers", a globally influential innovation center for science and technology and the building of Shanghai Pilot Free Trade Zone for a combined effect. It should undertake some major national functional carriers to create open cooperation platforms, enhance the factor agglomeration and radiation capabilities, and inject new vitality into the building of Shanghai into a global city. It is essential to fully meet the needs of market players, play the market's decisive role in the allocation of resources and the enterprises'role as main players, and effectively solve the demands of market players for two-way investment and bilateral economy and trade. It is necessary to take a long-and short-term combination approach for progressive roll-out. For fully meeting the new requirements of the national Belt and Road initiative and the achievement list of the Summit, joint efforts should be taken to prevent and control risks and lay a solid foundation for more farsighted development. Specifically, six key areas will be focused for acceleration.

First, specific project will be implemented for trade and investment facilitation. We will use the Shanghai Pilot Free Trade Zone as a carrier to improve the compatibility with the systems and rules of the B&R countries (regions). We will accelerate the construction of Shanghai Free Trade Port Zone and integrate the reforms in related fields such as imports and exports, international trade, shipping logistics and financial services in the core model of "zone-port integration, frontier opening and second-tier safe and efficient control". We will expedite the service trade innovation and development of Belt and Road initiative, prepare a negative list of cross-border trade in services in Shanghai, and gradually abandon or relax the service trade restrictions on modes of cross-border delivery and movement of natural persons.

Second, specific project will be implemented for financial openness cooperation. We will actively build RMB cross-border payment and settlement centers and promote the extensive use of RMB in trade, industrial investment and financial investment in the B&R countries (regions). We will improve the investment and financing service system targeting the Belt and Road, support the B&R countries (regions) in issuing RMB securities products such as Panda Bonds in Shanghai, and support high-quality domestic and overseas enterprises to develop by capitalizing on Shanghai capital market. We will step up bilateral and multilateral cooperation between the financial markets in Shanghai and B&R countries (regions), and support bilateral business and equity cooperation between the financial markets in Shanghai and the exchanges and registration & clearing institutions in the B&R countries (regions).

Third, special project will be implemented for enhanced interconnection function. We will further expand and improve the route and flight network layout, speed up the construction of an efficient and smooth global container ocean operation network and enhance the coverage and accessibility of Shanghai's aviation hub airline network. We will expedite the construction of an all-round multimodal transport combined system, promote the convergence of ocean-rail and air-train construction, actively develop ocean-rail combined transport, and strengthen the linkup between Shanghai's railway network and Central European and Central Asian railway networks. In addition, we should upgrade the service function level of such transport hubs such as seaports, airports and railways in an information-based approach.

Fourth, special project will be implemented for cooperation in science and technology innovation. We will establish the Belt and Road property-rights exchange center and technology transfer platform in Shanghai Pilot Free Trade Zone. In conjunction with B&R countries (regions), we will expand the technology transfer collaboration network, set up a technology transfer information platform and build a technology transfer center to promote the transfer and transformation of green technology. We will establish joint laboratories or joint research centers together with the B&R countries (regions) to join efforts on technologies, and create joint laboratories, technological innovation centers and engineering technology research centers.

Fifth, special project will be implemented for cooperation in people-to-people exchange. Relying on the China Shanghai International Arts Festival, we will integrate existing platform resources and strengthen the institutional development of cultural exchanges and cooperation with B&R countries (regions) to establish a national "Union of Silk Road International Arts Festival". We will deepen the mechanism of cooperation between Shanghai in terms of Shanghai International Film Festival, art galleries, museums, music creation and performance and B&R countries (regions) to further enrich and expand the cultural exchange and cooperation.

Sixth, special project will be implemented for think tank building. We will explore the creation of a national Silk Road information database and actively create a national large integrated database for different countries, cities and enterprises. We will deepen and perfect the Belt and Road think tank cooperation alliance and build a platform for strengthening resource integration, policy communication and talent exchange among the participating B&R countries (regions).

Shanghai International Think Tank Summit is celebrating its 7th anniversary. At the previous meetings, international think tank experts gave their insightful comments and suggestions on such topics as building an innovation center for science and technology in Shanghai and promoting international investment and trade facilitation. Such speeches have broadened our global perspective and strategic thinking, and some of them have been adopted by the municipal Party committee and government. I believe, with the aid of the Shanghai International Think Tank Exchange Center as an open research platform for policy-making consulting, exchanges between the think tanks at home and abroad will spark new ideas. Enterprises, think tanks and government representatives share international experience. Through interactive dialogues, practical ideas and solutions are explored as regards to how to play Shanghai's bridgehead role in the Belt and Road initiative, promoting international cooperation in productivity, exploring the construction of free trade ports, expanding market channels, enhancing personnel exchanges and training, and improving innovation capabilities.

KEYNOTE SPEECHES

主旨演讲

搭建超级贸易平台，发挥上海"桥头堡"作用

吴 琪

埃森哲全球副总裁、大中华区副主席

在埃森哲看来，搭建超级贸易平台对上海未来在"一带一路"倡议中发挥"桥头堡"作用而言，是非常重要的战略举措之一，也会成为上海一个重要的支柱性贸易平台。

为什么这么看？当前，全球经贸中心的发展正在面临着很大的变革。从最初基于港口、机场等基础设施形成的贸易中心，全球经贸中心现在正逐步转变为以金融服务为主导的相关贸易服务的金融中心。全球经贸中心，包括上海，目前正在经历这个阶段。下一代全球经贸中心将是新一代的数字化贸易生态中心，围绕这些贸易中心，将会形成一个全新的生态体系。

根据埃森哲研究和项目经验发现，目前，从全球范围看，发展最超前、最重要、最值得上海借鉴的案例之一的全球经贸中心是新加坡。新加坡不仅有"智慧国家"计划，而且正在实施"下一代贸易基础设施"建设，旨在通过数字化手段，把贸易环节中的不同参与方，包括货主、港口、物流公司、海关边检等，以及金融服务、保险，乃至在此基础上形成的创新生态，构成一个完整的生态体系。通过这个生态体系，推动新加坡在亚洲地区的贸易中心地位，甚至通过这样的平台，进一步推动新加坡自身的产业发展和升级。这个思路非常值得上海思考、借鉴。所以，数字化"一带一路"超级贸易平台，对于上海形成"桥头堡"地位可能是非常重要的发展方向。

从新加坡的发展进程看，它也经历了这样一个阶段。而且新加坡未来的数字化体系，不仅仅包括现在已有的贸易基础设施，该体系将会直接衔接到数字化港口、数字化机场和数字化政府上，并涉及一系列相应参与方的数字化，以及这些数字化体系之间的衔接。通过这些衔接，正好印证了埃森哲去年专门研究的"平台经济"的特点。要真正发挥平台经济的作用，本质上需要基于新的技术、数字化手段，使平台参与方能实现更大效率，更低的交易成本，带来放大作用。从新

加坡的发展规划来看，无论是国家数字化、基础设施数字化，乃至跟贸易基础设施相关的数字化，这几点的结合一定程度上预示着未来经贸中心重要的发展方向——基于原有的交通基础设施、贸易相关服务，包括金融等服务，再把这些服务内容进一步附加在一个更强有力、高效的平台上，使得它发挥更大的作用和产生更大的价值。

为什么我们说上海具备先天优势条件？除了上海已有的港口、机场等交通基础设施，以及相应比较完善的经贸中心地位外，在实现这个平台的过程中，上海应该在克服目前中国经贸便利性的弱点上，实施创新和突破。我们做了一个比较，比如和亚洲排名第一的新加坡和排名第三的中国香港相比，无论是从内部市场的衔接性、国际市场的衔接性、海关的效率、物流设施水平、物流服务水平、应用信息技术的水平，乃至监管环境等重要的维度看，中国跟这些领先的国家或地区，还是有着非常明显的差距，而且影响贸易的便利性和效率。在世界100多个国家里，中国在很多经贸领域仍然排名靠后，也就是说，中国为了实现"一带一路"倡议下在全球贸易环节中扮演更主要的地位，除了通过服务功能、超级平台实现效率提升以外，还需要解决目前面临的痛点问题。这些痛点问题的突破，是上海自贸试验区未来应该考虑的重点方向之一。

除此以外，我们希望推动贸易的发展，给中国，尤其是上海的经济发展、产业发展带来更多机会，带来更多投资和高水平的就业机会。除了贸易环境外，从商业开展的环境、效率上看，中国跟领先市场依然存在着比较明显的差距。在审批效率和登记方面，相比全球主要国家的投资环境、商业环境，中国在效率上，还有非常明显的差距和改进空间。这些痛点问题也可能是未来上海在形成和推动超级平台的建设过程中，需要着重思考如何解决的问题。

此外，我们认为，未来上海的超级贸易平台需要在三个方向有所突破：

（1）解决方案的设计。现在政府考虑推动超级贸易平台建设，更多是基于独立的功能，而且是基于现在的流程和需求来设计的，每个功能之间的衔接不强，甚至有割裂。未来，真正要想在生态体系下不断优化、不断提高效率，实现更智慧地发展，那平台就需要变得开放，不管是从功能还是技术角度。而且需要能集成更多相应的功能。还有平台本身的方案设计要考虑可计划性，这不是一步到位的，而是要能逐渐发展升级。

（2）设计思路。现在平台设计更多是基于政府当前的流程、职能和标准化的思路，未来从生态、平台角度考虑，要给平台参与者带来更大效率和价值，那么平台的设计流程和功能设计就需要围绕用户导向来设计。服务不同的企业，需要什么样的流程，要考虑"客户体验"。

（3）经贸促进。现在我们站在中国考虑平台的促进、发展问题，更多的是从中国跟其他国家之间相对固化的体系来分析的。未来站在"一带一路"、全球贸易的角度，要想成为"桥头堡"、发挥出真正的作用，则需要满足欧洲跟亚洲国家、美洲和亚洲国家，乃至亚洲国家间的相应的衔接和服务，形成多边的格局，才有可能实现平台更大的价值，从而实现"一带一路"的关键意义。

我们认为，这个平台应该由几个部分组成：

（1）基础功能。如贸易许可，我们需要思考如何通过数字化的手段实现贸易便利化。

（2）与贸易服务相关的功能。如何将资源整合到这个平台上，使平台上的相关客户能更高效地完成他们的交易。降低成本是我们需要关注的问题。

（3）围绕数字化平台，未来提供的服务应该是智慧化的、基于数据分析的，包括创新服务模式的平台。通过这种方式，新的业态、创新的服务内容，将使整个平台变得更有竞争力和吸引力。

如何发挥上海在"一带一路"
金融开放上的引领作用？

黄　佳

普华永道中国中区市场主管合伙人、上海首席合伙人

1. 上海金融开放的现状

在当前全球经济缓慢复苏的大背景下，加强区域合作是推动世界经济发展的重要动力，且为一种趋势。中国推出共建"一带一路"倡议，顺应世界多极化、经济全球化、文化多样化、社会信息化的潮流。党的十九大报告中再次明确，"一带一路"建设是国家总体长期的规划。习近平总书记也对上海提出了新的要求，把上海自由贸易试验区建设成为服务国家"一带一路"建设、推动市场主体走出去的桥头堡。

我们认为完善的金融服务体系是"一带一路"建设的重要支撑。上海在金融开放方面处于全国领先，从总体金融发展水平方面，根据英国智库 Z/Yen 集团发布的全球金融中心指数（GFCI），2017 年上海排名第 13，遥遥领先于"一带一路"沿线绝大多数的金融中心城市。上海与伦敦、纽约、新加坡、香港等世界主要金融中心相比，发展潜力巨大，广受全球认可，在市场成长、经济发展、科技创新方面均表现出较强的竞争优势。而同时，现状发展仍有所不足。总体来说，上海发展存在"重硬轻软"的问题。上海在商业环境方面与世界一流金融中心相比，仍有较大差距，具体体现在税赋、政府监管、客户保密、经济开放自由度、创业环境、经营风险等。上海的股票市场、债券市场、商品期货市场与一流国际金融中心相比，虽然在量上不存在太大差距，却存在质的不足。此外，上海的金融市场的开放程度和国际化程度还是不够，金融监管及法制化环境有待完善，经济开放自由度有待提高，金融产品、机制等创新亟须加强。

防止系统性金融风险也一直是中国领导层关注的重点。在 2017 年 7 月份召开的全国金融工作会议上，习近平强调，中国应该将国有企业——银行宽松信贷的主要受益者和坏债的主要来源——降杠杆作为"重中之重"，充分解决"僵

尸企业"，地方债务要终身追责。国际清算银行的数据显示，到 2016 年底，中国的总体债务水平是 GDP 的 257%，非金融企业杠杆率达到 166.3%，高于美国的 72.3%。为了解决这些问题，十九大报告中要求"深化金融体制改革，增强金融服务实体经济能力，提高直接融资比重，促进多层次资本市场健康发展"。在十九大期间召开的新闻发布会上，中国银行业监督管理委员会主席郭树清承诺将控制地方政府的资产负债表外债务，限制房地产开发商的资金来源，加强对金融市场的监督管理。7 月份新成立的"超级监管者"——金融稳定发展委员会，通过组织协调证券、银行和保险监管机关的应对措施，将会有助于完善金融风险管理。

所以，对于上海来说，既要控制金融风险，又要进一步提高金融市场国际化程度，以经贸合作为突破口，以金融开放为核心，在加强与"一带一路"沿线国家的金融合作方面起到引领作用。

2. 通过"一带一路"政策推动上海的金融开放

"一带一路"倡议的推动需要投入巨量资金，根据国务院发展研究中心估算，2016 年至 2020 年沿线国家基础设施投资需求至少在 10.6 万亿美元以上，这还不包括其他领域的投资。很显然，中国的银行再加上目前活跃在沿线国家的现有的以及新设立的多边金融机构，所能提供的贷款远远无法满足潜在需求。如何解决融资问题是推进"一带一路"倡议重大关键因素之一。

基于以上分析，我们建议：

第一，在股票和债券市场为沿线国家企业开辟融资通道。

2016 年两会的政府工作报告明确表示，支持外商投资企业在国内上市和发债。现实情况是，欧美发达国家本土股票和债券市场发展普遍比中国成熟，跨国外商投资企业如果选择在中国上市和发债可能更多考虑的中国本土市场发展的需求。

我们的统计数据显示，"一带一路"沿线国家（地区）所有的证券交易所企业股票市值没有一家可以与沪港深三地证券交易所的上市企业股票市值比拟，而且差距颇大（见图 1）。如果考虑到经济规模因素，新加坡和印度拥有一定的比较优势。

截至 2017 年 5 月 31 日，上交所上市企业总市值接近 30 万亿元人民币，合计约 4.4 万亿美元。2016 年福布斯全球企业 2 000 强榜单中，沿线国家共有 235 家企业上榜，总市值约 2.72 万亿美元。如果能吸引这 235 家企业在上交所上市，

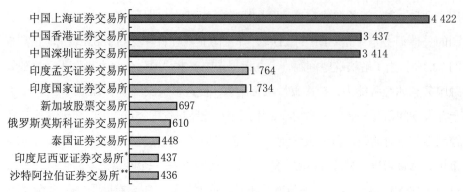

注：* 印度尼西亚证券交易所汇率为 2017 年 2 月 28 日收盘价；

　　** 沙特阿拉伯数据来自该国中央统计局，汇率为 2017 年 2 月 28 日收盘价。

资料来源：Wind，普华永道整理。

图 1　"一带一路"国家及中国前 10 大股票交易所上市企业股票市值

不但可以极大促进"一带一路"倡议的融资问题，也可能为上交所增加超过 3 万多亿美元（或 18 万亿元人民币）上市企业市值。此外，上交所还可能因此成为全球更加重要的证券交易所，也将推动和升级上海作为全球领先的金融中心地位，可以说是一举多得之重大战略性措施。

除了银行和股票市场，另外一个可以给"一带一路"倡议提供大量融资支持的，非债券市场莫属。2016 年中国债券市场的发行规模已经高达 36 万亿元人民币，合 5.29 万亿美元，在这样一个庞大的市场规模里面完全有条件为沿线国家和企业的融资开辟一条快速通道。再者，中央政府已经明确表示"支持沿线国家政府和信用等级较高的企业以及金融机构在中国境内发行人民币债券"。那么，上海如何扮演更加重要的角色？

我们建议上海推动以上交所为主要平台为"一带一路"倡议提供债券融资（首推人民币，兼顾美元），初期阶段把目标对象设定在信用评级较好的沿线国家政府和财务状况稳定的上市公司，即标准普尔评级在 A 级以上的 12 个国家，和福布斯 2 000 强榜单上 235 家财务状况良好的上榜企业。

最后，由于中国债券市场的监管相比股票市场复杂，推动以上交所为主要平台为"一带一路"沿线国家（地区）和企业提供债券融资，更方便协调中央相关监管部门，并商议制定政策、快速有效执行。

第二，人民币国际化优先考虑沿线经济体。

近来人民币经历了较大的波动，从 2015 年 8 月到 2016 年 12 月，人民币兑美元贬值，促使政府采取了一系列强有力的措施以控制日益加剧的资本外流。进入 2017 年以后，人民币兑美元开始升值。与此同时，从 2016 年 10 月起，人民币被正式纳入了国际货币基金组织的特别提款权货币篮子，这标志着人民币成为全球储备货币。

十九大报告中提出健全货币政策和宏观审慎政策双支柱调控框架，深化利率和汇率市场化改革。在十九大期间召开的新闻发布会上，中国人民银行行长周小川表示，政府将改革汇率形成机制，减少市场干预，稳步健全人民币资产的可及性。他还表示"沪港通""深港通"以及 2017 年 7 月推出的香港—上海间"债券通"，证明了中国继续扩大开放的承诺。

在人民币国际化的过程当中，上海作为在岸人民币交易中心一直发挥着举足轻重的作用，"一带一路"倡议的推进给人民币国际化带来了新机遇，我们建议上海继续发挥引领和示范作用。

前面建议的开放股票和债券市场给沿线国家企业和政府融资的方案中，首选人民币作为股票和债券发行的货币是一个多赢的举措。沿线国家及其企业融资获得的人民币资金，不但可以用在和中国的贸易、投资、与中资企业商业活动中，也可以在"一带一路"或其他区域流通。这将极大促进中国和这些国家的经济合作，同时促进和提升人民币国际化，还可以缓解国内的"资产荒"的困境，为居民和企业提供更多在国内的投资机会。

"一带一路"的发展将是一个长期而漫长的过程，人民币国际化虽然更早提出，但也需要较长时间。这两者都是未来中国经济与全球更深层次融合发展的关键因素。上海要成为中国首屈一指、全球领先的金融中心，"一带一路"人民币融资、结算中心的地位必不可少。如果能在几年时间里，让上海成为沿线国家（地区）股票和债券融资中心，不但可以极大提升上海在全球金融业务的市场份额，同时将把上海作为全球金融中心的地位推向一个全新高度。

第三，加速发展上海的金融科技。

全球金融科技的飞速发展为金融服务业带来了前所未有的冲击。金融科技这个在中国被称为"互联网金融"的行业的发展是上海推动"一带一路"建设突破的重要抓手，应加速发展互联网金融机制、健全监管体制机制、营造良好的环境。依托于中国在这方面巨大优势，上海无疑是站在了巨人的肩膀之上，拥有得天独厚的条件，上海已经充分认识到了互联网发展的重要性，并于 2015 年成立了上海互联网金融行业协会。我们建议上海致力于建设成为"一带一路"互联网金融中心，同时争取成为全球重要的互联网金融中心。

2017 年 5 月召开的"一带一路"国际合作高峰论坛提出"加强金融设施互联互通，创新投融资模式和平台，提高金融服务水平"。金融科技正在飞速发展，且已在许多方面都处于世界领先的地位。中国移动支付规模占据了全球的半壁江山，P2P 网络借贷（网贷）的余额更是占了全球总量的四分之三。加速发展上海的金融科技，可以为"一带一路"国家（地区）提供借鉴，在这些国家复制和推广，为"一带一路"倡议带来全新的互联网视角和内容。

普华永道 2017 年全球金融科技调查报告中显示了其带来的三大机遇和面临的三大挑战，可供参考。

（1）金融科技将从三方面带来机遇。

• 客户。金融科技低成本和无远弗届的特点，使金融机构得以将客户群体扩大至从前未获金融服务覆盖的群体。

• 产品与服务。客户的期望已从对产品的追求向体验至上转变，金融机构提供的产品和服务的重点，也将从简单和标准化，转变为创造个性化的体验。

• 渠道。在未来的五年里，实体分支机构的重要性将逐年下降，而电子渠道，尤其是移动渠道才是"王道"。

（2）金融科技的发展也面临了三方面的挑战。

• 竞争。竞争的加剧在所难免，不过比这个更重要的是，在互联网和科技行业存在的"赢家通吃"的模式，在金融业是否可行？

• 监管。监管是一把双刃剑，法规不仅需要与时俱进，更关键的是如何在鼓励创新和控制金融风险间取得平衡？

• 人才。在金融科技的竞争浪潮中，想要获得优势，需要的是复合型人才。金融机构应如何培养面向未来的人才？

（3）在金融科技的浪潮中，"合"是大势所趋，金融机构应对变革三个维度。

• 战略与理念。未来三到五年，金融机构倾向于通过加强内部研发和与金融科技公司合作来落实创新。

• 资源投入。金融机构对于新兴科技的热情非常高涨，他们愿意将接近三分之一的资源分配到金融科技相关项目。

• 行动方案。金融机构和金融科技公司有增强合作的主观意愿，但在合作中仍需进一步磨合，解决信息科技系统和商业模式差异等挑战。

面向人工智能、区块链和机器人流程自动化这未来的三项创新科技，将给金融业带来深远的变化（见图 2）。尽快掌握这些科技，并围绕其落实相应的配套技能，将使上海的金融机构在竞争中脱颖而出。

所以，金融科技首先要立足于"金融"的本质，而金融服务的变化与实体经济的发展息息相关。随着实体经济向信息化、智能化和个性化的商业模式和生活模式演变，未来的金融服务模式也将向 3.0 转型，而科技将是这个"新金融"模式的重要支柱。但在分享技术创新所带来的金融互联互通的同时，仍需坚持安全底线，防患于未然，建立稳定、可持续、风险可控的金融保障体系，创新投资和

图 2　未来的三次创新科技

融资模式，优化和完善互联网金融发展的环境。

3. 发挥自由贸易区桥头堡的引领作用，助力上海成为全国示范性"一带一路"建设智库

习近平总书记在十九大会议期间指出，中国经济已由高速增长转向高质量发展，在推动全面开放新格局下，以"一带一路"建设为重点，将赋予自由贸易试验区更大的改革自主权，积极探索建设自由贸易港之路。

上海自贸试验区正在研究推出以人民币定价的原油期货，这将提高中国在国际石油市场中的定价权以及人民币的国际地位，上海可以先行面向"一带一路"沿线国家（地区）推广这一业务，不但阻力小，而且可能取得意想不到的效果。

另外，基于上海自贸试验区已经取得的成绩，我们建议：继续在自贸区尝试金融创新业务以支持"一带一路"倡议，例如：在人民币跨境使用的过程中，特别关注"一带一路"沿线国家（地区），选择其中几个国家（地区）进行追踪研究，为人民币走向更多沿线国家（地区）积累经验；做跨境融资便利化的创新试点，一方面优先考虑中国企业"走出去"到沿线国家（地区）的投资项目，另一方面，尝试把这些国家（地区）条件成熟的项目"引进来"在自贸区融资。由于香港本身就是一个自贸区，很多方面的经验上海自贸试验区可以直接借鉴香港。

4. 结语

自由贸易港是自贸试验区的升级版，也是"一带一路"建设的助推器。在中

国经济转型面临关键节点和全球经济不确定性加剧的今天，上海有责任在金融开放创新方面成为全国示范性"一带一路"建设智库，发挥桥头堡的引领作用。自由贸易区、"一带一路"和金融开放，这三者是相互关联、彼此促进，同时都是改革开放的重要内容。金融要在确保安全的前提下，坚持开放，既要金融稳定，又要金融搞活。

普华永道一直以来都重视"一带一路"建设，借助公司全球网络资源，成立了"一带一路"全景平台。该平台以"一带一路"主要参与方为核心成员。以普华永道中国"一带一路"相关行业的核心服务团队为依托，通过与普华永道全球网络在沿线主要国家的"一带一路事业部"建立纽带，形成多行业、跨地区、全方位的"一带一路"全景平台。平台汇聚了在"一带一路"领域有深入研究的知名学者和智库、有投资实力和意向的各类型企业、投资机构、专业服务提供商以及"一带一路"国家的领事馆官员，相关政府、商会、协会的代表。普华永道作为平台的发起者，始终将广阔的全球网络资源和实务经验与成员分享。

"一带一路"是目前世界上跨度最长、最具潜力的合作带。该倡议的发展建议不但对中国经济整体发展是重大机遇，对于上海建设全球领先的金融中心也是至关重要的机会。"一带一路"为中国金融业开放提供了新的机遇，上海只有紧紧抓住每一次历史发展机遇，借助自我优势，搭建开放式多边投融资平台，引领推动"一带一路"沿线国家（地区）金融市场的双向开放。

互惠、互联、流动：上海成为"一带一路"的先锋

琼安娜

中国欧盟商会上海分会总经理

欧盟是中国"一带一路"倡议最重要的潜在合作伙伴。两大经济体不仅仅占据着欧亚大陆的两端，同时也是丝绸之路经济带和 21 世纪海上丝绸之路的起点和终点，双方更是对方最大的贸易伙伴之一。作为"一带一路"的桥头堡之一，欧盟欢迎"一带一路"倡议的成功实施，也期待能够在此倡议下加强和中国的经贸关系。

上海重要的地理位置和经济地位使其在"一带一路"中自然要扮演比其他城市更加突出的先锋作用。作为在沪欧洲工商界的代表和在一个上海生活了 15 年的市民，我想强调三个承载着我们期望和建议的关键词：互惠、互联和流动。

1. 互惠

"一带一路"倡议最首要的目的是连接沿线国家（地区），促进中国与沿线国家（地区）的交流，因此"一带一路"不应该成为一个单行线。

在欧盟商会 2016 年的建议书中我们引入了"互惠"的概念。相比中国企业在欧洲投资时面对较少的准入门槛，欧洲在华企业往往受到更大的准入限制。在市场准入方面缺少互惠性的问题在"一带一路"倡议下应该得到更大程度的重视。

荣鼎集团的一项研究报告指出，2017 年上半年中国在欧盟的投资持续保持高位，然而欧洲在华投资相较于 2016 年同期却下降了 23%。2017 年欧盟商会《商业信心调查》同样显示，61% 的受访企业认为市场准入门槛对他们在华业务的开展构成了显著影响。这样的状况不利于中欧双边贸易和投资关系的可持续发展，更不符合"一带一路"倡议的初衷。

今年早些时候，我们欣喜地看到国发 5 号文和国发 39 号文，以及上海地方

层面的 26 号文都在强调吸引外商投资的重要性。而新出台的《外商投资产业指导目录》和 2017 版上海自贸试验区负面清单也给投资者带来了一定程度的利好，并减少了部分行业的限制。然而，这些文件带来的积极势头似乎在减弱。因此，"一带一路"倡议承载着外国投资者对于这些在市场开放领域尚未兑现的承诺的希冀。

诚然，部分行业在进一步开放方面已经取得了骄人的进展，例如制药行业。在过去的一年中，我们见证了新药注册和审评审批领域取得的令人瞩目的突破，这也反映出中国政府在药品监管方面对标国际最高标准方面作出的努力。我们希望这种开放的态度和措施也可以在其他监管领域得以体现。

当然，开放的步伐需要迈得更大，特别是在"一带一路"背景下，金融行业应当更加开放。一个开放、多元、充满活力的金融行业不仅是上海升级成为全球金融中心的重要一步，更是"一带一路"得以成功实施的关键。一旦对于外资银行、期货经纪人、券商和基金管理机构的准入限制被取消，各类成熟且经验丰富的投资机构将入驻中国市场，这不仅有利于中国国内资本市场的良性发展，更将激励外资企业通过多元灵活的融资渠道参与到"一带一路"建设中。

2. 互联

一条道路最基本的功能即连接两地，促进货物流动。对于"一带一路"倡议而言更是如此，所以贸易便利化构成了倡议的核心。

上海已经在推动贸易便利化，改善物流基础设施和贸易监管环境方面做出了很多努力，这也得到了欧盟商会众多会员企业的一致认同。我们很高兴得知上海正计划在洋山港和浦东机场建立自由港区，它将成为融入更多功能，手续更简便，贸易监管标准更高的贸易示范区。

欧盟商会及其会员企业欢迎这一举措，同时也期待上海自由港能够在"一带一路"中起到引领作用。其中，物流企业长期呼吁并且会给自由港区带来更多实惠的一点是沿海捎带。

沿海捎带的概念可能对我们中很多人而言显得陌生，这其实是欧洲国际海运中的一个通行做法。如果在中国施行沿海捎带，国际班轮公司将可以把由中国运往他国的货物在中国港口进行本公司船舶间的转运。沿海捎带不仅可以帮助航运公司优化其航线网络、提高运营效率，更重要的是，它可以提升转运港口的吞吐量和营收，从总体上降低物流成本。

然而，中国目前仍然禁止国际航运公司开展沿海捎带。几年前，中籍外旗的船舶被允许在中国的自贸区内开展沿海捎带业务。相反，外籍船舶仍旧只能在诸如韩国和日本在内的周边国家换船转运。这不仅增加了运输成本和时间，同时也导致中国港口的收入流失到外国港口。

我们希望对外籍船舶沿海捎带的限制可以在上海自由港有所突破。这样，上海将有望成为前往东南亚、中东、非洲和欧洲货物的转运港口，而这些目的地正是21世纪海上丝绸之路的沿线国家。更重要的是，上海在国际航运网络中的地位将在与21世纪海上丝绸之路沿线国家加强互联互通的过程中得到显著提升，也将更有助于上海增强竞争力，实现其成为国际航运中心的目标。

3. 流动

一条道路的最终目的一定是连接并促进人民间的交流互动。众所周知，上海非常重视人才引进和保留，特别是上海有志成为未来全球科创中心的背景下。

我们很高兴地看到近期在此方面取得的一些积极进展。从2017年4月开始，新的统一的外国人工作许可制度将在全国推广，申请流程将变得更加透明、清晰。同时，我们也感受到了政府在控制污染和高房价，提升上海宜居和可负担程度方面做出的巨大努力。我坚信在上海将实现更高程度的人才交往和流动，成为"一带一路"沿线国家（地区）的人才高地。

除了人才的自由流动以外，信息和数据的自由流动同样值得关注。互联网接入和网速问题一直困扰着欧洲在华企业，也是阻碍世界各地青年人才选择来上海工作和生活的潜在因素。2017年欧盟商会《商业信心调查》显示，24%的受访者在与其总部、合作伙伴和客户间的数据和文件的传输过程中遇到困难，从而导致其运营成本上升。

在知识和信息时代下，"一带一路"倡议不应仅仅推动货物和人员等实体层面的流动，更应该成为信息快速稳定流动的载体。只有实现人才和数据的自由流动，上海才有望真正崛起成为一座基于知识的国际商业和创新中心城市。

作为欧洲在华工商业的代表，我们没有理由不去支持并拥抱这项同时惠及中欧的倡议。我们愿意持续贡献我们的知识和能力，在欧洲商界和政府间建立起桥梁，帮助上海在"一带一路"中发挥更大的桥头堡作用。

成为"一带一路"2.0 时代国际新贸易网络上的首席自由贸易港

吕文博

麦肯锡全球董事，大中华区政府事务与基础设施业务负责人

1. 世界经济面临深刻转型，"一带一路"迈入 2.0 时代

在前不久刚举行的 APEC 会议上，习近平主席在主旨演讲中提出世界经济正面临增长动能、全球发展方式、经济全球化进程、全球经济治理体系四个方面的深刻转变。的确，回顾过去一两年的全球形势，随着民粹主义和贸易保护思潮的重新抬头，既有的全球化和自由贸易格局正经受着极大的挑战。世界亟须创新的发展理念来构建新的国际贸易秩序以推进全球化进程的持续稳步健康发展。在此背景下，我们认为，中国基于共商共建共享理念提出并积极推进的"一带一路"倡议应积极加速迈入 2.0 时代。所谓"一带一路"2.0 时代，指的是运作机制市场化程度更高的阶段。如果说在"一带一路"倡议提出后的过去 4 年间，以政府和大型央企为主导的"国家队式"运作模式成功推动了多个建设项目的实施落地，那在中国"进一步走向世界、发展更高层次开放型经济"的新时期，"一带一路"2.0 阶段将侧重在经贸领域展开全方位、更深入的互通互联，倡议的复合性色彩将会得到更多重视，实现政策沟通、设施联通、贸易畅通、资金融通、民心相通的命运共同体。

2. "一带一路"2.0 时代下国际自由贸易港的新内涵

正因为原有的全球化和自由贸易格局正面临上述的深刻变化，所以我们认为伴随着"一带一路"进入 2.0 时代，作为国际贸易核心载体的自由贸易港也必将被赋予全新的内涵与功能。

首先，过去的国际自由贸易港是一个联结着两级世界的转口枢纽，它的功能主要是传导发达世界与发展中世界经济势能的中转站，简而言之即发展中国家生

产，发达国家消费，发展中国家输出资源，发达国家输出资本。但在以构建人类命运共同体为根本目标的"一带一路"2.0时代，各个国家将在平等的地位上互通共融，充分发挥各自的资源禀赋优势，以多种方式开展合作，共享机遇、互促发展。在这种新型的国际贸易格局中，自由贸易港就势必成为一张平等互惠网络中的关键结点，通过它，更好的产品、更优的服务可以真正地通达全球、普惠世界；通过它，资本的流动将更加畅通，在满足其逐利本性的同时也为富有潜力的新兴市场带来更好的发展机会，助推全球经济平衡可持续地发展。

其次，在互联网时代，全球贸易所承载的内容也在不断扩大。经济体之间的互联互通将不再是简单的物的交换、资本的流通。数据信息、知识创意，乃至发展理念和机制体制等无形要素的交互，在国际贸易交流中也正在占有越来越重要的地位。根据麦肯锡全球研究院2016发布的全球互联研究报告显示，过去十几年全球服务流与数据流的增速远高于物流及资本流增速。所以如果说过去评价自由贸易港是否成功的指标是转口贸易额或集装箱吞吐量，那"一带一路"2.0时代面向未来的自由贸易港也许还更应该看重数据交换量、专利交易额，甚至是创新理念和发展经验这些无形成果能通过一系列开放合作平台得以交流互通的辐射力和影响力。

正是基于上述对"一带一路"2.0时代下国际自由贸易港新内涵的理解，我们认为上海如果要更好地服务于"一带一路"建设，充分地发挥桥头堡作用，在建设自由贸易港的战略上不仅要对标国际最高标准，建成世界一流，更要充分着眼未来，敢于创出新路，力争成为"一带一路"2.0时代国际新贸易网络上的首席自由贸易港。

3. 如何理解"成为国际新贸易网络上的首席自由贸易港"的目标

如果要进一步诠释上海"成为国际新贸易网络上的首席自由贸易港"这一发展目标，我们觉得应该紧紧抓住两个关键词，即"首席自由贸易港"的"首席"两个字和"国际新贸易网络"中的这个"新"字，这两个关键词一个明确了上海自由贸易港的地位，一个提出了上海自由贸易港的特色。

首先，上海应该是一个"首席"的自由贸易港，是中国倡导下的国际自由贸易新秩序的代表。一方面，从经济地理的区位上看，上海是中国"一弓双箭"的区域经济发展大格局上的关键结点，是连接广袤的中国内陆与"一带一路"沿线国家（地区）的起始性节点，扮演着内通外连的首要角色，所以成为"首席"有着先天的优势与条件。另一方面，上海在当下提出建设自由贸易港，其所肩负的历史使命与 WTO 时代我们为了打开国门更好地融入世界贸易体系时已经大不相同，经过入世之后十余年的努力探索、改革与发展，中国已经成为全球第二大经济体，第一大出口国，是拉动全球经济发展，促进经贸互动的中坚力量，在新国际贸易秩序的构建中也必将发挥更加积极主动的引领作用。所以作为"一带一路"的桥头堡，我们不应该仅仅满足于作为对外开放的窗口，通过自由贸易港只是把窗开得更大了一点，我们应该代表中国在国际新贸易秩序的构建和推行中发挥表率和引领作用，在全方位扩大国际交流合作的同时，积极输出中国经验和中国模式，所以"首席"也代表我们应该积极主动地扮演的引领角色。

其次，上海引领建设的自由贸易港是"国际新贸易网络"上的自由贸易港。这个"新贸易网络"究竟"新"在哪里？这个"新"字意味着上海应该积极地承接落实我们在前面阐述的"一带一路"2.0 时代下国际自由贸易港的新内涵。上海不应该仅仅是简单地建设一个单纯向国际市场"开放"的自由贸易港，而是要走在世界前列，引领一个新的贸易体系的构建，与传统的自由贸易港相比形成自身的特色和模式上的超越。亚洲目前的自由贸易港，如中国香港、新加坡，主要依托港口的地理位置优势、税收优惠发展转口贸易。上海不能简单复制、取代这一类传统的自由贸易港模式，单纯以扩大贸易量为发展目标。而应有所突破、有所创新，在制度机制建设、贸易基础设施、全要素流通等方面做出全方位的垂范，构建一个新的贸易网络，使得各个国家能够真正获得便利的服务及有效的支持，共同分享"一带一路"2.0 建设的成果。

4. 制度建设与具体举措双管齐下，实现首席自由贸易港的愿景目标

我们认为，成为国际新贸易网络上的首席自由贸易港，一个总的建设原则是要找到自由与制度二者之间的最佳平衡点，建立以"最优规制"为基础的制度环境，在充分发挥市场力量，使各类资源要素充分流动的同时，完善制度保障以防范市场失灵，保证市场化机制平稳运作。这也是中国经验与中国模式在新型自由贸易港建设上的最佳体现。

不可否认，自由贸易港的要义首先在"自由"，即实现贸易经济活动的自由，其基础是建立一个自由而有序的市场，概括而言即全球的任何的交易主体都可以在这个市场中运用一切可能的贸易工具针对所有的商品和服务进行交换。自由贸易港不仅仅是实行普通贸易优惠政策的"出口加工区"，而应该是一个更加"开放"和"放权"的贸易港。这需要政府对外进一步向包括外资在内的各类市场主体开放准入范围，对内进一步放宽不必要的行政管制，用开放倒逼改革，用放权

助推活力，打造一个货物进出自由、投资自由、金融自由，充满市场活力的贸易港。

从国际经验看，公共政策向市场力量的放开是纽约、伦敦及东京等全球枢纽城市得以崛起的重要因素。不管是 20 世纪 70 年代美国通过修订资本市场法案推行金融服务自由化，80 年代英国伦敦全面彻底放宽金融机构并购限制的"大爆炸"（Big Bang），还是 90 年代末日本的"东京金融大爆炸"（Tokyo Big Bang）所推行的金融自由化改革方案，都可见政府规制的优化在有力促进市场发展，增强国际竞争力方面的巨大作用。

建立自由与制度平衡的"最优规制"在"一带一路"2.0 时代尤为重要。新时期下市场化运作机制的构建需要政府和市场两种力量的有机配合才能取得成功。对于政府而言，可以借助"新规制经济学"的理论基础，通过制度化的立法方式，实现对市场最优化的管理。这需要完善立法放松管制，减少货物贸易、服务贸易、投资、金融等领域的行政管制，放宽准入门槛，提高市场参与主体自由度。同时也需要对各类项目提供平台支持及系统的制度性保障，包括完善仲裁机制及风险控制体系，督促市场主体持续地、动态地披露真实信息，并加强公共安全、产权保护、公平竞争等关键领域的监管等，以更好服务于各类生产要素的自由流动与匹配，有效保障市场化机制的平稳运作。

在完善制度建设的基础上，我们还建议上海在市场化投融资体系建设、中国式创新成果输出以及国际化人才交流培养这三方面通过一系列的具体举措构筑服务"一带一路"的桥头堡。

首先，配合一带一路基建先行的特点，上海应该率先在基础设施金融方面率先推进跨国的市场化投融资体系建设，构建"符合银行担保条件的项目"（Bankable projects）投资平台。一带一路沿线国家的大型基础设施建设项目需要大规模的资金支持，但目前尚未建立起一套成熟的、可持续的投融资机制体系。上海在这方面可以先行一步，积极搭建项目融资平台，牵头建立国际顾问团队，并完善配套金融服务。第一，构建"一带一路"融资平台及交易市场，推进"符合银行担保条件的项目"等优质项目公开化，充分发挥市场的力量推进资金和项目的匹配；第二，由政府牵头，引入市场化的力量，搭建"一带一路"国际顾问团队，为市场主体提供项目支持，包括政策解读、法律咨询、风险评估等，加快项目开发进程，提高项目质量，开发系列"符合银行担保条件的项目"。第三，结合上海国际金融中心建设进程以及上海自贸区金融开放创新成果，吸引更多领先的国内外金融企业及服务机构入驻，完善跨境结算、保险、信用评估、国际仲裁等的多层次金融服务体系，为"一带一路"项目建设提供更加完备的金融配套服务。

其次，上海应当力争成为中国式创新经验及成果的输出地。中国作为一个新兴的大国，在发展过程中形成丰富的创新经验成果，尤其是结合本土市场特点，以客户为推动的产品及商业模式创新，在新兴发展中国家中有很高的推广价值。上海作为对外开放下中国企业"走出去"的窗口，在"一带一路"背景下应当更好发挥连接中国及新兴发展中国家的枢纽作用，推广中国式创新经验及成果。上海市政府可以从优化对外投资制度环境、搭建企业交流平台以及强化知识产权支持等方面促进中国式创新的经验与成果输出。第一，营造自由便利的投资制度环境。结合上海自贸区的建设成果，通过进一步减少对外投资政策限制，简化对外投资审批流程，提供税收优惠等措施，支持国内企业对"一带一路"沿线国家（地区）的投资和项目建设。第二，搭建企业交流平台，丰富企业交流活动，如定期开展"一带一路"投资贸易洽谈会，技术交流论坛等，使中国企业能够更深入了解新兴国家的市场情况，根据当地国家需求的进行产品开发及项目方案设计，更好的输出产品及服务，并增进发展理念、业务模式等创新经验成果的分享交流。第三，强化国际知识产权保护。随着"一带一路"建设推进，中国式创新的成果走向更多国家，也面临着更加激烈的市场竞争，知识产权的保驾护航尤显重要。但目前我国许多企业在国际知识产权保护方面的意识较为薄弱，也缺乏相关的维权经验和手段。上海应当关注强化知识产权服务体系建设，增强国内企业的专利保护意识，提供海外知识产权制度解读，知识产权纠纷专业协助等系列服务，保障中国企业的创新成果。

最后，关注国际化人才交流与培养的平台的建设。随着"一带一路"迈向2.0阶段，对人才亦提出更高要求，既需要行业的专业技术人才，也需要复合型的管理人才；既需要人才从我国"走出去"，也需要加强海外市场的国际人才及当地人才的引入。上海应当积极加强人才培育和交流平台建设，包括人才吸引、人才培育以及人才交流三大环节：第一，通过提供政策支持、税收优惠及津贴以及完善企业及人才基础设施及配套服务，吸引高素质人才参与"一带一路"建设。第二，推进人才培养，这既包括推动高校、智库、企业多方联动，培养适应"一带一路"建设需要的复合型人才，也包括积极承办援外培训项目，为"一带一路"沿线国家（地区）的人才搭建教育培训的平台。第三，以多元化的方式与沿线国家开展人才交流活动，如充分利用上海国际科技节、浦江创新论坛等平台，促进与沿线国家（地区）科技创新政策及管理经验的交流。

如何发挥上海在"一带一路"建设中的桥头堡作用——德勤的一点思考和贡献探讨

刘明华

德勤华东区主管合伙人

当前，世界正处于大发展大变革大调整的关键期；与此同时，我国经济也处在转变发展方式、优化经济结构、转换增长动力的攻关期。在此国内外形势正发生深刻复杂变化的宏观背景下，2013 年就提出的"一带一路"倡议也被赋予新的使命，将成为中国走向世界、提升全球话语权和影响力的重要途径。

首先，中国全球话语权和影响力的提升，是中国国际地位提升的必然结果。过去 5 年，中国对世界经济增长的贡献率始终保持在 30% 以上，国际社会希望中国在国际事务中发挥更大作用、在应对全球性挑战中承担更多责任，这也有利于维护未来中国在更紧密的全球合作中维护自身利益。

其次，中国全球话语权和影响力的提升，也是中国经济进入新常态后的必然选择。随着中国劳动力成本持续攀升，资源约束日益趋紧，环境承载能力接近上限，开放型经济传统竞争优势受到削弱，传统发展模式遭遇瓶颈；另一方面，中国人力资源丰富、市场规模庞大、基础设施比较完善、产业配套齐全，创新发展的制度环境和政策环境不断完善，开放型经济仍然具备综合竞争实力。面对经济全球化的必然趋势，通过掌握全球话语权，适时转换经济发展动力，顺势调整多方合作规则，将更有助于中国乃至世界适应新格局变化。

在此宏观背景下，相比过去 5 年，"一带一路"倡议侧重将至少在以下几方面有所升级：

（1）对中国制造而言，不仅仅是商品输出，更是标准/服务/品牌/技术输出。

（2）对中国经济而言，不仅仅是富裕产能转移释放，更是实现从追求规模速度向追求质量效益转型的软着陆缓冲。

（3）对区域合作而言，不仅仅是发展自身境内特殊经济区、自贸区，更是需要关注和拓展境外经济合作区。

（4）对政治外交而言，对于发展中国家，不仅仅只是资助扶贫，更是需要通过经济合作构建更为紧密的利益共同体；对于发达国家，不仅仅只是被动接入既有规则，更是共同协商谈判新的共赢规则。

在上述战略转型升级方向中，制定灵活开放、合作共赢的多边贸易规则是关键。近年来，WTO 的多哈规则日益衰弱，TPP 等多边自由贸易协定逐渐兴起，不断冲击 WTO 在世界贸易领域的统治地位。这也意味着，以往以西方国家为主的"单边价值规则输出"方式正在受到挑战。结合世界多极化、经济全球化、社会信息化、文化多样化的客观发展现状，借鉴邓小平"一国两制"构想，尊重各国各地区的文化差异和合理诉求，找到最大公约数，画出最大同心圆，用动态发展的眼光与方法去看待和处理多边关系，将有助于中国扩大同包括发展中国家和发达国家在内的各国利益交汇点，参与全球治理体系改革建设，发展积极的全球伙伴关系，进而有助于推动经济全球化朝着更加开放、包容、普惠、平衡、共赢的方向发展。

在此战略背景下，上海在新一轮"一带一路"倡议桥头堡的地位和重要性越发凸显，不仅体现在硬环境上（如区位交通、基础设施等），更体现在其软环境上。

外资特色突出：区别于同为一线城市的北京国资国企特色、深圳/广州民企与港资特色，上海对全球外商的集聚与融合程度最高，对外商的文化和合作习惯也最为熟悉。这为未来国际多边规则制定提供了良好的文化契合基础。

开放文化积淀：作为中国最早的开埠口岸，以及内地首个保税区、首个自贸区所在地，上海一直处在全国对外开放的前沿阵地，开放程度最高。灵活运用大家都能接受的各类商业手段，创造性解决各方分歧和现实难题，已经成为整座城市的发展习惯与价值共识。这为未来国际多边规则制定提供了良好的商业沟通基础。

市场要素集聚：作为中国的经济、金融、贸易、航运中心，以及中国具有国际影响力的科创中心，上海的国际市场化程度最高、市场要素集聚度最高。这为未来国际多边规则制定提供了良好的抓手项目基础。

国际品牌影响：上海在各类国际城市综合排名中，始终处于中国城市排名前列；此外，上海也是一系列国际合作的发起方/积极参与方（如上合组织）和重要的国际合作机构所在地（如金砖银行）。这为未来国际多变规则制定提供了良好的公关宣传基础。

综上所述，上海在新一轮"一带一路"建设中发挥的桥头堡作用，也将至少体现在以下几个方面：

探索各类多边规则与合作模式创新的桥头堡。不仅依托中国自身产业优势与领导地位，通过多边贸易有效整合和统筹各方资源，构建经济共同体，进一步发挥新兴市场和发展中国家对世界经济增长的主力贡献作用；也将代表广大新兴市场和发展中国家，与发达国家既有规则开展洽谈和对接，进而逐步构建多边贸易体制，推动建设开放型世界经济。

中国园区经济模式与经验向全球推广的桥头堡。无论是上海自贸试验区为代表的区域贸易模式，还是以张江、漕河泾为代表的园区经济模式，中国的园区经济模式创造了多项世界经济发展奇迹。在向"一带一路"国家（地区）输出成功经验、帮助伙伴国迅速发展和快速对接的同时，也能建立境外"根据地"，更有利于把握外资搭载的先进技术、经营理念、管理经验和市场机会，进而带动中国企业潜入全球产业链、价值链、创新链。而这本身也符合上海自身拓展开放空间的需要。

中国元素走向全球的桥头堡。构建开放型经济新体制，需要遵循一致性和多样性统一的原则。探索多边合作对外开放规则，也需循序渐进。上海的桥头堡价值，依托的是整个中国腹地经济；上海建设"一带一路"桥头堡，也不只是为了发展自家自留地，更是服务于整个国家对外开放战略，将成为中国元素走向全球铺设"高速公路"。

未来上海建设"一带一路"桥头堡，可分三步走：

（1）定规划：调研目标方向和潜在合作伙伴的背景信息及战略发展诉求，识别与上海及中国当下发展契合度较高、时机与条件较为成熟的优先对象开展顶层设计，明确多方共赢的合作模式和初步规范标准。

（2）搭平台：基于前期顶层设计框架，围绕先导合作切入点，导入相关资源，采用市场化运作方式开展合作，过程中不断优化完善相关规范标准。从具体项目入手，不断深化多方合作，扩大同心圆效应。

（3）铺网络：一方面，总结成功经验，扩展合作平台外延，建立跨境合作园区与服务节点，从而更深入地联动目标国市场需求和国情环境；另一方面，对接包括"长江经济带""粤港澳大湾区"在内的国内区域协同发展战略，打通腹地资源，帮助中国资源对接全球价值链网络，包括走出去、引进来，以及跨地域资源协同。

作为"一带一路"建设的桥头堡，上海未来发展需要具备更大的胸怀与格局，建设着力点需要从现有的营商环境构建，转变为将来的生态环境构建，侧重创新机制与规范标准的建立，而非仅仅局限于传统的招商引资项目导入。为了更好促进此转变，在一些传统运作领域，需要引入第三方专业机构，以价值为导向，促进政府和市场资源的有效对接。

以近期如何应对外商对中国对外资管理环境变化的焦虑为例。今年包括GSK、礼来等在内的几家外资研发中心陆续撤离中国或上海张江，在外资圈内引发诸多讨论；加上近期外籍人士工作签证系统正在更新调试，对原来流程操作周期影响较大，外媒纷纷猜测，中国对外资管理政策是否有了新的变化。虽然政府有传统的政策宣贯和媒体公关渠道，但从事件的及时反馈、解读视角、渠道管理等方面来看，若是能提前开展市场反应预判，把有些调整做在前面，或许公众反应会更好，一些做法也能化被动应对为主动引导。而这本身也是政府转变传统思维，通过市场化手段，与外资机构开展文化／思维模式对接的一种尝试。

综上所述，如何扮演好新的国际角色，承担与自身发展阶段相适应的责任，是中国不容回避的重要课题。而上海作为中国改革开放最前沿的旗手，如何因势利导、顺势而上，加大既有改革步伐，拓展自身发展空间的同时，也能帮助中国探索新时代背景下"一带一路"倡议新路径，真正发挥桥头堡作用。

上海："一带一路"的源泉

梅柏杰
世界银行社会、城市、农村和灾害风险管理全球发展实践局首席城市专家

上海是"一带一路"倡议的源头。上海35年人均GDP增长13倍，取得一系列成就：上海人均GDP是中国人均GDP的2倍；上海是长江经济带的关键；中国人口最多的城市；拥有全球最大的地铁系统；成功避免大城市病；世界前20的大城市。

上海对"一带一路"的贡献主要取决于如何应对全球"三大趋势"和"三大挑战"。"三大趋势"分别是：全球经济中心持续向东转移；服务业的全球化、持续创新；"银发海啸"——全球及地区人口老龄化加剧。"三大挑战"是：上海有机会成为全球生产网络的核心，但面临的竞争压力也会加剧；有机会加强服务业（如金融、研发、设计），但面临建设具有国际竞争力的人才储备的挑战；中国老龄化速度超过很多国家，而上海更快，必须找到新方法让老龄人口融入社会结构，而不是被孤立。

应对挑战一，需要提高生产力。投资和出口拉动经济增长已经接近极限，"简单"的改革已经不再有，提高生产能力愈发困难。国企为主导的经济缺乏创新力；劳动生产率较低，人力资源缺乏竞争力；较少的劳动人口在支撑更大的总人口。

应对挑战二，需要建立互联、高效、灵活的城市形态。上海的空间布局日益影响其竞争力和宜居性：城市扩张导致密度下降，经济距离加大，集聚效益减弱。低收入人群居住"边缘化"；附近地区无法应对气候变化。

应对挑战三，需要培养、吸引、留住人才。流动人口（占40%，每年增长35万以上）的融入情况不佳，说明人才和人力资本未充分利用，而快速人口老龄化将缩小劳动力队伍。一方面，流动人口不能平等地享受各种服务；另一方面，上海是全球生育率最低的城市之一，老年人口（60岁以上）与劳动年龄人口之比将很快低于1。

上海经济发展面临的主要挑战：没有形成有活力、竞争力的经济体；老龄人

口没有充足的设施与服务；缺少可承担得起的住房和面向大众的基本服务。

三大挑战虽然复杂，但有解决之道，应从结构、空间、社会三个方面形成城市发展战略。为成功发展奠定基础的三大工具为：利用市场有效激励；政策改革，提高国际竞争力；加强机构功能，巩固治理、协调。

三大转变：结构上，建立高生产力，建设创新型经济，从资本积累转变为提高生产力，培育创新、多元发展和推动服务业增长；空间上，打造互联、高效、灵活的城市，从零散的空间发展到扩大集聚经济并促进可持续发展；社会方面，建设开放、包容的城市，从吸纳农民工到融合家庭，提供平等的教育机会和可承担的住房，增强文化活力，扩大社会服务和社会保障，健全人力资源储备，促进创新，刺激消费。

提高生产率，创新拉动经济增长，实现由"中国制造"向"中国智造"的转变，促进经济多元发展，鼓励中小型企业市场参与；采取"以人为本"的政策，投资到人而非设施，改革国企；建立一个创新生态系统。

控制城市扩张，更有效地利用土地，提高城市密度，增强城市的集聚效益，同时使住房更加实惠，并保护环境，减缓气候变化。

促成转变的三大工具：市场工具，长三角城市之间土地供应和温室气体排放配额可交易；政策上，改革户口制度，改革国企，形成"竞争中立性"制度；机构上，整合区域层面的发展规划，协调土地利用、交通和城市战略，制定低碳能源稳步扩张的体制框架；创建一个强大、连贯的城市品牌。

围绕"产业赋能"推进上海经贸、金融创新，建设中国"一带一路"桥头堡

方寅亮

波士顿咨询公司全球资深董事经理

2013年秋天，习近平主席在哈萨克斯坦和印度尼西亚提出共建丝绸之路经济带和21世纪海上丝绸之路，即"一带一路"倡议。四年来，中国"一带一路"建设已取得初步成就。截至2017年8月，与我国签署共建"一带一路"合作协议的国家和国际组织已达69个，一系列部门间合作协议覆盖政策沟通、设施联通、贸易畅通、资金融通、民心相通，"五通"各领域，联合国大会、联合国安理会等重要决议也纳入"一带一路"建设内容，已有超千个重大项目逐步落地。另外，在贸易方面，我国"一带一路"贸易总额超过3万亿美元，工程承包在对外投资当中达到1 260亿美元，同比占新签合同额51.6%。在金融方面，自2016年1月开张以来，亚投行已批准了28个投资项目，发放贷款总额约30亿美元。

"一带一路"是一项庞大的工程，延伸国内18个省，覆盖沿线几十个国家。放眼未来，"一带一路"的深化落地也面临着诸多挑战。首先，从国内发展面临的挑战来看，"一带一路"成功的关键在于"互联互通"。不同行政区域都有本地利益，如果一些地区的地方保护主义色彩过于厚重，或者出现不同地区抢占"一带一路"红利，那么就会使"互联互通"的效果大打折扣。其中，相比较沿海发达地区，内陆地区纳入"互联互通"版图的挑战更为明显。

与国内的挑战相比，"一带一路"在国际上面临的挑战则更加艰巨。首先，沿线诸多国家的经济发展水平不高、市场发育程度较低，毕竟单方面实力资源有限，也面临着摊子大、后劲不足等风险。另外，一些国家政局本身就处在动荡之中，政府对社会的控制能力比较弱，而"一带一路"主要是高层政治之间的合作，看重的是与政府间的合作，选举政治本身就存在着很大的不确定性，一旦政府发生权力交替，就会存在终止"一带一路"项目的风险。在国际间合作方面，"一带一路"横跨亚欧非三大洲，沿线国家基础设施建设差

距较明显，如何在差距如此明显的环境下做到"统一"，简化投资程序，降低投资成本，这也是"一带一路"项目在实施过程中不得不考虑的问题。货币、交通工具、海关工作等领域的"不统一"为"一带一路"的实施增添了诸多风险。

这些挑战的问题本质在于供需信息的不透明、市场信息的不充足和流程标准的不统一，而问题的根源症结在于市场平台和整合服务的不足。

上海作为"一带一路"交汇点上能级最大的城市，是中国对外经济交往与发展空间要素的配置者，应肩负起通过金融经贸创新，疏解核心症结，建设中国"一带一路"桥头堡的重任。在金融经贸创新方面，上海应在过去服务跨国企业的基础上增加针对本土企业"走出去"的服务，聚集更多与"一带一路"新型经济体的相关机构和企业，不断提升针对新兴经济体企业的服务能力和服务模式。同时，作为"一带一路"的桥头堡，上海应通过帮助中亚、西亚、东南亚等"一带一路"沿线国家完整产业结构的契机，完成对本地和周边腹地产业的转移和升级改造。

且不论是2040年推进建设全球卓越城市，还是2020年打造"四个中心"，都与通过经贸与金融创新，推进中国"一带一路"发展一脉相承。上海作为建设中的国际经济、金融、贸易与航运中心之一，到2020年上海要基本建成与我国经济实力和人民币国际地位相适应的国际金融和贸易中心。基于已有的发展基础和比较优势，上海需进一步加快金融和贸易改革创新，提升市场功能，促进资金有序流动、增强配置全球市场资源能力和国际影响力。同时，推动上海作为国际金融、贸易中心与"一带一路"沿线国家和地区互联互通，通过创新手段打造面向"一带一路"、辐射全球的金融网络体系和支撑体系。另外，上海计划在2020年基本建成"四个中心"的基础上，到2040年建设成为综合性的全球城市。因此上海需深化金融、贸易、经济等领域创新，促进产业发展，多维度打造全球高地。

作为金融中心，上海在成长发展过程中取得领先，但在金融市场功能、产业支撑和服务水平上仍存在距离。近五年来，中国资本项目逐步开放，金融开放力度持续加大，上海国际金融中心全球地位稳步提高，由2010年的第八位逐步上升至2015年的第五位，一直保持稳定向好态势（见图1）。特别是成长性指标遥遥领先，连续多年处于第一位。但在金融市场功能上，上海在外汇市场的发展和成熟度方面较为领先，而在资本市场和银保市场领域尚落后于纽约、新加坡等老牌金融中心。在产业支撑上，上海的产业基础及跨国公司资源较完善，但在产业人才和景气度方面较为薄弱，体现在其产业创造力以及活力尚需加强。另外，在

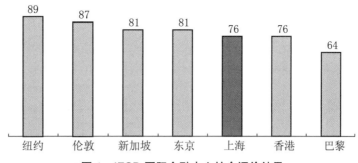

图1　IFCD 国际金融中心综合评价结果

服务水平上，上海作为国际金融中心的硬件支撑与纽约等领先金融中心发展水平差别不大，信息系统建设、工作环境和社会管理是衡量软性服务水平的重要指标，上海在软件服务方面仍需加强（见图2）。

作为贸易中心，上海在贸易规模上取得领先，但在服务功能、产业赋能角度上与全球领先水平仍有距离。近年来，世界贸易需求中心正向中国转移，世界经济格局的变化同我国经济政策的支持引导，帮助上海确立了国际贸易中心的地位，在规模上取得世界领先地位，上海港集装箱吞吐量连续7年位居世界港口第一（见图3）。但与此同时，上海距离向服务导向型的第三代国际航运和贸易中心转型中走在前列的伦敦、纽约、新加坡等城市，在软件服务和产业赋能上仍有很大差距。上海的自由贸易政策还处于起步阶段，贸易与周边产业间联系较弱，产业关联性和带动能力有待加强。另外，上海在航运交易、贸易融资、保险承保、保险保赔、金融租赁等服务功能上起步较晚，规模上也存在一定差距（见图4）。

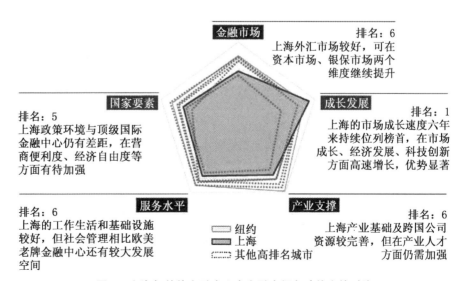

图2　上海与其他金融中心在金融市场各功能上的对比

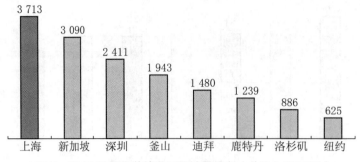

图3　2016世界集装箱港口吞吐量排名（单位：万TEU）

因此针对以上问题，上海作为"一带一路"国家的核心流量枢纽和资源配置中心之一，应充分发挥资金聚集、人才汇聚、物资流通的优势，充分发挥增值、扩散和配置的功能，真正通过以"市场机制"推进"实业赋能"，脚踏实地下好"一带一路"大棋局。"市场机制"是指通过设立创新性的市场交易平台，丰富要素市场种类，有效促进各类创新创业要素的流通与交易，促进市场在资源配置中发挥决定性作用。"实业赋能"是通过金融和贸易创新，推动功能型平台向服务型平台的转化，紧贴企业"走出去"的实际需求与挑战，切实有效地帮助实业"走出去"，实现外向落地。以市场机制服务实体经济，以此服务国家"一带一路"建设的同时，进一步提升金融、贸易中心在市场功能、产业功能上的支撑力度。

对此，针对上海贸易与金融发展，BCG深化以"市场机制"推进"实业赋能"的破题思路，提出四大创新构想。

围绕"市场机制"，BCG提出构建：

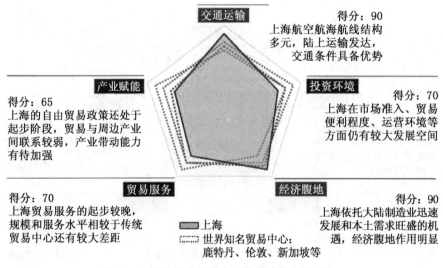

图4　上海与其他贸易中心在各功能上的对比

• 跨境虚拟币联盟：以人民币为虚拟币对应的储备兑换货币，在"一带一路"沿线国家（地区）中用于贸易结算、跨境支付和投资；使用虚拟币的国家享受上海给予的成员待遇。

• 多边项目交易市场：建设多边项目交易市场，交易所会员包括各国项目方、中国投资方、企业、银行等，各国会员将项目放到上海进行"挂牌"交易。

围绕"实业赋能"，BCG 提出：

• 整合服务平台：配合多边项目交易市场在上海建设"一带一路"整合服务平台，包括的功能如：跨境担保、跨境保险、跨境结算、法律服务、数据服务、税务服务、跨境尽职调查。

• 投资地信评指数：建立"一带一路"国家或者重点城市和地区的信用评价指数，成为"一带一路"国家投资和贸易的风向标。

针对"市场机制"，区块链技术被广泛认为将对全球经济和金融环境产生深远影响，为及早布局和受益，英格兰银行作为英国中央银行研究发行由央行主导的数字货币 RSCoin，致力于使整个金融系统更加高效、更具弹性，其设计框架及技术思路值得借鉴。框架上，引入虚拟货币促进贸易。英国央行引入不与美元挂钩的虚拟货币 RSCoin，直接充当不同货币间结汇的媒介，无需再转换成美元进行交割。此举既方便了非通用货币间的结汇问题，也通过与实体货币脱钩，避免了汇率波动和贬值风险。此外，通过 RSCoin 同时避免了通过其他跨境清算系统，极大程度上免除了清算所需的手续费用，减少了投资、贸易成本。技术思路上，英国央行采取了"高低区块"和"中心化"区别于比特币等一般传统虚拟货币，在效率和可控性上都有很大提升。RSCoin 采用双层区块，区分"底层区块"和"高层区块"，将每次交易的直接参与者从一般用户减少至商业银行用户，从而提高了业务处理速度。比特币系统的处理能力最高为 7 笔 / 秒，而 RSCoin 每秒可处理超过 2 000 笔交易，且业务处理速率随着直接参与者数量的增加线性增长。"中心化"是指英国央行掌握使用 RSCoin 系统的密钥，由央行控制数字货币的统一供应，承担的"管理者、调控者"角色。因此，不同于其他虚拟货币，RSCoin 拥有传统货币的可控性和国家信用背书，因而解决了虚拟货币无主权属性的问题，避免了货币超发和流动性危机。

针对"实业赋能"，新加坡自独立半个世纪以来所创造的一连串经济辉煌，政府提供一站式服务平台，支持对外投资，值得上海学习和借鉴。新加坡国土狭小、资源匮乏，由于有限的市场需求、充裕的资金以及过剩产能间的矛盾日益突出，新加坡制定了"七小时战略"，将七小时飞行范围内的国家和地区作为通商和经济发展的腹地，主要措施包括直接对外投资、建设海外工业园、自由贸易等。在之后的 30 余年里，新加坡的对外投资额逐年增长（除金融危机年份），并已完成从劳动密集型到资本—技术密集型再到高新技术产业、高附加值服务业的转变，几乎每 10 年就完成一次产业转型升级。其中，新加坡政府提供一站式服务平台，主要囊括交流服务、担保保险、人才咨询三个方面。针对交流服务，新加坡政府帮助企业建立与世界各国政府、组织、商业机构的联系，更针对企业进行"一对一"服务对接商业机会。2008 年一年，组织了超过 130 个代表团赴海外参观拜访，超过 400 家企业获益，帮助企业创造 170 亿新元海外销售收入，更组织了百余个各类贸易展览会。针对担保保险，政府为大型企业提供保险专项跨境保险业务，帮助企业有效管理跨境投资风险。同时，为中小企业提供跨境担保服务，在资金上给予支持，仅 2008 年一年就为 747 家企业提供 7 亿新元的担保和融资。在人才和咨询方面，政府成立了专门的一条龙咨询中心，包括法律、税收、金融、战略等，现已帮助超过 3 600 家企业受咨询成功在境外进行投资或建设工业园区。为了更好的服务广大中小企业，不仅为企业支付 50% 的咨询费用，更派遣咨询人员和中小企业负责人一起考察、研究市场。同时，开办多种人才培养学校，为企业输送对外投资所需贸易、战略、金融人才。

放眼全球，新加坡和英国是"市场机制"和"实业赋能"方向的先行者，为上海在经贸和金融领域的创新提供了方向。"一带一路"虽然面临巨大挑战，但是也存在着良好机遇，上海应肩负起通过"实业赋能"推进金融经贸创新的责任，服务国家"一带一路"建设的同时，进一步提升金融、贸易中心在产业功能上的支撑力度。

透过商务区经营的"一带一路"国际化管理人才的集聚和培育

天野宏欣

野村综研（上海）咨询有限公司副总经理

1. 中国企业"一带一路"发展的人才瓶颈

中国的"一带一路"建设在与多个国家双边和多边合作的基础上，正逐步开展着国际产能合作、自由贸易区合作等项目，并在"一带一路"经济圈内实现互利共赢的机制建设。通过丝路基金和亚洲基础设施投资银行的资金注入，带动"一带一路"各区域的直接投资，中国正在使双边和多边合作逐渐迈向可持续性发展的一个新阶段。越来越多的中国企业正在以"一带一路"建设为契机，实现其走出去战略，致力拓展全球市场；同时也有越来越多的海外企业开始着力中国市场的开拓以及与中国企业的合作发展，力图强化其全球事业。

已形成跨国事业布局的中国企业，以能源石化钢铁产业的各大企业、投资性企业，以及电子通信制造业为主，因较早进入国际市场，所以目前在海外市场已有一定规模性发展。而更多尚没有在全球市场开展业务的中国企业，则需要通过"一带一路"建设，战略性地开始海外市场的拓展。在这种多数中国企业仍处于走出去的发展阶段的状况下，今后中国企业拓展海外市场，除了需要解决投资贸易政策或资金课题以外，还需要解决企业在全球化发展格局中，如何提供能够掌控海外不同地区不同事业的经营管理人才的课题。

近年来，中国企业通过收购或参股国外企业引进国外技术或拓展海外事业的案例众多，但很多中国企业在收购参股的后续协调中，没能把国外的技术或模式很好地引进到该企业内部，或者很少有中国企业能够把自身的企业文化和理念根植国外企业当中，来发挥协同效应拓展海外事业，这样都会使中国企业在收购后无法掌控好国外企业，进而因无法形成事业上的协同合作，导致最终还是出让或股权转让等局面的发生。这些案例发生的根本原因，就是企业内部缺乏以中国企业的立场，管理并开拓国际事业领域的"国际化管理人才"。

上海是中国最早且最具规模对外开放的城市，有众多的外资企业集聚在此，也有无数的国际商务人才集聚在这里。但集聚在上海的国际商务人才，很多是偏向国外企业针对中国市场开拓中国业务的商务人才，或是对外进行投资、对外销售中国产品或服务的经贸人才，较少有诸如在"一带一路"国家（地区）进行国际化事业拓展的人才、管理经营收购后的海外企业的人才，或者作为中国企业内部多国籍小组的领导进行国际事业拓展的人才。

上海作为"一带一路"的桥头堡，应该着眼上述"一带一路"发展的人才瓶颈课题，充分发挥中国企业拓展海外市场时所需的国际化管理人才的集聚及培育功能（见表1）。

表1　上海的国际商务人才的事业领域偏重示意

对象事业领域 ＼ 人才所属企业	中国企业	外资企业
国内事业经营	人才资源丰富	人才资源丰富
对外贸易投资事业经营		
国外事业经营	人才资源缺乏	中国国内缺乏人才

2. 国际化管理人才所需的技能和素质

一般管理经营人才所需的技能和素质，按照美国管理学学者罗伯特·卡兹（Robert L.Katz）的定义，可总结为以下三大技能：

（1）技术性技能：能够完成组织内具体工作的技能。如，能够运用特定的程序、方法、技巧处理和解决实际问题的能力等。

（2）人际关系技能：能够与人共事，理解并激励他人的技能。如，能够以小组成员的身份有效地工作，并能够在自身领导的小组中建立起合作的能力等。

（3）概念性技能：能够对复杂的情况进行分析、诊断，并进行抽象和概念化的技能。如，能够提出新的想法和新的思想的能力，能够识别在某一个领域的决策对其他领域将产生何种影响的能力等。

除了上述三个基本技能之外，"国际化管理人才"还应需要具备以下两项重要能力：

（1）国际观：可从世界政治及经济的视角理解事业的定位和方向性。理解并认同与自身环境不同的价值观及文化。

（2）异种文化沟通能力：除运用语言能力之外，可顺利地与不同文化背景不同思想的人才进行深度交流沟通的能力。

为了培育具备此类能力的"国际化管理人才"，企业内部能否建立人力资源开发体系将至关重要。很多跨国公司在培育此类人才时有不同的举措，如日本企业因人员流动率不是很高，所以普遍会建构较为长期的人才培育计划，如从资浅阶段到资深阶段根据所处的事业环境提供较广泛的海外经验或海外培训，建立企业集团内跨国统一的人事制度，创造企业集团内跨国小组参与项目的机会，开展企业集团内建构跨国人际关系的活动等。

一个国际化城市也可以提供吸引国际化管理人才并使其成长的环境。上海一直以来提倡总部经济建设，并已经有一系列的鼓励政策让跨国公司的地区总部进驻到上海市内。随着上海市内的企业地区总部，从中国区总部扩大上升为亚洲总部、"一带一路"总部，乃至全球总部等，集聚在上海的经营管理人才的层次和厚度也必然会增加。而对于培养经营人才的"国际观"和"异种文化沟通能力"，除了引进总部经济等政策支持之外，还可以通过商务区的经营管理来实现单一企业无法进行投资的人才培育机制建设（见图1）。

	需配备的能力	集聚及培育方式
经营管理人才	技术性技能 概念性技能 人际关系技能	自身的经验 企业内外的培训课程 总部经济等政策激励
国际化管理人才	（除上述能力外） 国际观 异种文化沟通能力	（除上述能力外） 企业内的跨国人力资源体系 基于城市商务区经营的人才培育机制建设

图1 "国际化管理人才"所需的能力及集聚/培育方式

3. 城市如何吸引并培育国际管理人才

随着知识经济在全球范围内的扩展，公司白领人才今后将越来越没有必要集聚在特定区域的特定办公楼内工作。城市的商务区需要应对企业及办公人才的需求，战略性地通过区域管理构建吸引人才工作，并促进人才交流，实现创新的人才环境。

具体来说，工业经济发展模式下的企业活动的目的，主要在于安定的生产及供应，因此商务区的功能及配套需对应此类企业活动需求，配套安全大量的交通功能让员工可以定时上下班；需要有高效的动线让员工集聚或疏散；需要有足够的商务楼空间让全体员工一同工作；需要提供各个员工适当规格的办公空间，以及办公区周边功能满足大量员工的餐饮需求等。

而知识经济发展模式下的企业活动，则并不需要全体员工在相同的时间集聚在相同的地点，也不需要员工坐在按照规格设计的办公室内工作。而需要员工在办公空间内外与企业内部及外部的人才进行交谈、讨论、创新等知识交流活动，因此商务楼内外及整体商务区内都需要有足够的知识交流空间，也需要有可以刺激创新的活动空间、展示空间，以及满足知识性人才就业和生活的舒适空间等。

从"吸引人才"的观点来看，上海市众多的商务区虽然非常适合服务于工业经济发展模式下的各种企业活动，但现今需要有适合知识经济发展所需的商务环境来吸引全球多样的人才。为创造此类可吸引知识经济发展模式人才的商务区，无法由单一的开发商或物业管理公司来进行建设、开发及管理，而需要整个商务集聚区范围的相关政府、开发商、入驻企业等共同合作进行地区经营和建设。主要内容包括：建设运营知识交流环境、设计吸引人才的舒适空间，根据企业发展进行战略性区块再开发，引进创新功能、举办知识交流活动等。

从"培育国际化管理人才"的观点来看，除了上述的环境建设之外，更需要有针对性地促进人才交流的措施。为了拓宽于商务区就业的人才的国际视野、促进人才更了解多元异种的文化，并能实现更密切的跨文化交流，在政府、开发商、入驻企业等共同合作进行的地区经营中，应适当举办各种区域联合活动。比如，实施可拓宽商务人才国际视野的讲演或沙龙活动、能够了解不同文化、促进跨文化交流的社区活动等。

地区经营较多的案例偏向商业区域的地区经营，如整个商圈相关的政府、开发商、入驻商贸业联合组织一个经营体，进行该区域的空间舒适化建设、共同营销活动，以及共同节庆的举办等来吸引更多消费者前往该商圈，以实现个别商贸租户及业主的互利共赢。但也有如东京国际化管理人才聚集的东京站前 CBD 被称为大丸有地区（大手町—丸之内—有乐町）之类的高端商务办公区的共同经营案例，也是可以借鉴的。

因为东京是日本企业全球总部聚集的地区，国际化管理人才自然聚集在东京都心，但是随着知识经济的发展，即使在这个国际商务密集的大丸有地区，也在通过政府部门和民间部门的协调合作进行地区经营，使原本只是一个写字楼群体的商务区，逐渐变为适合知识化经济时代的经济、社会、环境和文化活动协调的综合性城市，并不断地举办推进适合企业人才需求的商务区活动。具体来说，从吸引人才方面，规划整个区域的高舒适度并易于交流的公共空间，提供办公或消费时可便捷使用的区域内交通，进行节庆、防灾、运动、环保等交流活动等。从培育人才方面，设置并经营促进国内外人才交流互动以及进行创新活动的平台，经营促进商务人士相互学习的"早间大学"，该学习平台还成为东京与郊区协同发展的项目启动据点，还有促进国际化管理人才多元考虑可持续发展的沙龙等（见表 2）。

表 2　东京大丸有地区的地区经营

区域经营的范围	东京都、千代田区（大手町—丸之内—有乐町）共约 120 公顷
进行区域经营的主体	东京都政府、千代田区政府 JR 东日本、大丸有地区开发商及业主企业约 90 家，以及多数大丸有地区进驻企业
"吸引人才"观点的措施	• 策划并实施城市可持续发展准则 • 区域内舒适的空间规划 • 区域内交通的运行 • 节庆、防灾、运动、环保等交流活动的实施 • 共同促销及品牌建构等共同商业活动
"培育人才"观点的措施	• 企业人才创新平台 • 学习社区（早间大学）活动 • 企业社会责任经营沙龙

4. 让上海成为"一带一路"国际管理人才建设桥头堡

已有多年历史的地区经营，也可理解为一个区域资源的共享经济。目前中国已经是全球共享经济最发达的国家之一，而上海市的商务集聚区作为中国国际商务人才资源最丰富的地方，更应该积极利用并共享上海市既有的资源，进一步发展商务区的地区经营模式，构建中国企业拓展经营国外市场时所需的国际化管理人才的集聚及培育机制，使上海成为服务于"一带一路"的人才建设桥头堡。

发挥"桥头堡"区位优势，上海全面推动"一带一路"建设

杨 洁

毕马威中国审计合伙人

2013 年以来，"一带一路"建设取得了举世瞩目的成就，一批有影响力的标志性项目逐步落地，来自中国和全球的领先企业和各类机构在倡议框架下积极开展基础设施、能源、装备制造、环保、金融等领域合作，推动了区域及世界经济的发展。

1."一带一路"沿线投资面临诸多挑战

随着"一带一路"倡议向纵深推进和鼓励措施不断出台，企业在沿线地区的业务拓展和投资活动愈加活跃。在服务客户的过程中我们发现，一方面"一带一路"倡议给企业带来了重大发展机遇，另一方面，企业在开展"一带一路"业务时也面临一些问题和挑战，这主要包括：

（1）信息匮乏和渠道不畅通。

很多有意在"一带一路"沿线开拓市场的企业都发现，由于有效信息的缺失或信息沟通渠道不畅，企业很难获得投资决策所需的核心资讯，包括中国和投资地政府在"一带一路"倡议下的优惠政策和合作框架、投资地最新的法律法规和行业监管条例、投资地支柱产业发展情况和未来规划、重点项目清单和针对重点行业的投资机会分析等。

（2）缺乏完整的产业链。

在目前开展"一带一路"投资的中国企业中，大多数是大型企业或央企，中小企业的参与度还不是很高，在投资行业上也多集中在基础设施、能源电力和公用事业等领域。在一定程度上出现了投资行业和地区集中、跟风式投资的情况，一方面使所投行业快速变成了竞争红海，利润率降低，另一方面也使产业链分工和布局不完整、产业配套能力有待完善的问题日益突出。

（3）针对"一带一路"投资优惠政策有待完善。

目前政府对于鼓励类的境外投资项目，在财政、税收、外汇管制、海关、信贷和保险等领域给予了相应的政策支持，有意愿开拓"一带一路"沿线市场的企业希望政府能够就"一带一路"项目也能够制定相应的鼓励政策，尤其是在项目审批、信贷、资金流动、保险理赔等环节采取措施，提高投资便利化水平。

（4）海外业务运营合规困境。

海外业务运营合规主要遇到的问题包括税务和社保缴纳等。企业在"一带一路"地区运营有时会遇到不该纳税而被征税、应少纳税而被多征税、税收优惠政策落实难、税收争端解决难等问题。在社保缴纳方面，一般情况下企业需要为在"一带一路"沿线开展工作的中国籍员工在海外和国内同时缴纳两份社保金，但在实际情况中，外派员工很难享受到海外社保待遇。

（5）投资风险大，管控难。

"一带一路"国家大多属于发展中国家，投资环境差别较大，项目运作也存在不规范的情况，这使得"一带一路"投资面临更为复杂和严峻的风险管理挑战。以汇兑风险为例，虽然有些"一带一路"项目签署的合同是以美元作为支付货币，但是合作方最后还是以当地货币支付项目款项，这就带来了巨大的汇兑风险，对人民币国际化的需求就显得更加迫切。

2. 利用上海区位优势推动"一带一路"建设

发挥上海推动"一带一路"建设的"桥头堡"作用，主要是以三个区位优势为出发点——国际金融中心、自贸区和自由港、跨国公司地区总部聚集地和长江经济带发展领头羊。

根据上海市"十三五"规划，到 2020 年，上海将基本建成具有全球资源配置能力的国际经济、金融、贸易、航运中心；在金融领域，将基本确立全球性人民币产品创新、交易、定价和清算中心地位。

上海自贸试验区成立四年来，积极打造法制化、国际化、便利化的营商环境，目前正在筹建自由贸易港，区域自主权将进一步加大。

此外，上海是内地跨国公司地区总部最为集中的城市，也是聚集了众多中小企业的长江经济带的地区发展领头羊，因此，在促进跨国公司和中小企业参与到"一带一路"建设的工作中拥有得天独厚的区位优势。

3. 上海发挥"桥头堡"作用的政策建议

在综合考虑企业开展"一带一路"投资面临的挑战的基础上，我们从上海区位优势出发提出以下建议，希望能为上海更好地发挥"一带一路"建设"桥头堡"的作用提供一些有益的思考。

（1）与"一带一路"沿线城市建立全面合作机制。

目前，多个国家级的"一带一路"合作框架已经达成，但城市间或行业间的较低层级的合作机制还有待建立和完善。上海可以考虑与"一带一路"沿线的主要城市或投资热点城市建立城市间的全面投资合作机制。

截至 2017 年年底，中国已累计与 86 个国家和国际组织签署了 100 份"一带一路"合作文件。上海可以考虑在这些国家级的合作协议框架下，与"一带一路"沿线重点城市建立城市间的全面合作机制体系，覆盖投融资和贸易促进、金融创新、联合培训和研究、建立互惠共赢的税收、关务、社保等监管和服务保障体系、建设信息和资源共享平台等，打造城市间经贸活动的"绿色通道"。

以自贸区为例，其实目前"一带一路"沿线很多国家和城市对于中国产业园区和自贸区的建设经验非常感兴趣，上海可以与这些城市开展合作，根据当地地理优势和产业发展特点，打造"一带一路"沿线自贸区链条，不仅能够促进链条上企业的投融资和贸易活动以及生产要素的自由流动，也能够带动当地经济发展，为各国民众带来福祉。

（2）建立与内陆地区省市"东西双向互济"合作机制。

在十九大报告中，习近平总书记提出"要以'一带一路'建设为重点"，"加强创新能力开放合作，形成陆海内外联动、东西双向互济的开放格局"。

与东部沿海地区相比，中国的内陆省市对外开放水平较为滞后，开放度较低，经济转型升级动力不足。"一带一路"倡议的提出打开了中国面向中亚、西亚、南亚的开放大门，使内陆省份由对外开放的末梢变为了前沿，面临巨大的发展机遇。然而，内陆省份在指导、引领和推动企业开展对外合作、建立自贸区等领域经验不足，面临人才和资金短缺的困难，短期内难以满足"一带一路"建设的需求。

上海可以考虑与内陆省市建立协作机制，比如陕西、重庆、四川、云南、新疆等，以优势互补、互利共赢、重点突破、市场主导、政府推动为原则，在人才、技术、资金、项目等领域开展交流合作，促进各地区开放型经济的协同发展，共同构建"东西双向互济"的合作与开放新格局。

（3）关注中小企业需求，建立全面投资促进服务体系。

上海可针对中小企业特点，重点关注中小企业需求，以此为基础建立全方位的"一带一路"服务体系。

在"一带一路"建设过程中，大型国有企业一直是主力军。但是在"一带一路"沿线存在一些还没有被大企业占领的细分市场，比如建筑建材、交通运输、餐饮旅游、跨境电商等，在这些领域内的产品和服务需求巨大。

中国有一些中小企业，尤其是中小型民营企业在某些细分领域内具有较强的竞争力，它们对市场变化较为敏感，决策机制灵活，研发周期短，可以为市场提供定制的产品和服务，或是凭借先进技术为大型项目提供配套支持和服务，与大企业一起形成完整的中国企业"一带一路"运营生态圈，从而推动上下游产业链和关联产业协同发展，建立完整的研发、生产和营销体系，提升区域产业配套能力和综合竞争力。

中小企业参与"一带一路"建设的途径可以包括与大企业、其他中小企业"抱团出海"，承担大型项目的一部分，或是积极参与到"一带一路"园区建设中来，完善园区的产业链分工与布局。

上海可以从以下几方面着手采取措施，促进中小企业开拓"一带一路"市场：

• 搭建"一带一路"信息服务平台：通过建立信息平台和举办各类活动，使中小企业能够及时了解"一带一路"相关政策和政府间双多边协议的最新进展，沿线各国建设规划和项目进展情况，投资地投资环境信息和风险提示，并为项目参与者提供项目推介和对接平台。

• 提供个性化的金融、咨询和培训服务：为中小企业提供个性化的金融和咨询服务，将企业需求与金融机构、中介和培训服务机构对接，为企业顺利开展"一带一路"服务保驾护航。

• 制定与实施促进投资的相关鼓励政策：了解企业开展"一带一路"投资时遇到的问题，探索、创新鼓励中小企业开展"一带一路"项目投资的配套扶持政策，包括融资支持、高新技术企业税收优惠、简化审批流程等，与投资地国监管部门联合探讨投资便利化措施，如跨境资金的自由流动、社保权益互认等。

4. 推动跨国公司与中资企业的合作与共赢

上海可以考虑发挥跨国公司地区总部集中的优势，促进中外企业的合作与共赢，助力中资企业在"一带一路"沿线拓展业务。

"一带一路"倡议不仅为中资企业带来了发展机遇，同时也为跨国公司提供了一个大展拳脚的舞台。跨国公司拥有先进、成熟的海外项目运营管理经验和全球化的信息和资源网络，中国企业可以充分利用跨国公司的这些优势弥补短板，实现转型，向产业链的高端进发，为顺利进入"一带一路"区域市场奠定良好的基础。比如，虽然中国的建筑承包商已经积累了丰富的海外大型工程、基础设施项目的开发和建设经验，但在从承包商向投资商、运营商转型的过程中仍然缺少可以借鉴的成功案例，面临不少困难。

此外，很多跨国公司也把"一带一路"倡议视为一个业务拓展的良机。一方面，跨国企业可以通过和中国企业携手开展"一带一路"项目，进入新市场，扩大业务规模。比如，一些全球领先的电子电气和工程设备提供商已经在多个"一带一路"沿线的 EPC 项目即工程总承包项目中与中国企业开展合作，提供技术和服务支持；另一方面，在"一带一路"倡议下，域内国家基础设施和公共服务水平提高，投资环境得到改善，政府支出和消费者收入增加，这都为跨国公司在当地开展投资和运营提供了便利条件。据我们了解，一些跨国公司已经制定了"一带一路"业务中、长期发展规划，预计未来还将会有更多跨国公司加大"一带一路"业务投入，在这个新的蓝海市场中赢得先机。

上海可以利用这个契机，深入了解跨国公司的疑虑和困难，一方面搭建跨国公司与"一带一路"项目的对接平台，引导投资的方向和行业，促进跨国公司与中资企业的合作与交流；另一方面可以从跨国公司实际需要出发，帮助跨国公司在上海的地区总部成为公司全球"一带一路"的投资和运营平台，更好地助力"一带一路"建设发展。

5. 开展融资机制和金融产品创新

货币自由兑换和资金自由流动是自贸区建设高效的"一带一路"投融资平台、扩大金融业双向开放的目标之一。上海自贸试验区挂牌四年多以来，开展了跨境融资和结算、投融资汇兑便利化、人民币跨境使用、外汇管理体系改革等一系列的金融创新试点，积累了丰富的理论和实践经验。在"一带一路"倡议下，自贸区可以进一步探索促进企业跨境业务的政策措施，为企业对外贸易和投资活动提供更加便捷的金融服务。

未来，自贸区可考虑加强金融政策创新力度，扩大自由贸易账户本外币一体化各项业务，挖掘自由贸易账户创新功能，完善自贸区分账核算单元体系。同时，在自贸区已建立的各类资产交易平台的基础上，鼓励金融产品创新，包括黄金、外汇、金融衍生品、保险保单、非标资产的产品创新，扩大境外人民币境内投资金融产品范围，支持人民币跨境双向流动。

此外，随着未来各项改革政策的进一步细化和落地，以及实施力度的增强，金融机构可协同政府部门在建设人民币全球服务体系和资本项目下可兑换方面不断深入改革，在区内设立银行、证券、保险等金融机构的分支机构和大型金融机构的业务总部，支持探索进一步扩大个人可兑换限额和开展区内非金融类企业在限额内的本外币可兑换试点，促进金融开放，为"一带一路"项目投资提供快捷、便利的金融服务。

6. 优化税收服务，深化税收合作

在境内外税务事项日益复杂、税收监管环境日趋严格的大背景下，税收问题逐渐成为影响企业"走出去"项目决策和海外业务运营绩效的一个重要因素。为使税收要素成为全面推动"一带一路"建设的"催化剂"，而非"拦路虎"，上海可以考虑采取以下措施帮助企业更好地"走出去"：

（1）优化针对参与"一带一路"建设企业的税收服务。2015年以来，国家税务总局陆续出台多项措施以服务"一带一路"建设。在贯彻落实国家税务总局文件规定的基础上，上海可以依托自身优势，为企业提供更加个性化的创新税收服务，比如，通过"12366"上海财税咨询服务热线，为企业提供有针对性的税收知识培训，包括"一带一路"国家一般税收和特定行业税收政策介绍、税收风险提示、最新涉外税收资讯等。

（2）为企业享受税收优惠提供绿色通道。为了更好地服务"一带一路"建设，政府为企业提供了诸多税收优惠政策，包括出口货物劳务退（免）税、跨境应税服务零税率或免税以及境外所得税收抵免等。因此，上海可以考虑通过设立特定服务窗口、简化执行程序、提高审批效率、提供相关咨询服务等为企业享受税收优惠提供绿色通道，使可以享受优惠政策的企业能够"应知尽知""应享尽享"。

（3）协助企业解决税务争端。建立企业跨境税务争端协调机制，协助开展"一带一路"业务的企业与当地税务机关和中国国家税务总局积极沟通，及时启动税务相互协商程序，以更好地为企业提供权益保护。

（4）深化城市间税务机关合作。在上文提及的城市间全面合作机制下，上海市税务机关可以与"一带一路"沿线的主要城市或投资热点城市税务机关建立定期会晤与沟通平台，以协助企业解决在当地运营时遇到的不该纳税而被征税、应少纳税而被多征税、税收优惠政策落实难等问题，通过深化合作共同提升税收治理能力。

安永对上海建设"一带一路"桥头堡的建议

张顺源

安永华中区国际税务部总监

"一带一路"是难得的历史机遇，上海可以充分运用其地理、自贸区制度创新、经济、产业以及人才聚集和科技创新等优势为"一带一路"建设出力，并成为服务"一带一路"的桥头堡，从而实现与"一带一路"沿线国家和地区的互联互通以进一步巩固和提升上海作为国际经济、金融、贸易、航运和科创中心的角色。

近年来，安永在"一带一路"市场积累了丰富的服务经验，过去三年安永已协助近 800 家中国企业在"一带一路"沿线国家（地区）进行投资和开展业务。基于我们的工作经验和观察，我们对上海如何服务"一带一路"建设，发挥桥头堡作用提出以下建议。

1. 打造综合性"一带一路"经贸投资促进服务平台

鉴于上海聚集了各国领事馆和政府机构、全球知名的金融和专业服务机构等，上海可建立一个全方位由各国领事馆和相关政府机构、国际化专业服务集群、保险和金融机构等组成的综合性"一带一路"经贸投资促进服务平台。该平台能为计划到"一带一路"沿线国家和地区进行投资和开展业务的企业提供一站式专业服务及信息分享，并在企业进行投资和开展业务的前、中、后阶段提供持续性的服务和支持，其中包括：

（1）前期阶段：提供投资和业务拓展机会信息；当地投资、经商和融资环境、当地市场、行业和供应链信息；投资风险和注意事项；当地法律、税务、优惠政策和相应的合规性要求；对外投资备案/审批相关的咨询和协助等。

（2）投资和开展业务阶段：引荐当地的相关政府机构；当地成功的中资企业和商会；协调企业到当地进行考察、为当地投资相关的审批、注册和优惠政策申请等工作提供支持；为企业在当地投资和经营过程中所面对的问题提供协助；提供当地市场、法规、风险信息动态等。

该"一带一路"服务平台可通过线上（网上联合办公平台）和线下（机构入驻）模式为企业提供支持服务。线下模式可以通过建立"一带一路"产业园引入相关部门和机构入驻，其中包括：

（1）上海市政府机构：在园内设立"一带一路"经贸投资促进服务平台协调办公室，负责牵头协调服务平台成员并提供指导意见。

（2）"一带一路"沿线国家（地区）的领事馆和政府机构：提供当地市场信息、法律法规和政策介绍、引荐当地的相关政府机构和提供协调支持工作。

（3）专业服务机构（如会计师事务所、律所、其他咨询机构等）、金融和保险机构：在园内开设办事处便于企业在园区内获得"一站式"咨询服务。

（4）"一带一路"沿线国家（地区）的中资商业协会：聚集当地的中资商会在园内设立联络处便于现有企业、新企业和计划到当地投资的企业进行有效交流和经验分享。同时也便于政府深入了解中资企业在当地的具体情况和问题、有效团结和凝聚当地中资企业的力量、改善当地经商环境、承担社会责任建立正面形象和提高影响力，间接地将桥头堡从上海延伸到当地为企业护航。

2."人文合作交流专项行动"之"升级打造走出去跨国经营人才培训工程"

针对"人文合作交流专项行动"之"升级打造走出去跨国经营人才培训工程"提出以下建议：

（1）对于即将被派遣到"一带一路"沿线国家和地区的人员："一带一路"沿线有 60 多个国家，大多为发展中国家，地缘政治格局复杂，各区域语言、文化、生活习惯大相径庭。因此为了培养更多跨国经营人才，做好被派遣到"一带一路"沿线国家（地区）的准备和应对在当地可能面对的问题，政府可运用上述建议的"一带一路"产业园入驻机构的资源，并与相应的大学和研究机构合作制定针对特定国家或区域的专项课程（如：法律法规、经商礼仪、文化习俗、语言、安全风险防范等课程）。

（2）对于所聘用的当地国籍高管人员：企业能够在"一带一路"沿线国家（地区）成功和永续经营的其中一个关键因素是与当地社会融合共进。企业在当地成长过程中将会聘用当地员工任职高管。因此为了培养当地国籍高管能够更容易地融入中国企业文化和作风，政府可与相应的大学和研究机构合作制定针对当地国籍高管人员的专项课程（如中国企业的经商礼仪、文化、中文等课程）。

3. 在上海打造"一带一路专板"

"一带一路"沿线大多为发展中国家，经济发展不稳定，同时也为企业带来商机。基于"一带一路"投资项目的风险相对较高，中资企业在当地投资经营的过程中可能会面对融资渠道短缺的问题。为了解决资金短缺问题和实行全民参与"一带一路"项目，政府可考虑打造"一带一路专板"，依据"减少限制、加强监管"的理念提出特殊的符合"一带一路"项目实际情况和收益分配周期的上市要求，具体包括：

（1）制定一套针对"一带一路"投资项目和相关企业的特别 IPO 审查标准和上市要求。

（2）组建专门审查团队或审查专员，加快对"一带一路"投资项目和相关企业的上市申请的审查及审批；针对符合条件的"一带一路"上市项目，安排单独的绿色上市通道以缩短上市等候时间。

"一带一路"的建设为中国与沿线国家和地区的合作打开了新局面，我们非常愿意为上海建设"一带一路"桥头堡出力，使得中资企业在"一带一路"沿线国家（地区）的投资能够安全和永续经营。

美国投资在支持"一带一路"中的角色与作用

欧　文

美中贸易全国委员会上海首席代表

1. 美国企业对支持"一带一路"的兴趣

"一带一路"战略启动后，许多美资企业都在从它们各自具有竞争优势的领域中寻找投资机会。比如，美中贸易全国委员会（USCBC）的一些会员公司已经成功地同中国企业在中国本土，以及其他"一带一路"国家缺乏管理经验、投资，或技术人才的项目中展开了合作。还有一些企业看到了与欧洲和中国国内其他"一带一路"沿线地区潜在客户的合作机会，如物流公司在船运服务和仓库贮存中的商机，以及服务业公司与中国中西部省份企业的合作机会。

虽然"一带一路"可能不会影响所有公司的区域战略，但会带来在中国发展新业务的机会。美中贸易全国委员会在 2016 年发表了一份关于公司如何从"一带一路"寻找商业机会的分析，也有不少公司分享了参与"一带一路"拓展业务的案例。

许多"一带一路"项目机会都是国内的，并且能从上海得到支持。尽管十多年前中国实施了"西部大开发"战略——修建高速公路、铁路、机场连接内陆和沿海——中国内陆省份的基础设施建设仍然落后于东部地区。因此，地方政府把"一带一路"看成吸引基础设施建设、制造业和服务业投资的机遇，因为可能通过"一带一路"规划获批新的项目。例如，一些支持基础设施建设的公司已经从四川、新疆、云南以及其他要建成"一带一路"重要枢纽的地区发现了新机遇。

2. 美国公司如何在"一带一路"与中方合作

为了能更好地抓住"一带一路"带来的商业机遇，一些公司考虑与中国企业合作。以下是一些国际企业参与"一带一路"并从中获益的方法：

（1）提供资金与金融服务。外资企业可以为在境外开展业务的中国公司提供资金支持。尽管已经有一些机构，如 AIIB 和丝路基金，会在"一带一路"项目上给予国内公司资金支持，不少美中贸易全国委员会的会员公司也投入资本和中国公司进行项目合作。金融服务公司也可以为参与"一带一路"项目的中国企业提供服务——比如为在"一带一路"沿线国家进行项目建设的中国公司提供商业保险。

（2）共享全球经验。美中贸易全国委员会的会员公司为中国商业伙伴们提供全球商业实践中的咨询服务，包括市场资讯、法律咨询、最佳实践、风险管理、人员培训和社区活动。例如，很多上海以及东部沿海主要城市的公司，在选择投资伙伴时，非常重视是否熟悉"一带一路"投资目的地，一些外资企业被认为是潜在的合作伙伴。

3. 上海的"一带一路"机遇

上海"一带一路"规划的主要政策包括，通过精简审批流程吸引外商投资，提供优惠政策以促进服务业发展，以及鼓励跨国公司设立地区总部，并充分发挥总部功能的多样性。这些努力能够有助于建立一个更加开放、透明的商业环境。上海"一带一路"规划可能带来的机遇还包括以下几点：

上海加快推进自由贸易试验区以及最近提出的自由贸易港建设，这会给上海带来更多的商业机会。

"一带一路"倡议中对服务业领域的促进，这将有机会为上海带来更多专业的服务和金融领域的专家人才。允许进一步开放服务业，也会推动上海经济的发展，并为"一带一路"提供更有利的支撑。

"一带一路"倡议下，上海大力推动电子商务发展，这有利于国内外企业将商品引入中国市场并销往"一带一路"国家（地区）。

我们希望上海能够有一个更加清晰的"一带一路"具体规划，这将会给中外企业都带来好处，这样它们能更好地了解如何参与支持。

4. 对于上海"一带一路"的政策建议

（1）营造中外企业公平透明的竞争环境。

① 平等待遇。中国境内和上海的外资企业应当在一个平等的基础上参与"一带一路"的项目和发展。只要是合法设立的公司，不论其归属的国籍，应当一视同仁，受到平等待遇。

② 确保行政审批和政府采购过程中的平等待遇。应减少行政许可壁垒，并确保在"一带一路"项目许可审查和批准环节中的公平待遇。有关"一带一路"项目的行政许可都应当排除对公司所有权的偏见，以统一的标准执行。应保证竞标和采购流程开放给可能参与"一带一路"项目的所有公司。

（2）减少贸易壁垒，强化全球贸易规则。

① 增加国际统一标准在对中国销售的商品和服务上的使用。国际统一标准在中国的使用能为中国消费者和最终用户享有最好的产品和服务提供保障，并确保中国的产品和服务能在"一带一路"国家及全球被接受且具有竞争力。上海应当推广有科学根据、透明，且以市场为导向的标准，并面向所有公司，包括本国、外国投资和国外的公司。

② 减少进口壁垒以促进消费和经济再平衡。中国保持着高进口关税和对多种消费品的消费税，以及在产品许可、分销、进口审查和特殊标准上的区别对待。减少对消费品的关税和消费税，并确保对国内和国外制造产品的公平待遇，将会是简单而有力的刺激国内消费的举措。国内消费的增加将有利于解决中国和"一带一路"国家之间的贸易不平衡，且利于减少物流成本。

（3）推动金融领域改革。

上海可以发展为"一带一路"项目提供本土和海外资金支持的金融中心。近年来中国限制资本外流的措施影响到了正常的商业交易和跨境支付，减少了市场信心和可预测性。上海应当在推动以市场主导的金融行业改革中起带头作用，这样将会为国内创造更多资本配置和回流的机会；允许大型外国金融机构的进入，会为世界第二大经济体和国际经济的进一步整合提供条件。

（4）强化创新环境。

① 推行有效的创新激励机制。继续实行创新激励政策以促进科研创新，如鼓励支持研发中心的设立，推动中国本土市场、"一带一路"国家和全球进行产品创新研发。

② 推行引进海外人才的政策。继续为海外人才在上海工作提供便利化的环境，并简化流程使国内外公司可以从"一带一路"以及全球引进人才。

③ 加强知识产权保护机制以及执法。完善的知识产权保护能带来互利。中国应当完善知识产权保护的相关法律法规，拓展资源以强化知识产权，并对侵犯知识产权的行为采取更严厉的惩罚措施。这样将会鼓励企业为中国市场带来更多创新产品，以应用于"一带一路"的本土和海外项目。

立体的"一带一路"：上海的角色和机会

陈英麟
高风咨询经理

1."一带一路"建设推动中国以及沿线国家经济发展和转型，与世界分享中国发展的红利

众所周知，"一带一路"是习近平主席自 2013 年 9 月到 10 月出访中亚和东南亚国家期间开始提出的重大倡议，亦是对外开放的总抓手和新引擎。古丝绸之路作为亚洲与欧洲互通互联的商贸大道，促进了古代东西方经济文化交流。如今国家大力推动的"一带一路"能为现代中国和沿线国家经济发展创造新的机遇，释放更多合作共赢的红利。

"一带一路"建设对中国经济的发展意义重大。首先，"一带一路"建设推动经济转型升级，通过对外开放参与国际分工与合作来提高中国商品质量和完善服务体系。不同于以往主打低端产品，如今沿着"一带一路"走出国门的更多是高新技术和创新产品和服务。中国现正与沿线国家积极合作共同消除贸易壁垒，并挖掘新的经济增长点。在 2016 年，中国对"一带一路"沿线国家的进出口额就高达 62 517 亿元人民币。这不仅有利于促进中国周边区域经济发展平衡，同时也提高了中国的国际影响力。

其次，"一带一路"建设开拓了行业投资机会。通过渐进式的大规模基础设施建设、资源能源开发利用、全方位贸易服务往来等合作方式，为中国资本市场带来多产业链和多行业的投资机会。由于"一带一路"沿线很多国家还处于欠发达状态，各国之间基础设施建设亟待升级。中国已与沿线大部分国家建立双边合作机制，合作领域涉及能源、交通、金融、旅游、基础设施等，力图推动各方共同发展，实现互惠互利，共同创造及培育新竞争优势。

随着全球化政治经济环境的快速变化和中国日益强大的影响力，国际社会期待听到中国的声音和方案。通过"一带一路"建设，中国积极参与全球治理，今后会在国际事务中发挥越来越大的作用，为世界输出更多"中国模式"。

2. 从"中国公司"跃升为"世界公司"的民营企业

"一带一路"建设也为中国企业，特别是民营企业，带来了巨大的发展机遇，但同时也会面临很大的挑战。

一方面，民营企业具有高的决策效率，与国企相比更能根据投资环境的改变及时地作出有利于企业发展的对外投资决策。而且，民营企业的创新欲望和能力都非常强，可以根据市场需求进行商业模式等方面的创新、以此开拓当地市场。民营企业应勇于尝试，而国际化恰恰是企业发展的必经之路。由于这些优势，民营企业在"一带一路"中的角色正变得日益重要。

但另一方面，现有的环境和条件还满足不了民营企业对信息全面性、及时性、有效性等方面的需求。而且，民营企业在跨国经营中将面临政治、经济、金融等方面的风险。这些风险和挑战的背后也意味着民营企业自身在走出去的过程中要在多方面进行战略思考和转型。

从大的趋势来看，目前民营企业的国际化正进入一个新的时代，即从"中国公司"到"世界公司"。而中国也已经进入一个新的以创新创业为代表的大时代，创新的背后代表着知识经济的到来，企业间竞争的焦点已经逐渐从有形资本转向无形资本，知识在企业价值创造中的作用日益凸显。在这个新的转折点，在这个创新知本时代，民营企业拥有了一个极佳的从中国公司跳跃到世界公司的机会。

"一带一路"倡议的全面实施，对于民营企业大跨步发展是一个很好的契机，借此机会从中国公司成长为世界公司，这对民营企业战略转型意义重大。民营企业成长为世界公司，软实力的打造至关重要。优秀的民营企业不但要能够整合硬实力，还要把软实力提升到全球层面上。

针对民营企业"走出去"，有一些具体的建议来帮助民营企业提升自身能力，增强国际竞争力：①民营企业要以全球视角，提升企业品牌认知和竞争力；②积极创新，提升企业整体治理水平；③积极培养跨文化人才，寻求更好的发展；④提高风险意识，健全风险防控机制；⑤建立跨境电商平台，实现全球业务运营；⑥加强企业外部多方合作，抱团出海；⑦民营企业与政府合作，提供奖学金共同打造人才培养平台；⑧大型民企带动中小民企"走出去"，促进产业链上下游"走出去"的协同发展；⑨打造高端智库，强化企业外脑资源，等等。

3. 立体的"一带一路"：软实力的知识平台

我们认为"一带一路"建设并非只是传统意义下为企业提供的硬实力机会，这是平面和线性的理解。实际上，对"一带一路"的解读应该是立体和非线性的。"一带一路"理应成为企业软实力的知识平台，即促进企业思考价值观、扩展国际视野进而实现战略转型。这立体的"一带一路"可以助力民营企业提升软实力知识，为民营企业实现跳跃式发展提供新的思路。

随着中国的商业环境变得越来越复杂和快速多变，中国很多企业都把创新的能力作为它们未来持续增长的核心竞争力。中国已经慢慢从过去的"山寨大国"转型升级为以创新主导的国家，不少中国原创的创新已经达到全球领先水平。在这"后山寨"时代，中国创新企业陆续"出海"探索海外市场的新机会，同时国外的企业也开始参考中国的创新企业，或是从中受到启发，出现"逆向山寨"的现象。尤其是在数字化领域，由于中国独特的互联网生态，不少中国企业已经成为全球领先的科技巨头之一，受世界注目和尊敬。无论是商业模式创新、组织创新甚至是技术创新，我们相信中国企业在未来将发展出更多思想领导力，启发和影响世界更多的企业。

所以，民营企业在思考国际化之时，不仅要考虑有形的东西，还要考虑这些无形的、摸不着的东西，以此全面提升企业竞争力，实现跳跃式发展。

4. 第三条路：数字化丝绸之路

从定义上，"一带一路"是指丝绸之路经济带和21世纪海上丝绸之路。随着虚拟经济在中国快速普及并与实体经济高度融合，我们认为"一带一路"也将跟随"互联网＋"思维发展出"第三条路"：一条虚拟的"数字化丝绸之路"。

中国企业将利用数字化商业模式和技术连接世界各地的企业和消费者，而这第三条路衍生的数字化经济将突破物理地域的限制。在未来，这条路的传播速度以及影响力甚至有可能比实体的更快更广。很多互联网公司，如阿里巴巴、腾讯、百度都在通过这条虚拟丝绸之路影响着世界，这是非常激动人心的。

比如说，马来西亚政府和印度尼西亚政府就聘请了马云担任其数字经济顾问，推动当地数字化转型升级。阿里巴巴跟宣布与马来西亚合作建设"数字自由贸易区"，联手打造中国以外的第一个"世界电子贸易平台"（eWTP）的试验区，旨在帮助全球发展中国家和最不发达国家、中小企业、年轻人更方便地进入全球市场、参与全球经济。阿里巴巴目标要在 2025 年服务全球 20 亿消费者，而其中至少有 10 亿来自海外，因此建立"数字化丝绸之路"对其极具战略意义。

数字化丝绸之路的发展需要线上线下的建设，包括信息基础建设、国际物流、跨境电商、智慧城市、数据安全和网络治理等环节。除了传统的数字化硬件和软件，一些中国本土的数字文化内容，如影视、手机游戏、音乐，文学、动漫等也可以借这第三条路出海。总之，独特的互联网生态和数字化创新将让中国成为行业标杆，向世界出口中国数字化创新。

5. 上海在"一带一路"建设中发挥桥头堡作用

上海在服务国家"一带一路"建设中有着明显的先发优势。首先，上海有着独特的历史背景和政治地位，是中国的经济和金融中心，又是对外开放的重要门户，在"一带一路"中具有"联通内外"的战略地位。透过发挥其区域竞争优势，联动长三角城市群及周边商业生态圈，上海能够成为帮助优秀中国企业走出去的关键节点。其次，过去发展"四个中心"（国际金融中心、经济中心、贸易中心、航运中心）及定位成全球科技创新中心的规划为上海奠定了良好的基础和竞争优势。未来此发展应与一带一路和其他国家战略互相融合，务求发挥一加一大于二的功能。第三，上海作为国际金融中心能为"一带一路"的建设提供融资和金融服务的支撑，而正在建设的自贸区更会成为中国未来自由贸易的新标杆。第四，上海国际化大都会的形象有助吸引全球顶尖人才，能助力"一带一路"人员往来，并基于上海自身的优势重点发展相关创新行业如金融科技和跨境电商等。

然而，上海该如何针对上述几个机会——民营企业、立体的"一带一路"、数字化丝绸之路——进一步把握"一带一路"带来的黄金机遇，发挥其桥头堡的作用？

首先，"一带一路"为企业同时带来了新的机遇和挑战，而更关键的问题是企业自身的战略眼界到底有多远和行动能力有多高。上海市政府应鼓励民营企业培养国际视野和生态思维来思考"一带一路"带来的机会。未来全球市场上的竞争不再仅仅是公司与公司之间的竞争，而更是生态系统与生态系统之间的竞争。生态系统内的参与者之间是多方共赢的，需要共同推动构建一个新型全球治理架构。民营企业要用国际视野来看待未来的颠覆式发展，从战略层面把对"一带一路"倡议的理解提升到一个高度，开始以构建全球生态的战略思维进行战略布局。虽然从"中国公司"到"世界公司"不可能一蹴而就，但这是未来的大趋势，通过把"一带一路"倡议和企业的长期发展规划结合起来真正参与国际治理，一些优秀的民营企业一定会走到这一步。

其次，上海市政府应鼓励民营企业通过"一带一路"积极打造软实力，成为世界商业思想领袖，全面提升企业竞争力，把经济和社会价值创造同时最大化。民营企业需要尝试超越传统观念，让企业有足够的社会责任感，成为世界公民，真正做到站在全球的角度思考问题。参与全球竞争与治理，并促进全球商业治理水平的提升。可喜的是，民营企业中已经有一小批领先的企业家走在前列，开始积极地参与全球治理方面的工作。

最后，上海市政府也应积极参与建设"数字化丝绸之路"，发挥引导角色打造有关数字化生态，扶持更多的创新型数字化初创企业成长，拉动更多的数字化企业"走出去"，推动跨国跨界合作。

2017年上海市政府发布的《上海服务国家"一带一路"建设发挥桥头堡作用行动方案》提出了六大专项行动指导性建议，分别围绕贸易投资便利化、金融开放合作、增强互联互通功能、科技创新合作、人文合作交流、智库建设六方面展开。我们相信未来更多的研究、建议和讨论将有助继续推动上海成为"一带一路"桥头堡的角色。

Building a Super Trade Platform to Play Shanghai's Bridgehead Role

Qi Wu

Senior Managing Director and Vice Chairman of ACCENTURE Greater China

In the opinion of ACCENTURE, the building of a super trade platform is one of the most important strategic initiatives for Shanghai to play its role as the "bridgehead" in the service of the future Belt and Road initiative. The super trade platform, itself, will also become a major pillar trade platform of Shanghai.

Why? Global economic and trading centers are undergoing big changes of development, from trade centers built up on infrastructure such as ports and airports to related trade service financial centers dominated by financial services. Global economic and trading centers, including Shanghai, are at this stage. The next generation of global economic and trading centers will be digital trade ecologic centers, surrounded which, a novel economical system will emerge.

From a global perspective, Singapore is one of the most advanced and most important global economic and trade centers for Shanghai's reference, according to studies and project findings of ACCENTURE. Despite "Smart Nation" initiative, Singapore is building the "next-generation trading infrastructure". The aim is to create an integrated ecosystem that connects participants in trading links, including shippers, ports, logistic companies, customs and border inspection, together with financial services and insurances, and even the innovative ecology formed on this basis through digital means. This ecosystem will promote Singapore's trade center status in Asia and will further drive Singapore's industrial development and upgrading. This thinking of development is worthy of reference by Shanghai. Therefore, building a digital super trade platform may be a vital development direction for Shanghai to act as a bridgehead in the service of the Belt and Road initiative.

Singapore also experienced this stage throughout its development course. The future digital system of Singapore will cover existing trading infrastructure, and directly link to its digital ports, airports and governments. This system also involves multiple stakeholders' digitalization as well as links between above digital systems. Such links just confirm the "platform economy" feature, a special topic studied by ACCENTURE last year. In essence, to make the platform economy really count, new technology and digital means are required to bring higher efficiency, lower transaction costs and amplified action for platform participants. From the development plan of Singapore, the combination of Digital Nation, digital infrastructure and digital trading infrastructure indicates a vital development direction of future economical and trading centers, creating a powerful and effective platform based on original transportation infrastructure, trade-related services (including financial services) for better work and higher value.

Shanghai has inherent advantages to build a super trade platform. Why? Given existing ports, airports and other transport infrastructure and its well-built status as a commercial and trade center, Shanghai shall improve its convenience of commerce and trade through innovation and breakthrough during its course to build a super trade platform. According to a comparison made by ACCENTURE between Chinese mainland and Singapore and Hong Kong SAR (rank No.1 and 3 respectively in Asia), there is a huge gap between Chinese mainland and other countries and regions in such major dimensions as domestic market connectivity, foreign market connectivity, customs efficiency, logistic facility & service level, application of technology information and supervision environment. This gap has influenced convenience and efficiency of trade. China ranks low in many commercial and trade fields among over 100 countries and regions around the world. Namely, to play a more important role in the global trade arena under the Belt and Road initiative, China shall improve its efficiency through service functions and super platforms and shall also solve a number of pain points. Tackling of these pain points will be a key consideration of China (Shanghai) Pilot Free Trade Zone (SHFTZ) during its future development course.

In addition, SHFTZ hopes to promote trade development, and bring China (especially Shanghai) more opportunities of economic and industrial development, more investments and high-level employment opportunities. Apart from trade environment, China also lags behind leading markets in commercial environment and efficiency. In terms of approval efficiency and registration, there is a sharp gap and room for improvement in efficiency of investment and commercial climates compared with major countries in the world. Top priority shall be given to thinking how to solve these pain points during the course of building and promoting the super platform in Shanghai.

Therefore, ACCENTURE believes that Shanghai needs to make breakthroughs in the following three platforms in building the super trade platform:

(1) Design of solutions. Currently, Shanghai municipal government promotes to build the super trade platform dependent more on independent function, and existing processes and demands. However, there are poor connections, even isolation, between different functions. In the future, for continuous optimization and efficiency improvement and for smarter development under the ecologic system, the platform shall become more open in both function and technology. In addition, the platform shall integrate an increasing number of functions. The platform solution shall be feasible, which cannot be done in one step, but allows for gradual development and upgrading.

(2) Design ideas. Current platform design is more relied on existing processes, functions and standardized ideas of the Government. However, in the perspective of ecology and platform, platform processes and functions shall be designed based on user-oriented principles to improve efficiency and increase values for platform participants. "customer experience" shall be considered for designing processes to serve different enterprises.

(3) Commercial and trading promotion. ACCENTURE, from China's perspective, considers platform promotion and development more on solidified system between China and other countries. In the future, from the points of the Belt and Road initiative and global trade, to play a real role of "bridgehead", Shanghai shall provide connections and services that meet requirements between European and Asian countries and between America and Asian Countries to form a multi-lateral pattern, thus creating higher values of platform and realizing the key implications of the Belt and Road initiative.

It is believed that this platform shall be composed of three parts below:

(1) Basic function. For example, trade permission. We need to think how to realize convenience in trade through digital means.

(2) Functions related to trade services. We need to consider how to integrate resources into this platform to enable platform users to effectively finish their

transactions. We need to focus on cost reduction.

(3) Surrounding digital platform, future services shall be intelligent and based on data analysis, including platforms under innovative service modes. Through such mode, new business model and innovative service contents, the entire platform will be more competitive and attractive.

Shanghai's Leading Role in the Opening-up of China's Financial Sector for the Belt and Road Initiative

Elton Huang

PwC Central China Markets Leader and PwC Shanghai Senior Partner

1. Shanghai's Current Macroeconomic Situation

2017 is a very special year. First, economic data released by major economies in 2017 have all showed a clear sign of positive growth for the first time since 2009. Second, BRIC countries' overall national economies have all registered positive growth for the first time in three years. Therefore, with the recovery and growth of the global economy, Shanghai should play a more important role which we will elaborate today in promoting the Belt and Road Initiative in such a favorable environment.

Against this backdrop, regional cooperation, essential for global economic development, has increasingly become a trend and the Belt and Road Initiative is a strategic move following this trend. As mentioned in the 19th NPC Report, the Belt and Road Initiative is one of China's overall long-term plans. Today, we will talk about the relationship between the development of the Shanghai international financial center and the Belt and Road Initiative.

2. Opening up Shanghai's Financial Sector

Against the backdrop that the world economy has been recovering slowly, regional cooperation has become one of the important drivers for global economic growth. Therefore, China put forward the Belt and Road Initiative should conform with the trend of political multi-polarization, economic globalization, cultural diversity and social informationization. As mentioned in the 19th NPC Report, the Belt and Road Initiative is one of China's overall long-term strategies and China's president Xi Jinping proposed Shanghai should build Shanghai Pilot Free Trade Zone to a bridgehead for the Belt and Road Initiative and helping market players go global.

It is believed that a sound financial service system is essential for the Belt and Road Initiative. According to the Development and Research Center of the State Council of China, the investment demand for the infrastructure construction in B&R countries from 2016 to 2020 will be more than 10.6 trillion U.S. dollars, which cannot only be funded by the government or several associations. Shanghai needs to raise funds through various channels in order to provide financial support for the Belt and Road Initiative. Shanghai outperforms its peers in the opening-up of financial sector. In terms of the overall financial development, Shanghai ranks 13th in 2017 according to the Global Financial Centers Index (GFCI) released by UK think tank Z/Yen Group, surpassing the vast majority of the financial cities along the Belt and Road. Compared with major financial centers in the world, such as London, New York, Singapore and Hong Kong, Shanghai has been widely recognized for its huge development potential, with a strong competitive advantage in market growth, economic development and technological innovation. Nevertheless, Shanghai is still facing the problem of inadequate and unbalanced development, lacking due attention to the importance of soft power. Shanghai still cannot rival world's top financial centers in terms of business environment. Specifically speaking, Shanghai lags behind in a vast array of areas such as taxation, government regulations, customer confidentiality, economic openness, entrepreneurial environment and business risk-taking. Compared with Shanghai and other world-class financial centers, there is not much differences in the quantity rather than the quality of the trades made in the stock, bond, commodity and futures markets. A more open international financial market with complete financial regulation and a better legal environment would be desirable. Moreover, Shanghai needs to further open up its economy and provide more innovative financing mechanisms and financial products.

Guarding against systemic financial risks is the eternal theme of the financial work of China's leadership. At the National Financial Work Conference held in July 2017, President Xi Jinping stressed that China should treat the deleveraging of state-owned enterprises (SOE), the major beneficiaries of the banks' easy credit and main source of bad debt, as "the priority of priorities", adequately deal with the "zombie enterprises", and hold officials accountable for a lifetime for building up debt at their respective regions. By the end of 2016, China's debt level was 257 percent of GDP, and the non-financial corporate leverage ratio stood at 166.3 percent, relative to the 72.3 percent in the United States. To address these problems, the 19th Party Congress report calls for "deepening institutional reform in the financial sector, making it better serve the real economy, increasing the proportion of direct financing, and promoting the healthy development of a multilevel capital market." At a press conference during the 19th Party Congress, Guo Shuqing, Chairman of China Banking Regulatory Commission (CBRC) pledged to step up supervision over the financial markets by curbing off-balance-sheet debts incurred by local governments and restricting funding sources for property developers.

In summary, it is necessary for Shanghai to control financial risks and increase the degree of internationalization of its financial market. Shanghai should remain committed to playing an important role in promoting financial cooperation with B&R countries through bolstering economic connectivity, trade cooperation and the further opening-up of the financial sector.

3. Promoting the Opening-up of Shanghai's Financial Sector through the Belt and Road Initiative

The Belt and Road Initiative needs a huge amount of finance. From 2016 to 2020, it is estimated by the Development Research Center of the State Council that the total funding needed for infrastructure development in Belt and Road countries will amount to $10.6 trillion, not alone the investment needed for other fields. Clearly, Chinese banks, coupled with the existing and newly established multilateral financial institutions currently active in the countries along the Belt and Road, cannot meet their potential needs for loans. Solving the financing problem is one of the key factors in promoting the Belt and Road Initiative.

Based on the analysis above, we suggest that:

First, opening up stock and bond markets and provide diverse financing channels for enterprises in B&R countries.

The Government work report approved at the National People's Congress in 2017 made it clear that it supports foreign investment enterprises to list in China's stock exchanges and issue bonds. However, the reality is that the local stock and bond markets of developed countries are more mature than those of China and hence, multinational enterprises are not keen to be financed in China.

As the data suggests, among all the stock exchanges in the B&R countries, none is comparable with those in Shanghai, Hong Kong and Shenzhen, in terms of total market values (Fig.1). If the scale of domestic market is taken into account, stock markets of Singapore and India have a comparative advantage among the B&R countries.

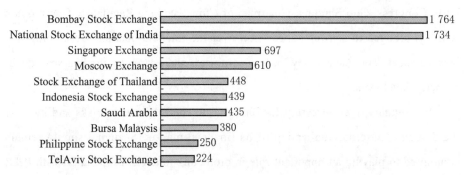

Fig.1　Top 10 stock exchanges in countries along the Belt and Road
(Unit: USD 1 billion) (by Feb. 2017)

As of May 31, 2017, the total market value of listed companies trading on the Shanghai Stock Exchange (SSE) amounted to nearly 30 trillion yuan, nearly 4.4 trillion US dollars. According to the Forbes 2016 "Global 2000", a total of 235 companies were from B&R countries, with a total market value of about 2.72 trillion US dollars. If these 235 companies were attracted to go public on the Shanghai Stock Exchange, it would not only greatly facilitate the financing of the Belt and Road Initiative, but also increase the market cap of over 3 trillion US dollars (or 18 trillion yuan) for SSE. SSE will become one of the most important stock exchanges, which will help Shanghai become one of the world's leading financial centers.

Apart from banks and stock markets, bond markets can also provide sustainable financing for the Belt and Road Initiative. In 2016, the value of the bond issued in mainland China rose to 36 trillion yuan ($5.29 trillion), which formed a huge bond market, making it easier for B&R countries and enterprises to finance directly through a fast track. Moreover, the central government has made it clear that it "supports the governments in B&R countries, companies with a higher credit rating and financial institutions that issue RMB bonds in China". So how does Shanghai play a more important role?

We recommend that Shanghai should build SSE into a major platform to provide bond financing for the Belt and Road Initiative (mostly RMB-denominated bonds and the rest is US dollar bonds). At the initial stage of the scheme, the target market will be the governments with high credit ratings and the listed company with stable financial statements, that is, governments in 12 countries with A+ credit rating assigned by Standard & Poor's and 235 companies listed on the Forbes 2000 with good financial position.

The Chinese bond market is more complicated than the stock market because of different regulations and stricter supervision, so promoting the SSE as a major platform to provide bond financing for B&R countries and enterprises will help the regulatory authorities of the Central Government negotiate and implement policies more promptly and effectively.

Second, promoting RMB internationalization in major economies of B&R.

The RMB experienced ups and downs recently, depreciating against the US dollar in real terms from August 2015 to December 2016, triggering the authorities to initiate a number of strong measures to curb rising capital outflow. Then it appreciated against the US dollar after entering 2017. Meantime, the RMB was admitted into the Special Drawing Rights basket of currencies of the IMF, effective from October 2016, which marks the RMB status as a global currency.

The 19th Party report calls for "improving the framework of regulation underpinned by monetary policy and macro-prudential policy" and making the interest rates and exchange rates become "more market-based". Zhou Xiaochuan, governor of the People's Bank of China, indicated at a press conference during the 19th Party Congress that the government would reform the generation mechanism for exchange rate, reduce market interventions and steadily improve the availability of RMB assets. He also cited that stock connects between Shanghai and Hong Kong with Shenzhen and the recent Shanghai—Hong Kong bond connect in July 2017 as examples of China's commitment to further opening up.

As an onshore RMB trading center, Shanghai has been playing an important role in the process of RMB internationalization. And now, it is important for Shanghai to be a bridgehead for the Belt and Road Initiative which has brought new opportunities for RMB internationalization.

It is a win-win decision to issue RMB-denominated stocks and bonds when China opens up its stock and bond markets and provides financing channels for enterprises and governments in the B&R countries. The RMB flowing into the enterprises and governments in the B&R countries could be used for trade, investment, commercial activities with Chinese governments and enterprises, and it will continue to be in circulation in other parts of the world. That will greatly promote the economic cooperation between China and these countries, strengthen the internationalization of Renminbi, release the problem of asset shortage and provide more investment opportunities in China for residents and enterprises.

Just like RMB's internationalization process, B&R development will be a long and slow process. But these two are the key drivers of China's future economic development and deeper integration with the world. In order to become one of the largest international financial centers, Shanghai should build itself into a center of finance and clearance firstly. If shanghai could become a center of finance and clearance for B&R countries in recent years, the market shares of Shanghai in the global financial sector will be greatly increased, pushing Shanghai towards one of the world-class financial centers.

Third, promoting the development of Shanghai's financial technology (FinTech).

The rapid development of global financial technology has had a profound impact on the financial services industry. In this context, the rise of FinTech (or Internet Finance) sector in China has provided opportunities for Shanghai to promote the Belt and Road Initiative through establishing online financial mechanisms, improving the regulatory mechanisms and creating a favorable financial environment. Mr. Wu from ACCENTURE has stressed the importance of digital infrastructure for nearly two thirds of the world's population living in over 60 countries along the Belt and Road contributed only about one third GDP of the total, showing the potential of the B&R market. Facing such a huge market, Shanghai, like standing on the shoulders of giants, have its unique advantages for leapfrog development. After realizing the importance of the online development, it set up the Association of Shanghai Internet Financial Industry in 2015. We suggest that Shanghai should remain committed to building itself into an Internet financial center along the Belt and Road and striving to become one of the largest international internet financial centers.

The Belt and Road Forum for International Cooperation held in Beijing in May 2017 called for "strengthening financial facilities connectivity, providing innovative platforms for investment and financing and improving accesses to financial services".

With the rapid development of FinTech, China has been developing rapidly and is world leading by several measures. China's digital payments account for half of the global volume and online peer-to-peer (P2P) lending accounts for three quarters of the global total. The rise of FinTech in Shanghai could a good example for the B&R countries, becoming a new driver for the development of the Belt and Road Initiative.

In the future, three innovative technologies of artificial intelligence, blockchain and robotic process automation will have a profound impact on the financial industry (Fig.2). Understanding their features and building capacity around them will enable Shanghai's financial institutions to stand out from the competition and provide customers with a more enjoyable experience, better products and more excellent services. That will also benefit the Belt and Road Initiative.

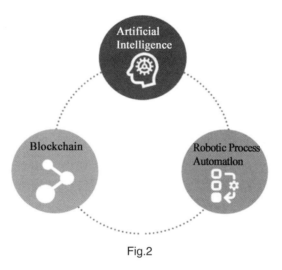

Fig.2

In summary, FinTech business model needs to follow the basis of financial services in order to be closely related to the development of the real economy. As the economy evolves to a digital, smart and personalized business model and lifestyle, financial services needs to transform to a 3.0 model. This means they need to evolve from a product and channel-oriented model to a customer-centered one, with technologies as an important pillar. However, as the increasing financial connectivity brought by technological innovation, we must still adhere to the bottom line of safety and take preventive measures to establish a stable, sustainable and risk-controllable financial security system. We should promote investment and financing innovations and improve the environment for the development of Internet Finance.

4. Giving Full Play to China（Shanghai）Pilot Free Trade Zone（FTZ）to Build a National Think Tank for the Development of the Belt and Road Initiative

President Xi Jinping proposed that China's economy has been transitioning from a phase of rapid growth to a stage of high-quality development at the recently concluded 19th CPC Congress. In a new era of reform and opening-up, China will prioritize the development of the Belt and Road Initiative and will delegate more power to lower levels to reform the Shanghai free trade zone and build a free trade port.

Shanghai free trade zone has played an important role as a pilot for the Belt and Road Initiative. For example, there are many regulation restrictions on China's trade platforms and cross-border trade. It is a good try to develop a regulatory sandbox in Shanghai to build an experimental environment without certain regulations, which also enable to encourage cross-border RMB settlement.

The FTZ China is preparing to launch its own yuan-based oil futures contract which will increase china' pricing power in global petrol industry and improve the status of RMB. Given that it is relatively easier to enter the markets in B&R countries, Shanghai could promote their oil futures to B&R countries firstly in order to receive a good response.

Based on the achievements that the FTZ has made so far, Shanghai should introduce more innovative financial services for the Belt and Road Initiative. To facilitate the use of RMB globally, Shanghai should prioritize B&R countries, while conducting follow-up surveys in some of these countries, to provide experience for the international use of RMB. To facilitate cross-border financing in shanghai, shanghai should encourage more Chinese enterprises to invest in B&R countries and help more B&R countries to finance for their promising and well-established projects in the FTZ.

5. Summary

The Shanghai Free Trade Port is one of the important drivers for the Belt and Road Initiative other than an upgraded version of Shanghai Pilot Free Trade Zone. Against the economic transformation of China and increasing uncertainties in the world economy, Shanghai should become a bridgehead and a national think-tank for the development of the Belt and Road Initiative in the opening-up and innovation of the financial sector. The development of the free trade zone, the Belt and Road Initiative and the financial opening-up is essential for China's reform and opening up. Shanghai should adhere to the opening-up of the financial sector and ensure a safe, stable and vibrant financing market.

Shanghai remains committed to building itself into an international financial center, promoting the internationalization of RMB in stock and security markets and developing Shanghai Pilot Free Trade Zone and Free Trade Port. It should take full advantage of the two "F", the International Financial Center and the Free Trade Zone to establish an open and multilateral financial trading platform for the Belt and Road Initiative.

The Belt and Road Initiative serves as the most promising cooperation strategy with the largest scale and scope in the world, providing an unprecedented opportunity for the development of China and the establishment of a world-class Shanghai international financial center. This initiative offers new opportunities for the opening-up of China's financial sector and Shanghai should seize the opportunity to build an open platform for multilateral investment and financing and promote the opening-up of financial markets along the Belt and Road.

Reciprocity, Connectivity, Mobility: Shanghai as a Pioneer in the Belt and Road Initiative

Ioana Kraft

General Manager of Shanghai Chapter, European Union Chamber of Commerce in China

The European Union Chamber of Commerce in China was founded in the year 2000. We represent the independent voice of the European business in China and work closely with both Chinese and European governments to create greater market access and a better business and regulatory environment in China.

The European Union is potentially the most important partner in the Belt and Road Initiative. The two economies, which mutually are among each other's top trading partners, sit at both ends of the Eurasian continent and occupy the endpoints of the Silk Road Economic Belt and the 21st Century Maritime Silk Road. As one of the two bridgeheads of the Belt and Road, the European Union welcomes a successful Belt and Road Initiative and looks forward to strengthening the economic and trading relationship with China via this initiative.

Given Shanghai's geographic and economic significance in China, it naturally bears more responsibility than any other cities to pioneer such initiative. As the representative of the European business community in Shanghai as well as a resident for almost 15 years, I would like to highlight three keywords that carry our expectations and recommendations: reciprocity, connectivity and mobility.

1. Reciprocity

First of all, reciprocity. The very purpose of creating the Belt and Road Initiative is to link all countries along the Belt and Road together and promote exchange between China and countries along the Belt and Road. Therefore, this should never be a one-way road.

In European Chamber's 2016 Position Paper, we introduced the concept of reciprocity. It states that, in contrast to Chinese companies who face few limitations when investing in Europe, European business face major market access barriers in China. Lack of reciprocity in access to the Chinese market remains an issue which needs to also be addressed in the context of the Belt and Road Initiative.

According to a research by the Rhodium Group, while Chinese investment into the EU continued to remain high in the first half of 2017, EU investment in China dropped 23 per cent from the first half of 2016 to the same period in 2017. Our 2017 Business Confidence Survey also shows that 61% of the respondents consider market access barriers to have the most significant impact for their business in China. This situation is not sustainable for the EU—China trading and investment relationship and is definitely not in line with the intention of the Belt and Road Initiative.

Earlier this year, we were excited to see the importance of attracting more foreign investment being emphasized in the Guofa No.5 and No.39 documents, as well as local documents like the Shanghai Document No.26. It is also recognizable that the newly released Foreign Investment Catalogue as well as the 2017 version of Pilot FTZ Negative List did bring some welcome clarity to investors and reduced the number of restricted industries. However, the momentum seems to have been diminishing. The Belt and Road Initiative therefore carries the hope of many foreign investors as the vehicle to boost the promised but yet fulfilled economic liberalization.

Admittedly, significant progresses have been made in several industries. Taking pharmaceutical industry as an example. Over the past 12 months, we have witnessed the most spectacular breakthrough in the new drug registration and approval regime, representing Chinese authorities' full commitment to aligning Chinese pharmaceutical supervisory system with the highest international standards. We hope such open attitude and practice could be also replicated in other heavily regulated industries.

However, more needs to be done. Let me address the financial sector as one area that needs to be further opened in the context of Belt and Road. An open, diverse and robust financial sector is not only the key to upgrading Shanghai to a global centre of finance but also to a successful Belt and Road Initiative. With market access restrictions on foreign banks, future brokers, securities houses and fund management companies being lifted, the influx of such highly sophisticated and experienced investors into the Chinese marketplace would not only contribute to the development of China's domestic capital market, but also incentivize foreign companies to partake in the Belt and Road Initiative projects, as they could have more diverse sources and flexible methods to finance.

2. Connectivity

Secondly, connectivity. The basic function of a road is to connect one place with another and facilitate free flow of goods. This is particularly true for the Belt and Road Initiative, as trade facilitation lies in its core.

In order to facilitate trade, Shanghai has made a lot of efforts in improving the infrastructure for logistics and regulatory environment for trade, which has been recognized by many of European Chamber members. It is inspiring to know that a free port in Yangshan Port and Pudong Airport is currently under planning. It is expected to integrate with more functions, more simplified and streamlined procedures, and higher standard of trade supervision.

The European Chamber and our members embrace this step forward and look forward to Shanghai free port playing a leading role in the Belt and Road Initiative. One aspect that our members in logistics sector have been advocating for a long time and is potentially beneficial to the performance of free port is international relay.

International relay may not sound familiar to many of us. However, it is a common practice in international shipping in Europe. In the context of China, it allows a company to carry cargo from China to an overseas destination on its own vessels and transferring the cargo from one vessel to another vessel owned by the same company in a Chinese port. International relay is beneficial to shipping companies as it helps optimize their route networks and enhance the operation efficiency. More importantly, international relay can also increase the throughput and revenue of ports where transshipment takes place and reduce the logistics cost in general.

However, such practice is still prohibited for foreign companies in China. Since a couple years ago, foreign-flagged ships with Chinese ownership have been allowed to practice international relay in China's FTZs. In contrast, foreign-owned ships still have to transship in surrounding countries such as Korea and Japan, which not only increases the shipping cost and time, but also leads Chinese ports to lose revenue to foreign ports.

We hope that restriction on international relay may eventually be lifted in a

Shanghai free port. As a result, Shanghai could become a hub for transshipment of cargos bound for South East Asia, Middle East, Africa and Europe, which exactly covers the destinations on the 21st Century Maritime Silk Road. More importantly, with strengthened connectivity with countries along the 21st Century Maritime Silk Road, Shanghai's position in the international shipping network will rise significantly, which will help Shanghai become more competitive and accomplish its goal as an international shipping centre.

3. Mobility

Last but not least, mobility. The ultimate purpose of a road is to connect and enable mobility of people. Shanghai fully recognizes the importance of talent attraction and retention, particularly as it envisages itself as a future global innovation centre.

We are pleased to see that progress has been made recently. Starting from April 2017, the new unified work permit for foreigners has been rolled out nationwide, giving more transparency and clarity to the application procedures. At the same time, we've seen the government's commitment to curbing pollution and the spiking housing price to make Shanghai more agreeable and affordable to live. Aiming at higher level of talent exchange and mobility, I'm sure Shanghai will become more attractive for talents along the Belt and Road.

In addition to free flow of talents, mobility needs also to be addressed in the context of free flow of information and data. Internet access and Internet speed issues continues to form a challenge for European business operating in China and is a potential obstacle to attract young global talents to work and live in Shanghai. According to our 2017 Business Confidence Survey, 24 percent of respondents report difficulties in exchanging data and documents with their headquarters, partners and customers, causing increasing cost for business.

In the era of knowledge and information, the Belt and Road Initiative should not only promote the physical flow of goods and people, but also serve as a vehicle that drives a fast and stable flow of information. Only if talent and free data flow is ensured can Shanghai truly thrive as a knowledge-based, international business and innovation centre.

In the 19th Party Congress that just concluded last month, Belt and Road Initiative has been written into the Party Constitution and will become the guideline for China's short- to mid-term strategy with regards to international relations. As part of European business in China, we have every reason to support and embrace this Initiative that mutually benefits Europe and China. We are willing to continuously contribute our knowledge and efforts as a channel between the government and European business community to help Shanghai better play the leading role in the Belt and Road Initiative that it deserves.

Become a Leading Free Trade Port in the Era of the B&R 2.0

Katrina Lv

Partner, Leader of Great China Public Sector and Infrastructure

Practice, McKinsey & Company

When recapping 2016, we see frequent "black swans" events globally: Brexit; Trump won the US election; "M5S" gaining momentum in Italy. These "black swans" events led to an undercurrent of "de-globalization" and rising trade protectionism. This serves as barrier to "B&R", an advocator to globalization and free trade. To face with the challenge, China has a bigger role to play. We believe that, "B&R 2.0" refers to a more sophisticated stage, with higher degree of market operation, which means positively engage market players, and screen investment projects with the force of market. Meanwhile, on both macro and micro levels, build up risk control system, and inter-disciplinary talent pool, deep-dive in overseas market, so as to jointly address disputes with partner countries, and positively lead new direction of economic globalization.

As B&R approaches V2.0, we'd see more sophisticated mechanism of market operation. Since its initial announcement, B&R has been echoed by over 100 countries. China has signed over 50 inter-governmental agreements with partner countries. In the past 3 years, based on joint consultations, a series of flagship infrastructures have been built, e.g. Jakarta-Bandung Hi-speed Rail of Indonesia, Hungary-Servia Rail, China-Laos Rail, as well as ports and infrastructures, as a steadfast step of B&R 1.0, and laid a solid basis for bi-lateral and multi-lateral cooperation. B&R 2.0 would focus on economic and trade area, to conduct all-round and in-depth connectivity, and further expand to social and cultural fields, and the "multi-dimensional" contents of the Initiative would be further emphasized. Accordingly, the current government and SOE based"national team" operation model, would transfer to more "market style" operation mechanism. In B&R 1.0, we see multiple projects implementation through inter-governmental coordination among partner countries. However, this cooperation model would face multiple challenges in B&R 2.0.

First of all, as major infrastructure projects are led by governments, SOEs and central companies during B&R 1.0, without positive participation from market entities. A mature and sustainable market operation is yet to come, so unable to support project identification and construction during B&R 2.0, which featured as multiple fields, multiple funding channels, and multiple stakeholders.

Second, the B&R partners are mainly developing countries, with risks such as economic imbalance. Meanwhile, these countries have strong local features in terms of culture, custom, business climate, legal and regulation, etc. However B&R projects typically have features as large funding gap, long return cycle and low yield (now mainly funded by long-term low-interest loan from Chinese government). As Chinese companies are still exploring "going out" journey, they typically lack of local knowledge and mature experience to control project risk.

As B&R approaches to V2.0, talent demand would be greater than ever: not only industrial professionals, but also management generalists; not only Chinese talents "going out", but also attract international and local talents "bring in".

For identification and building of hi-quality projects, market and government should complement one another for cooperation. In spite of the rich political and financial resources, governments lack of industry expertise and market operation system, thus unable to independently identify and build a series of "bankable projects" (qualified for bank guarantee). By contrast, companies accumulate industry knowhow and project experience, and at same time, have market-oriented organization and value. To bring market operation mechanism into B&R framework, we need not only leading role of government, but also positive participation of market entities. These entities should fully play their advantages, cooperate with government on hi-quality project identification and reservation. Furthermore, they could jointly push sustainable development of B&R, and fundamentally address the pain point of project funding.

To realize this goal, we propose government to cooperate with market entities on four initiatives as following: first, build a project development team, with rich industry knowhow, project building and execution experience, local market knowledge and diversified background; second, for different industries, build a measurement and benchmark system of "bankable projects", to push project approval standardization while considering industrial features and differentiations; third, through means like establishing joint functional committee, leveraging market oriented governance model, to create transparency in approval, optimize process progress, provide diversified funding channel for higher funding efficiency and quality, so as to accelerate project governance; fourth, for ongoing projects, ensure market operation degree in project management and post-investment technical support in execution level, so as to fully implement market operation value.

Lack of understanding of social, economic and business environment of foreign countries is a major challenge for Chinese companies to "Go Global". Chinese companies are not only short of experience in interacting with local governments, institutions and groups, but also lack of capabilities to respond to emergent risks in geopolitics, safety, laws and regulations and operations. This lack of governance on overseas risks often result in low efficiency and discounted impact of investment.

In our opinion, the market oriented "B&R 2.0" should build risk governance mechanism at both macro and micro level, with specialized market resources as key levers. At the macroeconomic level, government should play the safeguard role: proactively advocate and push forward the establishment of market-oriented risk assessment think-tanks (e.g., the EIU) which analyze, track and forecast the political, economic and industrial risks of countries along B&R with highly objective, independent and transparent risk models, and provide valuable references for upfront investment decision-making of government and companies. At the micro level of business operation, Chinese companies should proactively introduce localized, diversified overseas investment service partners into local markets to provide bespoke risk alert and protection services.

In this aspect, we already had one successful attempt made by a domestic leading industrial real estate operator. This year, this private player cooperated with local government, consortium and institutions of Indonesia, and jointly developed an industrial city in Indonesia. The company not only provided hardware services including industrial real estate development, infrastructure and residential community development, but also a series of "software services" for non-Indonesia companies (in particular Chinese companies) concerning risks when they invest locally. Specifically, these services included commercial consulting, HR capital service, and setting up a local advisory board to respond to operational risks like labor riots, to meet the needs of investors for investment risk control.

B&R Initiative aims at promoting connectivity of policies, facilities, trade and finance as well as people-to-people bonds. To achieve any of the above goals, suitable talents will always be the key. If companies want to succeed in farming overseas markets, they should gradually build the talent pipeline in stages. It is not only critical for company to achieve the short-term goal of entering the market, but also indispensable for it to survive and prosper in the long term.

In the early stage of "Go Global", companies should attract talents with global perspective and overseas market management experience, and equip itself with an international team with background in international finance, law and trade to quickly tap into overseas markets. In the longer term, what is more important is to accelerate the development of local talent pipeline, cultivate local talents and fully utilize them to truly fit into the local market. In a bigger picture, apart from developing China's own global talents and well utilizing the talents of target countries, Chinese players should collaborate with local governments and education institutions of countries along B&R to cultivate their own global talents, and regard B&R cross-border talent resources as a long-term investment for building presence overseas.

The first step that the above mentioned industrial real estate operator did for "Go Global" was to recruit professional managers with global perspectives from world leading consulting firms and MNCs to build a core team and develop overseas businesses. It then recruited excellent local talents in areas of corporate operation and government relations while carrying out the business, against the pain points of investors in local market development. The company aimed to build an interdisciplinary talent pipeline and create an inclusive working environment and corporate culture for both global and local talents.

As B&R Initiative deepens in the level of globalization, openness and its requirement for interdisciplinary talents, opportunities and challenges co-exist in the era of 2.0. The success of "B&R 2.0" must be the success of market-oriented operation, i.e. to achieve common prosperity with countries along "B&R 2.0" through market-oriented project selection, professional risk control and interdisciplinary team building that create synergy between market forces and government push.

Shanghai to Play the Role of "Bridgehead" under Belt and Road Initiative —Deloitte Insights

Minghua (Dora) Liu

Managing Partner of Eastern China, Audit Partner of Shanghai, China, Deloitte

With rapid changes and great revolution taking place throughout the world, China is also at a pivotal stage for transforming development model, improving economic structure, and fostering new drivers of growth. Against the backdrop of profound and complex changes both in China and overseas, the Belt and Road Initiative, since it's proposed in 2013, has been endowed with new missions, i.e. to be an important path for China to go global and have more say and bigger influence in the world.

Firstly, China having more say and bigger influence in the world reflects its rise on the global stage. In the past five years, China has maintained an over 30 percent contribution to global economic growth. The country is expected to play a greater role in international affairs and take more responsibilities in responding to global challenges. This will also enable China to protect its interests in closer global cooperation in the future.

Secondly, China having more say and bigger influence in the world echoes its entry into the economic New Normal. China is now facing various issues like the continuously increasing labour cost and resource constraints, the hard-to-bear environmental burdens, the weakening of traditional competitive strengths of open economy, and the challenges imposed on traditional development models. On the other hand, China boasts abundant labour resources, large markets, well-established infrastructure and supporting industries, as well as on-going improvement of the regimes and policies for innovation, all of which guarantee the comprehensive competitive strengths of open economy. It will be more helpful for China to better adapt to the new changes under the trend of globalization by securing its international standing, timely fostering new drivers of economic growth, and adjusting multi-party cooperation rules.

In light of the above, the Belt and Road Initiative will shift its focus regarding the following aspects since it was put forth 5 years ago:

(1) China's manufacturing will focus more on rule/service/brand/technology rather than just commodity.

(2) Chinese economy will focus more on the soft landing from a stage of pursing rapid growth and large scale to a stage of pursing high quality and great benefits, rather than just transferring and unleashing productivity.

(3) Regional cooperation will focus more on expanding overseas economic cooperation areas, rather than just developing domestic special economic areas/free trade zones.

(4) For political diplomacy with developing countries, the focus will be shifted to building a closer benefit community via economic cooperation rather than just providing assistance for poverty alleviation; for political diplomacy with developed countries, the focus will be shifted to negotiating new win-win rules rather than just accepting the existing rules.

The key to the abovementioned strategic transition is to formulate flexible and open multilateral trade rules for win-win cooperation. With Doha Round rules fading and multilateral free trade treaties like TPP rising in recent years, WTO's dominance over world trade has been threatened, including unilateral trade rules guided by western countries. Under the global trends of multi-polarity, economic globalization, IT application and cultural diversity, China should, referring to the principle of "one country, two systems", respect cultural differences and reasonable appeals of different countries and regions, seek for common grounds and convergence of interests, and treat and handle multilateral relations in a dynamic and evolving way. In doing so, China can expand common interests with other countries, take a part in reforming the global governance system, and actively develop global partnerships to make economic globalization more open, inclusive, and balanced so that the benefits are shared by all.

The new situation underlines the importance for Shanghai to play its role of bridgehead under Belt and Road Initiative, in terms of both tangible and intangible infrastructures.

(1) Top choice for foreign-owned enterprises: Different from Beijing featuring most of the SOEs and Shenzhen/Guangzhou featuring lots of private or Hong Kong

enterprises, Shanghai has always been the 1st choice of foreign investments and familiar to foreign investors, laying a solid foundation for cultural convergence in future international multilateral rule formulation.

(2) Open culture: As the first open port, bonded area as well as free trade zone in China, Shanghai has always been a pioneer in opening up to the world. In Shanghai, multilateral conflicts and problems are more likely to be handled through flexible and feasible business methods, laying a solid foundation for business communication in future international multilateral rule formulation.

(3) Market factors availability: As the national centre of economy, finance, trade and shipping, as well as the innovation base with global impact in China, Shanghai owns well-established international market with comprehensive market factors, laying a solid foundation for business opportunities in future international multilateral rule formulation.

(4) Global impact: Shanghai is always on the top list of international cities as a representative of Chinese cities. It also initiates and takes an active part in global cooperation (e.g. Shanghai Cooperation Organization), and is headquarter of many important international cooperation agencies (e.g. BRICS Development Bank), laying a solid foundation for positive propaganda in future international multilateral rule formulation.

In summary, Shanghai can play its role of bridgehead at the new stage of Belt and Road Initiative from the following aspects:

A bridgehead to explore various multilateral rules and innovative cooperation models: Leveraging China's industrial advantages and leadership, we can integrate and use various types of resources to build an economic community and enable emerging markets and developing countries to make further contribution to global economic growth. We can also negotiate the existing rules and develop cooperation with developed countries on behalf of most emerging markets and developing countries to create multilateral trade regimes and build an open world economy.

A bridgehead to promote the model and experience of Chinese park economy globally: Chinese park economy has made several records in global economic development, represented by Shanghai Pilot Free Trade Zone, Zhangjiang Hi-tech Park and Caohejing Hi-tech Park. We can share successful experience with the B&R countries and help partners with their development, meanwhile build overseas bases to better absorb foreign advanced technologies, business methods, management experience and marketing opportunities, bringing Chinese enterprises into global industrial chain, value chain and innovation chain. In doing so, Shanghai can also reach a higher level of opening up.

A bridgehead to introduce Chinese elements to the world: We should balance commonality and diversity in building a new open economy and explore opening up rules in multilateral cooperation step by step. Relying on China's hinterland, Shanghai will serve the national opening up policy and pave the way for Chinese elements to the world.

Shanghai can take three steps to play its role of bridgehead under Belt and Road Initiative:

(1) Designing plan: We should figure out the backgrounds and strategic appeals of potential partners, identify the priorities with high cultural convergence and good conditions for top-level design, and specify cooperation models and primary norms for multilateral win-win.

(2) Establishing platform: Based on the early-stage frame of top-level design, we should seize opportunities to import related resources, develop market-based cooperation and optimize norms. Multilateral cooperation can be enhanced by means of project to expand the convergence of interests.

(3) Building network: On the one hand, we should expand the cooperation platform and build overseas parks based on successful experience to better understand the environment and needs of target markets. On the other hand, we should take a part in synergetic development of the Yangtze Economic Belt and the Guangdong—Hong Kong—Macao Greater Bay Area and connect hinterland resources to better help China bring in and go global, as well as use cross-regional resources in a coordinated way.

As a bridgehead under the Belt and Road Initiative, Shanghai's future development should be based on a bigger picture. We should build an ecological environment apart from a business environment, and emphasize on building innovative systems and norms rather than just developing projects by attracting investments. In some traditional areas, the third-party professional firms should be introduced to promote effective value-oriented connection between the government and market.

Recently, foreign-owned enterprises are concerned about changes in foreign investment management in China. This year, heated discussion has aroused due to several global R&D centres of foreign-owned enterprises leaving China, including GSK and Eli Lilly. In addition, the application for foreigners' work visa is being upgraded in China and causes much inconvenience, resulting in various speculation of foreign media. In spite of the traditional channels for policy publicity and media relations, it would be better for the government to predict market response and make adjustments in advance for timely feedback, proper interpretation and channel management, thus gaining higher recognition from the public and taking the initiative. It will be an opportunity for the government to shift traditional thoughts and develop market-based cooperation with foreign agencies on culture or mind set.

It is the great importance for China to play a new international role and take corresponding responsibilities at this pivotal stage. Being the pioneer of China's opening up, Shanghai should serve as a bridgehead to seize the trend and accelerate the reforming speed for its own development as well as the new Belt and Road Initiative exploration.

Shanghai: Fountainhead of the Belt and Road Initiative

Barjor Mehta

Lead Urban Specialist, Social, Rural, Urban & Resilience

Global Practice, World Bank

The World Bank believes that Shanghai, as a fountainhead, is essentially important because for the fountain to be effective, the nozzle has to be effective. Over the past 35 years, Shanghai's per capita GDP has risen by 13 times. Shanghai has made a series of achievements: Shanghai's per capita GDP is twice as high as China's per capita GDP; Shanghai is the linchpin of the Yangtze River economic belt, China's most populous city and one of the world's top 20 global cities; Shanghai has the world's largest metro system; and successfully avoided common urban ills.

Shanghai's contribution to the Belt and Road Initiative will depends on how the city manages three mega-trends and three challenges. The three Global Mega-Trends are: Global economic center continues to move eastward; the globalization of service industries and continued innovation; and the Silver Tsunami—rapid aging globally and locally. The "three major challenges": Shanghai has the opportunity to build on central position in global production networks, but also the challenge of rising competition; there will be opportunities to gain ground in services (finance, R&D, design), but also the challenge of making human capital globally competitive; and China is aging faster than most and Shanghai even faster—must find new ways of integrating, not isolating, older residents into the social fabric of the city.

For challenge 1, we should enhance productivity. Power of investment and exports as the engine of growth is reaching its limits, while improvements in productivity are becoming more difficult as "easier" reforms have been exhausted. Cost of business as usual: the SOE-dominated economy lacks drive for innovation; labor productivity is low and human resources are not competitive; and the smaller working population is supporting a larger population.

For challenge 2, we should build connected, efficient, and resilient urban form. Shanghai's spatial layout increasingly impacts its competiveness and livability: urban sprawl has led to declining densities, increasing economic distance, and weakened agglomeration benefits. Sprawl led to weaker agglomeration economies. "Ghettoization" of low-income settlements at periphery and neighborhoods unable to cope with climate change.

For challenge 3, we should remain committed to nurturing, attracting and retaining talent. The poor integration of migrant families (40% of pop, growing by 350 000+per year) represents an underutilized source of talent and capital-while rapid aging will shrink the workforce. "Floating" population of migrants do not have equal access to public services and with one of the world's lowest fertility rates, Shanghai will soon have less than one person of working age for every senior resident (60+).

The main challenges Shanghai faces are the absence of a viable and competitive economy; the aging population without sufficient amenities and services; and the lack of affordable housing and basic services for the general public.

Although the three major challenges are complex, the solutions exist. Urban development strategies should be formed from the three aspects of structure, space and society. The three major instruments that help lay the foundation for continued success are: the effective use of market incentives; policy reforms to enhance global competitiveness; and enhancing governance and coordination.

We believe that there are three instruments that will help to lay the foundations for continued success if Shanghai could harness markets to incentivize efficiency, reform policy to become globally competitive and strengthen institutions to enhance governance and coordination. Let me explain, to achieve three transformations, Shanghai will have to have a structural transformation which is from capital accumulation to higher productivity, that is, nurturing innovation, diversification and growth of services. The second one is a spacial transformation. Shanghai should build a well-connected, resilient, and livable city, from fragmented spatial of sprawling, long and inefficient commutes development to an urban form that amplifies agglomeration economies and promotes sustainability. The third one is how Shanghai provides a welcoming and inclusive city for all who are living or want to live in Shanghai.

Increase productivity, promote innovation-led economic growth, realize the transformation from a "Maker of Products" to a "Creator of Ideas" and tradable services, promote greater diversity of businesses, including by opening up market to greater participation by vibrant SMEs; adopt a "People-centered Development" model that invests in people not just infrastructure and reform SOEs to level the playing field. Foster an innovation ecosystem and supporting institutions that connect ideas and entrepreneurs to funds, labor, and resources.

Limit sprawl, use land more efficiently, and increase densities to strengthen the city's agglomeration benefits, while making housing more affordable and protecting against climate change. When it harnesses the market to build a well-connected and livable city, Shanghai should use price signals to lead to more efficient patterns of land use and resource allocation which does not exist today. It also needs to use the sprawl management. There is nothing wrong with density and, as a matter of fact, the new growth of Shanghai will be seen as the same density remains. I know there is a lot of sensitivities towards it and Shanghai needs to address the problem, making housing more affordable.

We believe that there are three instruments that will help to lay the foundations for continued success if Shanghai could harness markets to incentivize efficiency, reform policy to become globally competitive and strengthen institutions to enhance governance and coordination. There are three tools to facilitate Shanghai's transformation:

Foster Markets: facilitate tradable land supply and GHG emissions quotas between YRD cities; Shanghai needs to foster institutions for regional integration to coordinate land use plans. In China, cities work independently of each other, but there is a culture of cooperation among the neighboring jurisdictions.

Reform Policy: reform Hukou; develop flexible and adaptive building codes and zoning regulations informed by land prices; and reform SOEs and adopt policy of "competitive neutrality".

Strengthen Institutions: integrate development planning at regional level to coordinate land use, transport, strategy; adopt institutional framework for coordinated expansion of low-carbon energy and support efforts towards creating a strong, coherent city brand.

If Shanghai could reach these goals, things would be much better. And for these transformations, Shanghai could use the tradable land supply, instead of debatable land pricing and incentivize building affordable units near transit which involves reforming the development policies. And of course, the residential permit system needs to be rethought because it will eventually impose tremendous challenges to the effectivities and productivity of the city of Shanghai. To strengthen the institutions, it could integrate development planning at regional level to coordinate land use, transport, strategy, adopt institutional framework for coordinated expansion of low-carbon energy and support efforts towards creating a strong, coherent city brand.

Promoting Shanghai's Trade and Financial Innovation by "Empowering Industry": Becoming a Pioneer for China's Belt and Road Initiative

Thomas Fang

Senior Principal, Boston Consulting Group（BCG）

1. Achievements of the Belt and Road Initiative

In autumn 2013, in Kazakhstan and Indonesia, President Xi Jinping proposed the establishment of the Silk Road Economic Belt and the 21st Century Maritime Silk Road, collectively known as the "Belt and Road Initiative". Over the past four years, China's Belt and Road development has achieved some initial successes. As of August 2017, 69 national and international organizations have signed cooperation agreements with China on building the "Belt and Road". China has signed a series of cross-sector cooperation agreements in a "five-pronged approach", covering policy coordination, road connectivity, unimpeded trade and flows of funds, and strengthened people-to-people ties. It has also included decisions from the UN General Assembly and the UN Security Council into the initiative. So far, it has put into motion more than 1 000 major projects. More than $3 trillion in trade has been carried out across the Belt and Road, and the value of engineering contracts in foreign investment has reached $126 bn, accounting for 51.6% of newly signed contracts. On the funding side, the AIIB has approved 28 investment projects since it began operations in January 2016, and a total of around $3 bn in loans.

2. Challenges of the Belt and Road Initiative

The Belt and Road Initiative is a grand undertaking that extends to 18 provinces in China and covers dozens of other countries. However, it also faces many challenges.

Given China's challenges in its own development, the key to the success of the initiative will lie in "interconnectivity". Each administrative region along the routes has its own local interests. If some areas introduce protectionist policies, it will be a challenge to achieve "interconnectivity." It will also be more difficult to include the inland areas than the more developed coastal areas of China.

Furthermore, the Belt and Road faces far greater challenges internationally. First, many of the countries on the routes are economically underdeveloped. China is not strong enough and does not have enough resources on its own to make the initiative a success, and there is a risk that the policy will become overstretched or that it will lose stamina. In addition, some countries on the routes are in political turmoil, and government control is weak. Since the Belt and Road Initiative is mainly based on high-level cooperation between governments, if there are power transitions in these governments, it would spell the end for the whole project.

The Belt and Road cross three continents: Asia, Europe and Africa. The level of the infrastructure is uneven in all the different countries along the routes. The major issue that the Belt and Road project has to consider in its implementation is how to achieve a level of "unity", despite development disparities, while simplifying investment procedures and reducing investment costs. Moreover, the lack of a unified currency, transport system and customs authority adds extra risk to the project.

The core issue is a lack of transparent information on supply and demand, a lack of market information and the inconsistency of processes and standards. The crux of the problem is the insufficient market platforms and poor integration of services.

3. Shanghai's Theoretical Breakthroughs that Can Guide the Belt and Road Initiative

Shanghai is the biggest powerhouse at the intersection of the Belt and Road, and it allocates the elements for China's foreign trade and development. It should be the pioneer for China's Belt and Road Initiative, and ease core issues through innovation in finance, economics and trade. Shanghai should serve multinational companies by providing services to help local companies "Go Global" and bring together relevant institutions and enterprises in the new Belt and Road economy, to improve the city's service capabilities and model for companies in emerging economies. At the same time,

Shanghai should transform and upgrade local inland industries by helping countries along the Belt and Road in Central Asia, West Asia and Southeast Asia to improve their industrial structure.

Shanghai's plans to build a world-class city by 2040 and build "four centers" by 2020, which will go hand-in-hand with the development of China's Belt and Road through economic, trade and financial innovations. It is an international economic, financial, trade and shipping center under construction. By 2020, it will have developed an international financial and trade center in line with China's economic strength and the international status of the renminbi. Based on its existing foundation of development and comparative advantages, Shanghai should accelerate financial and trade reform and innovation, enhance market functions, promote orderly flows of capital, and strengthen the allocation of resources and its international influence in the global market. At the same time, Shanghai should promote itself as an international financial and trade center, connected with other countries and regions along the Belt and Road. It should build an innovative financial network and support system with global influence.

Shanghai plans to become a comprehensive global city by 2040, after completing its "four centers" by 2020. Therefore, Shanghai must deepen its innovation in finance, trade and economics, promote industrial development, and become a global leader in many dimensions.

Shanghai is a leading financial center, however its financial market functions, industrial support and service still leave a lot to be desired. In the last five years, China has continued its financial liberalization, including liberalizing its capital account. Shanghai's global position as an international financial center has risen steadily from eighth place in 2010 to fifth place in 2015, maintaining a steady upward trend (Fig.1). Its growth indicators are far ahead of other cities, and the city has ranked first globally in this regard for many years in a row. Shanghai has a highly developed and mature foreign exchange market, but its capital, banking and insurance markets still lag behind established financial centers such as New York and Singapore. It has an established industry base and is home to a large number of multinational corporations. However, its talent base and market environment are weak. It need to strengthen its creativity and vitality. In terms of industry support, Shanghai is roughly on the same level as New York and other leading financial centers. IT system building, work environments and social management are important soft indicators for such service. Shanghai still needs

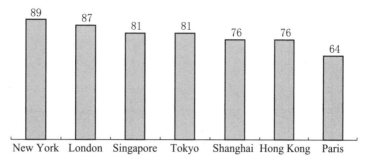

Fig. 1   International Financial Centers Development Index scores (IFCD)

to improve its software services capabilities (Fig.2).

Shanghai has grown as a center of trade, but the deficiencies in its services and its ability to "empower industry" still leave it far off the mark in becoming a global leader.

In recent years, the center of demand in world trade has been shifting to China. China's economic policies have guided changes in the global economic pattern, which have helped Shanghai establish its position as an international trading center and develop world-leading scale. Shanghai has ranked first among world ports for seven continuous years for its container throughput (Fig.3). However, Shanghai still lags far behind service-oriented third-generation international shipping and trading centers such as London, New York and Singapore in terms of its software services and ability to empower industry. Shanghai's free trade policy is still in its infancy, and the links between trade and its peripheral industries are weak. It needs to strengthen its links with and ability to drive industry. Moreover, Shanghai started to develop its shipping

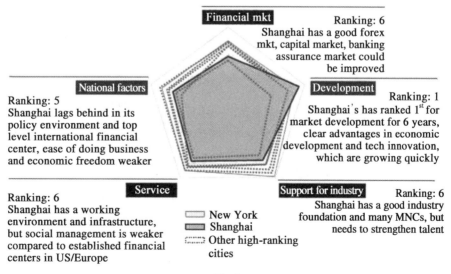

Fig.2

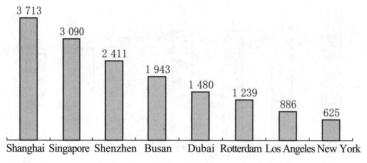

Fig.3 2016 ranking of world ports by container throughput (Unit: 10 000 TEU)

services, trade financing, insurance coverage, insurance claims, financial leasing and other service functions relatively late in comparison with other cities, and these functions are smaller in scale (Fig.4).

Shanghai is one of the core transport hubs and resource allocation centers for the Belt and Road countries. Therefore, to address the issues mentioned above, the city should capitalize on its advantages in accumulating capital, attracting talents, goods circulation and adding value, as well as its diffusion and allocation functions, so that it can empower industry by developing a market mechanism, and play a solid practical role in the Belt and Road layout.

The "market mechanism" refers to enriching the factors market by establishing an innovative trading platform to promote the circulation and trade of various elements of innovation and entrepreneurship, thereby enabling the market to play a decisive role in

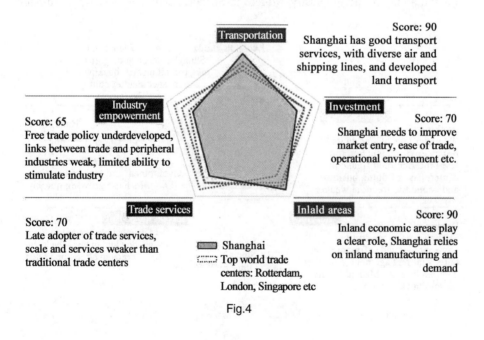

Fig.4

the allocation of resources.

"Empowering industry" means transforming from a functional platform to a service-oriented platform through innovation in finance and trade to meet the needs and challenges of companies "going global", and help them achieve success in overseas markets.

By serving the real economy through market mechanisms and thereby serving China's Belt and Road Initiative, Shanghai's financial and trade center will enhance its market and industry support functions.

4. BCG's Innovative Ideas on Economics, Trade and Financial Development

In response to Shanghai's development in trade and finance, BCG has put forward four innovative ideas to "empower industry" based on a "market mechanism."

To promote such a mechanism, BCG proposed the establishment of:

• A cross-border virtual currency union: an exchangeable virtual reserve currency corresponding to the RMB to use in trade settlement, cross-border payments and investment in Belt and Road countries. Countries that use the virtual currency would enjoy member benefits offered by Shanghai.

• A multilateral project exchange: the construction of multilateral project exchange market, the members of which would include project participants from Belt and Road countries, Chinese investors, enterprises and banks. Members from different countries would submit projects to be "listed" in Shanghai.

To promote "industry empowerment", BCG has proposed:

• An integrated services platform: the establishment of a Belt and Road integrated service platform in Shanghai, to work in concert with the multilateral project exchange. The platform would integrate functions such cross-border guarantees, cross-border insurance, cross-border settlement, legal services, data services, tax services and cross-border due diligence.

• An investment credit rating index:establish a credit rating index for countries or key cities and regions along the Belt and Road, which would become a benchmark for investment and trade.

5. The Significance of Global Best Practices for Shanghai

Blockchain technology can have a profound impact on the global economic and financial environment, and help to build a "market mechanism". In order to take action and benefit as soon as possible, the Bank of England, the UK's central bank, researched and issued the digital currency RSCoin, to increase the efficiency and flexibility of the financial system. The design framework and technical thinking behind this currency is worth studying.

The framework was to introduce a virtual currency to promote trade. The Bank of England introduced RSCoin, a virtual currency that is not pegged to the US dollar, as a direct medium for settlement between different currencies, without the need to convert to US dollars. This not only facilitates foreign exchange settlement between currencies in less common use, but also reduces the risk of exchange rate fluctuations and devaluation by decoupling the virtual currency from real currencies. In addition, RSCoin removes the need for other cross-border clearing systems, thus significantly reducing the processing fees required for settlement, and lowering investment and trade costs. Technically, the Bank of England has adopted "high and low-level blocks" and "centralization" technologies, which are much more efficient and controllable than traditional virtual currencies such as Bitcoin. By differentiating between the two levels of blocks, RSCoin reduces the number of direct participants in each transaction from general users to commercial bank users, thereby increasing the processing speed. Bitcoin systems can handle up to seven transactions per second, whereas RSCoin can process more than 2 000 per second, with transaction processing rates growing on a linear basis with the number of direct participants.

"Centralization" refers to the role played by the Bank of England in the RSCoin system. The central bank controls the supply of the digital currency, acting as the "manager and regulator". Therefore, unlike other virtual currencies, RSCoin has the controllability of traditional currencies and national credit endorsement, solving the problem of virtual currencies being non-sovereign currencies, as well as over-supply and liquidity crises.

There are also examples of empowering industry internationally that are worth drawing on. Since its independence half a century ago, Singapore has provided a one-stop service platform. Its support for foreign investment offers valuable lessons for

Shanghai. Due to its size, limited resources and limited market demand, abundant capital and excess capacity, Singapore has developed a "seven-hour strategy", targeting countries and regions within a seven-hour flight radius. The main measures under the policy include direct foreign investment, building overseas industrial parks and free trade. Over the next 30 years, Singapore's foreign investment increased every year (except during the financial crisis) and the country completed a shift from labor-intensive to capital and technology-intensive industry, and then to high-tech industry and high value-added service industry, approximately one industrial restructure and upgrade every 10 years. The Singapore government has provided a one-stop service platform, covering exchange services, collateral insurance, and talent consulting.

In terms of exchange services, the Singapore government helps companies establish contact with governments, organizations and commercial organizations across the world and provides "one-on-one" service for enterprises to take advantage of business opportunities. In 2008, Singapore organized overseas visits for more than 130 delegations, benefiting more than 400 companies, and helping them to create an overseas sales revenue of $17 billion and organizing more than 100 trade fairs. Under its guarantee insurance policies, the government provides special cross-border insurance business to help large insurance companies manage cross-border investment risks effectively. It also provides cross-border guarantee services and financial support for SMEs. In 2008 alone, it provided $700 million in guarantees and funding for 747 enterprises. In terms of personnel and consultation, the government has set up a dedicated one-stop consultation center, including laws, taxation, finance and strategy, and has helped more than 3 600 companies to invest or build industrial parks overseas. In order to serve SMEs more effectively, Singapore not only pays 50% of their consulting fees, but also sends consultants and executives from SMEs on study and market research tours. It also offers a variety of talent training schools to provide the trade, strategy and financial talent companies need for foreign investment.

Globally speaking, Singapore and the UK are forerunners in providing a "market mechanism" and "empowering industry". They provide a direction for Shanghai's economic, trade and financial innovation. While the Belt and Road Initiative faces challenges, it also offers tremendous opportunities. Shanghai should advance innovation in finance, economics and trade by empowering industry. As well as serving the country's Belt and Road development, Shanghai should enhance the capabilities of its financial and trade center to support industry.

Belt and Road Through Operation in Business Districts Pooling and Cultivation of International Management Personnel

Amano Hiroyasu

Vice President of Nomura Research Institute (NRI) Shanghai Limited

1. Talent bottlenecks facing Chinese enterprises during the development of the Belt and Road

Based on bilateral and multilateral cooperation with many countries, China's Belt and Road initiative is gradually implementing such projects as international cooperation in productivity and free trade zone cooperation, and is constructing mechanisms in the Belt and Road economic circle with mutual benefits and win-win results. With the direct investment to "Belt and Road" regions driven by the funding injection from the Silk Road Fund and the Asian Infrastructure Investment Bank, China is progressing bilateral and multilateral cooperation to a new stage of sustainable development. More Chinese enterprises are taking the opportunity offered by the Belt and Road initiative to realize their strategy of going global and are committed to expanding the global market. On the other hand, more overseas enterprises focus on developing the Chinese market and establishing partnership with Chinese enterprises, trying to strengthen their global business.

The Chinese enterprises that have laid out transnational business network are primarily major enterprises in the energy, petrochemical and steel industries, investment enterprises and electronic communications manufacturing enterprises. Thanks to early entry into the international market, they have established a certain presence in the overseas market. For more Chinese enterprises without footprint in the global market, they need to start strategic expansion of the overseas market through the Belt and Road initiative. Given that most Chinese enterprises are still at a preliminary stage of going global, it is essential for Chinese enterprises to figure out how to provide management personnel who are able to grasp different businesses at different foreign regions in their global development framework, in addition to solving the investment and trade policies or funding issues so as to develop the overseas market in the future.

In recent years, there were many cases of Chinese enterprises introducing foreign technologies or expanding overseas businesses through acquiring of taking up shares in foreign companies. However, many Chinese enterprises failed to introduce foreign technologies or models into them during the subsequent coordination of acquisition and participation, or few of them could root their own corporate culture and philosophy into foreign enterprises to exert the synergistic effect and expand their overseas businesses. This made Chinese enterprises unable to control foreign enterprises after acquisitions, resulting in the final grant or transfer of equity because of failure to form a synergistic cooperation in business. The rationale behind this is the lack of "international managers" who manage and develop international businesses based on the position of Chinese enterprises.

Shanghai is one of the earliest and largest cities opening to the outside world in China. It pools many foreign-funded enterprises as well as numerous international business professionals. However, many of those international business professionals in Shanghai tend to be business professionals for foreign enterprises seeking to open up their businesses in the Chinese market or foreign trade professionals for investing in foreign businesses or selling Chinese products or services abroad. There are few foreign trade professionals who expand international businesses in the Belt and Road regions, or talents who manage and operate the acquired overseas companies, or talents who develop international businesses as leaders of multi-national groups in Chinese enterprises.

As a bridgehead for the Belt and Road, Shanghai should focus on the talent bottleneck issue in the Belt and Road initiative and give full scope to its functions of pooling and nurturing international managers needed by Chinese enterprises to expand overseas markets (see Table 1).

Table 1　Diagram of international business professionals in Shanghai by business area

Enterprise for personnel / Target business area	Chinese enterprise	Foreign-funded enterprise
Domestic business	Abundant human resources	Abundant human resources
Foreign trade and investment business		
Foreign business	Deficient human resources	Lack of human resources in China

2. Skills and qualities required for international managers

The skills and qualities required for management and operation personnel are, in general, concluded into three areas as defined by American management scholar Robert L. Katz:

(1) Technical skills: ability to perform specific tasks within an organization. For example, the ability to use specific procedures, methods and techniques to deal with and solve practical problems.

(2) Human skills: ability to work well with other people, understand and motivate other people. For example, the ability to work effectively as a group member and to build cooperative effort within the team he leads.

(3) Conceptual skills: ability to analyze, diagnose, abstract and conceptualize complex situations. For example, the ability to come up with new ideas and new thoughts, and the ability to recognize what impact a decision made in one area will have on other areas.

In addition to the above three types of basic skills, "international managers" should also have the following two important abilities:

(1) Global perspective: ability to understand the orientation and direction of business from the perspective of world politics and economy. Ability to understand and recognize different values and cultures different from those in their own environment.

(2) Ability to communicate in different cultures: ability to have in-depth communication with people of different cultures and backgrounds in addition to language proficiency.

In order to foster "international managers" with such abilities, it will be crucial to establish a human resource development system within an enterprise. Many multinational companies take different moves as to cultivating such personnel. For example, Japanese companies tend to construct longer-term human resource develop programs because of the low turnover rate. They provide extensive overseas experience or training depending on their business environment from the junior to the senior stages, and establish a transnational uniform personnel system within enterprise groups. They create opportunities for transnational teams within enterprise groups to participate in projects and carry out activities to build transnational human relations within enterprise groups.

An international city can also provide an environment that attracts and develops international managers. Shanghai has all along advocated the construction of headquarters economy and has had a series of incentive policies in place for the regional headquarters of transnational companies to move to Shanghai. As the regional headquarters of enterprises in Shanghai expand from Chinese headquarters to Asian headquarters, the Belt and Road headquarters and even the global headquarters, the level and depth of management and operation personnel gathering in Shanghai are bound to upgrade. Apart from introducing headquarters economy and other policy supports, the managers can develop "global perspective" and "ability to communicate in different cultures" by managing and operating in business districts, a human resource development mechanism which cannot be invested in by any single enterprise (See Fig.1).

	Abilities required	Way to pool and cultivate
Management and operation personnel	Technical skills Conceptual skills Human skills	Experience Internal and external training courses Policy incentives like headquarters economy
International managers	(Except for the above abilities) Global perspective Ability to communicate in different cultures	(Except for the above abilities) Multinational human resources system within the enterprise Construction of human resources development mechanism based on operation in urban business districts

Fig.1　Abilities required for and the way to pool/cultivate "international managers"

3. The way for cities to attract and cultivate international managers

With the global expansion of the knowledge economy, it is less necessary for white-collar workers to work in a particular office building in a particular area in the future. The urban business districts need to respond to the needs of enterprise and office personnel by strategically building an environment to attract human resources, promote exchange of personnel and achieve innovation through regional management.

Specifically, the purpose of business activities under the model of industrial economic development lies primarily in the stable production and supply. Therefore, the functions and axillary facilities of the business districts should tailor to the needs of such enterprise activities, and provide safe, extensive transportation functions for workers to commute as scheduled. An efficient traffic flow is required for workers to gather or evacuate. Business building space should be enough to engage all workers together. Each worker is provided with sufficient office space, and the functions around the office area are available to meet the dining needs of many workers.

However, the business activities under the model of knowledge-based economy development do not require all workers to gather in the same place at the same time or to work in the office designed by specifications. Workers are required to exchange knowledge through conversation, discussion and innovation with people both inside and outside the enterprise inside and outside their office space. Therefore, sufficient knowledge exchange space is required both inside and outside the business building and the whole business district. Activity space and demonstration space are also needed to stimulate innovation, as well as comfortable space to meet the employment and living requirements of intellectuals.

From the perspective of "attracting personnel", while the business districts in Shanghai are well suited to serve various business activities under the model of industrial economic development, a business environment suitable for the development of a knowledge-based economy is now required to attract versatile personnel across the world. In order to create such a business district that can attract personnel under the model of knowledge-based economy development, it is impossible for a single developer or property management company to construct, develop and manage it. The regional business operation and construction can only be done by cooperative efforts from relevant government agencies, developers and move-in enterprises within the whole business district. This mainly involves: building and operating an environment for knowledge exchange and designing a comfortable space for attracting personnel; strategically re-developing blocks according to the development of enterprises; introducing innovative functions and holding knowledge exchange activities.

From the perspective of "nurturing international managers", more targeted measures are needed to promote personnel exchange, in addition to environment construction as stated above. In order to broaden the global perspective of personnel working in business districts, provide them better understanding of diverse and different cultures and achieve even closer cross-cultural exchanges, various regional joint activities should be conducted in the course of regional business operations by the cooperative efforts from the government agencies, developers, and move-in enterprises. Possible activities include lectures or salons that can broaden the global perspective of business personnel, and community activities that can provide insight into different cultures and promote cross-cultural communication.

Cases of regional business operations tend to take place in business districts. For example, a joint venture is organized by relevant government agencies, developers and move-in merchants within a business district, to attract more consumers to the district by constructing a comfortable space within the district, promote activities and organizing festivals, in order to achieve mutual benefits and win-win results between individual merchant tenants and owners. However, there are also cases in point in which joint operations take place in high-end business office districts like the former CBD of Tokyo Station, OMY district (Otemachi-Marunouchi-Yurakucho), where Tokyo's international managers are concentrated.

Since Tokyo is a place where Japanese enterprises locate their global headquarters, international managers naturally gather in the heart of Tokyo. However, with the development of knowledge-based economy, even in this international business-intensive district of OMY, operations are coordinated by cooperative efforts from the public and private sectors so that the business district, originally only an office building complex, gradually becomes a comprehensive city coordinated in terms of economic, social, environmental and cultural activities in the era of knowledge-based economy, and continuously organizes and promotes activities which meet the needs of enterprise talents. Specifically, in terms of attracting talented individuals, the business district plans for the entire highly comfortable area and easily accessible public space, provides convenient traffic for use during work or consumption, and organizes exchange activities such as festivals, disaster prevention, sports and environmental protection. In terms of nurturing talents, the business district sets up and operates a platform for promoting exchanges and interaction among domestic and foreign talented individuals as well as innovative activities. It operates a "Morning University" for business people to learn from each other. This platform also serves as a starting point of projects for collaborative development between Tokyo and suburbs. There are also salons enabling international managers to consider sustainable development (See Table 2).

Table 2　Regional business operations in OMY district, Tokyo

Scope of regional business operations	Otemachi, Marunouchi and Yurakucho in Chiyoda-ku, Tokyo, approximately 120 hectares
Regional operating entities	Tokyo Metropolitan Government, Chiyoda-ku District Government JR East, around 90 developers and owners in OMY district, and many enterprises moving in to OMY district
Measures for the perspective of "attracting talented individuals"	• Plan and implement guidelines for urban sustainable development • Plan comfortable space within the district • Operate transportation within the district • Carry out exchange activities such as festival, disaster prevention, sports and environmental protection • Conduct common business activities such as co-promotion and branding
Measures for the perspective of "cultivating talents"	• Innovative platform for enterprise talents • Learning community (Morning University) activities • Operate salons for corporate social responsibility

4. Playing Shanghai's bridgehead role in developing international managers for the "Belt and Road" initiative

Regional business operation, which has been going on for many years, can also be understood as a sharing economy of regional resources. At present, China is already one of the most developed countries in the world in terms of sharing economy. As a place with the most abundant resources of international business professionals in China, Shanghai's business cluster district should also make full use of the existing resources in Shanghai to further develop regional business operation model in its business districts and build up the mechanism for pooling and nurturing international managers needed by Chinese enterprises to expand their overseas markets so as to make Shanghai a bridgehead for serving the Belt and Road initiative in terms of personnel development.

Shanghai's Geographical Advantages Can Help the City Play a Bridging Role in Promoting the Belt and Road Initiative

Tracy Yang

Audit Partner, KPMG China

Since 2013, the Belt and Road Initiative has achieved remarkable results and a number of landmark projects have gradually been finalised. Leading companies and organisations from China and around the world are working together under the framework of the initiative in areas including infrastructure, energy, equipment manufacturing, environmental protection and finance, and have contributed to regional and global economic growth.

As one of the "Big Four" accounting firms and a leading financial advisor, KPMG has been actively involved in the Belt and Road Initiative, having served businesses in over 100 Belt and Road projects. Advising businesses how to expand their markets along the Belt and Road has become one of our top priorities, and our teams assist clients in tackling problems throughout the life cycle of projects. We will continue to allocate more resources in the future to ensure businesses succeed in their investing and operational activities.

1. Challenges of Investing in Countries along the Belt and Road

Business expansion and investing activities along the Belt and Road have been gaining momentum as the initiative has been widely promoted and incentives introduced on an ongoing basis. In the course of serving our clients, we have found that while the Belt and Road Initiative has brought great opportunities for companies, businesses also face some challenges in doing business along the Belt and Road. These mainly include:

(1) Poor access to information

Many enterprises interested in expanding their markets along the Belt and Road have found it very difficult to obtain the key information they need for investment decision-making, either because there is no useful information available or because the channels of communication are not open. Key information may include preferential policies and cooperation frameworks introduced and established by China and participating countries in the Belt and Road Initiative; the latest laws and industry regulations; the status of the development of and planning for key industries; lists of key projects; and an analysis of investment opportunities in key industries in host countries.

(2) Absence of a complete industry chain

At present, most Chinese players along the Belt and Road are large businesses or centrally owned enterprises, with limited participation of SMEs. In addition, their investments concentrate on infrastructure, energy, electricity and public utilities, which has resulted in a high concentration of investments in terms of both industry and region. This, along with the fact that companies tend to copy other companies' investments in terms of industry and region, has quickly created a lot of competition for these industries, thus reducing profit margins. This has also resulted in another prominent issue which is the inability to cover entire industry value chains, and the inability to provide sufficient producer services, components and parts in certain areas.

(3) Incentives for businesses investing in countries along the Belt and Road

The government has provided policy support in areas including finance, tax, foreign exchange control, customs clearance, credit and insurance for outbound investments it wants to encourage. Companies interested in exploring markets along the Belt and Road also expect incentive policies from the government, especially in areas such as project approval, credit, capital flow and insurance claims, to facilitate investments.

(4) Compliance in overseas operations

Taxation and social security contributions are the most common issues for compliance in overseas operations. Enterprises doing business along the Belt and Road may sometimes be subject to excessive taxation and are unable to enjoy tax incentives that they are entitled to. Some may therefore experience difficulties when resolving taxation disputes. Generally, they have to make social security contributions for Chinese employees working in countries along the Belt and Road in both China and the host country. However, international assignees rarely enjoy any social security benefits when working abroad.

(5) Big investment risks

Most of the countries along the Belt and Road are developing countries which differ greatly in terms of investment climate. Irregularities in project operations are not uncommon. To invest in countries along the Belt and Road, enterprises must be prepared for complicated and difficult risk management challenges. Take foreign exchange risk as an example. In some cases, though it is provided in the contracts that USD shall be the payment currency, the partners may ultimately still choose to pay in local currencies. This brings a big foreign exchange risk and makes the internationalisation of the RMB even more urgent.

2. Shanghai's Geographical Advantages for Promoting the Development of the Belt and Road

Shanghai is an international financial centre, a free trade zone and a free port. A leader in the Yangtze River Economic Belt, it is also home to many MNCs' regional headquarters. With its geographical advantages, it can play a bridging role in the development of the Belt and Road.

According to the city's 13th Five-Year Plan, Shanghai will basically become an international economic, financial, trade and shipping centre by 2020, with capabilities for global resource allocation. It will be a recognised global centre for the innovation, trading, pricing and clearing of RMB products.

Since its establishment four years ago, the Shanghai Pilot Free Trade Zone has been taking active measures to create a business climate that features the rule of law, facilitates investments and is in line with international practices. Shanghai is developing a free trade port, and greater autonomy is expected.

Shanghai is the Chinese city with the highest concentration of MNCs' regional headquarters, and is a leader in the Yangtze River Economic Belt where a large number of SMEs are growing their businesses. Such unique geographical advantages can enable the city to play a big role in involving multinationals and SMEs in the development of the Belt and Road.

3. Suggestions for Shanghai to Play a Bridging Role

After carefully considering the challenges businesses face in investing in countries along the Belt and Road, we would like to make the following suggestions based on Shanghai's geographical advantages, and hope they can offer some good ideas about how Shanghai can play a bridging role in developing the Belt and Road.

(1) Establish comprehensive cooperation mechanisms with cities along the Belt and Road.

Several international frameworks for cooperation under the Belt and Road Initiative have been finalised so far. However, cooperation mechanisms at lower levels, e.g. those between cities or across industries, have yet to be established or improved. Shanghai may consider entering into a comprehensive investment and cooperation mechanism with major or hotspot cities along the Belt and Road.

By the end of 2017, China had signed 100 cooperation agreements under the Belt and Road Initiative with 86 countries and international organisations. Shanghai can consider establishing a comprehensive cooperation mechanism with major cities along the Belt and Road under the framework of these cooperation agreements. The cooperation mechanism may cover investment and financing, trade promotion, financial innovation, joint training and research, the establishment of mutually beneficial regulatory and service systems (e.g. taxation, customs clearance and social security), and the setting up of information and resource sharing platforms, which can contribute to creating a green channel for economic and trade activities between cities.

Take free trade zones as an example. In fact, many countries and cities along the Belt and Road are interested in China's experience in developing industrial parks and free trade zones. Shanghai can cooperate with these cities and capitalise on its geographical advantages, while taking into consideration the characteristics of its own industrial development to create a chain of free trade zones along the Belt and Road. This will not only promote investing, financing and trading activities, and the free flow of factors of production along the chain, but will also be conducive to local economic development and the well-being of people in countries along the Belt and Road.

(2) Establish win-win cooperation mechanisms with inland provinces and cities.

"We should pursue the Belt and Road Initiative as a priority ... and increase openness and cooperation in building innovation capacity. With these efforts, we hope to make new ground in opening China further through links running eastward and westward, across land and over sea", said President Xi Jinping in the report delivered at the 19th Communist Party of China (CPC) National Congress.

Compared with eastern coastal areas, China's inland provinces and municipalities have been lagging behind in opening up to the outside world. The Belt and Road Initiative has opened China's gateway to central Asia, west Asia and south Asia. Inland provinces which used to be on the periphery of opening up are now at the forefront and face tremendous opportunities for development. However, they are inexperienced in guiding and encouraging businesses in international cooperation and in establishing free trade zones. As investors sometimes have difficulties finding qualified personnel and securing sufficient funds, they might find it challenging to secure local resources for their projects in landlocked provinces.

Shanghai may consider establishing cooperation mechanisms with inland provinces and cities such as Shaanxi, Chongqing, Sichuan, Yunnan and Xinjiang. They can use their complementary advantages to achieve win-win growth and make breakthroughs to solve strategic issues. In the process of cooperation, the market shall play a fundamental role, while the government promotes cooperation between participants. Exchanges and cooperation can be encouraged in the sourcing of talents, technology, fundraising and project implementation to promote the coordinated development of local economies and create a new pattern of win-win cooperation and opening up.

4. Focus on the Needs of SMEs and Establish a Comprehensive Service System for Promoting Investments

Shanghai can establish a comprehensive service system for Belt and Road projects based on the characteristics and needs of SMEs.

Large SOEs have always been major players in developing the Belt and Road. However, there are still some segments along the Belt and Road that have not been occupied by large enterprises, such as building materials, transportation, hospitality, and cross-border e-commerce, which means there is a huge demand for products and services.

Some SMEs in China, especially privately owned ones, are highly competitive in some segments. They are sensitive to changes in the market and flexible in their decision-making process, and their time to market is short. They are able to provide customised products and services, or provide supporting services for large projects with their advanced technologies. Together with large enterprises, they can form a complete Belt and Road business ecosystem for Chinese enterprises to promote the coordinated development of upstream and downstream industry chains; establish a complete R&D, production and marketing system; and enhance the supporting capabilities and overall competitiveness of local industries.

To participate in the development of the Belt and Road, SMEs may team up with large enterprises and other SMEs, play a part in large projects, or actively involve themselves in the construction of Belt and Road industrial parks to improve the division of labour in and the distribution of industry chains.

Shanghai may consider the following aspects to encourage SMEs to expand their markets along the Belt and Road:

• Set up a Belt and Road information service platform: An information platform can be established and activities held to ensure SMEs keep abreast of the latest developments in policies and intergovernmental multilateral agreements under the Belt and Road Initiative; development plans of countries and the progress of projects along the Belt and Road; information on the business climate of host countries; and risk warnings. With such a platform, participants can introduce their projects and engage with each other.

• Provide personalised financial, consulting and training services: The government can provide personalised financial and consulting services for SMEs, and match the needs of enterprises with financial institutions, intermediaries and training service agencies to ensure enterprises do business successfully along the Belt and Road.

• Introduce incentive policies to encourage investments: The government can look into the problems encountered by enterprises investing in countries along the Belt and Road, and explore and innovate supportive policies, including financing support, tax incentives for high-tech enterprises and the streamlining of approval procedures. It can work with the regulators of host countries to come up with measures to facilitate investments, such as the free flow of funds across borders and mutual recognition of social security rights.

• Promote win-win cooperation between multinational corporations and Chinese enterprises:

Shanghai is home to the regional headquarters of a large number of MNCs. It can use this advantage to promote win-win cooperation between Chinese and foreign enterprises and help Chinese enterprises expand their businesses along the Belt and Road.

The Belt and Road Initiative has not only brought opportunities for Chinese enterprises, but is also a platform for MNCs to utilise their strengths. In addition to mature overseas project operation and management experience, MNCs boast a global network of information and resources. Chinese enterprises can make full use of MNCs' strengths to assist with their own weaknesses, transform their businesses, move up the industry chain and get ready to enter local markets along the Belt and Road. For example, although Chinese contractors have earned rich experience in the development and construction of large overseas engineering and infrastructure projects, there are still few successful cases for them to learn from in the process of changing from contractors into investors and operators, and they encounter difficulties.

In the eyes of MNCs, the Belt and Road Initiative is also a good opportunity for business expansion. They can join forces with Chinese enterprises in undertaking Belt and Road projects to enter new markets and expand their businesses. For example, some of the world's leading providers of electrical and electronic equipment have cooperated with Chinese enterprises in EPC (engineering, procurement, and construction) projects in countries along the Belt and Road to provide technical support. Under the Belt and Road Initiative, the infrastructure, public services and business climate of countries in the region have improved. A big increase has been seen in government spending and consumers' income. All of this will help MNCs invest and operate locally. We have learned that some MNCs have formulated medium and long-term development plans based on the Belt and Road Initiative. More MNCs are expected to step up investments in countries along the Belt and Road to win a first-mover advantage.

Shanghai can take this opportunity to learn more about the concerns and difficulties of MNCs. It can also set up a platform which can act as a go-between for MNCs and Belt and Road projects, and promote cooperation between MNCs and Chinese enterprises. Shanghai can help MNC regional headquarters in Shanghai become the corporations' global Belt and Road investment and operation platform to boost the development of the Belt and Road.

5. Innovate in Terms of Financing Mechanisms and Financial Products

Currency convertibility and the free flow of funds are the goals of the Shanghai Pilot Free Trade Zone in establishing an effective investment and financing platform for Belt and Road projects and expanding the two-way opening up of the finance industry. Since its establishment more than four years ago, the Shanghai Pilot Free Trade Zone has conducted a series of experiments in financial innovation including cross-border financing and settlement, the facilitation of currency convertibility for investment and financing purposes, cross-border use of RMB, and reform of the foreign exchange management system, and has accumulated extensive theoretical knowledge and practical experience. Under the Belt and Road Initiative, the free trade zone can further explore policies and measures to promote cross-border business operations, and provide more accessible financial services for businesses in their overseas trade and investing activities.

In the future, the free trade zone may consider further innovating financial policies, expanding businesses relating to the integration of local and foreign currencies in free trade accounts, exploring the innovative functions of free trade accounts, and improving its Free Trade Accounting Unit (FTU). Also, based on the trading platforms that have already been established, the free trade zone can encourage innovation in financial products, including innovation in gold, foreign exchange, financial derivatives, insurance policies and non-standard assets, and expand the scope of onshore financial products that offshore RMB can invest in to facilitate the two-way cross-border flow of RMB.

In addition, as reform policies are further refined and finalised, and policy implementation is strengthened in the future, financial institutions can work with the government to deepen reforms in the context of building a global RMB service system and achieve capital account convertibility. Large financial institutions, such as banks, brokers and insurers, can establish branches and locate their headquarters in the free trade zone to explore the possibility of increasing personal foreign exchange limits and undertake pilot currency convertibility projects within stipulated limits for non-financial enterprises in Shanghai Pilot Free Trade Zone. This can contribute to the opening of the finance industry and provide easily accessible financial services for businesses investing in countries along the Belt and Road.

6. Optimise Tax Services and Deepen Cooperation between Tax Authorites

Tax matters are becoming increasingly complicated both at home and abroad. Tax authorities have also strengthened regulation. In such a context, tax issues have gradually become an important factor that influences the decision-making of enterprises "Going Out" and the performance of overseas business operations. In order to turn the tax factor into a "catalyst" for promoting the "Belt and Road" Initiative instead of a "stumbling block", Shanghai can consider the following measures to help businesses in their ventures abroad:

• Optimise tax services for enterprises participating in the Belt and Road Initiative: since 2015, the State Administration of Taxation has introduced a number of measures to provide support for the development of the Belt and Road. In addition to implementing the measures issued by the State Administration of Taxation, Shanghai can capitalise on its own advantages to provide enterprises with more personalised and innovative tax services. For example, Shanghai can provide targeted tax training for enterprises through the hotline for tax consulting services(12366), including an introduction of the general tax policies of countries along the Belt and Road and their tax policies for specific industries, tax risk warnings, and updates on tax regulations concerning overseas business activities.

• Set up green channels for enterprises entitled to tax incentives: in order to provide better support for the development of the Belt and Road, the government has introduced tax incentives for enterprises, including a tax refund(exemption) for the export of goods and services, zero tax rate or tax exemption for cross-border taxable services, and tax deduction for overseas income. Therefore, Shanghai can consider establishing green channels for enterprises entitled to tax incentives by setting up specific service windows, simplifying implementation procedures, improving the efficiency of review and approval, and providing related advisory services, so that all enterprises that are eligible for tax incentives are kept informed when there is a need for them to know, and enjoy the tax benefits they are entitled to.

• Assist companies in resolving tax disputes: Shanghai can set up a mechanism for coordinating cross-border tax disputes to assist enterprises doing business along the Belt and Road to actively communicate with local tax authorities and the State Administration of Taxation, and initiate mutual consultation procedures in a timely manner so as to protect the rights and interests of enterprises.

• Deepen cooperation between tax authorities: under the abovementioned comprehensive cooperation mechanisms, the Shanghai tax authorities can set up a platform to regularly meet and communicate with the tax authorities of major or hotspot cities along the 'Belt and Road'. This can help enterprises that have encountered difficulties in tax compliance or in claiming the tax benefits they are entitled to. Deepened cooperation can contribute to improving tax authorities' governance capabilities.

EY Suggestion to Shanghai Government on Building the "Bridgehead" for the Belt and Road

Shunyuan Zhang

Partner of Transaction Tax and China Tax Outbound Center, EY

The Belt and Road is a rare historical opportunity, Shanghai can make full use of its geographical position, institutional innovation of free trade zone, economy, industry, talent gathering, technology innovation and other advantages to support the construction of the Belt and Road to become the bridgehead to serve the Belt and Road, as well as to connect with countries and regions along the Belt and Road to further consolidate and enhance Shanghai's role as the center of international economic, financial, trade, shipping and scientific innovation.

In recent years, EY has accumulated its experiences in the Belt and Road market. In the past three years, EY has assisted nearly 800 Chinese companies to invest and do business in countries and regions along the Belt and Road. Based on our work experiences and observations, we hereby provide our suggestions on how Shanghai can play the bridgehead role in serving the The Belt and Road development:

1. Building a Comprehensive Belt and Road Economic and Trade Investment Promotion Service Platform

In view of many countries' consulate, government agencies, world famous financial and professional service agencies were located in Shanghai, Shanghai can consider to build a comprehensive economic and trade investment promotion service platform which consists of consulates, related government agencies, international professional service providers, insurance and financial institutions. The platform can provide one-stop professional services and information sharing to companies planning to invest and do business along the Belt and Road countries and regions, as well as provide continuous services and support for companies in investment all stages, which includes:

(1) Preparation Phase: Providing information on investment and business development opportunities; Local investment, business and financing environment, local market, industry and supply chain information; Investment risk and consideration; Local law, taxation, incentive policies and corresponding compliance requirements; Consultation and assistance related to the filing/approval for outbound investment.

(2) During investment and doing business phase: Referral of local government agencies, local successful Chinese companies and chambers of commerce; Coordinating companies to conduct local site visit and provide support for local investment related approvals, registration and incentive applications; Providing assistance to companies which face problems for local investment and business processes; Providing regular updates on local market, regulations and risk information.

The Belt and Road service platform can provide support services to online (online joint operation platform) and offline (joined institution) companies. Offline mode refers to bring in relevant departments and agencies to set up office in the Belt and Road industrial park, which includes:

(1) Shanghai municipal government agency: setting up the coordination office of the Belt and Road economic and trade investment promotion service platform, which can lead and coordinate service platform's members and provide guidance.

(2) Consulate and government agencies of countries and regions along the Belt and Road: Providing local market information, law regulations and policy introduction, referral of local government agencies to provide coordination and support work.

(3) Professional service providers (such as accounting firms, law firms and other advisory firms, etc.), financial and insurance institutions: establishing an office in the park to help companies have access to the one-stop services.

(4) Chinese chamber of commerce in the countries and regions along the Belt and Road: inviting local Chinese chamber of commerce to set up a liaison office in the park, which is convenient for existing companies and new companies planning to invest to communicate effectively and share experiences. At the same time, it can facilitate the government to have a deep understanding of Chinese companies' local situations and problems, effectively unite and cohesion force of local Chinese companies to improve the local business environment, bear social responsibility, establish a positive image

and improve their influence, indirectly extend the bridgehead from Shanghai to local.

2. Special Act for Cultural Exchange and Cooperation: Upgrading and Building a Training Program for Multinational Operation talents

The following suggestions are for the "upgrading and building a training program for multinational operation talents" from "special act for cultural exchange and cooperation":

(1) For those who are to be seconded to countries and regions along the Belt and Road: there are more than 60 countries along the Belt and Road, most of which are developing countries. The geopolitical situation is complex, and the regional languages, cultures and habits of life are also very different. In order to develop more multinational management talents, which needs them ready to beseconded to the countries and regions along the Belt and Road as well as respond to local problems if possible, the government can use resources (the platform discussed above) which has entered the industrial park of the Belt and Road and cooperate with relevant universities and research institutions to develop specific courses regarding specific countries and regions (such as: the laws and regulations, business etiquette, culture and custom, language, security risk prevention and other courses).

(2) For those executives who are local hired: integrating with local society is one of the key factors to the success and sustainable operation in countries and regions along the Belt and Road. The company will hire local employee as senior executives when it grows its local operations. Therefore, in order to help the local executives be more easily integrated into the Chinese company's culture and working style, the government can cooperate with relevant universities and research institutions in developing specific courses for these local executives. (such as: Chinese companies' business etiquette, culture and Chinese language courses).

3. Setting up a "Specialized Board Market for the Belt and Road" in Shanghai Stock Exchange

The Belt and Road are mostly consisting of developing countries, with unstable economic development environment, but which also brings business opportunities to companies. In view of the relatively high risk of the Belt and Road investment projects, Chinese companies may face shortage of financing channels for its local investment and operations. In order to solve funds shortage and make everyone participate in the Belt and Road project, the government can consider to set up specialized board of the Belt and Road in Shanghai Stock Exchange. On the basic concept of "reducing limit and strengthening supervision", the government can permit special criteria on listing requirements in considering of the Belt and Road project's actual conditions and income distribution cycle, details are as follow:

(1) Setting up special IPO review standards and listing requirements for the investment projects and companies related to the Belt and Road.

(2) Establishing a special review team or review commissioner to expedite the review and approval process of companies' listing applications for Belt and Road investment projects; for those eligible listing project of the Belt and Road, government can arrange a separate and green channel to shorten the listing waiting time.

The development of the Belt and Road opened a new era for China's cooperation with the countries and regions along the Belt and Road, we are willing to contribute to the development of the Belt and Road bridgehead in Shanghai, so as to keep investment security and sustainable management of Chinese companies in the countries and regions along the Belt and Road.

Role of US Investment to Support Shanghai's Belt and Road Goals

Owen Haacke

Chief Representative，Shanghai Office at US-China Business Council

1. US Company Interest in Supporting B&R

After the launch of the Belt and Road (B&R) initiative, many US companies are looking at investment opportunities in areas where they may have a competitive advantage to leverage. For example, some US-China Business Council (USCBC) members have been successful working with Chinese companies on the Belt and Road Inniative projects in China and in countries where Chinese companies may not have experience or the managerial, investment, or technological expertise. Other companies see opportunities to supply customers in Europe and other location from the Belt and Road Inniative-supported locations in China. Companies in logistics see opportunities in shipping services and warehousing, and service companies see opportunities with Chinese companies in central and western provinces that will be investing in OBOR countries.

While B&R may not affect regional strategy for all companies, there are opportunities to develop new business in China. USCBC published an overview in 2016 of how companies were seeking opportunities, but companies have since shared examples of how to expand business under the B&R umbrella.

Many the Belt and Road Inniative project opportunities are domestic, and can be supported from Shanghai. Although China promoted a "Go West" strategy over the past decade—building highways, railways, and airports to connect the inland to the coast—infrastructure in China's internal provinces continues to be less developed than eastern China. Provincial governments are looking at B&R as an opportunity to expand investment in infrastructure, manufacturing, and services, as they may be able to get approval for new projects tied to the B&R agenda. For example, companies supporting infrastructure development have discovered new opportunities in Sichuan, Xinjiang, Yunnan, and other provinces trying to become key logistical hubs for OBOR trade.

2. How US Companies Can Support the Belt and Road Inniative

To take advantage of B&R business expansion opportunities, some companies are considering partnering with Chinese businesses. Some of the ways that international firms participate in and benefit from B&R include:

• Providing Financing and Financial Services. Western companies can provide capital for Chinese companies doing business abroad. Although various institutions, such as the AIIB and the Silk Road Development Fund, assist domestic companies with financing for OBOR projects, several USCBC members have leveraged their capital to partner with Chinese companies on projects. Financial services companies are also able to provide services to Chinese companies with projects in B&R countries—for example, providing commercial insurance for Chinese companies setting up new projects in B&R countries.

• Sharing Global Experience. Experience in conducting global business position USCBC members to provide consulting services to Chinese business partners, including market intelligence, legal expertise, best practices, risk management, personnel training, and community engagement. Companies based in major east coast cities like Shanghai, emphasize the importance of working with partners familiar with OBOR investment destinations, some of which may be foreign companies with offices in China. One company was able to support a new project overseas where they had operations, but much of the collaboration occurred with their partner's headquarters in China.

3. the Belt and Road Inniative Opportunities in Shanghai

Key policy highlights of the Shanghai B&R plan include attracting foreign business by simplifying and streamlining the approval process for foreign investment enterprises, providing government incentives to foster the service sector, and encouraging multinational enterprises to diversify the functions of their regional headquarters in Shanghai. Working toward achieving such goals will help promote a more open and transparent business environment and help Shanghai achieve its economic goals. Some of the highlights in Shanghai's B&R plans include:

• Initiatives in Shanghai like the recently announced Free Trade Port and the existing Shanghai Pilot Free Trade Zone can serve as a launching point for further business opportunities if there are further openings and administrative reforms.

• Development of the services sector in Shanghai under the B&R initiative has the potential to bring more professional services and financial expertise to Shanghai. Allowing open participation in the services space will help Shanghai boost services as part of the economy, and be a services center for supporting B&R initiatives.

• Shanghai's promotion of ecommerce under the B&R initiative will bring opportunities for foreign and domestic companies to bring products into China and sell from China to B&R countries.

A transparent plan and strategy for B&R implementation in Shanghai and throughout China will be beneficial to both domestic and foreign companies so they can best identify how they can support and play positive role.

4. Policy Recommendations to Support B&R in Shanghai

(1) Promote a level, transparent playing field for foreign and domestic companies.

• Equal treatment. Foreign companies throughout China and Shanghai should be on an equal basis to contribute to B&R projects and development. Companies legally established under China's Company Law should all be treated equally by regulators, regardless of ownership nationality.

• Ensure equal treatment in licensing and procurement. Encourage further efforts to reduce licensing barriers and ensure equal treatment in licensing reviews and approvals for B&R projects. Licensing and other official approvals for B&R projects should be made without prejudice against type of ownership, without influence from competing entities, and with consistent interpretation. Ensure bidding and procurement process is clear and available to companies that may be able to support B&R projects.

(2) Reduce trade barriers, enforce globally accepted trade rules.

• Increase the use of internationally harmonized standards for goods and services sold in China. The use of internationally harmonized standards in China will ensure that Chinese consumers and end users have access to the best products and services, and that

Chinese products and services are accepted and competitive internationally—in B&R countries and across the globe. Shanghai should play a role in promoting science-based, fair, transparent, and market-led approaches to standards setting and development that are open to all companies regardless of nationality, including domestic, foreign-invested, and foreign-based manufacturers.

• Eliminate import barriers to facilitate economic rebalancing and consumption. China maintains high import duties and consumption taxes on a wide array of consumer goods, as well as differential treatment of imported goods through product licenses, distribution restrictions, import inspections, and unique standards. Reducing or eliminating tariffs and taxes on consumer goods and ensuring equitable treatment of domestic and foreign-made products would be a simple yet powerful stimulant of domestic consumption. An increase in domestic consumption may help address imbalances in trade flows between China and B&R countries that could help reduce logistical costs.

(3) Move forward with financial sector reforms.

Shanghai can serve as a financial hub for supporting B&R projects domestically and financing projects overseas. Recent moves to curb capital outflows from China are impacting normal business transactions and cross-border payments, reducing predictability and confidence. Shanghai should take lead in moving forward with market oriented financial sector reforms that would create more domestic opportunities for capital deployment and returns, allow greater foreign financial institution participation, and create conditions for better integration of the world's second-largest economy into the international economy.

(4) Strengthen the innovation environment.

• Promote effective innovation incentives in Shanghai. Continue to promote innovation incentive programs that would positively incentivize innovation activity such as the establishment of R&D centers that can support product development for the China domestic market, B&R countries, and globally.

• Promote policies that overseas talent to work in Shanghai. Continue policies that allow overseas talent to work in Shanghai, and work to streamline the process so domestic and foreign companies can bring in talent from B&R countries and from around the world to work in Shanghai.

• Continue to strengthen China's IPR regime and enforcement of IPR in China

Stronger IPR protection brings mutual benefits. China should continue to improve its IPR legal regime by updating laws and regulations to reflect the latest developments in IPR protection and enforcement. It should also continue to expand resources devoted to IPR enforcement and adopt stronger deterrents against IPR infringement. This will allow companies to bring more innovative products to the China market that can be used in B&R projects domestically and overseas.

The 3D Belt and Road Initiative: Roles and Opportunities of Shanghai

Alan Chan

Associate of Gao Feng Advisory Company

1. The Belt and Road Development Promotes Economic Development and Transformation of China and the Countries along the Belt and Road, and Shares Benefits of China's Development with the World

As we all know, the Belt and Road initiative was a top-level national strategy proposed during Chinese President Xi Jinping's visit to Central Asia and Southeast Asia in September and October of 2013, and it is becoming a crucial foothold and a new engine for opening up to the outside world. In the past, as a commercial tie between Asian and European countries, the ancient Silk Road had strengthened the economic and cultural exchanges between the East and the West. Today, the Belt and Road Initiative will bring greater opportunities and mutual benefits for cooperation between China and countries along the route.

It is of tremendous importance for China's economic development. Firstly, the Belt and Road development will push forward economic transformation and updating. Through its opening up, China will get involved in international division of labor and cooperation to improve its commodity quality and service system. Unlike the previous export model which mainly focused on low-end products, more high-tech and innovative products and services are now going global along the Belt and Road. China is striving to remove trade barriers in cooperation with countries along the Belt and Road and explore new economic growth areas. The import and export volume of China for countries along the Belt and Road reached up to RMB 6 251.7 billion in 2016. This enhances balanced economic development of countries and regions around China, and rise China's international influence.

Secondly, the Belt and Road development explores industrial investment opportunities. Through cooperation modes like progressive and large-scale infrastructure construction, reasonable exploitation of resources and energies and comprehensive trade service exchange, China's capital market is seeing more industrial chains and multi-industry investment chances. As many countries and regions along the Belt and Road are underdeveloped, they are in an urgent need to upgrade their infrastructure. A bilateral cooperation has been established between China and most countries and regions along the route, covering energy, traffic, finance, tourism and infrastructure. It is devoted to steer joint success of all parties and create new competitive advantages with mutual benefits.

With increasing change of political and economic globalization and greater influence of China, the international society expects more voices and initiatives from China. Through the Belt and Road development, China has taken an active part in global governance, and will play a greater role in international affairs by outputting more "Chinese modes".

2. "Going Global" of Private-owned Enterprises

The Belt and Road development also brings tremendous development opportunities and challenges for Chinese enterprises, in particular private-owned enterprises.

On the one hand, private-owned enterprises are efficient in decision-making. Compared with state-owned enterprises, they can make timely outbound investment decisions that help enterprise development based on changes of investment climate. In addition, thanks to strong creativity willingness and ability, private-owned enterprises can make innovation in commercial modes based on market demands to explore local market. Private-owned enterprises should act with courage to attempt. And internationalization is the only way for enterprise development. With these advantages, private-owned enterprises are becoming more important in the Belt and Road.

On the other hand, private-owned enterprises can hardly get comprehensive, timely and effective information required under existing environments and conditions. In addition, private-owned enterprises face political, economic and financial risks during multinational operation. Behind these risks and challenges, private-owned enterprises shall take overall strategic thinking and transformation during going global.

From large trend, private-owned enterprises are faced with a new era of internationalization to develop themselves from a "domestic company" to a "world company". China also enters a new era represented by innovation and entrepreneurship. Behind innovation comes the knowledge economy. The focus of competition among enterprises has changed from tangible capitals to intangible capitals. Knowledge is playing a prominent role in value creation of an enterprise. At this turning point and the era where innovation is critical, private-owned enterprises have a good opportunity to leap from a "domestic company" to a "world company".

The overall implementation of the Belt and Road initiative is a good chance for private-owned enterprises to leap ahead, and is of great importance for their strategic transformation into a world company. To achieve this, soft power is critical. Excellent private-owned enterprises shall integrate hard power and improve their soft power to global level.

To implement the "Going Global" strategy, some suggestions are proposed below to help private-owned enterprises improve their abilities and international competitiveness: ① The private-owned enterprises shall raise their brand recognition and competitiveness with global perspective; ② Make active efforts on innovation to improve overall governance; ③ Actively cultivate cross-culture talents to seek for better development; ④ Develop risk awareness and promote a sound risk control system; ⑤ Establish cross-border E-commerce platform for global operation of businesses; ⑥ Enhance external multi-cooperation and form closely knit groups when going overseas; ⑦ Cooperate with governments and provide scholarship to jointly build a talent cultivation platform; ⑧ Large-sized private-owned enterprises shall help small and middle-sized ones go global and promote coordinated development of "Going Global" of upstream and downstream of the industrial chain; and ⑨ Build high-end think tank to enhance "external brain" resources.

3. 3D Belt and Road Initiative: Knowledge Platform of Soft Power

We believe that the Belt and Road development is not to provide hard power opportunity for enterprises under traditional significance, which is an understanding at plane and linear level. In factor, the Belt and Road initiative shall be interpreted in a 3D and non-linear manner. The Belt and Road initiative shall be deemed as a knowledge platform of soft power for enterprises, which helps enterprises think their values and expand international views to achieve strategic transformation. This 3D Belt and Road initiative will help private-owned enterprises improve their knowledge in soft power and provide new thoughts for their leapfrog development.

As commercial environment in China is getting complex and rapid-changing, many enterprises in China see innovation as their core competitiveness in future growth. China is shifting from a "copy" nation to an innovation-based country; and many original innovations in China have reached international advanced level. In this "post-copy" era, innovation enterprises in China have "gone out" to explore new opportunities in overseas market. A "reverse-copy" emerges as overseas enterprises start to refer to innovation ideas and seek aspirations from China's enterprises. In particular, in digital field, a number of Chinese enterprises have developed into one of tech tycoons in the world due to specific Internet ecosystem in China, which attract great attention and respect from the world. In regardless of innovation in commercial mode, organization and technology, we believe that Chinese enterprises will increasingly present thought leadership to aspire and influence more enterprises around the globe.

Therefore, when thinking about internationalization, private-owned enterprises shall not only consider tangible things, but also consider intangible aspects to improve overall competitiveness and achieve leap development.

4. The Third Road: Digital Silk Road

By definition, the Belt and Road means the Silk Road Economic Belt and 21st Century Maritime Silk Road. As virtual economy gets increasingly popular and integrates with real economy, we think that a "third road" is developed for the Belt and Road following the thinking development of "Internet+": a virtual "digital silk road".

Chinese enterprises will connect enterprises and consumers across the world with digital commercial mode and technology. The digital economy derived from this third road will break physical geography limits. In the future, the road may show higher spreading speed and wider influence than real economy. It is inspiring that many Internet companies (such as Alibaba, Tencent and Baidu) are influencing the world through this virtual silk road.

For example, Malaysia Government and Indonesia Government have employed Jack Ma as their digital economic adviser to promote local digital transformation and upgrading. Alibaba announced to cooperate with Malaysia to build a "digital free trade zone" to jointly create the first pilot zone of "Electronic World Trade Platform" (eWTP) outside China. This will help developing countries, underdeveloped countries, small and middle-enterprises and young people around to world get involved in global market and global economy. Alibaba's target is to serve 2 billion consumers globally by 2025, including at least 1 billion overseas consumers. Therefore, the building of "digital silk road" is of great strategic importance to Alibaba.

To develop the digital silk road, online and offline construction are both needed, including information infrastructure construction, international logistics, cross-border e-commerce, smart city, data security and network governance. Apart from traditional digital hardware and software, some digital cultural contents in domestic China, such as film & television, mobile games, musics, literature and cartoon can go overseas through this third road. In a word, with unique Internet ecology and digital innovation, China has become industrial benchmark to export its digital innovation to the world.

5. Shanghai's Bridgehead Role in Building the Belt and Road Initiative

Shanghai enjoys significant first mover advantage in serving the building of national Belt and Road initiative. At first, Shanghai, with its unique historical background and political status, is the economic and financial center in China, and an important portal for opening-up. It has the strategic position for "connecting domestic and overseas" in the Belt and Road initiative. By taking advantages of its regional competitiveness, Shanghai will link urban agglomeration of Yangtze river delta and surrounding commercial ecosphere and become the key node to help excellent Chinese enterprises go out. Secondly, Shanghai was planned to be built into "four centers" (international financial enter, economic center, trade center and navigation center) and positioned as a global technological center. This lays a sound foundation and builds competitive advantage for Shanghai. In the future, this development shall be integrated with the Belt and Road initiative and other national strategies to achieve a result of

"1+1>2". Thirdly, Shanghai, as the international financial center, will provide financing and financial service supports for building the Belt and Road. China (Shanghai) Pilot Free Trade Zone under construction will become a new benchmark of free trade of China in the future. Fourthly, as a cosmopolitan city, Shanghai will attract top talents around the world to boost personnel exchange of the Belt and Road. Based on its advantages, Shanghai will focus on related innovative industries, such as financial technology and cross-border e-commerce.

However, faced with above opportunities-private-owned enterprises, 3D Belt and Road and digital silk road, how can Shanghai grasp great opportunities from the Belt and Road and give full play of its bridgehead role?

At first, the Belt and Road brings new opportunities and challenges for enterprises. The key for enterprises lie in their strategic prospect and action capability. Shanghai government shall encourage private-owned enterprises to foster international vision and ecological thinking to consider the opportunities brought by the Belt and Road. In the future, global competition is not only between companies but between ecosystems. Participants in the ecosystem shall be mutually-benefited to each other to jointly promote the construction of a new global governance structure. Private-owned enterprises shall consider disruptive development from international perspective, understand the Belt and Road initiative at a strategic level, and carry out strategic layout from the strategic thinking of building a global ecosystem. The process from a "domestic company" to a "world company" cannot be accomplished overnight. This is a big trend in the future that requires a combination of Belt and Road initiative and long-term development planning of enterprises. Only by participating in global governance can excellent private-owned enterprises achieve this target.

Secondly, Shanghai Government shall encourage private-owned enterprises to actively build soft power through the Belt and Road initiative, and become the global thinking leader to improve overall competitiveness and maximize economic and social value. Private-owned enterprises shall attempt to go beyond traditional opinions to bear more social responsibilities and become a global player to think from global perspective. Participate in global competitiveness and governance and promote overall global commercial governance level. The good news is that a small batch of leading private-owned enterprise entrepreneurs has taken the lead to actively participate in global governance.

Lastly, Shanghai government shall make active efforts on the building of "digital silk road" and play its leading role to build digital ecosystem. It shall support growth of more innovative digital start-ups and drive more digital enterprises to go out and promote cross-country and cross-sector cooperation.

The Action Plan for Shanghai's Bridgehead Role in Serving the National Belt and Road Initiative issued by Shanghai Government in 2017 has proposed six special plans to give guiding suggestions, including trade and investment facilitation, financial openness cooperation, enhanced interconnection function, scientific and technological cooperation, people-to-people and cultural exchanges and think tank building. We believe that more studies, suggestions and discussions in the future will boost Shanghai to become the bridgehead in the Belt and Road initiative.

ROUNDTABLE
DISCUSSION

圆桌讨论

主持人·MODERATOR

李剑腾 Leo Li
波士顿咨询公司全球合伙人兼董事总经理
Partner & Managing Director，Boston Consulting Group（BCG）

互动嘉宾·GUESTS
张 林 Lin Zhang
上海市交通委副主任
Deputy Director General of Shanghai Municipal Commission of Transportation

傅国庆 Guoqing Fu
上海市科委总工程师
Chief Engineer of Shanghai Science and Technology Committee（STCSM）

权 衡 Heng Quan
上海社科院世界经济研究所所长
Director of the Institute of World Economy of Shanghai Academy of Social Sciences（SASS）

桑 琦 Qi Sang
上海市商务委副巡视员
Deputy Inspector of Shanghai Municipal Commission of Commerce

赵文斌 Wenbin Zhao
上海市检验检疫局发展规划处处长
Director of the Development and Planning Division of Shanghai Entry-Exit Inspection and Quarantine Bureau

王德弟 Dedi Wang
上海市农委经济商务处处长
Director of the Economic and Commercial Division of Shanghai Agricultural Committee

谢善鸿 Shanhong Xie
上海市金融办金融发展协调处副处长
Deputy Director of the Development and Coordination Division of Shanghai Financial Services Office

张 宇 Yu Zhang
上海市外办政策研究室副处长
Deputy Director of the Policy Research Office of Foreign Affair Office of Shanghai Municipal People's Government

陈礼明 Liming Chen
锦江国际集团有限公司高级副总裁
Senior Vice President of Jin Jiang International（Holdings）Co., Ltd.

夏梅兴　Meixing Xia
上海电力股份有限公司副总经理
Vice General Manager of Shanghai Electric Power Company Limited

杨晓东　Xiaodong Yang
上汽集团国际业务部总经理
General Manager of the International Business Department, Shanghai Automotive Industry Corporation（SAIC MOTOR）

丁嵩冰　Songbing Ding
上港集团战略研究部总经理
General Manager of the Strategic Research Department, Shanghai International Port（Group）Co., Ltd.

华　黎　Li Hua
上海奥威科技开发有限公司董事长
Chairman of Shanghai Aowei Technology Development Co., Ltd.

桂　渐　Jian Gui
基仕伯中国区总裁
President of GCP Applied Technologies，China

王伟国　Weiguo Wang
西门子中国副总裁、上海和浙江公司总经理
Vice President at Siemens Ltd. China & General Manager of Shanghai and Zhejiang

陈　艳　Elaine Chen
霍尼韦尔亚太区政府事务总监
Director of Government Affairs, APAC at Honeywell Corporate

刘明华　Minghua Liu
德勤华东区主管合伙人
Managing Partner of Eastern China, Audit Partner of Shanghai, China, Deloitte

纪　纲　Gang Ji
罗兰贝格合伙人兼大中华区副总裁
Partner and Vice President of Roland Berger Greater China

杨　洁　Tracy Yang
毕马威中国审计合伙人
Audit Partner，KPMG China

乔依德　Yide Qiao
上海发展研究基金会副会长兼秘书长
Vice Chairman & Secretary General of Shanghai Development Research Foundation

李剑腾：从主旨演讲环节提到的超级贸易平台，到首席贸易港，以及我同事提出的实业赋能的观点，最终我们要出好的政策，还是需要到实践中，从实践中来、到实践中去。今天除了智库单位外，还有很多企业代表以及政府各个委办的领导。我们回到实践中，听听市场一线参与"一带一路"建设的企业，看看他们有什么困惑和疑问。尤其今天在座的企业代表，非常好地代表了上海"三三三"的经济组成结构，我们有国企代表，也有民企代表、外企代表。我们先从国企开始，听听大家在"一带一路"面临的困惑或疑问，再听听政府各委办的解答以及智库的思考。

丁嵩冰：我们国企作为"排头兵、先行者"，首先跟大家交流一下。我来自上港集团，上港集团经营的是上海港的公共集装箱码头和大多数的散杂货码头。如果说上海是"一带一路"建设的桥头堡，上港集团作为港口码头运营商，我们就是桥头堡的"排头兵"。经过这么多年的发展，我们跟许多咨询机构有合作，也得到了很多企业的支持。当前环境下，我们研究的一个重点是"自由贸易港"。

因为"自由贸易港"相关的细则还没有出来，所以把问题留给咨询公司。目前我们和两家咨询公司有业务关系，这个问题优先考虑埃森哲和德勤给我们回答解释？

我们的问题是，目前"自由贸易港"的相关政策中有很多细节没有明确，从我们的角度看，目前"自由贸易港"最值得期待的政策创新是什么？最难突破的政策创新是什么？最重要的政策创新是什么？

刘明华：在"自由贸易港"问题上。这个"自由贸易港"和现在我们的自贸区、现有的贸易便利度，到底有什么样的区别？升级版和突破在哪里？这非常重要，的确需要我们政府部门有更深刻的思考。

从现在看，我们认为结算以及货币是很大的一个挑战。如果"自由贸易港"只是仅限于在这样一个很小的范围里，那它的意义、作用和影响力，会有多大？把它的意义和影响力做得很大，对我们整个货币自由结算、金融体系，会造成什么影响？怎么突破？我们认为这些都有待深刻思考，不是上海市层面能决定的。从上海市的角度，从政策制定角度，我们需要跟中央提什么诉求？中央有什么先行先试的政策？这是很重要的。

李剑腾： 这个问题跟交通委、跟检验检疫局相关。两家单位有没有相关经验可以做一个回应？

张林： "自由贸易港"的方案正在完善和报批过程中，这不仅是企业的期待，也是上海的期待。目前大家共同期待的是"自由贸易港"较原来自由贸易区有真正的升级。这次汪洋副总理把我们上海的期待都已经说出来了，即境内关外资金自由、货物自由、人员自由。资金自由这个问题我们非常期待，单单只是自由贸易港里货物的自由，恐怕是不够的，因此希望资金自由这一块有所突破，特别是人民币离岸业务。

赵文斌： 原来我们做自由贸易试验区的时候就提出了"境内关外"。做自由贸易港方案还是回到"境内关外"四个字。当时做自贸试验区为什么没有真正实现"境内关外"这个定位？有很多因素。但自由贸易港一定要回到这个定位。所以讨论这个方案的时候，大家用得最多、最流行的四个字，就是"不忘初心"，还是要回到当时的设想中去。

另外自由贸易港标杆上，大家经常说"对照国际最高标准、最好水平"。我认为这句话体现在四个方面：

一是环境好。主要是加大公开性、透明度，其中最核心的是政策。在自贸试验区四年的发展中，负面清单在逐年减少。相信到了自由贸易港建设中，负面清单会更少。

二是效率更高。最重要的体现在"一线放开"。"一线放开"在上海自贸试验区相对做得还是不太够。相信今后的自由贸易港会在"一线放开"方面做得更好，包括现在提出的不报关、不完税、转口贸易不限制等政策。

三是安全问题。主要是二线的高效管理，同时进行大量风险管理、诚信管理，真正实现分门类管理。

四是在整个自由贸易港区的政策方面。这次出台的是初步方案，更期待今后方案会给上海多大的自主改革权，这对自由贸易港下一步的推动有积极意义。

乔依德：刚才大家讲到，希望自由贸易港中有金融的功能属性。我们回顾一下，上海自贸区虽然取得了很大进展，但仍有很多地方不尽如人意，主要体现在开放程度上，特别是金融这一块。因为金融不属于地方政府权力范围，主要集中在中央。

所以我的想法是，做自由港方案时要非常明确地提出在上海建立离岸金融中心。过去的讨论中就有很多争议，有人不太赞成在上海建立离岸金融中心。当时的理由是，资本账户会很快全面开放。这种情况下，上海再搞离岸金融中心，好像跟香港有冲突，也没有什么必要。但前几年就说资本账户到2015年"基本开放"，现在看来不会，我估计就算今后一两年、两三年也不会全部开放。如果这个判断成立，建议做自由港就要提出建立离岸人民币中心。这个定了以后，权力有了，资金池也解决了。否则这个事情解决不了。

李剑腾：这个问题归结起来，最难最值得期待，最要创新的，可能是同一个问题，就是如何基本围绕金融做一些突破。

丁嵩冰：我自问自答补充一点。这个问题我们之前也讨论过，对我们来说最值得期待的政策突破，可能是境内关外"一线放开，二线管住"，安全高效放开，这是最有可能率先突破的。

我认为金融创新方面最难突破。比如外汇自由汇兑，资金自由流出。因为我们现在的金融体量大而不强，很容易受到冲击。从2016年底开始加强外汇管制力度来看，也有这方面的考量。所以最难突破的，应该是金融方面的创新政策突破。

最重要的是税收政策。我们一直在争取这个方面的政策，但一直没有得到明确的回复或政策落地。我们对比了"一带一路"沿线国家，甚至全世界很多地方的自贸区政策后了解到，目前看起来没有哪个国家没有优惠政策。这不只是说关税的免征、缓交，甚至包括企业所得税，以及国家通行政策的优惠。比国内水平基本低5%—10%，甚至全部免征都有。最重要的政策之一还是税收政策。

总结一下。最值得期待的，境内关外，一线放开，二线管住。最重要的就是所得税政策。最难突破的，应该是金融政策。

李剑腾：国企已经提了非常好的问题。外企是不是也开个头？

王伟国：我是西门子中国有限公司的，作为外企，想问问政府对外企在"一带一路"建设中，尤其是发挥"桥头堡"作用，有没有什么期待？因为目前外企都是参与到国企"走出去"。除了这个角色外，政府对我们有什么其他的期待吗？

桑琦：你的问题，我理解下来，是问外企如何帮助上海本土企业到第三国或到"一带一路"沿线国家，共同合作，开拓市场。在沪外企大部分都是跨国公司的在沪子公司，所以刚开始来上海的时候，目标是国内市场。经过这么多年的发展后，外企在国内各个地方已经投资了很多项目，确实目前有一部分外企尝试到第三国去投资发展。

2017 年 1—10 月，在沪外资企业在第三国非金融类的直接投资项目金额达到 1.9 亿美元。这是非常好的一个苗头。在沪外资企业 2017 年 1—10 月新签的境外工程承包合同额达到 4.5 亿元人民币。这也是非常好的苗头。我们一方面希望在沪外资企业能走出去到第三国，特别是到"一带一路"沿线国家投资、承建工程项目。这是我们政府非常鼓励的。

针对外资企业的"走出去"，我们采取的是和国企、民企一视同仁的政策。首先体现在审批便利化方面，包括通关、检验检疫、外汇、政府部门的项目审批便利化措施。但外企想要超国民待遇，在现在的情况下不现实。第二方面，我们非常鼓励和支持在沪外资企业联合上海本土的国企、民企到第三国开展合作。特别是能共同到第三国或"一带一路"沿线国家去投资并购项目，组成项目联合体，共同在第三国或"一带一路"沿线国家去投标建设工程承包项目。这对所有企业是一视同仁的。第三方面，政府部门很重视在沪外资企业，特别是外资投资咨询公司、律师事务所、会计师事务所等专业服务企业、机构，帮助上海本土的国企、民企到第三国、"一带一路"国家投资项目、开展工程承包。因为你们在全球的布局已经历史悠久，有非常好的人脉和专业知识方面的积累，可以给我们本土企业提供非常好的专业服务和帮助。除了本土的国企、民企组成的"走出去"的信息互动联盟，我们还专门建立了上海企业"走出去"专业服务企业的联盟，每时每刻都可以通过新媒体、微信群交流各方面的投资、项目、政策的信息。几年坚持下来，成效还是蛮好的。

李剑腾：刚才领导非常强调的一点就是外企和内企是一视同仁。这是一个非常关键的问题。这对上海来讲，对在中国的外资企业，都是非常重要的一个问题。首先对上海，外企占上海经济的30%，建设"一带一路"的"桥头堡"，不可能不把外企包含在里面。另外，对很多外企来讲，今天中国业务可能已经占全球业务非常大的一个比重。下一步的增长，跟随着"一带一路"建设可能是非常重要的机会。当然，现在还处于早期，大家还在不断摸索。

除了刚才三位领导给的答案，我们各个智库有没有相关的理解？

纪纲： 这个问题非常好。外资企业在"一带一路"建设中扮演着重要角色，这是非常关键的。参与"一带一路"建设，有两个现象。首先看沿线65个国家，各个国家的情况都不一样。按国家分类梳理，经济走廊中，包括中亚、中巴、中蒙等，这些走廊活跃度不一样，中国企业在这些片区的经验也不一样。又如东南亚和中东，不管"一带一路"存不存在，这些市场的市场机制相对都比较完善了。外资企业的品牌非常好，而中国企业的品牌一般，外资企业应该跟中国企业合作，充分发挥外资企业的品牌能力、背书能力，以及对当地法规的管理能力。对"一带一路"建设最兴奋的实际是一些小国家，因为它急于发展，而大的国家对"一带一路"建设则有自己的政治考量。在这些区域，大量国企出海，外企扮演的是辅助、支持角色。因为这些片区很复杂，需要一个国家背书才能推动。这个时候外企应该是在项目管理方面提供大的支持。在不同项目中，国企、外企的角色应该是不一样的。

我是20世纪90年代中期跟着中国最大的能源企业"走出去"的，买油田、搞石油管道，亲身经历过中国企业在海外的巨大挑战。虽然今天我们知道怎么运营了，但在这些过程中我们国企依旧有很大困难。所以要如何发挥各自的优势？应在内部打造一个产业联盟，而且是政府搭台、各方资源相互自动配置的。

李剑腾： 大家对内外资的叫法将来可能会变，"一带一路"既然是国家倡议，肯定会是内外资企业将来重点关注的。

纪纲： 每个项目都是"一带一路"的关键载体。我们有的项目周期很长，未来如果项目出问题，对"一带一路"整体发展会有很大的伤害。智库的经验很重要。未来我们需要建立一个实操型的案例库，包括上港集团这些企业，把它们在项目操盘中所有的波折、挑战、"血泪史"会拿出来分享。以及OPPO、小米，这些民企做得非常好，它们是怎么进去的？包括吉利的投资，包括中东一些有巨大损失的项目，包括斯里兰卡的港口由于政府更迭给项目带来巨大的损失等，把这些项目拿出来分析，有很多指导性的意义。我们要建立这样的案例库，让每个经历过详细过程的人讲如何操盘。这是有实际意义的，不管它是什么类型的企业，抑或是投资成功与否。

刘明华：目前外企在"一带一路"的建设中非常有热情，而且也看到了很多的机遇。从政府角度来说，目前也不区分所谓的内资或外资。刚才商务委的领导也谈到了项目 PPP 合作的机制。前面我们也提倡由市场主导的政企合作，包括 NGO、PPP 这些模式。

打通信息壁垒是第一步。相信对很多外企、民企、国企来说，到底"一带一路"沿线国家现在有哪些项目机会或有什么需求，可能第一时间并不是非常清楚，那还怎么应对，怎么配最好的资源，做最佳的事情？我们建议可以加大政企合作平台，而且有一个对接的平台，类似 PMO 一样，建立相应的规则、信息发布以及应对。包括案例库，到底有什么经验教训，这些国家相应的法律法规、税务，是怎样的情况。目前我们有这样的"走出去"的联盟，但这个联盟现在是相对比较松散的结构。怎样做成一个机制化、真正的 PMO？有规则、有信息、有案例库，可以共同推进。这是我们提出的一个问题。

王伟国：今天我们讨论的是上海怎么在服务国家"一带一路"建设之中充当"桥头堡"，也就是对上海本身或政策层面的要求。所有东西都在摸索、创新，肯定有很多新的东西，所以拿出这个问题跟大家探讨，让上海在这当中成为"桥头堡"。

我们也碰到了其他的问题，比如各地建了不少创新中心，外资、内资也做了不少了。但怎么把创新中心信息平台做起来？我们做了开放式的平台，愿意跟各个企业、院校进行合作。信息怎么更透明？政府是不是有政策，把这个平台的消息公布出来让大家共同参与，使外企和当地企业能更好地结合起来，把资源用到最好？以后，我们也希望逐渐把"外企"这个名字拿掉。

李剑腾：不愧是领先的外企，已经在"一带一路"上已经做了一些思考和布局。这几年我们民营企业的崛起非常快，今天有两位民企代表在，也想听听你们遇到的困惑或问题。

华黎：民营企业还是"老三"。什么时候可以把"民营企业"去掉，跟"外资企业"一样？今天很荣幸能参加这么一个论坛，而且是智库高峰论坛。不管智库，还是高峰论坛，都要解决实际问题。有些问题在这个层面上是解决不掉的，但我们得提。

奥威科技是来自自贸试验区的高新技术企业。创业到现在 20 年，手里也有一些政府、上海市科委培育下早年布局的拿得出手的东西，现在在创建具有国际影响力的科技创新中心。我们在白俄罗斯明斯克建立了自己的生产和研发中心，首批入园日期是 2015 年 5 月 12 日，两国元首共同见证了 7 家企业入驻，我们是上海科技企业的代表。但是在实际操作过程中，我们遇到了很多问题，希望通过这个会议得到有关部门的帮助。

德勤公司讲得非常好，现在我们"走出去"的民营企业，肯定都是准备好了的，出去的不仅仅是产品，还是这么多年来的积累。"一带一路"建设的过程里有以下几点：

一是人民币结算问题。在实际操作过程中，出口创汇怎么创人民币？我们通过金融办把这个问题解决了。其中企业、高层都比较积极，但中间环节的配套政策还存在一定的问题。

二是中白工业园是我们国家在"一带一路"里最大的一个项目。已经扩展到 115 平方公里，有一个城市的大小，但在发展进程中我们也存在很多疑惑，比如，银行结算的时候，白俄罗斯竟然在"敏感国家"里；还有网点的问题，上海的银行，比如浦发银行、上海银行、交通银行，这些银行未来在海外的布局是怎样；中方员工的签证问题，中国香港的护照可以免签 158 个国家，而中国内地的护照原来可以免签 65 个，现在只有 62 个。这都是非常现实的问题。这些问题不解决，如何"走出去"？如何建立"桥头堡"？如何建设"一带一路"？

三是上海民营企业有实力参与到"一带一路"的建设中去，但遇到很多问题。比如，上海和有些国家之间没有直航的航班。现在我们发货都要先通过海运运送到其他地方，建交委能否提供改善的方法？中欧班列班次少、费用高，上海铁路要怎么融入，从而解决这个问题？既然是"桥头堡"，那么需要建立什么样的便利条件？还有自贸试验区和中外工业园如何对接？现在又有上海企业去了，包括国有企业上海建工，希望能解决这些具体问题。至于更高层次的税收等领域问题，这些我们有建议权，但解决不了。

最后，这些高新技术企业"走出去"以后，关于知识产权的保护和分享，上海会有哪些相关政策出台？包括针对知识产权的转移的政策。

李剑腾：民营企业非常实际，一下子提了很多问题。我们政府能不能回答？

张宇：不管是民营还是国有企业、外资企业，在"走出去"的过程中都会碰到包括资金、签证、人才交流等问题。但另一方面看，正是因为"走出去"、发展了，所以才推动了上海全方位的改革。原来没有出去、没有"一带一路"，现在意识到这些问题的重要性，然后再一步步推动政府和机制改革。

刚才提到的签证问题，其实政府在一步步做。这个权限就像金融权限一样是属于中央的，我们一直在关注这方面的情况，也在不断推动这方面的政策，包括免签、企业通关等，一直在跟相关国家进行沟通。关键的时间节点往往在于领导人出访，因为领导人访问的时候会带动和抓紧解决一批项目。对企业来说，应抓住关键时间节点，比如刚刚说的两地往返问题，你们掌握了这些信息后反馈给政府，政府为了推动两国关系，会把这些问题慢慢解决。很难说一下子解决这个问题，但政府确确实实在做这些方面的事情。

权衡：很具体的问题需要我们政府部门解决，宏观上我有几个体会。

第一，不管是国企、民企，还是外企，都讲到"走出去"的风险问题。我们去年做了一个"一带一路"的研究报告。对"一带一路"我们应该有一个判断，"走出去"不是普遍、全面的撒网，而要对沿线国家进行选择。有个概念，叫支点国家、支点城市，到产业园区，再到项目的落地。按照这样的逻辑，大致针对十几个国家能有把握地"走出去"。否则很多企业"走出去"会遇到很多问题，会有国内没有预料到的不确定问题。因此，首先要有比较、有评估、有选择，不是一下子就铺开地"走出去"。

第二，我们"走出去"到沿线国家，它们的税收怎么样？优惠不优惠？营商环境怎么样？我们研究发现，无论国际还是国内，对企业来说，从大的方面讲，"走出去"本身就是经济全球化的重要组成部分，背后都是市场化机制，以及追求利润最大化。这种情况下，不管国企、民企，还是外企，"走出去"要有竞争力，主要的并不是有多好的营商环境或便利性。我国2017年1—9月份的外贸增长，难道是营商环境有明显的有改善才带来这么大的贸易增长吗？这值得思考。最重要的是目前的国际环境，我们出去要盈利最终还是取决于企业自身的竞争力。在国际竞争中大家都是公平竞争的，倒不是说有什么优惠或其他。在国内，包括上海早期吸引外资，主要是靠税收优惠和优惠政策。而自贸试验区试图改变这个趋势，重点是创造公平竞争的营商环境。下一步，我们到别的国家，进行第三次或第四次国际产业转移，公平竞争的环境下，能不能盈利就看我们的创新和竞争能力。

第三，我们也对上海企业"走出去"做过一些研究和评估，发现上海的企业，特别是国企、外企，更有动力走出去。所谓有动力，就是在全球跨国公司的作用下追求利润。另一方面，在国内，特别是上海，面临成本上升的压力，所以在投资布局上有一定的考虑。

这对我们来说，最重要的是要像日本企业当年"走出去"一样，抱团"走出去"，而不是单个企业"走出去"。比如，日本株式会社这样的联盟。当然不是说政府作用不重要。沿线国家的规则、谈判，双边、多边关系要先走一步，这些谈好之后可以为企业"走出去"创造较好的平台和环境，减少企业的不稳定性，增加它们的可预期性和透明度。同时还需要政府将沿线国家自贸区的谈判和合作，以及投资贸易、金融规则确定下来，为企业"走出去"创造更好的条件。

李剑腾：企业"走出去"面临着种种困难，这也是预期中的，不断有问题出来，再不断去解决。这个过程中肯定有一部分是企业自己能解决的，有一部分是需要政府力量和政策慢慢解决的。

夏梅兴：我是上海电力股份公司的，有个案例可以分享一下。前两年我们投了马耳他的一个电力公司，这个项目被联合国开发计划署和商务部、国资委评为中国企业"走出去"的可持续发展案例，也是中央国资委企业"走出去"的成功案例。项目中我们跟一些咨询机构合作，把电价下降了25%。马耳他的总理认为我们上海电力和马耳他能源公司的合作项目是"中马经贸合作的典范"，评价比较高。

上海电力是百年老国企，南市、杨树浦、闵行的电力公司都是我们的下属企业。我们贯彻落实"一带一路"倡议，将其与百年国有老企业的转型结合起来，发展战略是将其与上海科创中心建设结合起来，制定创新型的国际化发展战略。去年，我们的海外利润已经占到了整个公司利润的20%，日本有我们的新能源项目，同时我们以马耳他作为据点，向南欧进行投资扩展。最近有个黑山新能源项目即将开工，在土耳其等地我们也有比较大的项目。

从这几年的实践情况来看，我们有一些难点：

第一，信息服务。"一带一路"沿线很多国家政治、经济、文化情况不一样，法律体系也不一样，而且多变，甚至有的地方政局也经常变。作为单个企业，在所有地方精耕细作，把所有情况都完全掌握透是很难的。所以我们建议，要发挥整体的作用，就是要共享、互动。外经贸委组织了一个联盟，这很好。我个人建议，政府是不是可以组建类似于日本贸易振兴机构的组织？在"一带一路"的重要节点，可以设一些分支专职机构，对该地进行长期、深入地跟踪，为企业提供全面的信息和服务，包括贸易、投资、人员来往。这是我个人的一个不成熟的想法。

第二，协调服务。从能源企业的角度讲，现在中国能源企业"走出去"，已经出现了恶性竞争的状况。在世界上很多地方，从工程到投资再到并购，国内企业自相残杀，这是非常不好的状况。而且因为恶性竞争，使中国有些企业在外面把中国的牌子做砸了。因为价格很低，项目品质不能保证，最终导致中国品牌信誉下降。不针对上海，但从整个国家来说，推进"走出去"的过程中，这个问题需要关注。应在市场机制下发挥行业协会的作用，制定一些规则。

第三，要进一步加强金融服务。金融是我们上海作为服务国家"一带一路"建设"桥头堡"的优势。但从全球资本的角度来说这个优势是不强的，如果上海不能在这方面表现出竞争力，那我国在"一带一路"建设上发挥的作用，就会被人看低。上海在金融、保险对"一带一路"建设的支撑作用方面有很大的提升空间。

李剑腾：上海电力分享了"走出去"的成功经验，也提出了很好的建议和问题。政府方面是不是作出一些回应？主要是两个方面。一个是在信息服务以及贸易促进方面能做什么事情？二是在提升金融服务的竞争力方面，可以考虑采取什么举措？

桑琦：刚才讲到马耳他的成功案例，非常巧，我专门到这个项目考察过，而且跟项目外方原来的业主总经理以及马耳他相关政府部门进行了座谈，确实像夏总所说这个项目非常成功。

所以引发了我一个问题，现在很多外资投资咨询机构在上海企业"走出去"的项目中，目前确实提供了很好的专业服务，但这些专业服务，可能比较集中在法律、会计、税务和项目前期尽职调查方面，这方面占的比重比较高。建议外资或内资投资咨询公司也可以把中国本土"走出去"项目中的成功案例，好好分析、总结一下，把里面的经验、教训梳理、提炼出来，然后通过培训宣传给我们未来将"走出去"的企业，为他们指明正确的道路。

夏总刚才提到的信息、协调服务，确实都是比较难的问题。对"走出去"企业提供信息服务，多年来政府部门，包括商务委和其他的机构一直在这方面做努力。比如，市政府专门成立了上海市对外投资促进中心，是双向投资。刚成立的时候，以招商引资为主，但最近几年随着"走出去"项目增多，在促进对外投资方面的工作比重力度也得到很大的加强，也在为企业提供很多信息服务。您提到在海外设办事处，上海市对外投资促进中心在海外设立了五个办事处，而且已经设立多年了，在不断发挥它的作用。但这里面有个矛盾，因为海外办事处都是地方财政资助，每年资助金额很大，要常派人员，所以在摸索怎么和已经"走出去"的上海成熟企业合作。还有上海"走出去"项目在当地已经很成熟时，能不能依托当地国家、企业的力量，将其作为上海对外投资促进中心的海外办事处？比如投资促进中心马耳他办事处。当然，这个要双方好好谈。这方面我们已经做了一定的尝试。

现在信息服务机构比较多但分散，把它集中到一个机构很难，集中起来后要保证质量和需求也很难。希望我们和"走出去"的企业、内外资投资咨询公司都好好研究，怎么更好地解决分散的问题。每年，各个国家的各种投资风险报告、国别政策报告都是财政拨款在出，网上也有公告，但效果到底如何？这确实是个问题。

刚才提到协调服务。中国企业"走出去"与外面投标项目恶性竞争，也是老大难问题。商务部、驻外大使馆商务处、承包工程商会、机电商会都有协调机制，多年来，这个协调机制确实发挥了一定的作用，但要尽善尽美很多地方还有待完善。被刷下来的投标企业很委屈、不买账，觉得协调机制不公平。这方面要好好研究，怎么建立一个有效协调境外项目恶性竞争的机制，要更加体现公正公平、透明的原则。

李剑腾：关于金融服务，金融办的同事有没有补充？

谢善鸿：我做点补充，首先，"一带一路"建设是金融服务实体经济的一个应有的任务，同时我们把"一带一路"建设看作上海建设国际金融中心和推进人民币"走出去"的一个重大机遇。这个前提下，上海有很多事情可以做。比如熊猫债的发行，资本市场和"一带一路"的相关资本市场的合作等。下一步，我们主要可能还是围绕着这些方面：

第一，市场方面，我们要发挥上海作为金融中心的优势，把上海打造成服务"一带一路"的投融资中心。大家也知道，"一带一路"有大量的金融需求，这样的金融需求不能单靠政策性的输血，更应该通过市场的力量来吸引国资、民资、外资等多渠道、多元化、多方式的资金。这个过程中，上海资本市场可以发挥很大的作用。同时"一带一路"的发展会产生许多红利，我们中国的投资者也能从"一带一路"的增长中获得收益，比如，熊猫债的发行要利用上海的资本市场，继续跟"一带一路"的资本市场开展合作。

第二，中国的金融机构怎样随着"一带一路"的推进继续"走出去"？奥威科技提到中资银行的海外布点问题，也是说"一带一路"沿线的有些国家有经济、金融欠发达的特点。我们认为，中国的金融机构在"一带一路"有发挥更大作用的空间，因为目前他们所处的阶段，可能正是我们前段时间所处的阶段。我们的发展经验可以根据当地的特点在"一带一路"的国家或地区进行一些移植。但我们也要看到一个现状，我们中资银行长期以来更多的是服务于国内，特别是上海本地银行，比如浦发银行，国际化程度和工商银行、建设银行、交通银行、中国银行这些国有大行来比，还是相对慢了一些。一些商业银行在香港、新加坡都开了，最近伦敦分行也要开业了，但在考虑"一带一路"国家当地的经济环境等各方面的环境，短期内没有列入考虑。同时我们银行在境外设立分行，要受监管部门的许可，有些计划性的安排。随着战略的推进，我们引导和鼓励中资银行把国际化的视野更多地放到"一带一路"国家或地区上。传统的路径是往经济、金融发达的地方布局，但"一带一路"建设中蕴含着巨大的发展机遇。建议大家关注前不久上海市政府印发的《"一带一路"行动方案》。这当中，金融是一个很重要的内容。《行动方案》有十个主要的方面，包括前面专家提到的好的建议、观点，我注意到《行动方案》中已经或多或少予以了吸收。《行动方案》的金融部分，我们研究已经持续一年多了。今天大家提的很多建议，跟我们也有相通的地方。在下一步的工作中，我们会继续把大家的观点结合起来，不断深化。

在金融服务相对不足的地方，金融办非常愿意发挥协调、推动作用。我相信，以我们中国的银行体量，一定能通过很多有效的办法解决这些问题。

再者，无论是"一带一路"、自由贸易港，还是金融中心建设，这都是十九大报告中提出的"构建开放经济新格局"的一部分，我们站在这个背景下考虑这些问题，相信会突破金融最难突破的局面。因为我感觉自由贸易港，不仅仅是自贸试验区的 3.0、4.0 版本，更应该是一个新的篇章，这是值得期待的。

乔依德：怎么鼓励上海金融机构"走出去"？现实情况是，浦发银行、上海银行的规模不大，要一下子"走出去"需要时间。这里面有两个问题，第一，公司治理或有些规定对走出去有阻碍。举个例子，浦发银行到哈萨克斯坦开会，是我帮他们联系的。据说国有企业要申请三个月出国，不好弄。第二，思想要开放、大胆一点。举个例子，中国银行、建设银行做得很好，中国银行本来总部在上海，后来迁到北京去了，为什么不能迁回来？现在有雄安中心，而非首都要利用这个机会，即使总部不能来，人民币业务总部至少要弄过来。一个金融中心没有大的商业银行怎么成为金融中心？利用上海自由贸易港这个契机，是有可能成功的，因为这是十九大报告中提的，要抓住这个机会。

谢善鸿： 国外金融机构到上海，我们觉得有这种可能性，我们可以朝这个方向努力。希望无论是专家还是学者，帮助我们一道呼吁、努力。

陈礼明： 目前，我们锦江国际集团是全球第五大酒店集团，主业是酒店、旅游和客运物流。在全球 67 个国家或地区布局的 8 800 家酒店中，在"一带一路"沿线有 200 家，未来我们可能还会布局更多酒店，达到四五百家。在全球范围，我们会达到 10 000 家酒店，100 万间客房。未来一到两年，我们可能在全球酒店产业里排位第三。我们认为，集团的全球布局、跨国经营，包括在"一带一路"的布局，主要还是从集团战略出发，这个战略是依据中国发展全球化趋势。

企业如果要做这件事情，首先自己要研究透，及时跟进，争取方方面面的支持。这两年，我们做了国际并购，利用国际并购的平台融合、融通起来，共同做"一带一路"的布局，外资、国资、民资哪个有优势就用哪个。现在锦江国际集团已经通过上市公司融合了民资、外资，利用所有机制的优势发挥作用。我们有 16 字方针，"经营不变，后台整合，优势互补，共同发展"。同样，处理对外关系时，一定要尊重当地法律、了解当地的风俗以及充分利用当地的优势（比如人才优势）。我们收购法国的平台，基本全部留用高管，我们派主要人员进去但是不替代，继续发挥他们的作用，利用法国在全球、中东"一带一路"的影响力，我们布局"一带一路"就会更顺畅。比如，通过上市公司平台收购了印度最大的酒店集团——Sarovar 集团。这样把南亚打开再到印度尼西亚、越南、东南亚。国内我们继续进行创新，建立了巴黎创新中心、上海创新中心，把原来公司好的品牌引进中国进行提升。旅游产业方面，中国有巨大的发展潜力，大量的国人需要在海外享用具有中国特色的服务，怎样优势结合布局？中国在"一带一路"的发展，就是发挥上海企业在"一带一路"建设中的桥头堡"突击队"作用，有优势、有条件的，先出去，以市场行为、企业行为运作。

有个建议，讨论"一带一路"建设中的"桥头堡"作用，上海责无旁贷。但这个过程中，一定不要遗漏了人文的桥头堡。商流、物流、资金流，更重要的是背后的人。要让人相信你、热爱你，可亲可敬，有很大一点就是文化的吸附能力。上海要有一个让人生活得更好的感染力，而且要有包容性。锦江国际集团也赞助了上海交响乐团、上海芭蕾舞团，上海的文化活动和我们锦江有关，但更和上海发展有关。让全世界的人愿意到上海，愿意相信你，你到那里去，人家愿意接受和欢迎你。这个文化实力，可能比"桥头堡"上的硬件更重要。硬件配置好了，我们更要配置软件。

傅国庆： 我谈几点有关科技创新方面的问题。

首先，"一带一路"沿线国家"走出去"，主体应该是企业。刚才听了大家的发言，有出去比较顺利的，也有不顺利的。首先企业要非常清楚知道自己有什么优势，不然"走出去"肯定是不成功的。"走出去"的过程中，一个是"走出去"，另一个是"引进来"。这些沿线国家不是什么都比我们落后、比我们不行，它们有些资源、技术、人才的优势，以及不错的理念，我们要向它们借鉴学习。这次有幸到中白工业园区看，它们开发的产品非常好，我们做增材制造，它们是做减材制造，跟我们不一样。

其次，从政府角度来说，政府怎么搭平台、提供服务？让这些企业能走得出去，走得放心、有收获？这是我们政府的职责。从信息角度来看，单靠一个企业，不可能了解那么多国家的情况，政府确实应该提供信息服务。政府确实已经在做了，我们都用网站、信息推送，但没人看。好多小微企业都不看这些信息，所以也没办法。但不管怎么说，政府的信息平台还是要搭。

再次，金融服务。企业"走出去"碰到很多问题。首先大企业的资金没有问题，但要是没有国家背景支持的项目，资金转出去谈何容易？我们讲"一带一路"五个"通"：金融要融通，没有这个融通后面是寸步难行。还有人才的流动也非常重要。哈萨克斯坦这次我也去了，他们的签证对我们是卡得很严的，他们的签证率只有我们的1/10。我们去3万人，他们跑到中国30万人，甚至300万人。所以，政策沟通非常重要。我希望不要造成我们"一头热、一头冷"的局面。我们请的这些专家，讲了很多，讨论得热热闹闹，但这些专家回去，有没有影响国家的决策层？今后"一带一路"的论坛，还要请一些他们的高官、前高官，把会场上各个专家的信息呼吁带回去，通过他们影响当局。五"通"里少一个"通"都不行，关键还是人员的流通。还有，我们能不能也在"一带一路"沿线国家搞一个青年创业家流通的绿色通道？

上海市科委这几年跟相关国家签署了不少合作协议，包括以色列、匈牙利、立陶宛、克罗地亚、白俄罗斯、芬兰、柬埔寨、越南等，这些合作协议主要目的是推动企业的交流合作，我觉得这个基础非常重要，没有一定的基础，说"走出去"就"走出去"是不行的。

最后我讲一个案例。科技部为发展中国家进行技术培训，交给了我们上海技术交易所，培训班基本都是东南亚东盟国家，教会他们做技术转移、技术贸易，等等。其中越南非常虚心，每次我们改革开放培训班都学，中国怎么做，他们回去就怎么弄。看我们技术转移非常好，参加培训以后就跟我们提出，能不能办专门的培训？我们就给他们专门培训，然后列入中越政府间合作项目里。之后他们还专门在胡志明市造了一幢技术转移大楼，包括整套人员培训的内容，都教他们做。这是基于前面的基础。我们不要太急，要把基础先打好。现在基础没有打好，像奥威科技，白俄罗斯不是说去就去，前面做了好几年的准备工作，基础已经打得很好了。

杨晓东：我们上汽的愿景是成为全球著名汽车公司，但现在还处于国际经营起步阶段。大家讲"走出去"，"走出去"不是很难，关键是走进去、走下去这后面两步。今天谈到项目很多都是 B2B 的，而汽车是 B2C 的，直接面向广大用户，没有办法要求当地政府、所有用户买我们的车。所以两个工作，一个，树品牌；第二，持续投入。

首先我们企业自身要强筋骨、练内功，但离不开政府搭台，包括人文。人文没有做好，要人家接受中国产品还是有难度的。关于政府搭台我提几个建议：

第一，"一带一路"建设主要集中在基建、能源、高铁领域，汽车产业好像没有。汽车产业的特点首先是 B2C，第二是带动当地的税收，还有就业。所以汽车产业应该作为"走出去"或"一带一路"的一个战略性产业。这对双方都是有利的。如果汽车能走出去、走进去、走下去，我相信其他都能做到。因为汽车产业链不光是平行的，还有垂直的，带动效应比较大。

第二，消费金融，刚才讲了很多投融资方面的内容，兵马未动粮草先行。海外消费一般 80% 都是消费融资，已经"走出去"的这些银行，它们对投资都比较有兴趣，但一讲消费，人都找不到了。所以消费金融怎么从政策角度上，支持走出去，也支持我们企业、财务公司走出去？现在有很多政策性限制。

第三，外汇管理，建议不要搞"一刀切"。针对确实想做成全球性的公司，还是要分层、个性化地管理。

第四，国有企业管理。比如能源管理、进出口领域，明天海外市场有个紧急任务，但是没有办法派人出去。因为一定要公派护照才能出去，都不敢奢望私人护照能出去。比如海外投资，一定要看项目的整体和长期性，不可能每个项目都成功。怎么激励国有企业"走出去"时放下思想包袱？我们和民企、外企比起来，竞争力还差。怎么进一步为国有企业松绑？要用市场机制推动。

最后就是自贸试验区的优势，要有进步。如果上海做不成资金池，还是要到香港或其他的地方解决贸易集散、资金融资和压汇、外汇风险管理等问题。

桂渐：整体来说，外资企业在中国这个市场还处于一个比较困惑的地位。基仕伯 1986 年就进中国，是中国第一家外商独资企业。我们应该是外资企业参与中国改革开放的先行者之一。我提几个意见：

第一，中国"一带一路"的项目，在外资企业的宣传不太够。虽然外资企业有针对"一带一路"的公司战略，但可能存在一些疑惑，比如，我们到底在其中可以起到什么作用？有什么参与机会？通过什么方式进行合作？面对什么样的市场和机会，外资企业具有一定的优势？

第二，从上海市政府和上海各个部委的宣传角度讲，还没有讲清楚上海在"一带一路"建设中到底要发挥什么样的"桥头堡"作用，能提供什么样的扶持和作用。上海市政府和上海美国商会、欧盟商会、德国商会、英国商会，是不是能建立定期的沟通机制？定期做一些宣传、组织一些论坛，来讨论在华外资企业怎么更好地加入"一带一路"建设，发挥什么作用。从这个角度看，上海有优势，因为上海有 1 200 多家外商投资企业的地区总部，全国除了北京以外，很难达到这个水平。

第三，宣传是第一位，推动是第二位，扶持是第三位。怎么推动外资企业参与到这个过程中，怎么和国有企业、民营企业一起"走出去"？外资企业的优势在于，在"一带一路"沿线国家，它们投资的脚步走得比较快和早，可能已经经历过文化上的差异、政策的影响，可以把它们的优势、经验，更好地分享给国有、民营企业，共同做一些平台的建设。最终这个平台需要通过政府来建立，各个成分进行参与，最后予以实现。

杨洁：上汽领导也提出，现在"走出去"最大的问题是后期的整合，我们去年跟市国资委围绕这个问题做过课题研究，的确有血泪史，就是前、中期都很好，后期需要注意。商务委领导提出，是不是智库里的咨询公司可以做定期培训，甚至案例库，涵盖投资前、投资中、投资后。但这个要请政府去牵头。因为信息渠道太多，对企业来讲不知道要看哪个好，所以政府需要整合信息来源，然后结合我们国际智库中所有的企业、中介机构、研究机构的经验。

我们现在在走全世界都没有走过的一条道路，所有的模式我们都可以创新。刚才商务委的领导提出，可以跟国企合作成立海外办事处。我觉得跟外企、民企、咨询机构都可以建立这样的办事处。在政府领导的平台下，怎么更好、更便捷、更经济有效地建立这样一个平台？

刚才讲到信息平台的问题，急需马上解决。因为这对我们发挥好"桥头堡"有至关重要的作用。我本人也在商务委对外投资的群里，这个群的确发挥了很大的作用，里面人数非常多。但针对中小型企业，很多企业还没有在群里。是不是政府可以推出一个上海政府建设相关的微信公众号？所有优惠政策都可以在这个公众号发布。

基于我本人和我们公司参与的100多个"一带一路"项目经验来看，企业的最大诉求还是税收优惠政策。据我了解，现在整个中国针对"一带一路"还并没有专门的税收优惠政策。希望政府后续会有所考量。

王德第：2015年国务院领导明确提出农业"走出去"应由农业部牵头。去年国务院办公厅专门下发了《关于促进农业对外合作的若干意见》。在这里有几个信息跟大家说一下。

我看到许多咨询公司都没有提到农业"走出去"，但事实上农业"走出去"中，上海走得非常好。2016年，统计数据显示，上海农业走出去投资达26.6亿美元，同比增长了62.6%，在整个中国农业走出去中，占到了2/3的比例。所以我们上海农业"走出去"，应该说发挥了"桥头堡"的作用。而且这个"走出去"跟在座的都有关，你们每天吃的东西，不管是新上海人还是老上海人，都吃到了我们好多农业"走出去"回来的东西。所以建议咨询公司好好研究农业"走出去"，怎么走法？十九大提出，我国社会主要矛盾已经转化为人民日益增长的对美好生活的需求和不平衡不充分的发展之间的矛盾。我们现在不是要吃"饱"，而是要吃"好"。

第一，在农业"走出去"方面遇到问题，我们农委义不容辞会协调海关、检疫、商务委相关部门，如果我们解决不了，我们会向农业部反映。27个在"一带一路"中"走出去"的企业都非常成功，不仅跟政府，而且跟当地的农民、老百姓都建立了非常好的关系。举个例子，我们青浦区当时养鸭养鸡，不知道养在哪里，别人建议在柬埔寨养，然后投资300万美元为当地提供了非常好的生态鸡和生态鸭。所以还是要多做接地气的事情。

第二，锦江在外面开了这么多酒店，总要吃的东西吧？我们在外面种粮、种菜、养猪、养牛的都很多，当地非常欢迎把我们的技术、当地技术结合起来。

陈艳：外资企业，特别是国际性大公司，在各个国家都有投资，上海作为"桥头堡"，应该是一个高地。在哪里做业务要看哪个地方的政策更适合我们。在上海建设"一带一路"高地的时候，我们非常建议上海能真正成为世界性的高地。具体原因在于，我们做具体业务的时候，发现上海运营的时间方面，跟香港、新加坡有一定的差距。

Leo Li: From the super trading platform mentioned in Keynote Speeches, to the chief trading port, and to my colleague's point of view on industrial empowerment, if we want to propose better policies, we should draw lessons from practice and make use of what we have learned in practice. Today, in addition to think tanks, there are also many business representatives and leaders of government departments. Let us return to practice and listen to the confusion and doubt of enterprises participating in the Belt and Road Initiative at the forefront of market. In particular, the business representatives present today epitomizes the economic composition of Shanghai "3+3+3" mode (i.e. 3 front-grounds, 3 middle-grounds and 3 backgrounds), including representatives of state-owned enterprises, private enterprises and foreign enterprises. First we will learn about the confusion or doubt that state-owned enterprises face in the Belt and Road Initiative and listen to the answers from government departments and the thoughts of think tanks.

Songbing Ding: First, it is our state-owned enterprises to share with you as the "bellwether & pioneer". I come from Shanghai International Port (Group) Co., Ltd. The Group mainly operates public container terminals and most bulk cargo terminals in the Port of Shanghai. If Shanghai is a bridgehead in the Belt and Road construction, then the Group, as a port terminal operator, is at the forefront of the bridgehead. After so many years of development, we have cooperated with many consulting agencies and also got the support from many enterprises. In the current environment, one of our focuses is the "Free Trade Port".

Because the rules related to the "Free Trade Port" have not been released yet, so we leave the questions to the consulting agencies. Now we have business relationship with two consulting agencies, Accenture and Deloitte, so we'd like to listen to their answers first.

Our questions include: at present, many details of the "Free Trade Port" policies are not clear. From our point of view, what are the most anticipated policy innovations for the "Free Trade Port"? What is the most difficult policy innovation? What is the most important policy innovation?

Minghua Liu: On the issue of the "Free Trade Port", what is the difference among the Free Trade Area and our existing free trade zone and the current trade facilitation? Where should be subject to upgrades and breakthroughs? It is very important and indeed requires deeper understanding of our government departments.

Now, we think that settlement and currency are big challenges. Imagine the significance, role and influence the "Free Trade Port" could have if the "Free Trade Port" is only limited in such a small range? What effect will a higher significance and influence cause on our currency free settlement and financial system? How to make any breakthrough? We think that it is not a matter that can be decided only by the Shanghai municipality and it needs to be profoundly considered. From the perspective of Shanghai municipality, or from the perspective of policy formulation, what appeals should we make to the central government? What kind of policies should be prior to carry and try with the central government? It is very important.

Leo Li: These questions are related to the municipal Commission of Transport and the Inspection and Quarantine Bureau. Would both units make responses by related references?

Lin Zhang: The plan of "Free Trade Port" is being improved and submitted for approval, which is not only the expectation of the enterprise, but also the expectation of Shanghai. At present, we all expect that the "Free Trade Port" will have a real upgrade from the original free trade area. Vice-Premier Wang Yang has already stated the expectation of Shanghai, i.e. freedom of funds, cargoes and personnel in areas inside the territory while outside the customs. We are very much looking forward to the question of fund freedom. As only the cargo freedom is probably not enough in the "Free Trade Port", we hope that there will be a breakthrough in fund freedom, especially the

RMB offshore business.

Wenbin Zhao: During our development of the pilot free trade zone, we have already proposed the concept of "inside the national border but outside the customs territory". While the "Free Trade Port" plan brings us back to the concept of "inside the national border but outside the customs territory". At that time, why did the Shanghai Pilot FTZ really not realize the positioning "inside the national border but outside the customs territory"? There are many factors. However, the "Free Trade Port" must return to this position. Therefore, when we discuss the plan, the most commonly used and popular term is "stay true to the mission", which means we should go back to the original assumptions.

In addition, as for the "Free Trade Port" benchmark, we often say "refer to the highest international standards and the best level". I think that this sentence is reflected in four aspects:

The first is a good environment. It is mainly to increase publicity and transparency, with polices as its core. In the four years of development in Shanghai Pilot FTZ, the negative lists have been decreasing year by year. I believe that the negative lists will be much less during construction of the "Free Trade Port".

The second is higher efficiency. It is mainly "to ease control on the first line", but the performance of China (Shanghai) Pilot FTZ in this aspect could be improved. I believe that the "Free Trade Port" in the future will do better to "ease control on the first line", including current policies on exemption of declaration and taxes, and unrestricted entrepot trade.

The third is security issues. Carry out second-tier efficient management along with risk management and integrity management, actually realizing the classified management.

The fourth is policies of the "Free Trade Port". It is the initial plan that is released recently. We expect that the future plan will give Shanghai greater autonomy in reform, which has a positive significance for the further development of the "Free Trade Port".

Yide Qiao: As we mentioned earlier, we hope that the "Free Trade Port" involves the financial sector. Let us recall that the China (Shanghai) Pilot Free Trade Zone has made great progress, but there are still many aspects below expectation, mainly including the degree of opening, and especially the financial sector. It is because that the finance sector is subject to the administration of central government instead of local government.

Therefore, my idea is that when making a plan for the "Free Trade Port", we must clearly propose to establish an offshore financial center in Shanghai. There have been many disputes in the past discussions. Some people are not in favor of establishing an offshore financial center in Shanghai. Their reason at that time was that the capital account would soon be fully liberalized. Under such circumstances, it seems that there is no need for Shanghai to establish an offshore financial center any more as it conflicts with that of Hong Kong. However, it is said a few years ago that the capital account would be "basically open" in 2015. However, it does not seem like that it will come true now. I don't think that it will be fully open in the next one or two or three years. If this judgment is made, it is suggested to set up an offshore RMB center for the "Free Trade Port". After it is set, the capital pool will be achieved along with governing power. Otherwise, this problem cannot be solved.

Leo Li: This problem can be summed up as follows: the most difficult, anticipated and innovative problem is how to make some basic breakthroughs in the financial sector.

Songbing Ding: I think to myself and would add that, this question has been discussed before, the most anticipated policy breakthrough for us may be "to ease control on the first line and to have control on the second line" under the concept of "inside the national border but outside the customs territory", and the aim to ease control in an effective and efficient way may be most likely to be broken through in the first place.

I think that the breakthrough is hardly to be made in financial innovation, such as decontrol of foreign exchange and free outflow of funds. Our financial system is vulnerable as it is large but not strong. Since the end of 2016, given considerations in this regard, the government has strengthened the control on foreign exchange. Therefore, the breakthrough of policy innovation in the financial sector should be the most difficult.

Above all, the tax policy is the most important issue. We have been striving for policy innovation in this area but have not been given a definite answer or learned about the implementation of policy. We have compared the FTA policies of countries along the Belt and Road and even other areas of the world, it seems that no country has no preferential policies at the moment. It includes the exemption and deferral of customs duties, and even incentives of corporate income taxes and national policies. In addition to the exemption and deferral of customs duties, it even includes incentives of corporate income taxes and national policies. They are basically 5%—10% lower than the domestic level or even be all exempted. One of the most important policies is still the tax policy.

In conclusion, the most anticipated policy breakthrough is "to ease control on the first line and to have control on the second line" under the concept of "inside the national border but outside the customs territory". The most important policy is the income tax policy. It is the financial policy that is the most difficult to be broken through.

Leo Li: State-owned enterprises have raised very good questions. How about foreign companies?

Weiguo Wang: I am from Siemens Ltd. China. As a member of foreign enterprise, I would like to ask if the government has any expectation of foreign enterprises participating in the Belt and Road construction, especially playing a role as a "bridgehead". Now foreign enterprises also play important roles in support of the "Going Out" policy of state-owned enterprises. In addition to this role, what other expectations does the government have for us?

Qi Sang: Your question, as I understand, is asking how foreign enterprises can help local enterprises in Shanghai go out to cooperate and explore new markets with a third country or countries along the Belt and Road. Most of the foreign enterprises in Shanghai are subsidiaries of multinational corporations, so they all aims to enter the domestic market just when they come to Shanghai. After so many years of development, foreign enterprises have invested in many projects throughout China. At present, some foreign enterprises indeed try to invest and develop in third countries.

From January to October 2017, the non-financial foreign enterprises in Shanghai have spent USD 190 million in direct investment projects to third countries. It is a very good sign. From January to October 2017, the amount of new engineering contracts executed by foreign enterprises in Shanghai reached RMB 450 million. It is also a very good sign. First, we hope that foreign enterprises in Shanghai can go out to third countries, especially to countries along the Belt and Road for investment and construction of engineering projects. It is highly encouraged by our government.

In response to the "Going Out" of foreign enterprises, we adopt a policy of equal treatment with state-owned enterprises and private enterprises. First of all, it is reflected in the facilitation of approvals, including facilitation measures for customs clearance, inspection and quarantine, foreign exchange, and project approval of government departments. However, the super-national treatment of foreign enterprises is unrealistic under the current circumstances. Second, we very much encourage and support the joint efforts among foreign enterprises, state-owned enterprises and private enterprises in Shanghai for cooperation in third countries. In particular, they can jointly go to third countries or countries along the Belt and Road to make invest in and acquire projects, and form a consortium of projects to jointly bid for construction projects in third countries or countries along the Belt and Road. It treats all enterprises equally. Third, government departments attach great importance to foreign enterprises in Shanghai, especially specialized service enterprises and institutions such as foreign-funded investment consulting firms, law firms and accounting firms, and help state-owned enterprises and private enterprises in Shanghai to invest in projects and execute construction contracts in third countries and countries along the Belt and Road. Your time-honored global layout, excellent network of contacts and expertise accumulated can provide our local enterprises with great professional services and supports. In addition to the "Going Out" interactive information alliance formed by local state-owned enterprises and private enterprises, we have also established an alliance of professional service enterprises for "Going Out" of Shanghai enterprises. We can communicate with each other through new media and WeChat groups all the time on investments, projects and policies. After several years, the effect of such practice is quite good.

Leo Li: What the leaders just emphasized is equal treatment between foreign and domestic enterprises. It is a very crucial problem. Both for Shanghai and foreign enterprises in China, it is also a very important problem. First of all, as for Shanghai, foreign enterprises account for 30% of Shanghai's economy. It is impossible to exclude foreign enterprises from building Shanghai as a "bridgehead" along the Belt and Road. In addition, to many foreign enterprises, their businesses in China today may already account for a very large proportion of their global businesses. The next step of growth, following the Belt and Road development, may be a very important opportunity. Of course, it is in early days, and everyone is still exploring.

In addition to the answers given by three leaders just now, could members of our think tanks share your understandings?

Gang Ji: It is a good question. It is crucial for foreign enterprises to play an important role in the development of the Belt and Road. There are two phenomena in enterprises participating in the Belt and Road development. First look at 65 countries along the Belt and Road, the situation in all countries is different. In terms of countries, the economic corridors, including Central Asia, China and Pakistan, China and Mongolia, have different degrees of activeness. The experience of Chinese enterprises in these areas is also different. Another example is Southeast Asia and the Middle East. No matter if the Belt and Road exists, their market mechanisms are relatively developed. Brands of foreign enterprises are influential while the brands of Chinese enterprises are common. Foreign enterprises should cooperate with Chinese enterprises to give full play to their brand competency, endorsement and management on local laws and regulations. Who would be the most excited about the Belt and Road development is some small countries as it is urgent for development while larger countries have their own political considerations on the Belt and Road development. In these areas, a large number of state-owned enterprises go global and foreign enterprises play an auxiliary and supportive role. Due to the complex situation of these areas, their development should be promoted by national endorsement. At the same time, foreign enterprises should provide great supports in project management. In different projects, the role of state-owned enterprises and foreign enterprises should also be different.

I was "Going Out" with the largest energy enterprise then in China in the mid-1990s and participated in oil fields procurement and other matters of oil pipelines, personally experiencing the enormous challenges Chinese enterprises faced overseas. Although we know how to operate enterprises today, our state-owned enterprises still face great difficulties in these processes. So how can we play our own advantages? An industry alliance should be built internally based on supports from government departments and automatically configured with different sources of resources.

Leo Li: What everyone calls the domestic and foreign investment may change in the future. Since the Belt and Road Initiative is a national initiative, it will certainly be the future focus of domestic and foreign enterprises.

Gang Ji: Each project is the key carrier of the Belt and Road Initiative. Some of our projects are long-term projects. If any problem occurs in the future, the overall development of the Belt and Road Initiative will be significantly affected. Experiences of think tanks are of great importance. In the future, we need to establish a practical case base involving enterprises like Shanghai International Port (Group) Co., Ltd., which shares all the twists and turns, challenges and sufferings they faced in project operation. In addition, private enterprises, such as OPPO and Xiaomi, have done very well. How did they get involved in the case base? Projects, including Geely investments, projects in Middle East suffering huge losses, and Sri Lanka's port project suffering huge losses due to change of ruling government, can be analyzed and shared to deliver guiding significance. We want to create such a case base, so that everyone who has undergone a detailed process can share their experiences in project operation. No matter what type of enterprises, or whether the investment is successful or not, it is of practical significance.

Minghua Liu: At present, foreign enterprises are very enthusiastic in the development of the Belt and Road and have also encountered many opportunities. From the government's point of view, there is currently no distinction between so-called domestic investment or foreign investment. The leadership of Shanghai Municipal Commission of Commerce just also talked about the mechanism of PPP cooperation. Earlier, we also advocated the market-led cooperation between government and enterprises, including NGO, PPP and other modes.

The first step is to eliminate information barriers. I believe that for many foreign enterprises, private enterprises and state-owned enterprises, perhaps it is not very clear for the first time that what project opportunities or needs exist in the countries along the

Belt and Road. Then how can they deal with them, allocate the best resources and do the best things? We suggest that we can expand the platform for cooperation between government and enterprises, and establish an alignment platform similar to PMO for corresponding rules, information release and responses. The case base is also included in the platform, showing what lessons learned, corresponding laws and regulations, and tax affairs in these countries would be like. Currently we have such a "Going Out" alliance, but this alliance is now relatively loosely structured. How to make an institutionalized and real PMO? We can jointly promote the work by rules, information and the case base. It is one of our questions.

Weiguo Wang: Today we are discussing how could Shanghai act as a "bridgehead" for the Belt and Road Initiative, that is, our demands on Shanghai itself or policies. We are seeking for exploration and innovation in all aspects, and there are certainly many new things, so we raise this question to discuss with you, in order to support Shanghai to become a "bridgehead" in the initiative.

We have also encountered other questions. For example, several innovation centers have been established with sufficient foreign and domestic investments. But how can we properly establish an information platform of innovation center? We have made an open platform for cooperation with various enterprises and institutions. How can we improve the transparency of information? Does the government have released any policy to publish the platform and invite everyone to participate in it so that foreign and local enterprises can better integrate their resources and use them best? Afterwards, we also hope to gradually eliminate the name of "foreign enterprise".

Leo Li: It is indeed a leading foreign enterprise as it has already had some thoughts and layout in the Belt and Road Initiative. In recent years, private enterprises have been rapidly developing. Today, two representatives of private enterprises are here and we would also like to hear the puzzles or problems they encountered.

Li Hua: Private enterprises still rank "third" in the market. When can we get rid of the title of "private enterprises" and be treated as the same as "foreign enterprises"? I am honored to participate in such a forum, especially a think tank summit forum. We must solve practical problems no matter in a think tank or a summit forum. Some problems cannot be solved at this level, but we must mention them.

Aowei Technology is a high-tech enterprise in the Free Trade Zone. It has been 20 years since its startup. Through its layout in early years under the support of the Shanghai municipality and Shanghai Science and Technology Committee, Aowei Technology now has something to be proud of and is creating a science and technology innovation center with international influences. We have set up our own production and R&D center in Minsk, Belarus and the first 7 enterprises has settled in the center on May 12, 2015 as witnessed by the heads of two countries. We are the representatives of Shanghai science and technology enterprises. However, during the actual operation, we have encountered many problems and we hope to get supports from competent departments through this forum.

First of all, the representative of Deloitte speaks very well. Now the "Going Out" private enterprises are certainly well prepared for export of products and experiences ambulated in past years. The process of Belt and Road development has the following points:

First, there are problems with RMB settlement. In actual operation, how can we earn RMB foreign exchange through exports? We solved this problem through the Finance Office. In the process, enterprises and their senior management are rather proactive, but there are still some problems with the supporting policies in the middle part.

Second, the China-Belarus Industrial Park is the largest project of China in the Belt and Road Initiative. The Park has expanded to 115 square kilometers, equal to the size of a city. However, in the process of development, we also have several doubts. For example, Belarus turns out to be a "sensitive country" in the bank settlement; as for bank outlets, we wonder what kind of overseas layout will Shanghai Pudong Development Bank, Bank of Shanghai, Bank of Communications and other banks in Shanghai plan to establish in the future; and as for visa of the mainland Chinese staff, holders of Hong Kong SAR passport are granted visa free access to 158 countries, while holders of the mainland Chinese passport are only granted visa free access to 62 countries (formerly 65). These are all very realistic problems. If these problems cannot be solved, how can we manage to "Go Out"? How to establish a "bridgehead"? How to construct the Belt and Road?

Third, private enterprises in Shanghai have the strength to participate in the construction of the Belt and Road but have encountered many problems. For example, there is no direct flight between Shanghai and some countries. Now we have to deliver cargoes to other places by shipping.Can the Construction and Transportation Commission provide a way to improve such situation? Given less frequent scheduling and higher cost of China Railway Express, how could Shanghai Railway integrate with the CR express so as to solve this problem? Since it is a "bridgehead", then what kinds of facilitating conditions need to be established? How can the Shanghai Pilot Free Trade Zone be aligned with the sino-foreign industrial park? Now, more Shanghai enterprises have gone out, including Shanghai Construction Group (a state-owned enterprise). We hope that these specific problems can be solved. As for high-level problems in respect of taxes and other fields, we have the right to make suggestions but cannot solve them.

Finally, after the "Going Out" of these hi-tech enterprises, what relevant policies will be released by the Shanghai municipality on the protection and sharing of intellectual property rights? Policies on the transfer of intellectual property are included.

Leo Li: Members from private enterprises are very realistic. They have raised several problems at a time. Can anyone from our government give an answer?

Yu Zhang: All private, state-owned or foreign enterprises may encounter problems in respect of funds, visas and exchange of talents during the process of "Going Out". On the other hand, it is precisely "Going Out" and development of enterprises that promote all-round reform in Shanghai. We are now aware of the importance of these problems and then step by step push forward the development of the "Going Out" and the Belt and Road Initiative that do not exist in the past, thus forcing reform in government and institutions in turn.

The visa problems just mentioned, in fact, are handled by the government step by step. This authority, like the financial authority, belongs to the central government. We have been paying attention to this aspect and are constantly pushing forward related policies, including visa exemption and corporate clearance. In addition, we have also been communicating with the countries concerned. The key time node often lies in the leaders' visit because leaders will drive and promptly handle a batch of projects during their visits. For enterprises, they should grasp the key time nodes, such as the just-mentioned round trips between two countries. When you have mastered and fed the information back to the government, in order to promote the relationship between two countries, the government will gradually solve these problems. It is hard to say that these problems can be solved at once, but the government is truly handling these things.

Heng Quan: As specific problems should be solved by government departments, I have a few experiences at the macro level.

First, all state-owned enterprises, private enterprises and foreign enterprises talk about the risks of "Going Out". We have prepared a research report on the Belt and Road Initiative last year. We should have a judgment on the Belt and Road Initiative as it is not a universal and comprehensive strategy for "Going Out". We must make choices about the countries along the Belt and Road. There is a concept involving from supporting countries and cities to industrial parks, and to the implementation of projects. In accordance with this logic, roughly a dozen countries can manage to "Go Out" with assurance. Otherwise, several enterprises going out will encounter many problems, including the uncertain problems that they have not anticipated in China. Therefore, we must first have a comparison, evaluation and choice, instead of "Going Out" at a stroke.

Second, when we go out to the countries along the Belt and Road, we should get to know their tax revenues, and find out what discounts are available there and how is their business environment? Our research shows that for both the international and domestic enterprises, "Going Out" itself, broadly speaking, is an important part of economic globalization. What is behind it is the market-oriented mechanisms and the pursuit of profit maximization. Under such circumstances, whether it is a state-owned enterprise, a private enterprise or a foreign enterprise, it is necessary to be competitive in the course of "Going Out" instead of having a good business environment or facilitation. Is the remarkable improvement in the business environment that brought about such a huge trade growth in the period between January and September 2017 in China? It is worth thinking. The most important thing is the current international environment, and our "Going Out" for profits eventually depends on our own competitiveness. In the international competition, we all compete with each other fairly, not to say that there is any preference or anything else. In China, we mainly relies on tax incentives and preferential policies, including Shanghai's early attempts to attract foreign investment.

However, the FTA seeks to change this trend by focusing on creating a fair playing field for businesses. Secondly, we will go to other countries to carry out the third or fourth international industrial transfer. Under the fair competitive environment, whether we can make profits depends on our innovation ability and competitiveness.

Thirdly, we have also conducted some research and assessments on the "Going Out" of Shanghai enterprises and find that private enterprises in Shanghai, especially state-owned enterprises and foreign enterprises, are even more motivated to go out. The so-called motivation means the pursuit of profits under the influence of global multinational corporations. On the other hand, enterprises in China, especially Shanghai, are facing the pressure of rising costs, therefore they will have certain considerations in the layout of investment.

For us, the most important thing is to go out as Japanese enterprises did in those years and we will go out along with other enterprises instead of going out all alone. For example, enterprise alliance like Japan Inc. Of course it is not to say that the role of the government is not important. The agreed rules, negotiations, bilateral and multilateral relations among the countries along the Belt and Road should be developed in advance, which can create a better platform and environment for the enterprises going out, reduce their instability and increase their predictability and transparency. At the same time, the government should also determine the negotiation and cooperation among the countries along the Belt and Road as well as investment, trading and financial rules, so as to create better conditions for the enterprises going out.

Leo Li: Enterprises going out are faced with all kinds of difficulties as expected. We will continuously solve those emerging problems. Some problems in this process are certainly solved by the enterprises themselves, while others should be gradually resolved by the government with policies.

Meixing Xia: I am from Shanghai Electric Power Co., Ltd. (SEP), and now I have a case to share with you. In the last two years, our company has invested in a power company in Malta, which was then awarded as a sustainable "Going Out" case of Chinese enterprises by the United Nations Development Program, the Ministry of Commerce of PRC and the State-owned Assets Supervision and Administration Commission of the State Council (SASAC), and also a successful "Going Out" case for the enterprises under SASAC. During the project implementation, we have cooperated with some consulting agencies to reduce the local electricity price by 25%. The Prime Minister of Malta believes that the cooperation project between SEP and Enemalta PLC is a "model for China-Malta economic and trade cooperation" and expresses his high compliment to such cooperation.

SEP is a century-old state-owned enterprise with affiliates over Nanshi, Yangshupu and Minhang, Shanghai. We have been committed to implementing the Belt and Road Initiative and combining it with the transformation of century-old state-owned enterprises. Our development strategy is to combine the Belt and Road Initiative with the construction of Shanghai Technology Innovation Center, so as to formulate innovative strategies of internationalization. Last year, our overseas profits already accounted for 20% of the Company's total profits. We have established new energy projects in Japan, and also invested in southern Europe with Malta as our stronghold. Recently, a new energy project in Montenegro is about to start, and we also have large projects in Turkey and other places.

During our recent practices, we have encountered some difficulties:

The first is information services. Many countries along the Belt and Road vary greatly and keep changing in respect of politics, economy, culture, legal system, and even political situation. As an individual enterprise, it is hard for us to work intensively in all places and comprehensively control everything. Therefore, we suggest that we should play an overall role in sharing and interacting. The Foreign Trade and Economic Committee has established an alliance. It is great. I personally suggest that the government should build an organization similar to the Japan External Trade Organization. At the important nodes along the Belt and Road, a number of branch offices can be set up to conduct long-term and in-depth tracking of the areas, and provide enterprises with comprehensive information and services in regard to trade, investment, and personnel exchanges. It is just an immature idea of my own.

The second is coordination services. From the perspective of energy enterprises, vicious competition has already existed in the "Going Out" process of Chinese energy enterprises. In many parts of the world, from engineering, investment to M&As, it is rather terrible to see domestic enterprises fighting each other. Because of the vicious competition, some Chinese enterprises have done nothing abroad but to ruin China's reputation. The quality of projects cannot be guaranteed due to extremely low price, which eventually leads to the declining reputation of China brands. From the perspective of China instead of Shanghai, this problem is in need of attention during the course of promoting the "Going Out" policy. The industry association should play its role under the market mechanism to formulate certain rules.

The third is further enhancement of financial services. The advantage of Shanghai, a "bridgehead" in the Belt and Road Initiative, lies in the finance sector. However, this advantage is not obvious in terms of global capital. If Shanghai is not competitive in this aspect, its role in the Belt and Road development will be looked down upon by other countries. In the finance and insurance sector, Shanghai still has great potential for improving its role of supporting the Belt and Road development.

Leo Li: SEP has shared its successful experiences in the Going Out Initiative and also put forward great suggestions and questions. Would any official of government give some responses? There are mainly two aspects. First, what can we do in terms of information services and trade promotion? Second, what measures should be taken to improve the competitiveness of financial services?

Qi Sang: Mr. Xia has just talked about SEP's success stories in Malta. Coincidentally, I once specially investigated this project and had an informal discussion with the former general manager of the project owner and officials of relevant government departments in Malta. Indeed, as Mr. Xia has said, this project is a great success.

However, a question comes to my mind: currently, many foreign investment consulting agencies do provide quality professional services in the "Going Out" process of Shanghai enterprises, but these professional services may be highly focused on such aspects as legal affairs, accounting, taxation and pre-project due diligence. It is suggested that foreign or domestic investment consulting agencies should analyze and summarize successful cases of the "Going Out" projects in China, and direct a right path for enterprises preparing to "Go Out" by summing up, training and disseminating their experiences and lessons.

The information and coordination services that Mr. Xia just mentioned are indeed difficult problems. Over the years, government departments, including the Shanghai Municipal Commission of Commerce (SMCC), and other institutions have been committed to this regard by providing information services to "Going Out" enterprises. For example, the Shanghai municipality has promoted the bilateral investments by setting up the Shanghai Foreign Investment Development Board (SFIDB). At the time of its establishment, SFIDB mainly focused on attracting investments, but in recent years, with the development of "Going Out" projects, SFIDB has also significantly strengthened its efforts in promoting investments abroad and provided many information services to enterprises. As for the overseas offices you mentioned, 5 overseas offices have been established by SFIDB for many years and continuously functioned. However, paradoxically, as these overseas offices are funded by local financial revenues, specific personnel should be assigned to manage such a large number of funds, it is necessary to explore how to cooperate with developed enterprises in Shanghai that have already "gone out". In addition, if Shanghai's "Going Out" projects have been maturely developed abroad, could they be considered as the overseas offices of SFIDB relying on the strength of local enterprises and governments? Take the Malta office of SFIDB for example. Certainly, this issue should be fully discussed between both parties. We have made some attempts in this regard.

Now, there are so many information service agencies that are dispersed all over the world, it is difficult not only to integrate them within one institution, but also to ensure their quality and demands after integration. I hope that the government departments can do some in-depth research and know how to better solve this problem along with "Going Out" enterprises and domestic and foreign investment consulting agencies. Every year in all countries, all kinds of investment risk reports and national policy reports are prepared out of financial allocations, and there are also announcements on line. But how well do they work? It is indeed a problem.

We have just mentioned the coordination services. Another long-standing problem also exists as Chinese "Going Out" enterprises are involved with vicious competition for overseas bidding projects. The coordination mechanism exists in the Ministry of Commerce, commercial counsellor's office of China embassy in foreign countries, China International Contractors Association, and the China Chamber of Commerce for Import and Export of Machinery and Electronic Products, which has played a certain role over the years, but there are still many areas to be perfected. The bidding enterprises which failed to win the bidding may feel wronged and unwilling to accept the results, and even think that the coordination mechanism is not fair. It is necessary to study well in this respect to find out how to establish a mechanism effectively coordinating the vicious competition among overseas projects so as to better reflect the principle of justice, equity and transparency.

Leo Li: Regarding financial services, are there any supplements from colleagues in the finance office?

Shanhong Xie: Let me add something else. First of all, the Belt and Road Initiative is a required task for the real economy of financial services, and we also see the Belt and Road development as a major opportunity for Shanghai to build an international financial center and promote the "Going Out" of RMB. Under this premise, there are many things to do in Shanghai, such as the issuance of Panda bonds, and cooperation between general capital markets and those associated with the Belt and Road Initiative. Next, we may mainly focus on these aspects:

First, in the marketplace, we must take full advantage of Shanghai as a financial center and build Shanghai into an investment and financing center serving the Belt and Road Initiative. As we all know, the Belt and Road Initiative requires a large amount of financial investment, which should be achieved by attracting state-owned, private and foreign funds, and other multi-channel, diversified and multi-mode funds instead of relying on policy-based investment alone. The capital market in Shanghai may play a great role in this process. In addition, the implementation of the Belt and Road Initiative will generate plenty of dividends and Chinese investors will also be able to benefit from its development. For instance, the issuance of Panda bonds should utilize the capital market in Shanghai to continue its cooperation with the capital markets associated with the Belt and Road Initiative.

Second, how can Chinese financial institutions continue to "Go Out" along with the Belt and Road? Aowei Technology has mentioned the overseas distribution of Chinese-funded banks. It also said that some countries along the Belt and Road have the characteristics of being under-developed economically and financially. In our view, China's financial institutions still have more room to play a larger role in the Belt and Road Initiative as they are now in the stage where we might have been in the previous period. Our development experiences can be transplanted in the countries or regions along the Belt and Road according to their local characteristics. However, we also have to see the fact that our Chinese-funded banks have long been mainly serving the markets in China, especially Shanghai Pudong Development Bank (SPDB) and other local banks in Shanghai, and the internationalization degree of SPDB is relatively lower than that of state-owned banks such as ICBC, CCB, BOCOM and BOC. Some commercial banks have launched branches in Hong Kong and Singapore, and most recently in London. However, considering the local economic conditions and other factors, no commercial bank has planned to set up branches in the countries along the Belt and Road in a short term. Besides, Chinese-funded banks have set up branches abroad subject to the approval of regulatory authorities, and have also proposed some planning arrangements. With the advancing of strategies, we will guide and encourage Chinese-funded banks to place much emphasis on the countries and regions along the Belt and Road in the drive for internationalization. The traditional route is to deploy branches in economically and financially well-developed places. However, huge opportunities exist in the implementation of the Belt and Road Initiative. I suggest everyone could read the *Action Plan for the Belt and Road Initiative* recently issued by the Shanghai municipality. In the Plan, the finance sector is of great importance. The Plan mainly contains 10 aspects. I also note that the Plan has more or less absorbed the good suggestions and ideas previously mentioned by experts. Our study has been going on for more than a year against the financial section of the Plan. Many of the suggestions you have today are similar to those held by us. Next, we will continue to combine our views for further deepening.

Where financial services are relatively inadequate, the Finance Office is very willing to play a coordinating and facilitating role. I believe that given the considerable scale of our Chinese banks, we can surely solve these problems by taking many effective measures.

Moreover, the construction of the Belt and Road, the Free Trade Port or the financial center is part of "Building a new pattern of open economy" set forth in the report of the 19th National Congress of CPC. Under the context, I believe that we will overcome the biggest difficulty taking these issues into consideration. It is because that, in my opinion, the Free Trade Port is not only the version 3.0 & 4.0 of the FTZ, but also a new chapter worthy of our expectation.

Yide Qiao: How to encourage financial institutions in Shanghai to "Go Out"?

The reality is that SPDB and BOS still need time to "Go Out" given their limited scale. There are two problems. First, corporate governance or some regulations have impeded their "Going Out". For example, I made the contacts with the organizer when the staff of SPDB is planned to attend the meeting held in Kazakhstan. It is said that the staff of state-owned enterprises are difficult to be approved to travel abroad for three months. Second, we should have an open mind and be bolder. For example, BOC and CCB have done well in this area. BOC was originally headquartered in Shanghai and later moved to Beijing, and now we want to relocate it back to Shanghai? To utilize the opportunity of establishing Xiong'an New Area, Shanghai, as a non-capital city, should at least take back the RMB business division of BOC even if its headquarters cannot be relocated. How can a financial center without large commercial banks be a financial center? We are likely to succeed given the opportunity of establishing the Free Trade Port in Shanghai, as this plan is proposed in the report of the 19th CPC National Congress. We must seize this opportunity.

Shanhong Xie: We think that it is possible to attract foreign financial institutions to enter the market in Shanghai, and we can work toward such a direction. We hope that both experts and scholars can work with us to make our voices heard.

Liming Chen: Jin Jiang International (Group) Company Limited is the world's fifth largest hotel group, and our main businesses include hospitality, tourism and passenger transport. We have 8 800 properties in 67 countries or regions around the world, of which 200 properties are located along the Belt and Road. In the future, we may also launch more properties ranging from 400 to 500. Globally, we will have 10 000 properties containing 1 million guest rooms. In the next one or two years, we may also rank third in the global hotel industry. We believe that the Group's global layout and multinational operations, including its layout along the Belt and Road, mainly proceed from the Group's strategies, which are based on the globalization trend in China.

Enterprises getting involved must first study all aspects and follow them up in a timely manner, and strive for supports from all parties concerned. In the past two years, we have carried out several international M&As, using the platform of international M&As to facilitate our integration and financing. We have also jointly implemented the

Belt and Road Initiative and utilized foreign, state-owned and private funds based on their advantages. Now, Jin Jiang International (Group) Company Limited has combined the private and foreign funds through listed companies and fully utilized them based on all advantages of the mechanism. We have always committed to the principle of "unchanged businesses, integrated background, complementary advantages and joint development". Similarly, when dealing with foreign relations, we must respect local laws, get to know local customs and make full use of local advantages (such as talent advantages). All senior executives are basically retained when we acquired a French platform, and they will continue to play their roles instead of being replaced by the major personnel assigned by us. Given the influences of France on the world and the Belt and Road in the Middle East, our layout along the Belt and Road will be more efficient. For example, we have acquired the Sarovar Group, the largest hotel group in India, through a listed company platform. Therefore, we have opened the market in South Asia, and then Indonesia, Vietnam and Southeast Asia. Domestically, we have been committed to innovation and establishing the Paris Innovation Center and the Shanghai Innovation Center, so as to introduce and further develop originally good brands into China. As for the tourism industry, China has enormous potential for its development as a large number of Chinese people need to enjoy services with Chinese characteristics overseas. How could we combine advantages with our layout? The implementation of the Belt and Road Initiative in China is to give play to the pioneering role of Shanghai enterprises as the bridgehead of the Belt and Road Initiative. Those enterprises with advantages and conditions may first "go out" and operate with market behavior and business behavior.

I think that Shanghai is obliged to discuss the role of bridgehead in the Belt and Road Initiative. But in this process, the culture of bridgehead must not be ignored. As for business flow, logistics and capital flow, what is more important is the people behind them. To make people believe in, love and respect you, it is important to form a cultural adsorption capacity. Shanghai should be more inclusive, and convince people that they will live a better life here. Jin Jiang International (Group) Company Limited has also sponsored the Shanghai Symphony Orchestra and the Shanghai Ballet. The cultural activities carried out in Shanghai are associated with the Group, but more about the development of Shanghai. We should attract people from all over the world to come to Shanghai and would like to believe in you. No matter where you go, people there are willing to accept and welcome you. This cultural strength may be more important than the hardware of the "bridgehead". With developed hardware, we also have to acquire quality software.

Guoqing Fu: I would like to talk about some issues on technical innovation.

First of all, enterprises should be the subject for the "Going Out" of countries along the Belt and Road. As your speeches indicated, some enterprises have went out successfully, while others not. First of all, enterprises must know very well what advantages they have, otherwise their "Going Out" will certainly fail. In the "Going Out" process, one is to "Go Out" and the other is to "Bring in". Not all of these countries along the Belt and Road lag behind or are inferior to China. They have some advantages in resources, technologies and talents, as well as good ideas that we must learn from. Recently, we were fortunate to visit the China—Belarus Industrial Park. The products they developed are very good. Different from our additive manufacturing, what they are doing is subtractive manufacturing.

Second, from the perspective of government, how could we set up a platform and provide services? How could we help enterprises go out with confidence and make gains? It is the responsibility of our government. From the perspective of information, it is impossible to understand the situation in so many countries only relying on a single enterprise. The government should indeed provide information services. The government has already been trying to do something. We have released messages through the website and information push service, but no one seems to notice them. Many small and micro enterprises do not care about these messages, and there is nothing we can do about it. But in any case, we still have to establisha government information platform.

Third, financial services. Enterprises have encountered many problems during the process of "Going Out". First of all, large enterprises have no problem with funds, but how easy will it be to transfer funds abroad if no project is supported by the government departments? As for the "Five Passes" (i.e. policy coordination, facilities connectivity, unimpeded trade, financial integration and people-to-people bonds) in the Belt and Road Initiative, you can't get much of anything done without financial integration, and the flow of talents is also very important. I also went to Kazakhstan this time. It imposes tighter visa restrictions for Chinese visitors. Their visa acceptance rate is only

1/10 of ours, which means 300 000 or even 3 million Kazakhstan people may have been to China while only 30 000 Chinese people can travel to Kazakhstan. Therefore, the policy coordination is of great importance. I hope it is not our one-sided enthusiasm. The experts we invited have talked a lot and delivered impassioned speeches. But could these experts affect the decision making of their countries when they come back home? In the future, we should invite their top officials and former officials to attend the Belt and Road forums, so as to bring experts' information and suggestions back to the countries and influence their authorities. No one in the "Five Passes" can be ignored, and the key is the flow of talents. In addition, could we establish a green channel for the flow of young entrepreneurs in the countries along the Belt and Road?

The Shanghai Municipal Science and Technology Commission has executed a number of cooperation agreements with relevant countries in recent years, including Israel, Hungary, Lithuania, Croatia, Belarus, Finland, Cambodia, Vietnam, etc. The main purpose of these cooperation agreements is to promote the exchange and cooperation among enterprises. I think these measures have laid an important foundation, without which, the "Going Out" policy will not work.

Finally, I will talk about a case. In order to provide technical trainings to developing countries, the Shanghai Technology Transfer Exchange is entrusted by the Ministry of Science and Technology to provide training courses to the ASEAN countries in Southeast Asia on technology transfer, technology trade, etc. Among them, the personnel from Vietnam are very open-minded. They have participated in every training course on reform and opening up, and will do everything that China has done before. As they noticed the effect of technology transfer, after attending those trainings, they asked us if we could provide a special training on the technology transfer. We then carry out a special training for them and included it in the China-Vietnam intergovernmental cooperation projects. Later, they specifically set up a technology transfer building in Ho Chi Minh City and prepared all the things as guided by us, even including the staff training. This is based on the previous foundation. We cannot be so hurried, as the foundation should be laid first. Taking the Aowei Technology as example, if a solid foundation has not been laid, we cannot start our cooperation with Belarus as expected. Now, the foundation actually works well as we have done several years of preparation in advance.

Xiaodong Yang: The vision of SAIC Motor is to become a world-renowned motor company, but it is still at the initial stage of international operations. Everyone talks about "Going Out", but the subsequent steps, "Going In" and "Going Further", are more important and difficult than the "Going Out". Today, many of enterprises operate based on B2B. However, the motor enterprises operate based on B2C and are directly accessible to a large number of users, therefore there is no way to require the local government and all users to buy our cars. So we have to first establish the image of our brand and then continue to make investments.

First of all, our enterprise must enhance its structure and internal strength, but the supports of local government, including cultural supports, are also indispensable. It is still difficult to have local people accept Chinese products if the cultural inputs have not been prepared well. With regard to the government supports, I would like to make several suggestions:

First, the implementation of the Belt and Road Initiative mainly focuses on infrastructure, energy and high-speed rail, with nothing to do with the automobile industry. Characteristics of the automobile industry include B2C first, and then promotion of local taxes and employment. Therefore, the automobile industry should be considered as a strategic industry for the "Going Out" or the Belt and Road Initiative. It is beneficial to both sides. If the automobile industry can "Go Out", "Go in" and "Go Further", I believe others can also make it. Because the automobile industry chain is not only parallel, but also vertical, its driving effect is relatively significant.

The second is consumer finance. I have just talked a lot about investment and financing. Old saying says: food and fodder should go ahead of troops and horses. In general, 80% of overseas consumption is consumer finance. Those banks that have already "went out" are more interested in investment than consumption. No one would like to talk about consumption. So how could the consumer finance, from a policy point of view, support the "Going Out" policy, and support the enterprises and finance companies to "Go Out"? There are many policy restrictions now.

The third is foreign exchange management. It is recommended not to engage in the "one size fits all" approach. Enterprises that actually plan to become globalized still need to be managed in a layered and personalized manner.

The fourth is management of state-owned enterprises. For example, in the areas of energy management and import & export, no one can be assigned to go abroad if there is an urgent task in any overseas market tomorrow. It is because employees of state-owned enterprises cannot go abroad unless they have obtained the Public Affairs Passport. No one would dream of traveling abroad with his/her private passport. For example, overseas investment must be based on the integral and long-term nature of projects. It is unlikely that every project will succeed. How to encourage state-owned enterprises to unload their negative thoughts during the "Going Out" process? State-owned enterprises are still less competitive than private and foreign enterprises. How could state-owned enterprises be further unloaded? It should be promoted by the market mechanism.

The last is the advantage of Shanghai Pilot Free Trade Zone and there must be progress. If Shanghai cannot set up the capital pool, it still has to solve such problems as trade distribution, capital financing, foreign exchange detaining, foreign exchange risk management, etc. in Hong Kong or other places.

Jian Gui: On the whole, foreign enterprises are still in a confused position in the Chinese market. As China's first exclusively foreign-owned enterprise, GCP Applied Technologies entered the Chinese market in 1986. We may be one of the foreign enterprises pioneering in China's reform and opening up. I would like to make a few comments:

Firstly, the Belt and Road Initiative of China is not sufficiently publicized among foreign enterprises. Although foreign enterprises have proposed corporate strategies against the Belt and Road Initiative, certain doubts may still exist. For example, what roles could we play in the process? What opportunities do we have to participate in the Initiative? In what ways could we cooperate with each other? With what kind of markets and opportunities could enterprises have certain advantages?

Secondly, from the publicity perspective of the Shanghai municipality and its departments or commissions, it has not yet made it clear what kind of roles should Shanghai play as a "bridgehead" in the Belt and Road development and what kind of supports Shanghai can provide. Could the Shanghai municipality establish a regular communication mechanism with the AmCham Shanghai, the European Union Chamber of Commerce in China, the German Chamber of Commerce in China and the British Chambers of Commerce in China? The government should give good publicity and organize forums to discuss how foreign enterprises in China can better participate in the implementation of the Belt and Road Initiative and what roles could they play in the process. From this perspective, Shanghai has its own advantages as Shanghai is home to 1 200 regional headquarters of foreign enterprises. Except for Beijing, no other cities in China can catch it up.

Thirdly, the publicity should rank first, while the promotion and supports rank second and third. How could we promote the participation of foreign enterprises in this process, and help them "Go Out" together with state-owned and private enterprises? The advantage of foreign enterprises is that, in the countries along the Belt and Road, their investment moves faster and sooner, and would have experienced the cultural differences and policy influences. They can better share their advantages and experiences with state-owned and private enterprises, so as to jointly build a platform. Ultimately, this platform needs to be established by the government with supports from all parties concerned, before it is finally implemented.

Tracy Yang: The leadership of SAIC Motor also pointed out that the biggest problem in "Going Out" is the later integration. Last year, we have worked with the municipal SASAC to research on this issue and found out its miserable past. Specifically, things are going well in the early and middle stages, while attentions should be paid to the later stage. The leadership of SMCC proposed that the consulting agencies in the think tank can provide regular trainings or even the case base, covering pre-investment, investment, and post-investment issues. But it requires the government to take the lead. As enterprises cannot decide which information channel is better due to its large quantity, the government needs to integrate information sources and then combine them with experiences of all enterprises, intermediary agencies and research institutions in our international think tanks.

We are now following a path that the whole world has not gone through, which means we can innovate all the modes. The leadership of SMCC has just suggested that we can cooperate with state-owned enterprises to set up overseas offices. I think that such offices can also be established with foreign enterprises, private enterprises and consulting agencies. Under the government-led platform, how could such offices be established better, more convenient, and more cost-effectively?

The issue of information platform just mentioned needs to be solved immediately, as it is crucial for us to play the role of a "bridgehead". I am also a member of the foreign investment group organized by SMCC, which has indeed played a great role and contains a large number of members. However, few members of the group are from the small and medium-sized enterprises. Is it possible for the government to launch an official WeChat account to publicize the efforts Shanghai municipality has made to build the "bridgehead" of the Belt and Road development? All preferential policies can be issued on this official account.

Based on the experience of more than 100 Belt and Road projects that I and SAIC Motor have participated in, the greatest aspiration of enterprises is still the tax incentives. As far as I know, there is still no preferential tax policy specific in China as a whole. I hope the government will consider it later.

Dedi Wang: In 2015, the leaders of the State Council clearly stated that the "Going Out" of agriculture should be led by the Ministry of Agriculture. Last year, the General Office of the State Council specially issued the *Several Opinions on Promoting Agricultural Cooperation with Foreign Countries*. Here are a few messages to tell you.

I noticed that many consulting agencies did not mention the "Going Out" of agriculture. But in fact, Shanghai has done very well in the "Going Out" of agriculture. In 2016, statistical data showed that Shanghai's investment in the "Going Out" of agriculture reached USD 2.66 billion, an increase of 62.6% year-on-year, accounting for 2/3 of the total investment in the "Going Out" of agriculture throughout China. Therefore, Shanghai may have played the role of "bridgehead" in the "Going Out" of agriculture. Moreover, the "Going Out" of agriculture is related to all of us. What you eat every day, no matter you are immigrants or natives in Shanghai, is partly the products derived from the "Going Out" of agriculture. Therefore, I suggest consulting agencies study what is the "Going Out" of agriculture and how could the agriculture "Go Out". The 19th CPC National Congress proposes that our social contradictions are now involved with the people's growing desire for a better life. We want to eat "well" instead of being "full".

Firstly, if any problem occurs in the "Going Out" of agriculture, the Shanghai Municipal Agricultural Commission will be bound to solve such problem by coordinating with the Shanghai Customs, Shanghai Entry-Exit Inspection and Quarantine Bureau, SMCC and competent departments, otherwise we will report it to the Ministry of Agriculture. Total 27 enterprises that "went out" along with the Belt and Road have succeeded in establishing a good relationship not only with the local government but also with local farmers and people. For example, the government of Qingpu District once planned to raise some ducks and chickens, but we cannot find any proper place to raise them. As others suggested us to raise these ducks and chickens in Cambodia, we then invested USD 3 million to provide locals with quality ecological chickens and ducks. So, we should work more in a practical and realistic manner.

Secondly, Jin Jiang International (Group) Company Limited also has its demands on food as the Group has launched so many properties around the world. During the process of "Going Out" of agriculture, we have produced abroad lots of grains and vegetables in addition to pigs and cows. Local people are very welcome to combine our technologies with local skills.

Elaine Chen: Foreign enterprises, especially large international enterprises, have investments in various countries. As a "bridgehead" of the Belt and Road, Shanghai should be a highland for them. Where to conduct businesses depends on whose policies are more suitable for us. As Shanghai is building itself as a highland for the Belt and Road, we strongly recommend that Shanghai can truly become a global highland. The specific reason is that when we were conducting specific businesses, we found that there was a certain gap in service time between Shanghai and Hong Kong or Singapore.

SUMMARY STATEMENT

总结发言

李剑腾　Leo Li

波士顿咨询公司全球合伙人兼董事总经理

Partner and Managing Director of

Boston Consulting Group（BCG）

今天下午总体围绕三个问题在讨论：第一，从 2013 年提出"一带一路"倡议，走到今天，到底有什么不一样？第二，"一带一路"发展到今天，再往后走会有什么挑战？第三，上海发挥好"桥头堡"作用，到底能做什么事情？

通过四年的摸索，"一带一路"建设进入 2.0 版本，那么 2.0 版和 1.0 版到底有什么区别？在 1.0 版本中更多的是有"国家队"参与，主要是政府间合作、以国企参与为主。2.0 版本，第一个变化，就是要更多的发挥市场主体的作用，实现全面互联互通。第二方面，要向质量、效益转变。第三方面，从内容上讲，原来更多的是商品输出和销售，未来 2.0 版本，希望看到的是标准、服务以及品牌的输出。

此外，从区域角度看，1.0 版本更多是针对自贸区、境内区域的开放，到 2.0 版本更多是从"走出去"到在国外境外建立合作开发区域。这是讨论"一带一路"建设在新 2.0 版本下的基本前提。

在这样的前提下，目前"一带一路"建设我们面临的问题主要包括以下几个方面：首先，沿线国家和地区的发展参差不齐，尤其是基础设施，要实现互联互通。第一步是互联，但基础设施只要投钱，比较容易解决。更多是互通的问题，连起来以后，怎么互通？怎么把要素连接在"一带一路"中才能比较好地流动起来？其次，信息不对称，渠道不畅，以及沿线国家相对产业链不完整。跟金融一样，大家喜欢去相对发达的地区，这对我们"一带一路"建设恰恰是重要的机会，去发达经济体不愿意去的地方。最后，各个地方的法规不一样，涉及各种合规、经营风险的问题，这是往后"一带一路"建设往前走的根本的矛盾。

今天我们讲上海怎么发挥"桥头堡"的作用。首先，上海本身拥有世界级的空港、海港和铁路港以及金融港，"一带一路"的主要城市节点中，没有一个城市有这么好的基础，这些使上海在"一带一路"建设中发挥着不可替代的作用。上海跟东京、纽约不一样的是，对内，我们连接广袤的腹地，不光是长三角，通过长江经济带，我们有广阔的腹地；对外，我们有相关国家的融合。如果要进一步用好、用活流量枢纽，要抓住先行先试的政策优势。概括一下，就是刚才各个专家、智库以及讨论环节提出的要做的事情，主要是三个方面：

第一，自由市场制度和规则的建立。今天我们很多规则不完善，很多制度没有，所以不可能做到"法不禁止即可为"。首先是制度完善，包括金融问题、信息问题，要把规则先建立起来，当规则完善到一定的程度，才有可能变成一个自由的市场制度。

第二，金融、投融资体系建设。"一带一路"建设中第一件事，就是要连起来，连起来本身的基建投入非常大，有十多万亿美元的需求。从今天的融资投资体系讲，很难支持这样大的资金需求。刚才很多智库提到非常实际、可操作的一些手段，包括建立符合银行担保条件的担保平台，还有沿线国家官方虚拟货币，把股票和债券市场为沿线国家开放等等，这些都是非常好的、能在金融体系建设上有突破的点。

第三，创新信息和交流平台的建设。包括沿线国家项目信息，企业本身相关的交流，科研成果的转化等，以及中国经验的输出。不管是中国民营企业还是外资企业，中国过去 30 年的发展，大家都积累了非常好的经验，比如通过园区模式发展经济，如何针对本地的需求做一些支付能力不那么高的产品，以及通过多元化的层级满足相对多元化的需求等。这些都是沿线国家需要的经验。不管是外企还是民企都可以做，当然政府可以做一些牵头工作。人才培养上，以往我们做的大多是外资企业引进来，往后我们更多的是需要走到"一带一路"沿线的企业中，进行外向型人才的培养。

最后，补充一下个人观点。今天我们讲的是"一带一路"。第一，看历史上的丝绸之路，这个"桥头堡"是谁？是我们盛唐时期的长安。长安当时对中亚以及亚洲地区，都有非常大的影响。今天去日本，还能看到唐朝留下的一些东西。这并不是说楼建得多高，路建得多好，更多是软实力的影响。所以今天在硬件建设的基础上，我们不要忽视对文化、制度的建设以及文化和制度跟大家之间的联系。第二，从未来的角度看，现在是改革开放 2.0 版本，2050 年前后中国会是什么样？上海会是什么样？大家可以放开畅想，但有一点不变，今天科技的变革，包括互联网、人工智能、区块链等，这些在今天建设的互联互通里必须前瞻性地考虑到。往往我们对一个城市或一个经济体的发展，会高估一两年的发展，但往往会低估二三十年的发展。所以在现在的"一带一路"建设中，不光要考虑到当前需要解决的问题，更多要考虑未来科技革命带给我们的影响。这里，我们需要做一些事情，比如洋山港已经运用了一些先进的技术建立了全球第一个无人港，在"一带一路"建设中，还有很多类似的领域可以前瞻性地应用。

This afternoon, we will discuss three questions in general: first, compared with the Belt and Road Initiative proposed in 2013, what is changed now? Second, what challenges will the Belt and Road Initiative encounter in the future? Third, what results will Shanghai achieve by playing its role as a "bridgehead"?

After four years of exploration, the Belt and Road Initiative has developed into the version 2.0. What is the difference between the version 2.0 and the version 1.0? The version 1.0 is more about the "national" participation, mainly including government-to-government cooperation and participation of state-owned enterprises. The first change in version 2.0 is to make more use of the market subjects and achieve comprehensive interconnection. The second change is to focus more on quality and efficiency. The third change, from the content point of view, is expected to cover output of standards, services and brands in the version 2.0, as the version 1.0 is more of commodity output and sales.

Fourth, from a regional perspective, the version 1.0 is more specific to the opening up of the free trade zones and territories, and the version 2.0 focuses more on establishing cooperative development zones abroad than the "Going Out". This is the basic premise for discussing the Belt and Road Initiative under the version 2.0.

Under this premise, the problems we currently face in the Belt and Road Initiative mainly include the following aspects: Firstly, the development of the countries and regions along the Belt and Road is not the same, especially their infrastructure. It is required to achieve interconnection among them. The first step is to interconnect their infrastructure, which can be easily solved by simply investing funds. More problems lie in intercommunication. How could we achieve intercommunication among them when their infrastructure is interconnected? How could we connect elements to the Belt and Road so that these elements can work better? Secondly, information asymmetry, impeded channels, and incomplete relative industry chains of the countries along the Belt and Road. Like the finance sector, everybody would like to travel to relatively developed regions. However, it is in turn an important opportunity for us to implement the Belt and Road Initiative in places where advanced economies would like to avoid. Finally, laws and regulations vary from place to place, involving compliance and operation risks. It is a fundamental contradiction against the future development of the Belt and Road Initiative.

Today we will talk about how could Shanghai play the role of a "bridgehead". First of all, Shanghai itself has world-class airports, seaports, railway ports and financial harbors. None of the major cities and nodes of the Belt and Road have such a good foundation, which makes Shanghai have an irreplaceable role in the Belt and Road Initiative. As we can see, Shanghai is different from Tokyo and New York. Domestically, Shanghai connects with vast hinterlands like the Yangtze River Delta, and boasts a vast backland along with the Yangtze River Economic Belt; overseas, Shanghai also integrates with related countries. If we want to make better use of this traffic hub, we must seize the advantages to carry out and try policies preferentially. In conclusion, the things that experts, think tanks and discussion sessions have proposed to do mainly include:

Firstly, establishment of the system and rules on free market. Today, given imperfect current rules and lack of systems, it is impossible to say that "absence of legal prohibition means freedom". First we should perfect the system by solving the financial and information issues, and then set up relevant rules. Only when the rules are perfected to a certain degree, would it become an unrestricted market system.

Secondly, establishment of financial, investment and financing system. The first thing in the implementation of the Belt and Road Initiative is to interconnect existing infrastructure, which requires a large amount of investment (more than USD 10 trillion). From the view of current financing and investment system, it is difficult to support such a large capital requirement. Just now many think tanks have mentioned some very practical and operational means, including establishing a guarantee platform that meets the guarantee conditions of bank; launching official virtual currencies of the countries along the Belt and Road; opening the stock and bond markets to the countries along the Belt and Road, etc. These means are very effective, which can make certain breakthroughs during the establishment of the financial system.

Thirdly, construction of innovative information and communication platforms. It includes the project information of the countries along the Belt and Road, exchanges related to enterprises, transformation of scientific achievements, and output of Chinese experiences. In the development over the past 30 years, both Chinese private enterprises and foreign enterprises have accumulated plenty of good experience, such as developing the economy by the park model; making products that are affordable to locals; and meeting relatively diverse needs through diversified systems. These are the experience that the countries along the Belt and Road need. Both foreign and private enterprises can learn from such experience, and the government can also take the lead. In terms of personnel training, what we have done in the past is to introduce foreign enterprises to the domestic market. In the future, we will need to cultivate world-oriented talents for the enterprises along the Belt and Road.

Finally, I would like to add my own opinions. Today we are talking about the Belt and Road Initiative. Firstly, who was this "bridgehead" of the Silk Road in the history? It was Chang'an during the Tang Dynasty. Chang'an had a very large influence on Central Asia and other Asian regions at the time. If you go to Japan now, you can still notice some things inherited from the Tang Dynasty, which does not mean that our buildings and roads are more splendid than others. It is more about the influence of soft power. So today, on the basis of hardware construction, we should not neglect the establishment of culture and systems, as well as the connection between us and the culture and systems. Secondly, from the perspective of the future, it is now the version 2.0 of reform and opening up. What will China be like around 2050? What will Shanghai be like? Everyone can let go of imagination, but there is one thing that remains unchanged, that is, current technological changes, including the Internet, artificial intelligence, block chain, etc., must be taken into account proactively in the interconnection under construction. During the development of a city or an economy, we will often overestimate its development within one or two years, while underestimating its development within two or three decades. Therefore, in the current implementation of the Belt and Road Initiative, it is not only necessary to consider the current problems that need to be solved, but also to consider the impact that the future technological revolution will bring us. We need to do something. For example, Yangshan Port has already applied some advanced technologies to establish the world's first unmanned port. There are many such things that can be proactively used in the Belt and Road Initiative.

CONFERENCE REVIEW

峰会综述

1. 目前"一带一路"建设呈现出转型升级的势头

麦肯锡、波士顿和德勤的专家关注到，目前"一带一路"建设正在迅速升级，上海要把握其中的三个重大转变：一是参与主体正在从以政府部门和国企为主向全部经济主体深入参与转变；市场开始发挥重要作用，出现了互联互通的态势。上海社科院和上汽集团的专家指出，完善国企参与"一带一路"的激励机制，用市场经济方式，从考核个别项目转变为考核整体长期效益，政府把精力转移到搭平台、造环境、创条件、减少不稳定性等，这些要求也越来越紧迫。二是具体推进领域正在从单纯商品贸易和产能合作，向提升服务、完善服务标准、品牌、技术和创新等方面转型，推进内容正在进一步拓展和细化。高风咨询的专家认为，目前我国在沿线国家（地区）投资和开展经贸合作的企业主要是有高新技术、创新产品和现代服务能力的企业，完全不同于过去主打低端产品的企业，对贸易服务的质量效益要求也越来越高。三是沿线经贸合作正在突破国家地区范围，出现了跨国跨地区的经济区和自贸区等方面的合作，国内多种经济主体正在"走出去"，开拓境外合作开发的区域。

波士顿、埃森哲、野村和锦江集团的专家认为，上海要发挥"桥头堡"作用，应积极探索多边合作的规则和模式，搭建中国元素与世界经验融合的桥头堡，具体地说，上海应建设完善市场制度和规则的"桥头堡"、数字化的"桥头堡"、人才培养和人文交流的"桥头堡"。

2. 在沪国际智库和国内外企业参与"一带一路"建设的主要诉求

目前，国内外智库已经广泛涉及国内外企业参与的"一带一路"项目，例如，毕马威和安永分别为沿线 100 多个和 800 多个企业项目提供专业服务。专家们概括了市场和企业的具体诉求。一是加强沿线地区的联动协调。上港集团、基仕伯和美中贸易委员会提到，市场普遍希望上海的自由贸易港和外企聚集等优势能与"一带一路"建设在战略上实现联动。奥威科技、上海电力公司的专家提出，国内外企业对加强国内企业中方员工签证、上海铁路融入中欧班列、上海自由贸易港和沿线国家和地区的园区对接、避免恶性竞争等具体问题上的协调，有比较强烈需求。二是加大金融对基础设施建设的支持力度。普华永道和波士顿的专家强调，目前主要依赖多边金融机构贷款的形式，已远不能满足"一带一路"沿线的基础设施融资的需求，国内外企业越来越希望上海改变金融大而不强的状况，提升金融市场和产业服务功能。麦肯锡的专家提到，企业对提供法律仲裁、信用风控等制度性保障的需求日益凸现。三是突破信息壁垒。基仕伯、上海电力公司和西门子的专家认为，缺乏信息渠道和内容已经成为企业有效参与"一带一路"建设的瓶颈与障碍；上海在整合沿线国家和地区的市场信息，搭建更透明及时和有效互动的信息平台，实现信息资源最大化利用上还有很大空间。毕马威的专家特别反映，企业仍难获得沿线国家和地区有关合作文件、法律法规、战略规划和优惠政策信息。根据其《2017 商业信心调查》，欧盟商会的专家提出，约四分之一的欧盟商会会员企业认为与总部和客户之间的信息传递不够畅通。

3. 国际智库与市场主体提出的对策建议

国内外智库和有关企业的专家，根据上海发挥服务国家"一带一路"建设"桥头堡"作用所要求的连通性、前沿性等方面，提出了三个方面的对策建议。

（1）发挥贸易连通枢纽作用，建设首席自由贸易港、超级贸易平台和第三代"服务性港口"。

麦肯锡、埃森哲和波士顿的专家建议，为发挥服务国家"一带一路"建设"桥头堡"作用，上海要根据"首席"和"新"的标准，实现自由与制度的平衡，建设自由贸易港；要基于贸易和金融中心的基础设施和贸易服务能力，打造更加开放、用户导向、相互衔接和可持续拓展的、有新一代数字化贸易生态中心特点的超级贸易平台；要顺应国际贸易由在岸贸易向转口贸易、离岸贸易和期货贸易转变的发展趋势，借鉴新加坡"智慧国家"和"下一代贸易基础设施"计划经验，建设第三代"服务性港口"，实现参与各方更大效率和更低成本。

（2）发挥自贸试验区金融开放的先行先试作用，加快提升上海融资服务能力。

普华永道的专家认为，加快金融和投融资改革，是中国在"一带一路"沿线提升融合力和影响力的关键因素，上海应发挥自贸试验区金融服务实体经济"走出去"的前沿示范作用，加快向沿线国家（地区）和企业开放资本市场（例如发行绿色债和双创债）、沿线优先推进人民币国际化和加速在沿线的金融科技布局（以先进技术手段，推广沿线受益的金融科技优势）。上海市金融办的专家强调，加强资本市场合作，建沿线投融资中心，增强上海吸引全球资金的能力。上海发展研究基金会、上港集团、美中贸易委员会和德勤的专家提出，上海要依托"一带一路"倡议，争取人民币总部业务，在自由贸易港建设人民币离岸中心，率先推进结算和汇兑等金融改革。波士顿、麦肯锡、安永和德勤的专家分别提出了在上海建立"一带一路"沿线跨境虚拟币联盟、符合银行融资条件的项目投资平台、上交所"一带一路"专板和非标金融市场的建议。毕马威和普华永道的专家提出，要加强沿线人民币跨境使用追踪研究。

（3）提升为市场企业参与"一带一路"提供服务的能力。

毕马威、德勤、安永、罗兰贝格、波士顿咨询和上海市商务委的专家建议，上海与沿线和内陆省市建立"东西双向互济"等合作机制、政企合作办事机构和多边建设项目交易市场；为参与"一带一路"的企业，集聚整合政府与市场资源，提供全方位和综合性的规划、建设、信用、投资和信息服务。在"东西双向互济"协作上，要以优势互补、互利共赢、重点突破、市场主导、政府推动为原则，引领和推动内陆省市人才、技术、资金、项目等领域对外交流合作，帮助打开了面向中南亚大门，使内陆省份由开放的末梢转变为前沿。罗兰贝格的专家具体强调，要建立"一带一路"沿线投资贸易项目案例库和加强项目研究，为中外资、中小企业和民企提供经验指导。毕马威的专家建议，帮助企业克服双重纳税和社保金交纳享用等问题，解决企业税务争端，深化"一带一路"沿线城市间税收监管合作要成为上海服务"一带一路"企业的重点。高风咨询的专家认为，在民企从"中国公司"向"世界公司"转变过程中，上海要加强培育民企的国际视野和生态思维，帮助其把握"一带一路"建设机遇。世界银行、野村和安永的专家再次提出，为有利推动"一带一路"倡议，上海要注意控制住房成本、改革户籍居留政策、完善城市规划和依托商务区，形成"兼容、共存的营商环境"，集聚和培育国际化管理人才。

1. The Current Rapid Escalation in Belt and Road Initiative

Experts from Mckinsey & Company, BCG and Deloitte are concerned that the Belt and Road initiative is rapidly escalating during which Shanghai must grasp three major changes: Firstly, the participants are changing from mainly state-owned enterprises to all economic subjects; the market has started to play an important role and produced a situation of interconnection. Experts from Shanghai Academy of Social Sciences and SAIC point out that it is also becoming increasingly urgent to improve the incentive mechanism in participation of the Belt and Road development for SOEs, use the market-oriented economy method to change from evaluating individual projects to evaluate overall long-term benefits. loosen state-owned enterprises up and put down their burden, and shift the government's efforts to building platforms, creating environment and conditions and reducing instability. Secondly, the specific areas to be promoted are being transformed from simply commodity trade and productivity cooperation to service promotion, improvement of service standards, branding, technology and innovation. The contents are being further expanded and refined. Experts from Gao Feng Advisory believe that the enterprises that China invest and corporate with along the Belt and Road initiative are mainly those with high-tech, innovative products and modern service capabilities, a situation completely different from the past when low-end products dominate. The demand for quality and efficiency of trade services is also getting ever higher. Thirdly, the economic and trade cooperation along the initiative is expanding beyond the territory to result in cooperation in terms of cross-border economic zones and free trade zones. Various economic subjects in China are "Going Global" and developing overseas cooperation and development areas.

As stated by experts in BCG, Accenture, Nomura and Jin Jiang Hotel, to fully play the bridgehead role, Shanghai should actively explore modes of multilateral cooperation rules and become the bridgehead of Chinese elements and worldwide experience. Specifically, Shanghai is tasked with building bridgehead for better market system and rules, for digitalization, and for personnel training and humanities exchange.

2. The Key Demands of the International Think Tanks and Enterprises at Home and Abroad in Participating the Belt and Road Initiative

At present, think tanks at home and abroad have extensively involved in the Belt and Road projects of domestic and foreign enterprises. For example, KPMG and Ernst & Young provide professional services for projects of 100 and 800+ enterprises in the B&R countries (regions) respectively. Experts sum up the specific demands of markets and enterprises. The first is to strengthen linkage and coordination along the B&R regions. SIPG, GCP and the U.S.—China Business Council mention the general expectations of markets that the advantages of Shanghai in free trade port and the gathering of foreign enterprises could be strategically linked to the Belt and Road initiative. Experts from Aowei Technology and Shanghai Electric Power point out domestic and international enterprises have strong demands for better coordination of such issues as visas for Chinese employees in domestic enterprises, the integration of Shanghai Railway into the China—EU trains, the connections of parks in the free trade zone and in B&R countries and regions, and the avoidance of vicious competition. The second is to increase financial support for infrastructure construction. Experts from PwC and BCG emphasize that the current reliance on the loans from multilateral financial institutions is far behind the demand for infrastructure financing in B&R countries and regions. Enterprises both at home and abroad increasingly expect Shanghai to change its current status in the financial industry characterized by big size but weak competitiveness, and to improve the service functions in the financial markets and industries. Mckinsey & Company experts mention an increasingly prominent need of enterprises for providing institutional guarantees such as legal arbitration and credit risk control. The third is to break through information barriers. According to experts from GCP, Shanghai Electric Power and Siemens, the lack of information channels and contents has become a major obstacle for enterprises to effectively participate in the Belt and Road initiative; Shanghai has a long way to go toward consolidating market information in B&R countries and regions, establishing a more transparent, timely and effectively interactive information platform, and maximizing information resources. KPMG experts report, in particular, that it is still difficult for enterprises to obtain information on cooperation documents, laws and regulations, strategic planning and preferential policies in the B&R countries. According to its Business Confidence Survey (2017), experts from EU Chamber of Commerce pointed out that about a quarter of US businessmen believe there is an obstacle to information transfer between their headquarters and their customers.

3. Recommendations and Suggestions from International Think Tanks and Market Entities

Experts from domestic and foreign think tanks and related enterprises have put forward three suggestions on connectivity and frontier issues in order to play Shanghai's bridgehead role in the development of the Belt and Road initiative.

(1) Building a principal Free Trade Port, a super trade platform and a third version of service-oriented port to play Shanghai's pivotal role in promoting international trade.

Experts from McKinsey & Company, Accenture and BCG suggest that for Shanghai to play its bridgehead role in the Belt and Road development, it should strike a balance between freedom and system and build a free trade port according to the standard for "principal" and "new". Based on the infrastructure and trade services capabilities of the trade and financial centers, Shanghai should further create a more open, user-oriented, interlinked and sustainable super trade platform which is characterized by a new generation digital trade eco-center. Shanghai should promote the shift of international trade from onshore to re-export and offshore trade. By learning from Singapore's experience with "Smart Nation" and "next-generation trade infrastructure" program, Shanghai will build the third generation "service ports" to achieve greater efficiency and lower costs for all parties involved.

(2) Playing a leading role in the opening up of the financial sector and improving financial services in Shanghai.

PwC experts believe that speeding up reforms in finance and investment & financing is a key factor for China to form soft power in the B&R countries and regions. Shanghai should encourage the financial services and real economy to go global through Shanghai Pilot Free Trade Zone and expedite the opening up of capital markets to B&R countries and enterprises (for instance, by issuing green bonds and innovative startup company bonds), giving priority to the internationalization of RMB and accelerating the layout of finance and technology among the B&R countries (to promote advanced financial technology in order to benefit more B&R countries and regions). Experts from Shanghai Municipal Financial Service Office stress that Shanghai should strengthen its capability to attract global capital through more cooperation in capital market and the establishment of the investment and financing centers in the B&R countries and regions. Experts from Shanghai Development Research Foundation, SIPG, US—China Business Council and Deloitte suggest that Shanghai should rely on the Belt and Road initiative to win RMB headquarters transactions, set up RMB offshore center in the free trade port and lead financial reforms in settlement and exchange. Experts from BCG, McKinsey & Company, Ernst & Young and Deloitte advise establishing a cross-border virtual currency union among the B&R countries in Shanghai, a project investment platform that meets the requirements of bank financing, a special board for the Belt and Road initiative in Shanghai Stock Exchange and a non-standard financial market. Experts from KPMG and PwC propose the need for deeper follow-up research on cross-border RMB usage in B&R countries.

(3) Improving the ability to provide services for markets and enterprises to participate in the Belt and Road initiative.

Experts from KPMG, Deloitte, Ernst & Young, Roland Berger, BCG and Shanghai Municipal Commission of Commerce propose that Shanghai should establish cooperation mechanisms such as " the two-way mutual benefits between the East and the West" with B&R countries and other inland provinces and cities, and set up offices for cooperation between government and enterprises and multilateral construction project trading markets. Shanghai should gather and integrate government market resources, and provide all-round, comprehensive planning, building, credit, investment and information services for enterprises involving in the Belt and Road initiative. The East and the West should be complementary, make breakthroughs in the key points, and strengthen market-oriented cooperation promoted by the local government for the two-way mutual benefits between the East and the West. Shanghai should lead and promote the exchanges and cooperation in terms of talent, technology, funds, and projects in inland provinces and cities, and help accelerate the opening up of the inland provinces to South and Central Asia. Roland Berger experts emphasize the creation of database of project cases in B&R countries to provide experience guidance for Chinese and foreign-funded enterprises, small and medium-sized enterprises and private enterprises. KPMG experts suggest that Shanghai should focus on helping enterprises overcome double taxation and social security benefits, resolve tax disputes among enterprises, and deepen cooperation in tax supervision and administration among cities which are the focus of Shanghai's efforts in the Belt and Road Initiative. Gao Feng Advisory Company experts believe that in the process of transforming private enterprises from "Chinese companies" to "world companies", Shanghai should step up its efforts to foster the international perspective and ecological thinking of private enterprises and help them grasp the strategic opportunities brought about by the Belt and Road initiative. Expects from The World Bank, Nomura Research Institute and Ernst & Young restate that in order to facilitate the Belt and Road initiative, Shanghai should control and lower the housing cost, reform the household registration and residence policies, improve urban planning and base itself on commercial areas, forming a "compatible and coexisting environment" to pool and cultivate international management talents.

RESEARCH PAPERS

研究成果

全球金融治理和"一带一路"建设

乔依德

上海发展研究基金会副会长兼秘书长

"一带一路"建设既是我国进一步对外开放的平台,也是继续推进经济全球化的重要平台。它的主要内容可以用"五通"来概括,即:政策沟通、设施联通、贸易畅通、资金融通和民心相通。就像血液给人体带来了氧气和营养,资金融通也给整个"一带一路"建设带来了活力和养分,所以它是"一带一路"建设不可或缺的重要组成部分。

资金融通涉及各方面的问题。例如,资金从哪里来? 如何筹集? 什么金融机构来运作? 资金通向哪个领域? 这些跨境的资金应该如何监测和管理? 资金应该以什么货币计价和结算? 对资金流入国的国际收支会有什么影响? 这些问题都不是孤立的,都与一个更大的金融框架有关,也就是跟国际货币金融体系相关。因为构成这个体系的规章制定、机构设置和制度安排等无不直接或间接地规定了解决上述问题的政策、方法和途径。

二战以后,布雷顿森林会议建立了以解决国际收支问题为宗旨的国际货币基金组织(IMF)和以提供开发援助为宗旨的世界银行,同时以金汇兑形式确立了美元的主导地位。虽然在 20 世纪 20 年代初,美元与黄金挂钩、其他货币与美元挂钩的双挂钩金融安排已经破局。但是美元占主导地位的局面并未改变。应该承认,这样一个全球货币金融体系对于战后全球经济贸易的发展,对于推动经济全球化是起了积极作用的。但是同时,我们也应看到,它也存在着一些缺陷。例如,发展中国家代表性不足、防止金融风险能力不够、包容性缺乏等。在全球金融危机以后,各国和国际经济界进行了一系列努力,旨在改善全球金融治理,消除或减缓上述种种缺陷。例如,G20 在 2010 年峰会上通过了 IMF 份额和治理改革。经过曲折和反复,该方案终于在 2015 年得到了实施,包括中国在内的发展中国家的投票权有所增加,但这是远远不够的。特别是,该体系的根本缺陷,即:一国的主权货币充当了全球的信用货币,并未得到改变。该国货币当局(美联储)只会从本国经济需要出发来决定货币政策,这样的政策有可能与全球的经济需要产生冲突。这也是造成全球金融危机的深层次原因。

资金融通是"一带一路"建设本身所要求的。首先,"一带一路"倡议的重心是基础设施建设,沿线国家对于基础设施投资有着巨大的需求,而"一带一路"途经国家多为发展中国家,大多没有充足的国内储蓄,不能解决基础设施投资所需的资金。根据亚洲开发银行预测,未来 10 年,亚洲基础设施投资需要8.22 万亿美元,即每年需要新增投入 8 200 亿美元基础设施资金。其次,"一带一路"也引发了巨大的产能合作融资需求,为我国企业"走出去"、产业转型升级创造了机会。再次,"一带一路"倡议还衍生了其他融资相关需求,包括与沿线国家金融机构开展金融合作、金融产品创新等方面的需求。

如此大规模的跨境融资需求其本身就有进一步完善全球金融治理的动因,同时它又为进一步改善全球金融治理提供了一个新的机会。随着经济全球化过程,在过去一二十年,包括中国在内的发展中国家有了很大的发展,它们对全球经济增长的贡献已经达到 70%。为了打破这样一种经济格局和现有国际金融机构话语权的不对称,产生了一系列新的国际金融机构,如亚投行、金砖发展银行、应急储备安排(CRA)等。它们可以在"一带一路"当中发挥非常积极的作用。在这个过程中,这些新的金融机构本身也能得到发展、增强和提高。这样对现在的国际金融机构是一个很好的补充和有力的促进,能够使国际货币金融体系趋向更为公平、更有包容性。

在资金融通中涉及资金结算的问题。现在"一带一路"沿线一些国家已经开始使用本币结算。这就减少了对美元的过分依赖,有利于减缓外部的金融冲击。这样的货币多极化既反映了客观需要,同时也可能是全球货币体系演变的趋势。一般认为,在中期(15—20 年以后)很可能会出现三足鼎立的储备货币,也就是美元、欧元和人民币为主要储备货币的体系。

"一带一路"的资金融通的巨大需求也会扩大人民币的跨境使用。2016 年 10月,人民币正式纳入 SDR 篮子,提高了人民币的国际地位。IMF 最新公布的数据显示,以人民币计价的外汇储备资产已经达到 845.1 亿美元,占全球外汇储备资产的 1.07%。尽管比例不大,但已经有了很好的起点。随着"一带一路"建设的进一步开展,人民币进一步跨境使用也是指日可待的。历史有时会给人们一些启示,尽管布雷顿森林体系确立了美元的主导地位,但这个主导地位真正起作用却主要是由于马歇尔计划的推动。毫无疑问,"一带一路"建设和马歇尔计划的本质是完全不同的,但这也是一个跨国的经济计划,有可能为人民币国际化创造更好的条件。

"一带一路"建设使沿线国家,特别是发展中国家受益。"一带一路""五通"

的实现有利于提高它们的经济实力，使它们的金融市场更加完善，经济更有韧性，更能抵御外部冲击，从而对稳定全球金融体系起到积极作用。

上面讲了"一带一路"建设会有利于全球金融治理改革，反过来，全球金融治理改革又将推动"一带一路"建设。现在 IMF 正在进行第十五次份额评估，预期发展中国家投票权和发言权将会进一步增加。另外，金融危机以后，作为改革全球金融治理的一个重要部分，现在正在加强全球金融安全网建设。全球金融安全网包括自我保险（储备资产）、双边融资机制（央行货币互换）、区域融资安排（RFA）和 IMF 多边融资机制五个部分，IMF 在其中起到主导作用。去年 IMF 与清迈协议进行了第一次防风险的操练，这将加强 IMF 与 RFA 之间的合作。全球金融安全网的加强对"一带一路"的资金融通起到了保护网的作用。最近，国际金融界对跨境资金的监测和管理给予高度重视，这也可说是全球金融治理的一个部分。跨境资本包括 FDI、证券投资和其他投资。其中，FDI 对接受国是非常有利的，同时它对利率变化的敏感度比较小。在其他两部分中，也有一些长期的超过一年以上的融资，对利率变化也不敏感。去除这部分的资金以后，我们可以把剩下部分定义为会快速移动的资本（QMC）。它们对发展中国家的冲击比较大，需要给予足够的重视。正像周小川行长在两会的新闻发布会上把资金分成实体性的投资和金融性的资金流动。对跨境资本的进一步分类、监测和管理无疑将会有利于"一带一路"中的资金融通。

总而言之，就其本质而言，全球金融治理结构改革和"一带一路"建设是可以相互促进的。关键在于我们应该认识到这一点，并以市场为基础的政策主动引导两者相互促进，共同获利。

上海长江经济带"龙头"和"一带一路"建设"桥头"的耦合效应分析

李延均　郑　义

上海立信会计金融学院"一带一路"研究院

1. 引言

党的十九大报告将"促进我国产业迈向全球价值链中高端，培育若干世界级先进制造业集群"作为贯彻新发展理念，建设现代化经济体系的重要目标和任务之一。上海作为长江经济带的"龙头"和服务国家"一带一路"建设的"桥头堡"则是完成前述国家任务的重要载体。上海地处长江入海口，居龙头之位，通江达海，交通区位得天独厚，是长江经济带中经济活动最密集、经济效益最高、对外开放程度最高的城市。其作为长江经济带的"龙头"和服务国家"一带一路"建设的"桥头（堡）"的双重使命，在国家对外开放的大格局及长江经济带"东中西联动"中具有举足轻重的战略地位。

"一带一路"倡议提出前，黄金水道一路向东，上海无疑是域内经济"龙头"和外向经济"桥头"；"一带一路"倡议提出后，《长江经济带发展规划纲要》明确指出，要打造长江经济带三大增长极，推行长江经济带首尾两端的开发开放（即上海对外海运走廊、成渝城市群向西的中欧经济走廊）战略，龙头还是龙头，龙尾业已成为"豹尾"。势必弱化上海对长江经济带其他城市的辐射，威胁其龙头地位，也可能会冲击上海作为开放的前哨，渐趋淡化其桥头功能。作为双重角色叠加的上海如何做到1+1>2? 如何做到"两头"都要强，最大限度地减少两者间的对冲效应，实现龙头和桥头的耦合效应，业已成为决策者和学界亟待解决的课题。

基于此，本文以"耦合"为切入点，剖析"桥头"对冲"龙头"的制约机制，理清"龙头"耦合"桥头"的内在机理，提出通过龙头企业、"链主"企业及成熟的金融市场来实现耦合效应的路径与对策。

2. "桥头"对冲"龙头"的机理

上海作为服务国家"一带一路"建设的"桥头堡"，充分体现国家战略，有着强烈的政治担当。但是要把服务国家"一带一路"建设与"四个中心"、上海自贸试验区建设等国家战略有机整合，发挥战略叠加效应，是一项考验决策层智慧的新课题。

一方面，上海作为对外开放的前哨，除了要巩固传统的东南亚、中西亚等"老朋友"之外，上海还要善于开创结识"新伙伴"。要率先打开湄澜流域、孟加拉湾及欧盟市场，使上海成为我国向东对外开放的桥头堡，形成货物和服务贸易同步、国际和国内市场相互融通的发展格局，成为连接长江流域腹地和国际市场的枢纽节点。以更好地服务于其长江经济带中的"龙头"地位。

另一方面，上海在海外市场激活以后，攻城略地，需"守成"海外市场，以"桥头"壮大"龙头"。但是由于拥有"龙头"经济地位的上海没有匹配性的"龙头"企业，结局可能演变成上海搭台唱戏，中西部坐收门票。笔者认为，上海作为服务国家"一带一路"建设的"桥头堡"，承担对外开放的前哨，会在一定程度上弱化其对长江经济带中其他城市的辐射作用，威胁到其"龙头"地位，甚至出现"桥头"与"龙头"相悖的情形。

机制如下："一带一路"建设的"桥头堡"功能趋强→对外开放升级→中西部城市中高端需求外流→弱化上海对中西部城市的辐射→上海"龙头"地位下降，阻滞长江经济带产业升级。

3. "龙头"加固"桥头"的机制

长江经济带有群有带，条中嵌块，串块成带。长江经济带中的大、中、小城市以其在条带中的差异化功能和个性化服务，布局合理，天然一体。城市间一体化程度较高，空间分布上相对集中，业已形成以分工、协作、共享为特征的世界第六大城市发展命运共同体。

上海作为长江经济带这一世界级城市群的中枢，集现代工业职能、商业金融职能、外贸门户职能和文化先导职能于一身。上海不仅要凸显其长三角的"龙头"功能，而且要发挥中心城市的辐射作用，以"龙头"加固"桥头"。龙头地位是关键，桥头功能是结果，两者间双向因果制约。

机制如下：上海作为长江经济带的"龙头"地位凸显→聚焦制造业中的资

本、技术密集环节，以其产品内分工的链条地位实现功能升级和结构优化→与中西部城市精准定位，良性竞争，从产业内分工、产品内分工走向工序分工，依据各自资源禀赋优势和历史文化传统等因素协同推进，错位发展→渐次实现梯队升级→中西部城市对上海的中高端需求扩大→倒逼上海以其高端人才云集、科研院所密集和先行先试的政策优势，增强上海消化吸收国际前沿技术的能力，同时驱动上海原创技术创新和成果转化→加固上海作为国家一带一路建设中"桥头堡"的地位。

4."桥头"耦合"龙头"的路径

就经济总量而言，上海作为世界第六大城市群和长经济带中最重要的增长极毋庸置疑，但是就细分的产业而言，上海不具有极强比较优势的产业，从数据上看，具有较强比较优势的产业主要是服装、纺织、机械和运输设备制造业（这三个产业的 RCA 指数都大于 1），显而易见，上海在国际贸易中处于比较优势地位的主要还是劳动密集型产业，这与期望中的"四个中心"还有不少差距。一句话，上海有经济"龙头"地位，但是其拥有的龙头企业、"链主"企业十分匮乏，基础设施、交通枢纽、城市规模等硬件自不待言，但是在当下能真正体现出城市竞争力的软实力，上海还有漫长的路要走。基于前述"桥头"对冲"龙头"的机理以及"龙头"加固"桥头"的机制分析，笔者认为"桥头"耦合"龙头"的路径有三个层面：

首先，"龙头"城市需要"龙头"企业。"龙头"企业应该是世界级的龙头企业，在先进制造业所涵盖的各行业中处于领先地位。不仅要求其产出、资产等总体规模指标要在全世界细分行业中排名前列，而且要求其利润、技术、品牌等绩效指标要居于全世界同行业的领先水平。因此，要完全靠自身力量培育这么多的"龙头"企业不现实，我们要从地理区位、政策红利等角度大力引进世界级的"龙头"企业，首先争取设立"龙头"企业分公司，进而积极引进设立"龙头"企业的研发、营销等关键职能部门，最终实现"龙头"企业落户上海，近似总部经济。

其次，积极培育"链主"企业。改革开放 40 年来，国内企业通过加入西方跨国公司主导的全球价值链获得了成长的机会，甚至有些企业攀升到了全球价值链的最高端，成为"链主"企业。但是大多数企业在向全球价值链向中高端攀升过程中，均不同程度地遭遇到天花板。不仅会遭遇西方国家"链主"企业的"狙击"，甚至被后者所俘获。基于此，本土企业必须充分利用长江经济带以及整个国家庞大的内需市场，主动构建自身主导的国家价值链，成长为"链主式"企业，始于服务国内市场出发，逐步拓展到海外市场，最终成长为全新的全球价值链。要充分利用长江经济带的现有产业基础，重点培育电子信息、高端装备、汽车、家电、纺织服装这 5 大世界级制造业集群。

最后，规范金融市场，落实金融服务于实体经济。金融市场的完善也能够同时助推我国产业迈向全球价值链的中高端和培育世界级先进制造业集群。这种同时助推作用之所以能够实现，其理论支撑是完善的金融市场能在本土"链主式"企业的快速成长过程中扮演无法替代的重要作用。

世界经济发展历史也表明，制造业发达的国家必然有与之相适应的完善的金融市场体系，健全的金融市场会显著降低企业的融资难度和成本。也只有完善的金融市场才会发现这些潜在的"龙头"企业和"链主"企业，向其配置金融资源，为其从幼稚阶段逐步走向快速成长阶段及成熟阶段。世界级先进制造业集群的培育过程中，一方面，完善的金融市场会加速"链主式"企业和"龙头"企业的壮大，为其构建自身主导的国家价值链和全球价值链提供源源不断的金融资源支撑，另一方面，完善的金融市场还会直接服务于全球价值链上的一系列支撑企业和相关企业，促进其与"链主式"企业共同壮大。

做好自由贸易港离岸人民币业务
服务"一带一路"建设

丁剑平

上海财经大学上海国际金融中心研究院

1. 离岸金融业务将予以自由贸易港更大的创新空间

上海在全力推进自贸试验区和科创中心建设两项国家战略，初步体现了当好排头兵、先行者的要求。上海是全国最大的金融中心，汇聚着所有的金融市场。在开放和监管方面已经积累了大量的数据和经验，最早就提出了"放得最开、管得最细、服务最精准"方向。一直在以有效的"管"保障有力的"放"，突出服务在前的理念。自贸区核心任务是制度创新。来降低企业的成本，已有 100 多项创新制度在全国推广。作为自贸区的延伸的自由贸易港更是将全球产业链中的物流环节掌控住，同时将在金融上予以支持。

党的十九大报告提出"赋予自由贸易试验区更大的改革自主权，探索建设自由贸易港"。自由贸易港是指在国家与地区境内、海关管理关卡之外的，允许境外货物、资金自由进出的港口区。除了货物贸易在"一线"不缴纳关税和其他进出口税之外，尝试资金自由进出将是提升其活力的关键所在（见表 1）。外汇和投资管理便利、与自由贸易相关的贸易金融、航运金融、外汇支付结算等配套措施也要相继跟上。其中离岸金融政策创新将是改革空间所在。

表 1　上海自由贸易港在金融领域可以探索的方面

领　域	上海自由贸易港（目前）	全球自由贸易港
资本市场开放	尚未完全开放，虽然有了"沪港通"，再冲刺"沪伦通"。	完全开放：开立买卖证券账户就可以随时交易；债券市场流动性强。
对外融资自由度	还有额度限制存在。	不仅对借贷没有额度限制，还提供特色服务。
货币自由兑换	还有额度和目的限制存在。	完全取消外汇管制。
全方位的金融服务	正在协调各种金融要素市场之中。	可提供全方位保险、结算、融资租赁、项目融资服务。

2. "效率第一"是自由贸易港离岸人民币业务的特征

由于目前人民币在资本项目下仍受到严格管制，上海自贸区在融资便利、汇兑自由、人民币跨境使用、放开利率、外汇管制等方面还需要进一步放开，逐步推动金融创新，同时要做好金融机构监管和金融风险防范工作。自由贸易港在金融领域的"试水"也将涉及融资汇兑自由、资金进出自由、贸易结算自由和金融服务发达。

自由贸易港可作为离岸人民币业务的突破口，通过全球产业链的"咽喉"（物流环节），为中国在对"一带一路"等对外投资中提供全面的买方信贷、项目融资、杠杆收购、资金结算等多种金融服务（见图1）。可以获得"纲举目张"的效果。通过制度创新，通过产品创新、服务创新、组织创新来推动离岸市场和在岸市场的协调发展。区别与自贸区人民币离岸业务，自由贸易港的人民币离岸业务更加突出"效率第一"。

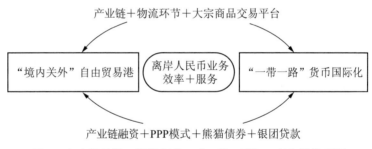

图1 自由贸易港—离岸金融—"一带一路"三者之间关系图

自由贸易港金融的特点就是"效率"，能够最快的满足各类机构和个人的投融资需求，向他们提供最佳的时间匹配的"量体裁衣"结构创新产品。评级机构和各类资产管理机构的专业化组合提供投融资便利和一站式金融服务。也就是金融产品与各类（税务、保险等）服务"打包"（见表2）。非居民的金融业务一定与离岸人民币业务高度相关。此外，自由贸易港金融还涉及为客户编制预算、短期和长期规划、现金收入和支付、债务管理、固定资产、内外审计、采购、财务申报等。为此要满足上述金融要素和制度创新要优先进入自由贸易港。"打包"（捆绑式）产品必然要与非居民的离岸人民币业务牵连在一起。离岸人民币业务势必涉及流动性和衍生品的协同。其中在岸人民币在期限种类上以及离岸人民币在规模上还有许多可以"探索"的事情。就目前来说，两个市场都有其"短板"。

表 2　离岸金融可以"打包"服务的环节

服务大类	具体服务细节
税收服务	个人、商务、公司、工资单、会计、E申请、国别和区域等
私人保险服务	车辆、家庭、生命、健康、房车、承租、助动车、船只等
商务服务	商业地产、债务、工人团体、团体健康、退休金等
老年服务	补充医疗保险、维权、最终费用、急救护理、预先计划等

而上述"打包"（捆绑式）产品必然要与非居民的离岸人民币业务牵连在一起。离岸人民币业务势必涉及流动性和衍生品的协同。就目前来说在岸与离岸人民币市场的流动性和衍生品现状如表 3。

其中在岸人民币在期限种类上以及离岸人民币在规模上还有许多可以"探索"的事情。两个市场都有"短板"。

表 3　人民币离岸可交割、离岸无本金交割远期及在岸可交割市场的流动性情况

	离岸人民币市场	离岸 NDF 市场	在岸人民币市场
外汇现货			
期限	现货（T+2 交割）	无	T+2 value spot
日内交易量（十亿美元）	2—3	无	20—50
单位交易规模（百万美元）	5—15	无	10—20
外汇远期			
期限	O/N-12m，18m，24m	T/N-12m	O/N-2y
日内交易量（亿美元）	3—5	4—5	6—10
单位交易规模（百万美元）	0.1	10—50	7—10
外汇期权			
期限	O/N-2y	O/N-3y	O/N-2y
日内交易量（百万美元）	70—300	250—300	1400—2000
单位交易规模（百万美元）	10—20	50	20—30

3. 自由贸易港离岸业务有助于"一带一路"的人民币国际化

上海金融市场如何支持"一带一路"？就目前来说，股市"沪港通"如何拓展到"沪伦通"？离岸债券市场如何扩大"熊猫债"的规模？上海银行业如何创新"银团贷款"？离岸人民币市场的扩容是不可避免的一环。中国朝着更加开放

方向前进，而离岸人民币的扩容对人民币汇率稳定是否会产生冲击？2015年至2017年初中国确实是通过对离岸人民币的流动性调节来避免其对在岸人民币汇率的冲击。而今后如何避免两者之间的矛盾？一边要扩容人民币离岸产品，一边要维持人民币汇率的稳定。然而对外开放将以更大的步伐向前迈步。离岸人民币规模扩大是无疑的。靠通过离岸人民币流动性控制来稳定人民币汇率的方法不可持续。

解决这一矛盾的焦点是金融监管的精准定位。上海自贸试验区账户在新时期要在功能和规模上提升。随着大数据和科技金融创新，新型支付结算方式与账户都有"创新空间"。上海各个金融产品交易平台账户（身份）与海关商品编码HS二分位数/四分位数细分行业如何匹配？更加精准监管与上海自由贸易港的"境内关外"（一线放开，二线管住）结合。海关保税区、全球物流是生产与消费的环节。物流金融是未来上海创新的空间。涉外自由贸易港"开放与监管"的核心还是自由贸易账户的拓展，上海自贸试验区账户在全国各个自贸区推进还在止步不前。主要原因还是资金池的规模不大，对企业来说实施成本较高。效率较低。资金调拨滞后时间偏长。这些问题将随着自由贸易港的离岸业务的创新解决。

"一带一路"的倡议将进一步促进沿线各国与中国的经济贸易往来，构造人民币在"一带一路"沿线区域的货币区网络外部性，提高人民币在这些区域国际贸易和国际金融的"货币锚"地位，这将会是人民币国际化过程中关键性的一步。国际货币体系中理想货币锚的根本作用在于降低一国及世界贸易和金融往来中交易费用的潜在能力，对于锚货币国而言，本国的海外贸易、投资汇兑风险也能大幅降低。

"一带一路"沿线还有不少国家的汇率管制较为严格，外汇市场不发达，中国企业主体的经营收支或出口收支如果以当地货币为主，企业可能很难利用当地金融市场来对冲汇率风险，在"一带一路"建设中的作用充分发挥人民币本币的作用有现实需求。为降低企业面临的汇率风险，中国在"一带一路"国家推进实施货币直接交易，并与沿线国家实行货币的区域直接交易。人民银行还与相关国家货币当局开展了包括本币互换、人民币清算等在内的一系列合作机制安排。在自由贸易港推进离岸人民币业务将有助于上述目的的实现。本文发现：跨国的加工贸易和产业链重组可能让区域参照货币出现新特征（见表4）。表现在独联体对人民币汇率参照的极为显著和东盟对人民币参照的不显著。为此还需以更新的视角去分析。

表 4　本文对"一带一路"国家地区货币与人民币的关系研究面板样本

所属区域	国　　家	国家数量
北亚	蒙古	1
东南亚	新加坡、马来西亚、印度尼西亚、缅甸、泰国、老挝、柬埔寨、越南、文莱、菲律宾	10
南亚	印度、巴基斯坦、孟加拉国、阿富汗、斯里兰卡、马尔代夫、尼泊尔、不丹	8
西亚北非	伊朗、伊拉克、土耳其、叙利亚、约旦、以色列、埃及、沙特阿拉伯、巴林、卡塔尔、也门、阿曼、阿拉伯联合酋长国、科威特、黎巴嫩、塞浦路斯	16
中亚	哈萨克斯坦、乌兹别克、土库曼、塔吉克、吉尔吉斯	5
独联体国家	俄罗斯、乌克兰、白俄罗斯、格鲁吉亚、阿塞拜疆、亚美尼亚、摩尔多瓦	7
中东欧	爱沙尼亚、拉脱维亚、立陶宛、捷克、匈牙利、波兰、斯洛文尼亚、克罗地亚、黑山、塞尔维亚、阿尔巴尼亚、罗马尼亚、保加利亚、马其顿王国、斯洛伐克、比利时	16

"一带一路"货币是否参照人民币的研究结论如下：

首先，市场规模决定货币参照权重。随着中国经济的发展，"一带一路"国家总体上增加了参照人民币汇率的波动权重（也就是相对降低了其对 SDR 的其他货币的份额）。但这还远远不能撼动美元和欧元的地位。尤其各国对巨大的美国市场的依赖是绝对的，压倒一切的。这不是随着地理距离远近和政治关系好坏来改变的。国际贸易中的"引力模型"难以解释这类现象。

其次，历史痕迹难以抹去。原来殖民地货币参照宗主国货币、货币集团的影子还继续存在，表现在南亚国家 8 国（印度、巴基斯坦、孟加拉国、阿富汗、斯里兰卡、马尔代夫、尼泊尔、不丹）对英镑参照的权重还是显著的。前苏联（独联体国家诸如乌克兰、白俄罗斯、格鲁吉亚、阿塞拜疆、亚美尼亚、摩尔多瓦）对卢布的参照在统计上依然显著。

再次，要获取大宗商品的定价权。那些大宗商品用美元定价的国家（诸如伊朗、伊拉克、叙利亚、约旦、埃及、沙特阿拉伯、巴林、卡塔尔、也门、阿曼、阿拉伯联合酋长国、科威特等）很难摆脱对参照美元的依赖。此外，它们对主要石油消费国货币的参照多数也是显著的。

最后，跨国的加工贸易和产业链重组可能让区域参照货币出现新特征。表现在独联体对人民币汇率参照的极为显著和东盟对人民币参照的不显著。为此还需以更新的视角去分析。

上海自贸试验区建设"一带一路"海外投资风险管理中心的思考[*]

尹 晨

复旦大学上海自贸区综合研究院

海外投资风险管理日益成为"一带一路"战略推进中的痛点和难点问题。建设"一带一路"桥头堡是上海自贸试验区的重要战略任务。上海自贸试验区可以结合其战略定位和自身优势,以建设"一带一路"投资风险管理中心为突破口,推进"一带一路"桥头堡建设。

1. 引言

2013 年,习近平主席在中亚和东南亚进行国事访问期间,提出共同建设"丝绸之路经济带"和"21 世纪海上丝绸之路"的倡议,拉开了"一带一路"建设的序幕。2015 年,由国家发展改革委、外交部、商务部联合发布的《推动共建丝绸之路经济带和 21 世纪海上丝绸之路的愿景与行动》,标志着"一带一路"建设进入全面推进的崭新局面。2017 年 5 月,习近平主席在"一带一路"国际合作高峰论坛上发表重要讲话,指出在过去的 4 年,"一带一路"倡议已取得重大进展,今后将继续围绕建设"和平之路、繁荣之路、开放之路、创新之路、文明之路"的重点积极部署各项工作。

"一带一路"沿线国家和地区大多经济水平相对落后,投资需求巨大,但国内金融市场发展相对滞后、投融资能力不强,因此对海外投资的需求较大。在整体加快"走出去"的大背景下,中国企业积极参与"一带一路"建设,海外投资不断增加。据商务部统计,2013 年,中国企业共对"一带一路"沿线国家

---

* 本文是国家社科项目"中国(上海)自由贸易试验区先行先试与经验复制推广研究",上海市政府决策咨询课题"美国退出 TPP 后上海自贸试验区深化发展研究",上海市社科规划系列课题"新形势下进一步提升上海自贸试验区开放度研究",以及上海高校智库内涵建设计划项目的阶段性成果。

直接投资 134 亿美元；2014 年为 125 亿美元；2015 年达到 148 亿美元，同比增长 18%。截至 2016 年末，中国企业已经在"一带一路"沿线 20 多个国家建立了 56 个经贸合作区，累计投资超过 185 亿美元，为东道国增加了近 11 亿美元的税收和 18 万个就业岗位[①]。中国企业对"一带一路"沿线的海外投资有效促进了"一带一路"倡议的深入推进。

但我们也要看到，"一带一路"沿线的海外投资在经历前段时间持续增长后，2016 年后有所波动。2016 年，中国企业对"一带一路"沿线国家直接投资 145 亿美元，同比下滑 2%。[②]2017 年 1—3 月，我国企业共对"一带一路"沿线的直接投资 29.5 亿美元，同比下降 17.8%。[③] 这一方面是由于国际经济形势不确定性提高后，中国对资本流出实施了越来越严厉的管制；另一方面，中国企业在"走出去"过程中遭遇或认识到越来越多的风险也是重要原因。越来越多的中国企业认识到了海外投资风险管理的重要性和紧迫性。

2017 年 3 月末，国务院发布《全面深化中国（上海）自由贸易试验区改革开放方案》（以下简称《全面深改方案》），开启上海自贸试验区 3.0 版新篇章。方案中明确要求上海自贸试验区应"成为服务国家'一带一路'建设、推动市场主体走出去的桥头堡"。上海自贸试验区担当"一带一路"桥头堡，就需要充分发挥上海的优势，集中力量解决国家"一带一路"战略实施过程中的痛点和难点问题。服务国家战略，依托上海优势，上海自贸试验区可以以构建"一带一路"投资风险管理中心为突破口，推进上海自贸试验区"一带一路"桥头堡的建设。

2. "一带一路"海外投资风险及其管理的现状分析

（1）"一带一路"海外投资风险现状。

根据美国企业研究所和传统基金会的统计，2005 年 1 月至 2014 年 6 月，中国企业海外投资发生在"一带一路"沿线国家和地区的风险案例共 33 起（占同期全部海外投资风险案例总数的 25.4%），涉及金额 565.2 亿美元（占同期全部海外投资风险案例涉及金额的 24.0%），涉及 20 个国家，每起案例平均涉案金额 17.1 亿美元。[④] 从以上案例情况来看，中国企业海外投资风险在"一

---

① 数据源自商务部网站。

② 数据来源：《2016 年中国企业对"一带一路"沿线国家非金融类直接投资 145.3 亿美元》中商情报网 2017 年 2 月 15 日。

③ 数据源自商务部网站。

④ 数据来源：李锋，《"一带一路"沿线国家的投资风险与应对策略》，《中国流通经济》，2016 年第 2 期，第 115—121 页。

带一路"沿线的东南亚、南亚、西亚、中亚、中东欧等地区都有发生。结合中国现代关系研究院李伟主编的《"一带一路"沿线国家安全风险地图》，"一带一路"沿线的东南亚、南亚、西亚、中亚、独联体等地区国家综合安全风险较高。

进一步来看，"一带一路"沿线海外投资风险的主要特点是各种风险交织重叠，组合风险高。"一带一路"沿线的风险种类繁多，既包括宏观的政治风险、经济风险、金融风险、宗教风险、法律风险、环境风险、社会风险、传统和非传统的安全风险等，也包括微观的贯穿事前事中事后的项目运营风险、管理风险、财务风险等。上述风险还往往交织重叠在一起，增加了风险的复杂性。

"一带一路"沿线国家沿线政治、种族、宗教等各类环境复杂，在高风险地区，政治、经济、社会等宏观风险同时存在并相互交叉。比如中东地区，战乱破坏、宗教冲突、恐怖主义等风险因素交织，诱发一系列宏观风险，导致国家总体风险系数高。

宏观风险和微观风险也往往交织组合。由于语言、宗教、文化、习惯等方面的差异，同时受东道国教育、制度、市场发育等因素限制，中资企业海外投资项目往往在公司治理模式、员工的本地化、激励和约束机制等方面存在较大的磨合问题；受制于经济和金融发展程度，中资企业海外投资项目在资金融通、风险分散等方面也缺乏更多的选择；受制于制度、市场和信息透明度，中资企业海外投资项目在进行市场调研、可行性分析时也会遭遇诸多障碍；而项目运营风险、财务风险管理不善或处理失误，又可能与宗教、社会乃至政治风险叠加，可能演变加剧成公共事件，难以挽回。

以下两个典型案例可以充分说明"一带一路"风险的组合特性。

中国海外工程有限责任公司（简称中海外）2009年中标承建波兰A2高速公路A、C标段。项目中标后遭遇组合风险。首先是宏观经济风险，筹建期间国际和欧洲经济形势改善，包括钢材、沥青、沙子等原材料价格不断上涨，导致建造成本不断提高；其次是管理风险，中海外为开拓欧洲市场，急于求成，以政府预算一半的报价中标，项目推进中中波双方工作人员因语言障碍而导致工作效率低下；第三是环境风险，中海外未考虑到项目建设将穿越的波兰自然保护区，在实际施工时因建设便于珍稀动物转移的多处通道而必须提高建造成本。2011年中海外被迫放弃该项目，并承担1.885亿欧元的赔偿。

中国万宝矿业有限公司与缅甸联邦经济控股公司合作开发的缅甸莱比塘铜矿在2012年3月开工后不久就因抗议事件而停工，于2015年1月复工、2016年3月投产。在项目建设中，中资企业遭遇系列风险，包括：环境风险，为应对破坏环境的指控，项目公司预提基金用于矿坑回填和生态恢复工作；经济风险，为应对村民和抗议者在征地补偿、就业安置、移民搬迁等反面的指控，项目公司提高了相应的标准；宗教风险，项目公司追加投资对矿山区域内的佛教遗址进行了保护；政治风险，项目建设期间缅甸恰逢政局动荡，抗议事件起初由一些村民不满土地补偿金而引发，此后随着外部政治势力的不断介入，整个事件成为缅甸不同政治势力角力的舞台，导致停工期不断延长。

事实上，中国企业"一带一路"在海外投资遭遇的风险，大多数都具有组合风险的特点。

（2）"一带一路"海外投资风险管理现状。

我国在"一带一路"海外投资风险管理层面的建设正处于起步阶段。

中国正全面推进与"一带一路"国家高水平自贸区（FTA）网络的建设，努力为贸易和投资提供双边或多边政策和规则保护。截至 2017 年 8 月 1 日，中国与"一带一路"沿线国家和地区签署了 4 个 FTA，分别为中国—格鲁吉亚、中国—巴基斯坦、中国—新加坡 FTA 和中国—东盟升级版 FTA，此外 7 个 FTA（包括升级版）正在谈判，4 个 FTA 正在研究。中国正在大力推进区域全面经济伙伴关系（RCEP）的谈判。

在重大海外投资项目出现风险时，中国政府也采取了外交手段加以干预，比如希腊比雷埃夫斯港项目、缅甸莱比塘铜矿项目等。商务部、外交部、中国驻"一带一路"国家和地区的使领馆、智库都开始定期发布"一带一路"沿线国家和地区的国情、经济、金融、贸易、投资等信息，并定期发布"一带一路"国别风险报告。

中国牵头组建的亚洲基础设施开发银行、金砖国家新开发银行、丝路基金、中俄投资基金、中国—中东欧基金，以及国家开发银行等单边或多边开发性金融机构已经成立并开始介入"一带一路"的投融资。中国出口信用保险公司提供包括政治风险保险在内的海外投资保险业务。

越来越多的中国企业也开始认识到了海外投资风险管理的重要性和紧迫性。越来越多的企业开始利用咨询和中介服务开展尽职调查，加强对项目的风险评估；采取产业链合作的方式或加入国际产能合作区，与其他企业"抱团出海"；采取更切合所在国实际的企业治理模式，提高本土化比例；加大在保险、法律咨询等风险管理方面的投入。

但是，我国"一带一路"海外投资风险管理无论是距离国际先进水平，还是距离"走出去"企业的需求，都还有比较大的差距。国内不少地方政府都建立了企业"走出去"综合服务平台，不少研究机构和智库也在为企业"走出去"提供目的地国家和地区的信息，但大部分信息都是一般性信息，且高度雷同，海外投资风险管理所需的全面的、深入的、精准的、定制化的信息非常缺乏。服务机构和平台之间信息和资源不联通、不能共享，企业进行风险评估只看到局部或某些模块的信息，不同地方的企业由于信息不通而前赴后继重复犯同样的错误或掉进同样的陷阱。缺乏国际化、专业化和市场化的服务机构与人才。比如，海外投资保险业务目前主要还是依赖中国出口信用保险公司，专业从事海外投资保险业务的国际化、专业化的内资市场主体还没有；现有的内资市场化专业服务机构业务主要在国内，与企业"陪伴出海"的还很少；高校、智库等为政府提供的决策咨询比较多，但为企业"走出去"提供定制化决策咨询很少，激励机制、运作模式、观念意识等还跟不上市场的需要；对小语种、小民族（种族）、小国家的法律等精通的人才严重缺乏。

3. 上海自贸试验区的责任与条件

"一带一路"建设，是我国今后相当长一个时期对外开放和对外合作的管总规划。十九大报告提出"要以'一带一路'建设为重点，坚持引进来和走出去并重，遵循共商共建共享原则，加强创新能力开放合作，形成陆海内外联动、东西双向互济的开放格局。"而把上海自贸试验区建设成为服务国家"一带一路"建设、推动市场主体走出去的桥头堡，是党和国家在全局高度对上海提出的新要求。[①]

上海自贸试验区的设立的初衷，就是为国家全面深化改革和进一步扩大开放探索新路径、积累新经验。上海自贸试验区的角色就是开放的破冰船、改革的挖掘机，以及改革开放排头兵中的排头兵、创新发展先行者中的先行者。上海自贸试验区建设"一带一路"桥头堡，同样必须站在国家全局的高度，勇于担当，"大胆试、大胆闯"，聚焦"一带一路"建设中的痛点和难点。"一带一路"海外投资风险管理问题就是一个事关全局的痛点和难点。

同时，凭借投资便利化、贸易便利化、金融开放与创新、综合服务与营商环境等优势，上海自贸试验区已经成为中国企业"走出去"，包括到"一带一路"沿线海外投资最重要的平台之一。截至 2016 年末，上海自贸试验区已经办结境外投资项目累计 1 577 个，中方投资额累计 546 多亿美元，其中，在新加坡、捷克、俄罗斯、印度等 25 个"一带一路"沿线国家和地区投资项目 108 个，中方

---

① 转引自《上海服务国家"一带一路"建设发挥桥头堡作用行动方案》。

投资额累计 26.3 亿美元。① 从问题导向、企业需求导向出发，上海自贸试验区也有责任积极探索海外投资风险管理的制度创新和政策措施系统集成，以更好地为企业服务，更好地保护海外投资利益。

上海自贸试验区也有先行先试探索"一带一路"海外风险管理的若干优势。

首先，上海自贸试验区大胆探索与国际投资贸易通行规则相衔接的制度创新体系，在以负面清单管理为核心的投资管理制度、以贸易便利化为重点的贸易监管制度以及多元化国际商事争端解决机制等方面形成了一定的经验成果，在国内不同层面复制推广的同时，也一定程度上具备了在"一带一路"沿线复制推广的条件。

其次，上海自贸试验区与上海国际金融中心建设联动，建成了包括股票、债券、货币、外汇、商品期货、金融期货与场外衍生品、黄金、保险等在内的较为完备的金融要素市场体系，初步形成了全球性人民币产品创新、交易、定价和清算中心。上海自贸试验区金融市场国际化程度不断提升，金砖国家新开发银行、全球中央对手方协会等相继落户上海，沪港通、债券通先后运行，熊猫债发行规模稳步提升；各类外资金融机构总数超过 430 家，占上海金融机构总数的 30% 左右，② 截至 2017 年 6 月，14 个"一带一路"沿线国家和地区在上海共设立 13 家外资银行分行和 10 家代表处。③ 上海自贸试验区初步建成包括原保险、再保险、保险资管和保险中介等多元化的保险市场体系，2015 年出口信用保险向"一带一路"沿线 58 个国家和地区的 4 882 个客户提供买方授信额度 42.2 亿美元，支持承保 74 亿美元。④

第三，上海自贸试验区地处上海，而上海拥有丰富的涉外资源和研究咨询资源，第三方服务机构集聚。目前，上海已经与境外 64 个城市建立了友好城市关系，其中 22 个城市处于"一带一路"沿线；75 个国家在上海设立领事馆，其中 34 个国家处于"一带一路"沿线。上海高校林立，其中 985 高校就有 4 所，各类综合性和专业性的智库、研究机构众多，国家首批 25 家高端智库建设试点单位中上海就有 2 家。上海拥有大量中外资的法律、会计、审计、咨询、税务等第三方服务机构，仅上海自贸试验区境外投资服务平台就囊括了法律、金融、财税、保险、投资促进等 40 余家第三方机构。

① 数据来源：上海市人民政府新闻办公室，《2017 年 4 月 1 日市政府新闻发布会：上海自贸试验区制度创新成果及建设推进情况》，2017 年 4 月 1 日。

② 数据来源：《上海国际金融中心建设顺利推进　全球城市高"含金量"从何而来？》，《新民晚报》2017 年 4 月 10 日。

③ 数据来源：《"一带一路"沿线国家和地区银行在沪机构增多》，中国新闻网 2017 年 7 月 21 日。

④ 数据来源：《上海保监局：上海已形成现代保险市场体系》，中国证券网 2016 年 3 月 28 日。

4. 上海自贸试验区建设国家级风险管理中心的建议

上海自贸试验区建设应该服务国家战略，聚焦"一带一路"海外投资风险管理这一痛点和难点，利用自身优势，对接市场主体需求，承接一批国家重大功能性载体，打造一批开放型合作平台。其中，建设国家级"一带一路"海外投资风险管理中心可以成为突破口。具体而言，可以在以下几个方面进行先行先试。

（1）贡献制度性公共产品，防控规则风险和法律风险。

全球经济治理的核心是规则和制度的制定。全球经济治理在很大程度上是用和平手段争夺对国际规则的制定权和解释权，并借此维护自身的最大利益。近年来，国际投资贸易规则正在经历重大重构，美国主导了 TPP、TTIP、TiSA 和美式 BIT 等新的投资贸易规则的制定，其核心目的就是维护和强化国际规则的主导权，以新的符合自身比较优势的国际规则来保护自身的贸易和投资利益。中国积极参与全球化和全球经济治理，以"一带一路"建设为突破口，推动构建人类命运共同体，也需要以议题、规则和制度来体现和落实"开放、包容、普惠、平衡、共赢"的发展理念，以不断升级的多边规则来提升国际投资利益的保护，应对国际投资面临的法律风险和规则风险。

已经运行四年多的上海自贸试验区已经在以负面清单管理为核心的投资管理制度、以贸易便利化为重点的贸易监管制度以及多元化国际商事争端解决机制等方面形成了一定的经验和制度创新成果。下一步，上海自贸试验区不仅要继续深化和扩大改革与开放试点，而且要及时将经验、做法和措施这些"珍珠"进行整合、提炼和提升，形成"项链"性质的制度性成果，为中国与"一带一路"沿线国家和地区进行双边和多边的 FTA 甚至 BIT 谈判、推进 RCEP 谈判提供议题和文本贡献，争取早日形成有利于保护贸易和投资权益的、有约束力和执行力的制度和规则体系，以防控海外投资的规则风险和法律风险。

（2）深化多边合作，丰富多边风险管控架构。

对"一带一路"海外投资风险的管理，除了加强风险识别、风险预警、风险分散等，丰富多边风险管控架构也是重要内容。在这个方面，国家层面已经有了一些顶层设计，上海自贸试验区可以利用自身国际化程度和对外开放度高的优势，积极创造条件加速推进相关设计落地。

2015 年，金砖五国在乌法峰会上首次提出要设立金砖国家独立的评级机构，并在《果阿宣言》中得到进一步确认。[①] 目前，金砖五国已召集多次会议，对拟设立的评级机构采取的商业模式、相关算法等进行讨论。上海自贸试验区应积极争取将独立于现有标普、穆迪和惠誉三大评级机构的金砖国家评级机构总部设立在上海自贸试验区，并以此为突破口，推进新国际评级机构在"一带一路"沿线的资信调查、评级和服务业务。同时，支持符合条件的企业面向"一带一路"沿线国家和地区开展信用评级服务，逐步培育和建立具有国际影响力的信用评级机构和体系。

投资担保是海外投资风险分散的重要机制。目前国际上主要的多边投资担保机构是世界银行多边投资担保机构（MIGA）。[②] 国家层面正在考虑牵头设立新型多边投资担保机构，有专家建议配套亚洲基础设施投资银行，新设亚洲基础设施投资保险公司或类似的新型多边投资担保机构。上海自贸试验区可以积极跟踪这一设想的发展，积极创造机会推进其在上海自贸试验区落地。

海外投资风险管理需要国际化的争端解决机制。目前看，中国主导设立专门的、国际化的"一带一路"争端解决机制和机构是大势所趋。上海自贸试验区可以进一步完善国际争端多元解决机制，推进实施国际通行争议解决方式，探索境外仲裁机构与上海仲裁机构的多元化合作模式，打造国际化仲裁服务品牌，争取将"一带一路"国际仲裁中心设立在上海自贸试验区。

从现有的经验来看，吸引多边金融机构或主权基金参与也是一种有效的海外投资风险管理和分散的途径。上海自贸试验区应更好地支持总部位于区内的金砖国家新开发银行的发展，同时在国家相关部门的支持下，吸引世界银行下属国际金融公司、亚洲开发银行、亚洲基础设施投资银行、伊斯兰开发银行、美洲开发银行、欧洲复兴开发银行等多边政策性或开发性金融机构，以及沙特主权基金、新加坡淡马锡、阿布扎比主权基金、迪拜主权基金等主要主权基金在上海自贸试验区设立分支机构或办事处，方便中国企业在"一带一路"海外投资过程中采取多元股权、债权股权组合、银团贷款等复合投融资方式，分散管理投资风险。

（3）与金融中心建设联动，加强金融综合服务。

上海自贸试验区与上海国际金融中心建设联动，可以在深化金融服务领域为"一带一路"海外风险管理作出贡献。

---

① 《果阿宣言》提出："为进一步加强全球治理架构，我们欢迎专家探讨设立一个市场主导、独立的金砖国家评级机构的可能性。"

② MIGA 即世界银行多边投资担保机构（Multilateral Investment Guarantee Agency），一般进行通过向投资者和贷款者提供政治风险担保，或通过提供技术援助协助发展中国家吸引私人投资的业务。

多元化融资是有效管理海外投资风险的重要方法。上海自贸试验区可以进一步支持"一带一路"沿线国家或地区企业在上海证券交易所和银行间债券市场发行熊猫债等人民币证券产品，大力发展"一带一路"人民币国际债券市场。上海自贸试验区可以总结债券通和沪港通的经验，与"一带一路"沿线重要的证券市场先开展债券市场的互联互通，等条件成熟后再逐渐开展股票市场的互联互通。上海自贸试验区可以探索设立"一带一路"金融资产管理公司，优化"一带一路"金融资产配置和处置。上海自贸试验区还可以探索境外信贷资产证券化（ABS）试点，吸引境内外金融机构和机构投资者共同参与。

上海自贸试验区应鼓励和支持上海国际保险中心的建设。可以进一步拓展上海保险交易所的功能，争取早日开设保交所"国际板"，吸引国际金融机构参与，创新国际保险交易产品，提高其国际风险分散的功能；支持中资保险公司在"一带一路"沿线国家和地区开办分支机构，支持中资保险公司与当地保险公司和跨国保险公司开展全方位合作；支持区内境内外保险机构创新海外投资保险产品，为企业海外投资、产品技术输出、承接"一带一路"重大工程提供综合保险服务；进一步鼓励区内发展再保险机构和再保险业务。

上海自贸试验区可以积极响应国家提出的金融服务网络化布局的设想，一方面完善条件，吸引"一带一路"沿线国家和地区的金融机构在上海自贸试验区设立分支机构，另一方面，鼓励和支持中资金融机构在"一带一路"沿线布局网点，或通过代理行方式促进服务联通。

上海自贸试验区还应加强对参与"一带一路"的金融机构和企业的金融监管要求，比如强化压力测试、"三反"（反洗钱、反恐融资、反逃税）等要求，强制要求将限额管理、系统监控、风险预警、风险评估、风险报告等嵌入自由贸易账户分账核算系统。

（4）大胆探索，促进专业服务业的发展。

专业服务业在海外投资风险管理中发挥着重要的作用。前文已经提到，目前，国际化、专业化、市场化的服务机构缺乏是瓶颈。

上海自贸试验区应结合外资管理模式的创新，进一步扩大海外投资风险管理相关服务业的有序开放，特别是保险、资信、律师、会计、税务、咨询等领域的开放，以开放促进竞争，在开放、竞争和学习中培养和训练国际化和专业化的人才，在开放、竞争和学习中鼓励和培育专业化、市场化、国际化的海外投资风险管理机构，进而鼓励和支持这些机构与"走出去"的企业一道"抱团出海"，到"一带一路"沿线国家和地区开展投资风险管理相关的专业服务。

上海自贸试验区还应鼓励专业服务机构在做精做强本专业的同时，积极向产业链两端延伸。比如，注册在上海自贸试验区的江泰保险经纪公司已经开始从金融保险出发，整合境内外保险、会计、律师、投融资等服务，为中小企业的跨境投资提供当地尽职调查、风险规避咨询等延伸服务。上海自贸试验区可以采取鼓励性的政策，培育保险公司、咨询公司、评级公司等延展产业链，发展成为综合性的投资风险管理机构。

上海自贸试验区还可以积极争取国家相关部门的支持，试点设立专业海外安保企业，加强与"一带一路"沿线国家和地区政府和企业的合作，寻找机会在"一带一路"沿线参与甚至创办海外安保业务，让"经贸合作、安保先行"从口号变为现实。

（5）其他方面的探索。

上海自贸试验区还可以在其他方面加强探索。

上海自贸试验区应进一步做实驻外机构。2015年上海自贸试验区依托上海市外国投资促进中心在海外设立了6个办事处。除了可以在"一带一路"沿线重要国家和地区继续新设办事处以外，上海自贸试验区更要做实驻外机构，将政府服务前移，直接在海外投资一线做好服务工作，强化与当地政府、商会、侨团的联系，加强与使领馆的协作，在加强投资促进的同时强化风险防控服务。

目前，上海已经与境外64个城市建立了市级的友好城市关系，其中"一带一路"沿线有22个城市。上海自贸试验区可以利用上海与友好城市已有的交往基础，依托上海国际文化大都市建设，搭建更多文化艺术、教育培训、卫生医疗、旅游体育等交流机制和平台，全面提升与"一带一路"沿线国家和地区的人文合作交流水平，巩固和提升民间友谊与合作，为海外投资风险管理赢取人心。

上海自贸试验区可以以问题导向、企业需求导向，探索更加有效的激励机制，鼓励和吸引高校、智库和其他研究机构提供有针对性、操作性的"一带一路"风险预警、风险评估、风险管理等决策和咨询服务。同时加强风险教育。上海自贸试验区可以仿效金融开放和创新案例定期发布的做法，由相关部门联合行业协会、智库等持续搜集、整理、加工"一带一路"海外投资风险管理的成功经验和典型案例，定期（建议每半年）公开发布，对相关市场主体加以教育和警示。

"一带一路"倡议下上海电力装备制造企业"走出去"策略研究[*]

张世翔　　林艺璇

上海电力学院经济与管理学院

"一带一路"倡议可以推动沿线国家能源系统的互联互通，对于全球能源生产和消费方式的变革、保障相关国家能源安全、促进全球经济复苏等方面具有重要的战略意义和现实意义。电力装备制造企业"走出去"战略与"一带一路"建设、供给侧改革等紧密关联。当前，我国电力装备产业正处于从"跟跑并跑者"到"并跑领跑者"角色转变的关键时期，但电力装备产业发展也存在一些不容忽视的问题，正视并解决这些问题，是我国电力装备产业从"大"向"强"转变的必由之路。从我国电力装备制造企业目前所面临的技术差距、压力风险、产能过剩、技术标准等问题出发，以典型企业引导中小型企业发展，结合上海电气集团案例分析以及我国电气装备制造产业发展现状，提出我国电力装备制造企业"走出去"的可行性策略建议。

电力装备制造产业是"一带一路"建设中至关重要的战略性产业，区域内协同发展空间较大。2006 年到 2016 年，我国发电设备年产量已经连续 10 年超过 1 亿千瓦，占全球发电设备产量的 50% 以上，重点电力设备出口额占全球比重超过 45%，我国已经是电力装备生产制造和出口第一大国。"一带一路"沿线国家或地区对电力基础设施建设的需求在不断高涨，国内电力装备制造企业借力"一带一路"契机"走出去"，不但能够使发展实现创新式成长和跨越式突破，并且能高效地推动国内电力装备制造产业结构的升级，提升电力装备制造企业整体的核心能力。

1. 我国电力装备制造企业"走出去"的时代背景

在日趋变化的复杂形势下我国通过"一带一路"倡议一步步融入欧亚大陆，

---

* 本文为上海市教委科研创新重点项目（14ZS146）；上海市哲学社会科学规划课题（2013BGL016）；上海高校人文社会科学重点研究基地建设项目（WKJD15004）；中国工程院咨询研究重点项目（2016-XZ-29）。收稿日期为 2017 年 11 月 13 日。

并且不断创新尝试占据经济发展制高点。基础设施产业链是"一带一路"建设中的重中之重，而"一带一路"沿线国家对于基础设施建设的需求均极其旺盛，且基础设施建设需求也直接带动了上下游产业企业走向世界。随着"一带一路"倡议的深入实施，电力装备以整套设备、工程总承包形式出口潜力巨大。

（1）"一带一路"倡议为我国电力装备制造企业提供新机遇。

首先，沿线国家电力建设基础设施市场需求较大。"一带一路"沿线国家主要以发展中国家及新兴经济体为主，其中大部分国家或者地区基础设施以及经济发展水平较为落后，经济实力形成固定资本不足，无能力修建维护基础设施，从而迫切需要外部资金来解决基础设施的问题。再加上这些发展中国家中不少存在政治局势动荡问题，这对该国的基础设施建设更是雪上加霜，所以大多数外部资金都不敢冒险投入这些基础建设落后的国家。但电力发展是每个地区经济社会发展的血液，没有电气化就没有工业化、城镇化、信息化。这些国家对电力建设中电力设备制造的需求保持较快地增长，为我国电力装备制造产业"走出去"提供了难得的海外发展机会。据有关统计和预测，"一带一路"沿线大部分国家线损率超过 20%，远高于我国 6.64% 的线损率水平，电网改造升级有望拉动配网一二次设备企业海外市场需求。非水可再生能源需求量持续提升，海外风电、光伏、核电市场新增需求也是不容小觑。我国电力装备制造产业"走出去"将很大限度上推动这些国家的电力建设，推进整体基础设施建设，促进这些国家的全面的经济发展，互联互通，互惠互利，所以我国应发挥电力装备制造产业的发展优势，积极主动地投入到沿线国家中。

其次，电力装备制造产业技术输出具备广阔的发展空间。"一带一路"东起朝气蓬勃的亚太经济圈，西至经济水平较高的欧洲经济圈，中部沿线地带是一条具备发展潜力的经济带。可见，"一带一路"沿线国家间经济发展水平具有较大的差距，并且与我国差异明显。部分"一带一路"沿线国家经济发展水平滞后限制了电力的开发利用，电力短缺反向进一步制约经济发展，使相关国家陷入经济收入恶性循环。这些也意味着"一带一路"沿线国家具有很大的发展潜力与发展空间。经过多年的发展，我国已拥有全球比较完备的电力装备制造体系和产品体系，以及一批竞争力较强的高端电力装备制造新技术和新产品，制造产业技术海外溢出效应已凸显。这种多方的利益诉求契合与优势互补的现状督促着我国与"一带一路"沿线国家进行电力装备产能合作。

（2）电力装备制造产业的突破进展。

首先，电力装备技术水平不断提高。以拥有自主知识产权的大型发电成套装备、特高压输变电成套装备、智能电网用成套装备等为代表的电力装备已经达到国际领先水平，其中具有标志性的重大技术装备及产品包括：发电设备中的 1 000 兆瓦级超超临界火电机组、700 兆瓦及以上水电机组、1 000 兆瓦级的核电机组等；300 兆瓦 F 级重型燃气轮机；输变电设备中的 1 000 千伏特高压交流输电成套设备、±800 千伏特高压直流输电成套设备、智能电网用输变电成套设备；关键核心零部件中的超超临界火电机组和大型核电机组用安全阀、大型发电机组用保护断路器、5 英寸 7 200 伏 /3 000 安、6 英寸 8 500 伏 /4 000—4 750 安电控晶闸管、±800 千伏及以下电压等级直流输电换流阀，等等。

其次，电力装备支撑国家重大工程建设能力显著增强。经过 30 多年的不懈努力，坚持"产、学、研、用"相结合，通过引进技术消化吸收再创新，我国成功研制出一批适合我国国情、国际领先的电力装备，并已先后应用于河南沁北 600 兆瓦超临界火电工程、浙江玉环 10 000 兆瓦超超临界火电工程、宁夏灵武 1 000 兆瓦超超临界空冷火电工程、四川白马超超临界循环流化床工程、三峡水电工程、向家坝水电工程、岭澳二期核电工程、三门核电工程、官厅—兰州东 ±750 千伏交流输变电工程、向家坝—上海 ±800 千伏特高压直流输电工程等一批国家重大工程建设，有力地确保了国家"西电东送"能源战略的顺利实施，成为支撑国家重大工程项目建设的中坚力量。

再者，我国现逐步成为名副其实的电力装备制造大国。从 2006 年到 2016 年，我国发电设备年产量连续 10 年超过 1 亿千瓦，占全球发电设备产量的 50% 以上；到 2016 年底，我国发电设备装机容量已达到 16 亿千瓦，已超过美国位居世界第一。自 2008 年开始，变压器年产量连续 8 年超过 10 亿千伏安。2014 年以来，电力设备制造业发展取得了重要进展。受应用领域需求向好、技术创新能力显著、重大装备有所突破、产业结构调整过程明显加快等利好因素影响，我国已进入世界电力装备制造大国行列。未来随着国家不断增大对电源、电网的建设

表 1　2010—2015 年中国电力设备制造业规模

年份	企业数（个）	资产总额（亿元）	同比增长（%）
2010	26 161	27 326.56	24.73
2011	18 301	33 025.24	23.62
2012	19 808	38 544.74	10.69
2013	18 652	39 330.62	9.33
2014	19 079	43 370.73	9.57
2015	19 632	45 125.06	8.39

资料来源：中国机械工业联合会。

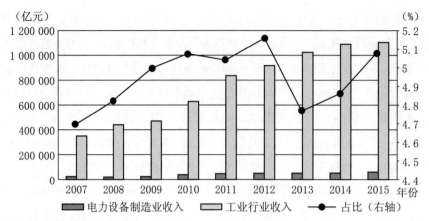

资料来源：中国机械工业联合会。

图1　2007—2015年中国电力设备制造业营业收入

投入，电力设备的市场需求还将明显增长。2015年我国电力设备制造业实现工业产值超过5万亿元，主营业务收入5.33万亿，实现利润3 112亿元，进出口总额1 649亿元，行业规模不断增大（见表1、图1和图2）。

（3）电力装备制造企业"走出去"的必要性。

首先，响应国家"一带一路"倡议的积极倡导，抓住战略发展机遇。国内电力装备制造企业从"一带一路"倡议中获得了良好的政治支持以及与境外项目投资合作的难得机会。"一带一路"倡议有望为电网建设投资带来新机遇，加快国产化电力设备全球推广，促进海外清洁可再生能源市场需求增长。在"一带一路"背景下，实施电力装备制造合作，有助于深化对外关系，尤其是加强与沿线国家的经济技术合作，扩大中国在高科技产业领域的国际影响力和话语权。

其次，提升自主创新能力及技术进步，提高利润、就业量，促进行业及相关产业的持续发展。电力装备制造业作为国民经济中发、输、变、配、用电多

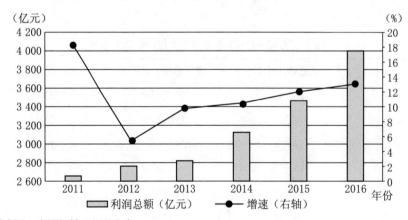

资料来源：中国机械工业联合会。

图2　2011—2016年中国电力设备制造业利润总额及增速

个领域、环节提供电力部件的关键产业，对于自主创新提高竞争力的需求和紧迫感日益上升。行业及相关产业能否持续发展的关键在于其创新能力及技术的进步。我国制造业从"大"向"强"的转变、由"中国制造"向"中国创造"的转变需要电力装备制造业"走出去"这个重要推动力，不仅可以使电力装备制造产业本身获得更大发展，同时可以带动上下游诸多产业的发展和外贸结构的合理化。

2. 国内电力装备制造企业"走出去"的主要形式

一般来说，"走出去"往往要跨越地理界线，需通过人才引进、合作研发、贸易投资、跨国并购、合资经营、工程承包等方式和途径。践行"一带一路"倡议以及走出去是大型企业实现"全球化"的重要途径，是民营企业的重大机遇，是中小型企业实现升级发展的一条关键之路。电力装备制造行业"走出去"强调的是电力企业、装备制造企业、电力建设企业一起"抱团出海"，同时防止国内企业同质化恶性竞争。并且通过建立国际化融资平台，建立国际营销网络等方式，实现产品国际化发展研究利用产业基金、国有资本收益等方式，推动电气装备中优势产能走出去，支持海外投资并购。在电力设备企业"走出去"初期，大型电力设备集团和西部边疆地区地域优势更加突出，终端能源计量设备也占据一定市场空间；随着"一带一路"倡议对电力能源基础设施升级与特许经营权模式推广，电力设备企业有望实现全面出海，更看好现金流充足、产品序列覆盖全面的企业，依托集团切入海外项目 EPC 和运营的商业模式，以及智能终端（电表 / 充电桩 / 能源管理系统）和新能源发电海外市场的新增需求。从单一设备出口到海外项目特许经营权，看好提前布局海外市场渠道的上市公司。

近年来电力设备企业走出去主要有以下几种方式：一是靠近市场供应端建厂，如防爆产品主要为煤矿和石化产业服务，国内有些企业便在伊朗设厂，更好地为前端市场提供直接服务；二是在原材料前端设厂，如国内一些特种变压器企业去铜价低的非洲开工厂；三是直接在海外兼并企业。商业模式从传统的单一设备采购逐渐向提供成套解决方案进行过渡，其中 BOT、BOO、PPP、EPC 等模式不断增多。而 PPP（Public-Private-Partnership）模式，即"公共部门—私人企业—合作"模式，其基本运行方式是通过采购的形式，政府部门与中标单位组建特定目的公司，双方通过签署合同规范权利与义务，并由组建后的公司负责筹集资金再进行建设和经营项目。由于民营私人企业的加入大大减轻了

表 2   PPP 模式在电力企业项目管理中的运作

项目类型	益　　处
核电项目	有利于我国对国外先进技术的引进，以及对先进管理观念的吸取，并且能够强化政府的控制能力。在保证项目质量安全的同时，保证核电项目的技术性。
水电项目	既能够拓展项目的融资方式，又能够分散项目的融资风险。在 PPP 模式中，政府的优势作用能够对项目进行合理的帮助，促使项目能够实现更好的融资。
风电项目	对于优化水电项目的融资结构具有极强的积极意义，能够推进电力企业的可持续性发展；电力项目能够实现对融资来源的良性管理。

政府部门的资金负担，因此 PPP 模式符合"一带一路"沿线基本特征。特别在专用设备和电气机械及器材制造产品等属于大型设备、重大项目的领域引入PPP 模式，具有重大的应用价值，它们具备以 PPP 模式"走出去"的自身特质（见表 2、表 3）。

　　国家电网从 2007 年开始积极倡导国家的"走出去"政策，不断开拓海外市场，从菲律宾、巴西等发展中国家向意大利、葡萄牙、澳大利亚等发达国家布局，从劳动力输出向技术与管理跨越（见表 4）。参股国外电力公司输配电网运营权，有利于推动国内设备厂商走出国门，与国内推行的增量配网电力体制改革有异曲同工之处，是有效打破垄断与设备输出的重要途径。

表 3   国内外涉及电力装备制造产品的 PPP 模式项目成功案例

案例名称	行业（大类）	时　间	地　区	结　果
国　内				
中国太平—中广核核电项目债权计划	电气机械及器材	2012 年开始	中国广东	进行中
全国首个光伏扶贫 PPP 项目	电气机械及器材	2014 年开始	中国安徽	成功
酒泉市城区热电联产集中供热项目	电气机械及器材	2009 年开始 2014 年完工	中国甘肃	成功
国　外				
波兰波兹南市政垃圾热处理厂项目	电气机械及器材	2004 年开始 2013 年完成	波兰、欧盟	成功
英国欣克利角 C 核电项目	电气机械及器材	2016 年开始	中国、英国、法国	进行中
中国水电建设集团国际工程有限公司约旦红海项目	电气机械及器材	2012 年开始	中国、约旦	进行中

资料来源：根据相关公开资料整理所得，统计时间截至 2017 年 9 月。

表 4　国家电网技术与管理输出跨越

年　份	重　大　事　项
2007	与菲律宾企业组成联合体以 39.5 亿美元报价获得 25 年特许经营权
2010	投资 9.89 亿美元获得巴西 7 家输电公司以及其输电资产 30 年特许经营权
2012	收购澳大利亚南澳大利亚州一家电力供应商 41% 股份
2012	3.87 亿欧元收购葡萄牙国家能源公司 25% 股份
2014	收购新加坡能源澳洲资产股权，包括 SPIAA60% 股权和 SPAusNet19.9% 股权
2014	投资 20 亿欧元收购意大利全国电网 35% 股权
2016	埃及 EETC500KV 国家主干网升级输电工程合同签署
2016	与俄罗斯电网公司签署双方设立合资公司开展电网业务的股东协议
2016	收购希腊国家电力公司输电网输电运营公司 24% 股权

资料来源：根据相关公开资料整理所得，统计时间截至 2017 年 9 月。

3. 我国电力装备制造企业"走出去"的现状

（1）国内电力装备制造企业"走出去"现状。

2015 年，主要输配电设备企业海外业务持续增长，特变电工、中国西电海外业务收入占比高达 21.6% 和 10.9%；受益智能电网建设全球化推进，智能电表出口稳中有增，并涌现出海兴电力这样的龙头企业。2016 年，除上海电气电站集团工程产业在埃及、印度尼西亚、孟加拉国获得一批订单外，上海电气服务产业也在海外有所斩获，电站锅炉获得菲律宾项目分包合同。此外，由东方电气集团设计、制造、施工的波黑斯坦纳瑞项目投入商业运行，这是我国和波黑正式建交以来的第一个大型基础设施合作项目，也是我国企业在欧洲独立设计和施工的第一个火电总承包项目；哈电集团把目标定位在抢占海外高端和新业务领域，在走出去的基础上推动企业走上去，与世界先进企业同台竞争。其电站工程从最初建设在越南、巴基斯坦、菲律宾、印度尼西亚等传统市场，逐渐向中东、南美、土耳其及周边的东欧市场等高端电力市场挺进（见表 5）。

从对外贸易来看，电力设备制造业进出口规模均有所减少（见图 3）。具体来看，2015 年，我国电力设备国产化率持续提高，进口替代效应进一步增强，进口增速由 2014 年的 1.73% 下降至 −10.75%；由于全球经济复苏乏力，外需持续疲软，电力设备出口额增速由 2014 年的 6.95% 大幅下降至 −3.51%。进入 2016 年后，电力设备的内外需不足及进口替代效应进一步延续，全年进口额和出口额仍负增长，但增速大幅下滑态势得到缓解，增速分别为 −6% 和 −2%。

表5 部分电力装备"走出去"项目

年份	项目	相关企业	设 备	参与模式
2013	柬埔寨桑河二级水电站	华能集团	水电设备	项目建设和管理
2014	风力发电变压器抢占埃塞俄比亚主要市场	泰开集团	风电设备	设立分支机构+产品出口
2014	越南永兴燃煤电厂EPC合同	中国能建	火电设备	总承包+运营
2015	白俄罗斯风力发电装置	中国华仪电气股份公司	风电设备	产品出口
2015	巴西美丽山二期项目	国家电网	国产电力设备	投资+承包+运营
2015	切尔纳诺德核电三、四号机组全寿命期框架协议	中广核	核电设备	协议共识合作谅解备忘录
2015	南非库贝赫核电站的更换项目	上海电气	核电主设备	分包制造
2016	巴西杰瑞水电站	东方电机	水电设备	总承包+运营
2016	巴基斯坦默拉直流输电项目	国家电网	输电设备	项目合作协议
2016	连云港风力发电塔架出口英国	重山风力设备有限公司	风电设备	产品出口
2016	布莱斯海上风力发电项目	三菱维斯塔斯风电公司	风电设备	产品出口
2016	黑山MOZURA风电项目	上海电力公司	风电设备	投资+承包+运营

资料来源：根据相关公开资料整理所得，统计时间截至2017年9月。

（2）国内电力装备制造龙头企业的"走出去"现状。

以上海电气集团为例，"走出去"动作不断，2016年8月上海电气及下属全资子公司上海电气香港有限公司与4家交易方（合计持有TEC4的100%股权）

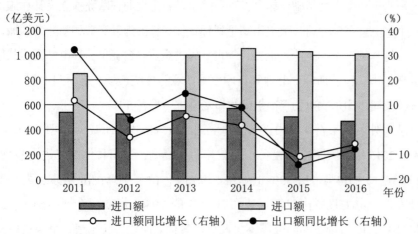

资料来源：中国机械工业联合会。

图3 2011—2016年中国电力设备制造业进出口状况

签订了股权收购协议。并且公司正致力于能源及智能制造业务的拓展，未来通过创新协同、产品多样化、积极开拓市场等多个方面促进公司与被收购方的共同发展。过去7年中国电力设备已占印度新增电力设备市场约四成份额，印度目前成为中国电力设备最大的海外出口市场。近些年来伴随着经济的迅速发展，印度的电力需求也在大幅度地增长，但其本土电力装备制造商供应能力有限，因此我国电力设备可以利用这个机会发展印度市场。据印度电力部统计，2012年到2017年，印度已开工建设的装机容量为7.6万兆瓦，其中超过六成的设备由中国制造商提供。其中包括上海电气和哈尔滨电气等中国主要发电设备制造商都已进入印度市场。上海电气将印度开拓成为最大的海外市场，目前已拥有12个电站建设项目并完成装机容量达2万兆瓦，占到我国出口印度电力设备的半壁江山。

"十二五"以来，上海坚持服务国家装备制造业发展战略，整合资源，发挥优势，不断推进装备制造业高端化发展，在许多方面取得显著成效。根据上海海关2017年1月发布的数据显示，以出口机电产品为例，2016年上海海关关区对"一带一路"沿线国家出口机电产品8 506.80亿元，2017年1—6月机电产品出口总值为4 423.21亿元，占出口总值的70.6%，比重提高1.2个百分点，占比重大。

随着智能电网建设和能源互联网的推进及发展，电路信息流将从单向性转向多向性、从链条化转向网络化，但是这些都要通过电力装备来支撑。2016年9月，上海市商务委员会、经济与信息化委员会授予临港地区"上海装备走出去和国际产能合作示范基地"，从而积极推动本土龙头装备制造企业和重点机构的发展，并鞭策龙头企业带动中小企业共同发展。未来逐步开展其他区域的示范基地建设，并积极发挥包括临港在内示范基地的示范带头作用，使其成为上海甚至中国装备"走出去"的标杆。

4. 影响我国电力装备制造企业"走出去"的因素

（1）国内电力装备制造技术。

大部分电力装备制造企业的发展现状仍然具有"大却不强"的特点。强烈依赖进口的关键核心技术和薄弱的自主创新能力，进而导致产品的附加值低，处于全球价值链的低端。如煤电机组环保技术、大型抽水蓄能机组、重型燃气轮机的叶片、输变电成套装备技术以及新型高温超导输变电设备等，虽技术的引进使国内的生产制造得到了自我实现，但多数是在进行仿造。另有关键零部件、材料及配套体系严重依赖于进口。同时跟国外一些重大装备的可靠性、能耗指标相比，国内大部分电力装备制造企业存在一定差距。因此需要切实加强宏观调控和需求结构改善将倒逼电力设备制造业向高端化、绿色化转型。

（2）国内电力装备制造企业现存发展问题。

模糊的并购目的、急功近利的心态、缺乏专业经验以及认识不足都容易使企业陷入困境。北上广深等一、二线城市不断升高的生活、商务成本导致技术工人、复合型人才流失严重，进出比例不协调，企业人力成本压力加重，并且在某些领域的高端创新型复合人才十分缺乏。所以留住人才并且培养综合性人才，让强大的智力支持企业"走出去"，助力"一带一路"建设成功。

（3）技术应用的难度。

中国技术标准和规范很多时候没有运用在许多产品出口和技术输出的过程中，主要是因为中国标准大多数根据经验或实验数据来直接规定参数，从而在国外不同环境下的适应性比较差，以及国内外不同企业的恶性竞争问题，这都不利于企业在海外的健康发展。这意味着我国加速构建国内标准化技术机构联动机制，结合国际国内产业和科技的最新发展动态，推动更多的中国自主创新、优势特色技术成为国际标准。

（4）东道主国家给予的环境条件。

在"走出去"过程中不可避免地要面对来自其他发达国家进行技术竞争和市场竞争的过程中存在贸易摩擦、盲目竞争的压力。恐怖主义、极端组织势力、武装分裂等危险存在于中东地区如叙利亚、黎巴嫩、阿富汗和巴基斯坦等国家中，使安全问题、经济风险集聚，同时包括项目管理、施工安全等内部控制风险也是潜在的。企业实现本地化经营和发展，不可避免地要注意项目投资建设和运营一体化、设备生产和营销一体化、资源整合等问题，还有文化融合、人员就业、环境保护等问题。切实加强对东道主国家安全性的研究，在有效管控风险的前提下，大力打造责任和命运共同体，倡导可持续发展观迫在眉睫。

5. 推进我国电力装备制造企业在"一带一路"倡议下"走出去"的建议

集中力量办大事的制度优势和我国大国大市场优势越来越成为我们企业发展成长的中坚力量，我国电力装备制造企业应充分利用这些优势，不局限于将高铁、核电装备制造集中在少数几家国有企业，应大中小企业抱成一团紧密联合，有效形成创新合力，防止被国外企业逐个击破，并且走上"高端引领、重点突破、分步推进"之路，打造自己品牌，抢占市场，形成装备企业自身品牌效应。经过笔者的调查研究，认为我国电力装备制造企业"走出去"可以实施四阶段战略对策。

（1）品牌战略，升级转型。

企业首先进行自身品牌的战略定位，同时要强化以自主知识产权为核心的国际竞争能力。与国内的大专院校、科研院所建立"产学研"研发体系，密切联系系统集成商加大智能制造系统解决方案研发，积极开展国际合作，引进消化技术，不断促进技术进步，使得内部效应最大化。中小电力装备制造企业前期可以通过建立友好关系，利用友好关系介绍自己的品牌，加入驻外的中国商会，通过跟中国公司接触了解寻找更多的经营合作机会；然后注重产品标牌统一化，让顾客和合作伙伴更好地记住集团的品牌；积极参与投标，最重要目的不只是谋求中标而是寻找向顾客推介品牌的机会。在适应不同国家环境的同时，学习借鉴国内成功企业及海外成功企业经验。

同时，要引起相关政府管理部门的足够重视，各司其职，通力配合好，组织推动基础科学研究，整合各方资源形成优势。我国相比于发达国家而言，中小制造企业数量多而且劳动密集型企业所占比例较高，同时存在信息化程度普遍不高的问题。因此，政府、企业等协力推进互联网与制造业融合发展，应该采取因地制宜、差异化实施的方案。

（2）以点带面，一点多赢。

电力装备企业技术产品差异化的主要脉络和导向是未来输变电工程的建设和后续经营。因此电力装备企业应加快进行由单纯的设备供货商向以设备供货为基础的国际能源建设工程总承包商的角色转变。企业培育产品的市场竞争力可以通过不断的产业升级、技术进步、发展转型，并通过提高产品质量服务于品牌优势来实现。

政府可以考虑使用更加机动和市场化的手段，积极发挥驻"一带一路"沿线国家或城市间的代表处、办事处的信息情报和事务服务作用，并且组织落实新技术、新装备示范工程，然后在试点示范基础上形成电力装备数字化研发设计与制造一体化的新模式加快推广，为中小电力装备制造企业在海外的发展做好坚强的后盾。对接亚太示范电子口岸网络，积极推进国际贸易"单一窗口"与"一带一路"沿线口岸的信息互换和服务共享。加大政策支持和引导力度，尤其是电力装备优势明显的区域和企业。成为制造强国最好的外在体现就是打造一批具有品牌、企业文化、规模、技术、资金、质量优势且能够与 GE、SIEMENS 旗鼓相当的大型企业集团。而上海电气企业集团就是通过采用集约式的发展体制构架，其中主营业务高度集中、品牌文化高度统一、核心资源和核心能力的高度聚集，形成"恒星"企业的关键竞争力。"恒星"核心吸引力和辐射力带来多种行业的

"行星""卫星"式企业围绕其运转，值得借鉴。

（3）探寻契机，持续盈利。

在初步的成功下，积极巩固公司与东道主本土企业（比如沿线国家的电力集团、电力设备公司等）的合作关系，主要措施是促进双方领导层的互访和加强双方的技术交流。充分利用品牌优势和中国制造的成本优势，积极开拓巴西、墨西哥等新兴市场，巩固原占有的市场。

在"一带一路"不断带来的契机下，政府可在积极推动优化业务流程的同时提高服务的效率，并且不断地探索和落地外商投资合作管理模式和相关政策制度，成为企业"走出去"的支撑力量。电力装备制造行业、电力建设行业及协会要加强经验宣传与推广力度，促进典型经验的推广应用。

（4）共赢理念，协同发展。

在条件成熟的市场成立全资境外子公司，实现境外公司本地化的商业运作，才能更好实现跨国合作、国际经营。在"走出去"过程中，企业应该充分考虑东道国的经济状况和实际需求，坚持互利共赢、共同发展的理念，并尽可能促进当地经济社会生态的可持续发展。在"一带一路"建设中，民营企业发挥着越来越突出的作用，中小型企业抱团共同进军发达国家、产业投资的高端化趋势较显著。三亿重工、华为、长城、联想、吉利等大型民营企业在"走出去"的过程中取得了好成果。

上海自贸试验区深化服务
"一带一路"的制度创新

张建华

上海对外经贸大学国际经贸所

2008 年的国际金融危机使世界经济增长一直呈下降趋势，我国的经济增速虽然高于世界平均水平，但是下降幅度更大且有收敛于世界经济增速的迹象，表明我国和世界的经济增长都到了一个新的阶段。为了保持新阶段的中高速经济增长，必须探寻潜在的增长动力。建立上海自贸试验区和提出"一带一路"倡议是通过深化改革开放探索增长新动力的两个努力。由于"一带一路"是我国新时代对外开放合作的重点且具有开放性，因此以制度创新服务"一带一路"倡议就成为上海自贸试验区改革开放工作的内在要求。

1. 两个国家规划的内在一致性

从上海自贸试验区建设方案和"一带一路"倡议的决策背景、决策性质及其核心要求中，都能看到两个规划的联动。比如，二者都是在新时代提出的新国家发展愿景，在性质上都是党中央、国务院作出的重大决策，在时间上都是在 2013 年提出的。

（1）"一带一路"是上海自贸试验区的深耕领域。

2013 年 9 月、2015 年 4 月和 2017 年 3 月，国务院就上海自贸试验区分别印发了三个方案，指出上海自贸试验区是在新形势下为国家全面深化改革和扩大开放探索新途径、积累新经验的重要举措，同时根据国内经济发展需要及应对国际经济新变化提出了具有明显阶段性特征的任务，其标志性用语是上海自贸试验区的"建立""进一步深化"和"全面深化"，显然它承载的功能是动态的。

自贸区承载的核心任务是制度创新，包括四个方面：转变政府职能（深化行政审批制度改革、提升事中事后监管能力和建立法制化营商环境）、构建外资管理新模式（探索外商投资准入前国民待遇加负面清单管理模式）、扩大服务业开放（包括服务业和金融业）以及促进贸易投资便利化。这几个方面是相互配合、相互促进的，没有政府职能转变就无法适应改革开放的新要求，没有深化改革的要求就不知道政府职能转变的方向，没有扩大开放的要求就不知道如何探索构建新的外资管理模式。因此，上海自贸试验区先行先试积累的成功经验对国家深化改革开放至关重要。

2015年"方案"提出自贸试验区要构建开放型经济新体制和探索区域经济合作新模式两个任务，如果说前一个任务是对上述四个方面制度创新内容概括的话，那么后者具体来说指的是推进长江经济带的合作发展。尽管该方案也提出，自贸区要推动"一带一路"建设，但是由于"一带一路"方案也是刚刚推出（2015年3月），在顶层设计中还没有在这两个战略之间建立明确的联系。比如，在国际贸易"单一窗口"建设方面，仅提出探索长三角区域国际贸易"单一窗口"建设，推动长江经济带通关一体化。

在2017年的"方案"中就特别提出了上海自贸试验区要主动服务"一带一路"的具体内容，"创新合作发展模式，成为服务国家'一带一路'建设、推动市场主体走出去的桥头堡"。与此呼应，2017年10月，上海市政府发布了《上海服务国家"一带一路"建设发挥桥头堡作用行动方案》，提出以自贸区制度创新为载体，在经贸合作、金融服务、基础设施建设、人文交流和人才培训以及全球友城和跨国公司合作等方面服务"一带一路"。十九大报告指出，要以"一带一路"建设为重点，坚持引进来和走出去并重，遵循共商共建共享原则，加强创新能力开放合作，形成陆海内外联动、东西双向互济的开放格局；把"一带一路"打造成国际合作新平台。如此两个国家战略不仅水到渠成地结合在一起，而且服务"一带一路"成为探索全面深化改革开放的深耕领域。

（2）两个国家规划的联动点。

我们把2017年方案第五部分的三条内容分解为12点，并把它们与"一带一路"倡议中的内容匹配，找出了两个方案中的联动点（即共同点）和不同点（表1）。很容易看出，上海自贸试验区改革开放任务包括了"一带一路"倡议中的大多数内容，尤其是投资贸易便利化和金融服务是两个规划方案共同的建设任务。"一带一路"倡议中含有国务院2017年上海自贸试验区方案中没有的内容，比如在"一带一路"倡议中的民心相通部分的多数内容在上海发布的服务方案中均给予了回应。此外，根据表1中对我国与沿线国家经贸状况的比较分析，我们认为减少双边贸易不平衡或者推动彼此优势产业互补也应该成为上海自贸试验区探索深化改革开放的任务。

表 1　上海自贸试验区与"一带一路"建设的联动点

2017 自贸试验区方案第五部分	2017 自贸试验区方案其他部分	2015 "一带一路" 倡议
目标要求：成为桥头堡，搭建开放合作新平台，建设资源配置功能枢纽，发挥辐射带动作用	目标要求：建成国际高标准自由贸易园区，健全投资管理、贸易监管、金融服务和政府管理体系	目标要求：实现区域基础设施更加完善；高标准自由贸易区网络基本形成；人文交流更加广深
（二十）以高标准便利化措施促进经贸合作		
1. 推进"单一窗口"与沿线口岸的信息互换和服务共享。	（六）建成国际先进水平"单一窗口"。（十三）实施贸易便利化新规则。	贸易畅通：着力解决投资贸易便利化问题，商建自贸区；海关及双多边合作；加快"单一窗口"建设；拓宽和优化贸易；拓展投资领域；推动新兴产业合作；优化产业链分工布局；扩大服务业相互开放。
2. 率先探索互联互通监管合作新模式。	（七）建立海关综合监管新模式。（八）建立检验检疫风险分类监管综合评定机制。（九）建立具有国际竞争力的创新产业监管模式。	
3. 加快建设门户复合型国际航空枢纽。		设施联通：提升道路通达水平；建立运输协调机制；口岸和航空基础设施建设等。
4. 促进港口合作形成亚太供应链中心枢纽。		
5. 建立综合性对外投资促进机构和境外投资公共信息服务平台。	（十四）创新跨境服务贸易管理模式。	
6. 打造产权交易中心与技术转移平台促进产业科技合作。	（十）优化创新要素市场配置机制。（十一）健全知识产权保护和运用体系。	贸易畅通：同上。民心相通：科技合作，提升科技创新能力。
7. 积极推进国际产能和建设能力合作。		贸易畅通、设施联通：同上。
（二十一）增强"一带一路"金融服务功能		
8. 推动上海金融中心与沿线金融市场合作联通。	（十五）进一步深化金融开放创新。	资金融通：推进亚洲货币稳定、投融资和信用体系建设；扩大货币互换和结算；开放亚洲债券市场；亚投行、金砖银行、丝路基金；支持境内外发行人民币债券；金融监管、风险应对及信用合作。
9. 利用境内外人民币资产为沿线重大项目提供融资服务。		
10. 发展综合保险服务"走出去"。		
11. 支持金砖国家新开发银行。		
（二十二）探索具有国际竞争力的离岸税制安排		
12. 探索服务贸易创新试点扩围税收政策。		贸易畅通：同上。

2. 自贸区服务"一带一路"建设的现状与深化

自"一带一路"倡议实施以来，就成为了上海自贸试验区改革开放的一个重点任务，时至今日，在服务"一带一路"建设上已经取得了不俗的成绩，但未来仍需要以制度创新深化联动。

（2）自贸区服务"一带一路"建设的现状与问题。

上海自贸试验区对接和服务"一带一路"建设的进展如下：一是扩大与沿线国家的贸易和投资。中国（上海）自贸试验区成立四年来，与沿线国家之间的走出去和引进来项目3 000多个，贸易增速保持在22%以上。沿线已有52个国家在浦东投资，投资企业3 012个，合同外资115.8亿美元；自贸试验区对捷克和印度尼西亚等25国的投资近40亿美元。二是建立专门促进机制。设立"一带一路"进口商品国别馆，扩大沿线国家优质商品进口。三是开展科技创新合作。与以色列、俄罗斯和新加坡等国联合建立跨国孵化器；引进了浦俄论坛、亚太科技创新展览等活动，搭建跨境项目交流平台。四是搭建企业走出去服务平台。在自贸试验区境外投资服务平台增设服务"一带一路"专栏，与东盟法律服务联盟签约以推动律师、会计、咨询和评估等专业服务力量跟随企业一起走，设立"一带一路"技术贸易措施企业服务中心，在认证认可、标准计量等方面与沿线国家开展更多合作交流。

上海自贸试验区服务"一带一路"建设的这些举措很好地反映了"方案"的要求。当对照上海自贸试验区改革开放的核心任务和两个国家规划的联动点时，我们认为，自贸区在对接"一带一路"倡议上仍有许多需要深挖的空间，不能满足于现有规则之内的投资贸易或经贸合作，满足于已有做法不是自贸区的任务。自贸区的核心任务是制度创新探索，就是以"一带一路"建设为重点，遵循引进来走出去并重和共商共建共享的原则，通过与有关国家的投资贸易制度和规则谈判，搭建起高水平的贸易和投资自由化便利化国际平台，使这个平台成为我国发展高层次开放型经济和推动开放性世界经济建设的有力抓手。

（2）自贸区深化服务"一带一路"建设的制度创新框架。

当国内和国际经贸环境发生变化的时候，或者为了超越现状而需要改变目前经贸环境的时候，制度创新首当其冲。制度创新本质上是改变对现有制度结构中某些制度的路径依赖，从而形成新的制度结构，以保证经贸活动朝着有利于经济结构调整和经济增长的方向变化。

在国务院发布的2017年上海自贸试验区深改方案中，提出建立国际上最高标准、最好水平的自贸区，这是对自贸试验区制度创新提出了最高要求，也是对建设"一带一路"国际平台的最高要求，其实质是最大限度地实现贸易和投资的自由化便利化政策。达到这两个"最"的要求必然使制度创新达到如下理想的结果：吸纳国际上现行的最高和最好标准的贸易规则；创建超越现有国际经贸规则的更高水平的规则；通过与单个国家经贸谈判构建的一对一规则，其中就包括"一带一路"沿线国家。可以预期，如果上海自贸试验区在这三个方面成功地建立起最高标准、最好水平的自贸区和"一带一路"合作平台，那么一个适应国内和国际经贸新形势要求的、开放型经济新体制也就构建成功了，不仅能够极大地促进我国的经济发展，而且也能够遏制国际贸易投资保护主义趋势，使世界经济和贸易回到开放合作的轨道。

制度创新是制度学习和制度创造的结合，是"我需要"与"他需要"的结合，但归根结底是"我创造"。国际经贸领域的制度创新也是如此。上海自贸试验区通过"一带一路"进行的制度创造包括三个方面：一是双边或多边谈判，这是制度创造的源起；二是横向的制度扩展，即把现有双边或多边的制度成果借鉴到与沿线国家的双边或多边谈判中；三是纵向的制度变革，即根据达成的双边或多边国际投资贸易规则，来调整国内相关法律和政策，达到以开放促改革。

在当前的国际经贸背景下，上海自贸试验区基于"一带一路"的制度创新既有机遇也有挑战，其中的机遇有：尽管世界经济增长困难，但是发展中国家谋求开放发展的愿望没有改变甚至更强烈；虽然发达国家和其他一些国家倾向于国际投资贸易保护主义，但是仍然需要投资和出口，特别是不论是这些国家的政府还是企业都看到了"一带一路"潜在的巨大投资贸易机遇，如多数发达国家愿意成为亚投行发起成员；一些发展中国家希望学习我国经济发展的成功经验；在全球多边投资贸易体制出现困难的条件下，双边或区域体制成为趋势。其挑战有：发达国家趋向于贸易投资保护主义和民粹主义，沿线各国国情不同决定了对与我国经贸合作中投资贸易规则的要求不同，受到现有一些国际性组织的制约，一些国家对我国固有的偏见，用开放创新的制度成果改变在传统规则中固化的政府和企业行为也不容易。

但是毫无疑问，上海自贸试验区基于"一带一路"的成功制度创新对于建设我国现代化经济体系和开放型世界经济都具有划时代意义。首先，强化了上海的"桥头堡"服务功能。成功的制度创新最直接的效果是进一步提升上海城市综合服务功能，发展更高层次的开放型经济，从而增强服务"一带一路"建设"桥头堡"的能级。其次，推进贸易强国建设。自贸试验区的制度创新、特别是赋予自贸试验区更大改革自主权，有利于拓展和深化对外贸易、培育贸易新业态和新模式，形成面向全球的贸易、投融资、生产和服务网络，从而培育经贸合作和竞争新优势。第三，推动构建人类命运共同体。自贸试验区与沿线国家达成的投资贸易或经贸合作规则的实用性、先进性和代表性，不仅超越了被废弃的 TPP，而且还为未来扩展和对接其他非沿线国家或国际组织做好制度储备。第四，形成国际共同发展新动力。中国与"一带一路"沿线国家的经贸合作不仅具有通常意义上的贸易投资性质，还具有通过基础设施建设、产能合作、科技创新合作以及人力资源培训等措施带动这些国家，特别是低收入国家与我国共同发展的性质。

3. 自贸试验区深化制度创新的经济基础

尽管搭建最高标准、最好水平的"一带一路"国际经贸活动平台过程中，上海自贸试验区会遇到许多挑战，但根本性的挑战还是来自沿线国家经济发展的状态和要求，一个最优的贸易和投资自由化便利化规则一定是符合彼此利益最大化预期的，因此本部分着重分析沿线国家的经济发展特征。

（1）沿线国家的经济概况。

"一带一路"倡议是一个开放的倡议，没有明确的边界和国家数量，学术界普遍的看法是包括我国在内共有 65 个国家，占世界国家数的 1/3。根据世界银行的分类，有 16 个高收入国家、21 个中高收入国家、20 个中低收入国家以及 7 个低收入国家。这是一个以中等收入、发展中国家和转型国家为主体的国家集合，那些最发达的国家均不在此列。世界经济论坛把驱动经济增长的动力分为要素驱动、效率驱动和创新驱动三类，沿线国家经济增长的阶段性特征如表 2。比较这两个分类发现，在 16 个高收入国家中，有一半属于创新驱动发展的国家，其他国家处于要素驱动和效率驱动的阶段或者向高一级阶段转型的发展状态。这暗含着不同发展阶段的国家对投资、贸易或者跨国经贸合作的要求是不同的。

2016 年，64 个国家的总人口是 46.1 亿，[①]占世界人口的 62%；其中，有 36 个国家的人口不超过 100 万，文莱和马尔代夫是人口最少的两个国家，分别只有 40 万；有 21 个国家的人口不超过 1 000 万；有 5 个国家的人口不超过 3 亿；中国和印度的人口总量就超过 27 亿，占 65 个国家的 58.6%。

2016 年，63 个国家的 GDP 总量是 23.3 万亿美元，[②]占世界 GDP 总量的 30.9%；人均 GDP 是 5 074 美元，是世界人均 GDP 的 50%。人均收入水平在

---

① 缺少巴勒斯坦的数据。
② 缺少叙利亚和巴勒斯坦的数据。

表 2　国家经济发展阶段

阶段 1 要素驱动	从阶段 1 向阶段 2 转型	阶段 2 效率驱动	从阶段 2 向阶段 3 转型	阶段 3 创新驱动
孟加拉国	阿塞拜疆	阿尔巴尼亚	克罗地亚	巴林
柬埔寨	不丹	亚美尼亚	匈牙利	捷克
印度	文莱	波黑	拉脱维亚	爱沙尼亚
吉尔吉斯斯坦	哈萨克斯坦	保加利亚	黎巴嫩	以色列
老挝	科威特	中国	立陶宛	卡塔尔
摩尔多瓦	蒙古	埃及	马来西亚	新加坡
尼泊尔	菲律宾	格鲁吉亚	阿曼	斯洛文尼亚
巴基斯坦	俄罗斯	印度尼西亚	波兰	阿联酋
塔吉克斯坦	乌克兰	伊朗	沙特阿拉伯	
也门	越南	约旦	斯洛伐克	
		马其顿	土耳其	
		黑山		
		罗马尼亚		
		塞尔维亚		
		斯里兰卡		
		泰国		

资料来源：世界经济论坛《全球竞争力报告》（2016），第 38 页。说明：缺少 10 个国家的资料。

1 万—6 万美元之间的有 19 个国家，在 0.5 万—1 万美元之间的有 13 个国家，在 1 000—5 000 美元之间的有 27 个国家，其余 4 个国家人均收入不足 1 000 美元，人均收入最高的卡塔尔和人均收入最低的阿富汗相差 104 倍。

在经济增长速度超过人口增长速度的时候，人均收入水平必然提高，并且在人口规模较小的条件下很容易提高国民收入水平。比如，卡塔尔的人口为 260 万，在 2000—2016 年间，GDP 年均增速达到 12.1%，是沿线国家增速最高的，2016 年人均收入为 5.9 万美元、也是最高的。人口大国不具备这样的经济特征，像中国，同期年均增速是 9.9%，但人均收入只接近于卡塔尔的 14%。

（2）产业结构特征。

在一个给定的时期内，一国的产业结构反映了其要素禀赋结构特征和经济增长阶段特征。长期看，在开放竞争的条件下，经济的发展反应于经济规模扩大（人均收入水平提高）和产业结构高级化，其中隐含的一个前提是，产出占比趋于减少的产业变得越来越强大，并为其他产业的发展提供稳定的基础，同时必须有相应的要素禀赋结构升级给予支持。但是一些国家的产业结构演变因受发展战略、资源、人口和市场规模的制约表现出明显的异质性，表现为产业结构扭曲、产业结构长期停滞，其人均收入水平也难以提高。

就产业结构现状看，2016 年，在有数据的 55 个国家中，有 38 个国家的农业产出和工业产出的占比都超过世界平均水平，[①] 有 25 个国家的制造业产出占比高于世界平均水平，服务业产出占比超过世界平均水平的只有 7 个国家，所以多数国家的产业结构落后于世界水平。

历史地看，在 2005—2016 年的 11 年间，沿线国家产业结构变化有两个突出特征：一个是大多数国家产业结构的服务业化，一个是少数国家产业结构的快速工业化（见表 3）。从表中看出，有 44 个国家的服务业产出占比呈现增加趋势，只有 4 个国家的服务业产出占比略微减少；37 个国家的农业和工业产出占比都趋于减少，其中包括 35 个国家的制造业产出占比下降，具有明显的去工业化特征。在这期间，有 15 个国家的工业和 13 个国家的制造业在产业结构中的产出占比增加了，增长速度最快的当数缅甸、越南[②] 和乌兹别克斯坦等国家，前两个国家的制造业发展成就在国际上非常抢眼，而后者在非制造工业领域增速很快。

表 3 "一带一路"沿线国家产业结构特征（2005—2016 年）

	产出占比没有变化的国家数		产出占比减少的国家数		产出占比增加的国家数
农业	10	占比在 0%—10% 之间	37	缅甸和吉尔吉斯斯坦分别下降了 19% 和 17%	8	最多的也只增加了 4% 的产出，如巴基斯坦、乌克兰
工业	2	保加利亚和约旦最高占比 28%—29%	37	沙特减少了 19%	15	缅甸和乌兹别克斯坦分别增加了 12% 和 12%
制造业	6	斯洛文尼亚最高占比 24%	35	马来西亚下降了 8%	13	缅甸增加了 8%
服务业	7	占比在 42%—69% 之间	4	减幅最大的马其顿下降了 5%	44	马来西亚、卡塔尔和沙特增幅在 10%—19%

资料来源：根据世界银行的《世界发展指数》（2017）统计。说明：表中列出的国家是变化幅度最大的。

与发达国家发展路径不同的是，沿线一些国家的产业结构服务化并不是建立在发达的农业或制造业基础上的。在农业领域，2000—2015 年间，除 6 个国家的农业生产率下降外，其余 53 个国家的农业生产率都有不同程度（1%—469%）

---

① 2016 年，农业、工业、制造业和服务业产出结构（%）的世界平均水平是 4：27：15：69。

② 尽管缺少越南 2005 年的数据，从而无法与 2016 年比较，但是根据日常观察能作出这样的判断。

的提高，有 39 个国家的提高幅度超过了世界平均提高的幅度（39.9%）。这直接导致了大多数国家（41 个）高于世界平均水平（2 179 美元）。然而，一些高收入国家的农业生产率非常低，如中东欧国家的波兰、匈牙利等。我国的农业生产率不仅低而且提高缓慢，与多数沿线国家相比不具有比较优势。相比之下，我国最有竞争优势的是制造业，从 2011 年以来制造业增加值规模稳居世界第一，2015 年总规模是 2.87 万亿美元，占世界总量的约 1/4（24.6%），沿线其他 64 个国家加起来也只占我国的 63.5%。

沿线国家和我国在制造业上的这种差距隐含重要的经济和发展意义，即双向国际产能合作和促进发展中国家的经济发展。对于一些国家来说，有些产业在本国投资和生产既不具有规模经济或范围经济的优势，也不具有比较优势，引进中国的部分产能是最好的方式；同时，这些国家的某一产业想获得规模或者范围经济的优势，可以把生产和研发基地放在中国，而后把产品再出口到本国，这是一种双向产能合作。产能合作对发展中国家的本质意义在于，弥补制造业缺失或者促进结构升级以获得经济社会的发展。

（3）贸易特征。

2016 年，沿线 65 个国家贸易总额是 13.3 万亿美元，占世界的 31.9%；其中货物贸易总额是 10.9 万亿美元，服务贸易是 2.4 万亿美元，分别占相应世界贸易总量的 33.7% 和 25.3%。与世界总体情况相比有三个特征：与 65 个国家经济总规模占世界份额（30.9%）一致，与人口总量占国际份额（62%）显著不相称，服务贸易相比于货物贸易规模较小。由此可得，沿线国家间贸易有巨大的潜力，在提高贸易总量的同时，重视发展服务贸易。

在过去的十多年（2005—2016 年）里，沿线国家的贸易相当活跃，绝大多数国家的进出口增长速度都高于最发达的国家，但各国之间的贸易增速、贸易顺差或逆差的差别都极大。沿线国家最突出的贸易品是制造业和原材料，超过一半的国家以制造业为主，13 个国家以原材料为主，另有 5 个国家以食品为主，这也是贸易顺差的主要来源。只有两个国家（马尔代夫和黎巴嫩）的服务贸易额超过货物贸易，服务贸易逆差最大的国家是我国。沿线各国服务出口和进口最有竞争力的产业都是旅行、计算机和信息通信服务以及运输。

比较"一带一路"沿线国家的贸易便利化看出，以中国为标杆，有 21 个国家的加权平均关税高于我国，而 42 个国家的低于我国；相对于绝大多数国家来说，我国的物流绩效指数是非常高的，与以色列、捷克处于同一水平，高于我国水平的只有新加坡和阿联酋。

沿线 65 国在 2011—2016 年间，年均外商直接投资（FDI）4 329.4 亿美元，对外直接投资 2 826.2 亿美元，分别占世界总规模的 27.4% 和 19.6%，对外资的需要大于对外部投资，或者说绝大多数国家只有有限的或者还没有对外投资的能力。在这些国家中，中国是最大的 FDI 流入和流出国，分别占 65 个国家总量的 29.5% 和 41.5%。

就我国与沿线国家的贸易情况而言，通过与可得数据的 21 个国家的对比有以下几个特征：我国是周边国家最大的贸易伙伴；不是中东欧国家主要的贸易伙伴，我国占其贸易总额在 1.8%—4.4% 之间，并且这些国家对我国的贸易大多是逆差；沿线国家对我国出口相对多元化，最多的三类产品是矿产品、机电产品和劳动密集型产品，而从我国进口最多的是清一色机电产品。

"一带一路"沿线国家的国情和经济发展差异是巨大的，由此决定了各国对贸易投资要求在规模、结构及性质等方面的多样性，这些要求必定也会反映当前国际贸易投资的一些趋势（比如保护主义）。一些沿线国家都有相对稳定的国际贸易投资格局，比如中东欧国家传统的最大、最便捷的贸易伙伴是欧洲其他国家，我国要成为其最主要的贸易伙伴显然需要长期持续努力。发展要求的异质性、国际贸易投资的不利趋势以及一国传统的贸易投资格局都是上海自贸试验区搭建"一带一路"贸易投资自由化便利化规则平台的挑战。

4. 自贸区深化"一带一路"建设制度创新的思路

上海自贸试验区建立最高标准、最好水平自贸区的过程也是打造"一带一路"贸易投资自由化便利化平台的过程，应当根据"我需要、我创造"的原则，着重于构建基于如下要求的国际经贸规则框架：培育我国在国际经贸规则重构中的主导作用、有利于我国建立现代化经济体系、推动建设开放型世界经济和人类命运共同体。

首先，定义最高标准、最好水平自贸区规则。上海自贸试验区就投资贸易或者经贸合作等，既要吸纳沿线国家的自贸区的最高最好经验，又要主动与沿线国家共同谈判和定义最高最好标准的双边或多边经贸规则。这样的规则应该使现在由欧美发达国家主导的投资贸易规则相形见绌，以激发国际社会对新规则的向心力。

其次，掌握国际经贸规则重建主导权。在当前全球治理体系和国际秩序重建的时代，像我国这样的国家如果失去新规则制定权，那么在新治理体系和新秩序建好之后的世界里，必将是一个二三流国家。因此，上海自贸试验区以"一带一路"为重点着力创建的最高最好自贸区规则应当而且必须成为新国际经贸秩序的核心内容，唯如此才能发挥主导作用。

第三，扩大提升我国经济发展的新动能。尽管凭借改革开放使我国短期内迅速地融入了全球经济体系，但仍处于全球价值链的低端，获得的国际收益较低。建设现代化经济体系需要构建新国际经济关系改变这种状态，通过自贸区服务"一带一路"探索建立的国际经贸新规则，集聚和用好全球创新资源，加快培育国际经贸竞合新优势，建立起以我为主的全球价值链，为我国经济转型升级提供新动能。

5. 自贸区深化"一带一路"建设制度创新的对策建议

只有知道身居何处，才能知道去往何方。上海自贸试验区和"一带一路"倡议的实施都还处于初级阶段，实现预期目标将走过漫长且艰辛的路程，但千里之行始于足下，上文的分析为我们提示了如下可能的政策建议。

第一，以自由港建设为抓手。十九大报告指出，赋予自贸区更大改革自主权，探索建设自由贸易港。这是对建设最高标准、最好水平自贸区的新要求。上海自贸试验区要立足自身优势，在政府职能、贸易投资规则、金融、科技创新等商事仲裁等方面以最高标准和最好水平与沿线国家全面对接和提升。

第二，探索可持续的产能合作规则。由于沿线国家在国土面积、人口数量、价值观念、收入水平和资源禀赋等方面差异巨大，企业不能一窝蜂似的对其投资和贸易，经验表明一些小国对我国的一些企业不计后果、不计影响的投资贸易很反感。所以，自贸区应因地制宜地与沿线国家就产能合作探索建立适合当地特点的合作方式、规模和规则。

第三，强化服务业的对外贸易。扩大服务业的开放和出口是自贸区的重点任务，相对于商品的出口来说，服务出口相形见绌。同时，针对我国服务进口的不足，要最大幅度地放宽服务贸易限制，依托传统制造业改造升级、高新技术产业发展和科技创新开放合作，着力推动以现代服务业为核心的服务贸易。

第四，探索城市与园区合作新模式。城市（包括港口）是合作的节点，园区是合作的载体。园区经济是我国经济发展的一个成功经验，也成为走出去的一种方式，但本文想强调的是，园区经济是我国国情的产物，要把其形成和运作的模式一成不变的搬到其他国家，成功的可能性不是很大。上海自贸区要做的就是，与沿线国家合作探索适合当地的园区模式。这样的园区经济无疑是我国园区经济的创新和变种。

第五，强化基础设施建设和效率。上海拥有的区位、规则、人才以及城市的中心性等在服务"一带一路"倡议上具有显著的领先优势。不足的是，即使与沿线一些国家的城市相比，上海还存在明显的不足，比如物流的便捷性不如新加坡，上海的全球城市能力与最顶尖的城市如伦敦、纽约及东京等还存在明显的差距。所以，上海应当继续强化基础设施建设和全球城市能力，着力提高物流效率和跨境电子商务能力。

发挥上海桥头堡作用，建设"一带一路"人才培养体系探索

辛　格　　夏　璐

上海财经大学　中国人民大学

改革开放近 40 年以来，在中国共产党领导下，我国经济增长取得了举世瞩目的成功，为世界经济发展作出了巨大贡献。2013 年习近平总书记提出共建"丝绸之路经济带"和"21 世纪海上丝绸之路"的重大倡议，为全球经贸发展再注入新的活力。"一带一路"倡议具有时代意义，对密切我国同中亚、南亚周边国家以及欧亚国家的经贸关系，深化区域交流合作，维护周边环境，统筹发展等都有重大意义。为了更好地切实推进"一带一路"建设，需要建设全面综合的人才培养体系，以培养大批能够进行跨文化理解与沟通、具有国际视野的高素质人才。

在 2015 年《推动共建丝绸之路经济带和 21 世纪海上丝绸之路的愿景与行动》(以下简称《愿景与行动》)发布前后，关于"一带一路"战略实施的人才问题逐渐成为各界讨论的焦点话题。随后发布的《关于做好新时期教育对外开放工作的若干意见》和《推进共建"一带一路"教育行动》，将拔尖创新人才、非通用语种人才、国际组织人才、国别和区域研究人才和来华杰出人才五大类人才列为重点培养方向。2016 年 9 月 27 日在中央政治局学习会上，习近平总书记又强调：参与全球治理需要一大批熟悉党和国家方针政策、了解我国国情、具有全球视野、熟练运用外语、通晓国际规则、精通国际谈判的专业人才。由此可见，随着国家发展和国力强盛，中国对各种人才尤其是国际化人才的需求日益增强。

"一带一路"建设开展四年以来，"政策沟通、设施联通、贸易畅通、资金融通、民心相通"仍为全面努力的目标。与沿线 60 多个国家的多维度相通，人才是关键支撑。一方面，"一带一路"倡议的推行离不开熟练掌握外语、通晓国际规则、了解国际发展并知晓地区政治经济的专业人才；另一方面，"一带一路"在沿线国家的推行也离不开通晓中国事务，对中国有更强认同感，能准确理解我国需求的他国人才。因此，"一带一路"的人才培养，既包括我国人才与政治社

会经济精英的培养，也包括对"一带一路"沿线国家的人才与精英培养。培养这两类人才正是上海各高等院校、专业智库和高级人才培训机构应该积极思索并主动应对的问题。笔者认为，在推进"一带一路"建设的人才培养体系构建方面，上海已经具备的优势和条件以及在今后工作的着力点体现在以下几方面。

1. 上海培养"一带一路"国际化人才与精英队伍的主要优势

"一带一路"倡议的顺利实施，尤其要达至"民心相通"，离不开国际化人才的培养。正如中国高等教育学会会长瞿振元认为，"需要培养一批具有较好的国际交往能力，具有较好社会影响力与社会声誉，能经常往来于各国间的民间人士、文化使者，他们通过非政府组织（NGO）志愿者、学术研究、文化交流等方式进入到整个社会的肌体中，才能达到民心相通"。因此，在本国本地的人才培养既需要关注年轻人才也要关注社会精英。

首先，"一带一路"倡议所重点关注的贸易和金融领域，都需要高校在培养相应人才方面有创新有进展。上海高校可结合上海本地优质的金融与贸易资源，给学生提供更多实习实践的机会，真正培养出有扎实知识功底，又有实战经验和创新能力的人才，结合"一带一路"理念进一步推动上海自贸试验区的发展。

其次，"一带一路"沿线国家的历史传统、语言文字、风俗习惯等不尽相同。经济、金融、贸易方面的人才固然重要，但也不能忽略对语言文学、小语种、相应国别史、国际政治方面人才的培养。现实是，在人文和社会科学领域，我国与沿线国家的往来不多，很多大学甚至没有相应的教学人员，也谈不上人才培养。教育部的统计数据显示，我国 2010 年—2013 年外语专业招生的 20 个"丝路"小语种中，11 个语种的每个语种在读学生不足 100 人。而希腊语、希伯来语、乌尔都语、孟加拉语、尼泊尔语、普什图语、僧伽罗语和菲律宾语等 8 个语种均不足 50 人。随着"一带一路"倡议的实施，小语种人才的需求量必然会上升。就上海来说，虽然上海高校资源丰富，但除了上海外国语大学外，很多综合性重点大学都缺失这方面的师资与教育计划，这与上海作为服务国家"一带一路"建设桥头堡的地位与作用很不相称。

当然，推动"一带一路"倡议，掌握相关语言、文化仅是第一步。除新设相关专业外，还可从更高层次上培养人才，比如打破现有学科分类，实现"一带一路"复合型人才培养。除了培养"复语种"即一人可以掌握几门语言，更可把"多语种+"作为一种战略，即如上海外国语大学在探索"多语种＋多技能"的机制。

在北京，已跻身世界一流大学的北京大学、清华大学等，已作出有鲜明特色的国际化人才培养定位，比如北京大学本科人才培养的目标是"为国家和民族培养具有国际视野、在各行业起引领作用、具有创新精神和实践能力的高素质人才。"

这些都可以为上海众综合性高校所借鉴。比如，资源丰沛的高校可申请设立"一带一路"研究生甚至本科学位，学生需要在就读期间，完成包括金融、贸易、经济、语言、历史、政治等课程；同时，不同专业的学生和教师、研究人员可整合于新设立的"一带一路"研究院。这样不仅可以从体制建设上保证培养出跨学科复合型的人才，而且对多学科在"一带一路"方面的聚合性研究提供了场所。

2. 上海培养沿线国家的重点着力方向

中央三部委发布的《愿景与行动》中称，要"扩大相互间留学生规模，开展合作办学，中国每年向沿线国家提供 1 万个政府奖学金名额"。培养"一带一路"沿线国家的留学生和社会精英对中国的感情是巩固、加强中国和其他国家友好关系的必要举措。对于沿线国家人才，上海高校和其他研究培训机构可对留学生和已工作公务人员分别培养。

（1）留学生培养。制度化培养人才的第一步是要搞好学位点建设。如何建好沿线国家来华留学生的学位点值得思考。目前，北京大学、浙江大学等高校均已开设了面向一带一路沿线国家的硕士点项目。在上海，更多高校可设立类似培养项目，不仅面向华侨更要面向其他"一带一路"的 60 余个国家的优秀学生扩大生源，并加强来华留学生和中国社会的互动，促进年轻人的相互深度了解。

（2）海外公务人员培训课程。"一带一路"倡议成功的必要条件是获得沿线国家的认可与支持。虽然倡议的内容多以经贸和金融为主，但是政府官员的站台依然非常重要。2016 年 8 月由上海市外办和上海交大人文学院汉语国际教育中心合办的第二节非洲有成外事官员培训班，来自非洲的六名官员不仅参与了精心为他们设计的有关中华文化、中国国情与上海发展等课程，同时也参观了新基建、国有企业、基层政府和农业基地，从经济、社会、政治、历史、文化等各个方面进行了了解。类似这样邀请海外官员来中国培训应继续推广下去。在过去几十年，中国的各层级公务人员曾赴美国、欧洲、亚洲发达地区学习先进管理技术，并深入了解当地的文化、政治、经济与社会发展状况。如今，中国发展进入了新高度，为响应"一带一路"倡议，也可以邀请其他国家的公务人员来更多了解中国，学习借鉴中国经验。

因此，在培训课程设置上，笔者认为除了基本政府管理技能以外，更重要的是增强相关官员对中国的政治、经济、社会发展的全面认知，以培养对中国更强的认同感，在国家决策方面形成更多的"知华派"和"友华派"。

3. 上海高校智库和中国精英的能动性

向沿线国家派遣留学生与访问学者也是建构"一带一路"人才培养体系的重要环节。在过去几十年，我国的人才很多去了北美、欧洲和日本学习，很少有在沿线国家留学。在未来，比如国家公派留学基金可以向"一带一路"沿线国家适当倾斜，上海市政府也应积极与教育部合作派遣愿意了解、有志学习、积极投身"一带一路"建设的不同学科人才和学者到"一带一路"沿线国家当地进行进修。

除此之外，长时间的实地考察同样重要。只有长期在国外留学、工作的经历，才能真正了解、理解所在国的社情民意，这一原则对于国内"一带一路"所经的地区同样有效。要鼓励进行实地考察，而不是纸面作业，或走马观花、蜻蜓点水般的所谓调研。这也从另一方面要求培养出的人才既具有学科专业能力，又具有实地获取信息、分析信息能力，符合"一带一路"倡议需要、知行合一。另外，"一带一路"沿线国家有些国情复杂，政局变化很难预期，社会内部地区、阶层、宗教派系差异性大，官方外交不可能全面了解民间需求与广泛民意，而需要民间外交人才通过学术研究、NGO 志愿者、文化交流等方式深入了解整个社会的运行肌理。

4. 上海构建合作办学或短期合作培训项目等培养平台的储备条件

2015 年中科院院长白春礼曾表示："我们有意与'一带一路'沿线国家和地区的科学家建立联盟，共同商讨沿线国家和区域发展，从科学角度支撑'一带一路'。"2016 年 4 月中共中央办公厅、国务院办公厅印发的《关于做好新时期教育对外开放工作的若干意见》强调要"形成重点推进、合作共赢的教育对外开放局面"；随后，教育部于同年 7 月细化出台《推进共建"一带一路"教育行动》，积极倡导沿线国家构建"一带一路"教育共同体。在同年 7 月下旬的中国—东盟教育周上，教育部部长陈宝生和贵州省领导又共同提出成立"'一带一路'人才培养校企联盟"，50 多家高校与百余家中资企业已加入该联盟。其目标是通过校企合作，搭建平台，共同培养服务国际化、本地化的专业人才。由此可见，从国家层面到地方政府，都在积极推进高等教育的中外合作办学。

很多研究表明，在与欧美等地区的主要发达国家教育合作过程中，从早期的优质生源到后期的优秀人才都呈现出"一边倒"的"输出""外流"现象，我国一直处于不平衡合作的弱势一方，属于优质教育资源的需求方和被供给方。而"一带一路"倡议对于中外合作办学而言可谓恰逢其时：一是可吸引沿线各国留学生，深挖国际生源市场，培养具有一定中国情怀、深刻理解"一带一路"倡议需求的本土人才；二是通过中外合作打造的科研平台和决策智库来为"一带一路"倡议的深入实施提供智力支持和咨询服务；三是合作办学中培养的中方人才，也可输送到亟须建设与治理的沿线国家去就业、构建更紧密合作关系。

上海市政府和教委有丰富的与海外高校合作的办学经验，比如上海有教育部正式批准的第一所中美合办大学——上海纽约大学，迄今为上海乃至国家发展培养了大量人才。在此经验基础上，政府应大力鼓励上海的高校也更多走出去，发挥上海的地域优势，与当地高校合作或共同设立科研机构，培养服务"一带一路"的人才。除了有能力和资源在海外合作办学的高校和教育机构外，其他高校也可尝试短期的交换生项目或夏令营冬令营等，今日的学生是国家未来发展的依托，他们年轻时的交流体验也会对未来与中国的积极互动产生影响。

Global Financial Governance and the Belt and Road Initiative

Yide Qiao

Vice Chairman & Secretary General of Shanghai Development Research Foundation

The Belt and Road initiative is a platform for China to further expand and deepen its opening-up, and to advance economic globalization. The main contents can be summarized in five aspects: policy coordination, facilities connectivity, unimpeded trade, financial integration and people-to-people bond. As blood brings oxygen and nutrients to the body, financial integration vitalizes and nourishes the Belt and Road initiative, therefore, being an indispensable of this initiative.

Financial integration relates to a variety of problems. For example, where does the fund come from? How to collect the fund? What's the financial institution in charge of operation? Where does the fund flow to? How to monitor and manage cross-border funds? What's the currency for fund pricing and settling? What's the influence on the international balance of payment of the recipient country? These problems are not isolated, and are related to a bigger financial framework, namely, the international monetary and financial system. The reason is that the rule preparation, institutional set-up and systematic arrangement of this system will, directly or indirectly, influence policies, methods and solutions of the above problems.

After the World War II, the Bretton Woods Conference created the International Monetary Fund (IMF) in charge of balance of payments and the World Bank for development assistance. Besides, US dollar was established as the global currency in the form of gold exchange. Despite the fact that the US dollar was tied to gold and all other currencies were tied to the US dollar has frayed since 1970s, the US dollar remains dominant. It should be admitted that this global monetary and financial system has played an active role in global economic and trade development after the WWII, and in promoting economic globalization. We should notice, however, that this system has its shortcomings. For example, developing nations are under-represented. The ability to prevent financial risk and inclusiveness remains to be improved. After the global financial crisis, all countries and the international economic circle have stepped up efforts for improving global financial governance, and eliminating or removing such shortcomings. For example, G20 Summit of 2010 agreed on IMF quota and governance reform. After twists and turns, the IMF's quota and governance reform plan was finally implemented in 2015, witnessing increase of the votes of developing countries, including China. However, this is far from enough. In particular, the fundamental flaw of the system that the global credit currency is the sovereign currency of a certain country remains unchanged. The monetary authority (Federal Reserve Board) of this country would only decide currency policies on the basis of its own economic needs, which may clash with global economic demands. This is also the deep cause of global financial crisis.

Financial integration is what the Belt and Road initiative calls for. Firstly, infrastructure construction is the strategic core of the Belt and Road initiative, where B&R countries have enormous demands for infrastructure construction investment. However, most of them are developing countries and have insufficient domestic savings to fund infrastructure construction. According to the forecasts of Asian Development Bank (ADB), in the next 10 years, the investment into the Asian infrastructure construction will need USD 8.22 trillion. That is to say, each year, there needs to be a new investment of USD 820 billion for the infrastructure. Secondly, the Belt and Road initiative boosts huge financing demands for production capacity cooperation, creates opportunities of "Going Global" and industrial transformation and upgrading for Chinese enterprises. Thirdly, the Belt and Road initiative derives other financing demands, including financial cooperation with financing institutions of the B&R countries, and financial product innovation.

Such a huge-sized cross-border financing demand has its motivation for further improving global financial governance. In turn, it provides new opportunity for such improvement. During the process of economic globalization, developing countries including China have developed a lot in the past 10 and 20 years, and contributed 70% of global economic growth. To break asymmetry in this economic pattern and voice of existing international financial institution, a series of new international financial institutions come into being, such as Asian Infrastructure Investment Bank (AIIB),

BRICS Development Bank and Contingent Reserve Arrangement (CRA), which can play active roles in the Belt and Road initiative. During this process, these financial institutions will be developed and improved. This supplements and promotes existing international financial institutions, and builds a more fair and inclusive international monetary and financial system.

Financial integration involves fund settlement. Currently, some countries along the Belt and Road begin to use local currency for settlement. Therefore, there is less dependence on US dollar, and it is good for eliminating external financial shock. This currency multipolarity reflects objective requirement and may also be the evolution tendency of international monetary system. It is generally believed that a global reserve currency system dominated by USD, EURO and RMB is likely to appear in the mid-term (15—20 years later).

Enormous appetite from financial integration of the Belt and Road also expands cross-border application of RMB. In October 2016, the inclusion of RMB in the Special Drawing Rights (SDR) basket marked an improving status of RMB in the world. According to latest data published by IMF, foreign exchange reserves which were identified in the RMB reached USD 84.51 billion, accounting for 1.07% of the world's total foreign reserves. This is a good starting point yet the proportion is small. As the Belt and Road initiative develops, further cross-border use of RMB is just around the corner. Sometimes, history gives us some enlightenment. Though established by Bretton Woods System, the dominance of USD was actually driven by the Marshall Plan. Undoubtedly, the Belt and Road initiative is totally different from the Marshall Plan in essence. However, it is an international economic plan and may create better conditions for RMB's internationalization.

The Belt and Road initiative will benefit B&R countries, in particular developing countries. With achievements of policy coordination, facilities connectivity, unimpeded trade, financial integration and people-to-people bonds, countries along the Belt and Road will see stronger economic strength, improved financial market and more flexible economy, and become more resilient to external impact, thus playing an active role in stabilizing global financial system.

As mentioned above, the Belt and Road initiative will help reform of global financial governance. In return, this reform will promote the Belt and Road initiative also. Currently, IMF is undertaking the 15th review of quotas, and it is estimated that developing countries will have more votes and more say. In addition, after the financial crisis, the Global Financial Safety Nets (GFSN), as an important part of global financial governance reform, is strengthened. GFSN encompasses self-insurance (reserves), bilateral arrangements (swap lines between central banks), regional financing arrangements (RFA) and IMF multilateral financing mechanism, among which, IMF plays the leading role. Last year, IMF and Chiang Mai initiative made an initial test for risk prevention, which enhanced cooperation between IMF and RFA. Improved GFSN serves as a protection net for financial integration of the Belt and Road. Recently, the international financial circle gives priority to the monitoring and management of cross-border capitals, which can be seemed as a part of global financial governance. Cross-border capital includes foreign direct investment (FDI), security investment and other investments. Among them, FDI is very favorable for recipients and is less vulnerable to interest rate change. As to security investment and other investments, some long-term (over one-year) financings are also not sensitive to interest rate change. The rest is called quick-moving capital (QMC). QMC has big impact on developing countries and needs enough attention. Zhou Xiaochuan, the Governor of the People's Bank of China, divided capital into substantive investment and financial capital flow in the NPC & CPPCC press conference. Further classification, monitoring and management of cross-border capitals will undoubtedly promote financial integration of the Belt and Road.

All in all, the reform of global financial governance structure and the Belt and Road initiative, in nature, can be mutually reinforced. The key is that we should recognize this and actively guide their mutual promotion and mutual profit with market-oriented policies.

Analysis of Coupling Effect of the "Leader" of Shanghai Yangtze River Delta Economic Belt and the "Bridgehead" of the Belt and Road Initiative

Yanjun Li   Yi Zheng

Research Institute of the Belt and Road of the Shanghai Lixin

University of Accounting and Finance

1. Introduction

According to the 19th National Congress of the Communist Party of China, one of the important goals and tasks of applying a new vision of development and developing a modernized economy is that "we will move Chinese industries up to the medium-high end of the global value chain, and foster a number of world-class advanced manufacturing clusters". As the "leader" of the Yangtze River Economic Belt and the "bridgehead" in serving the Belt and Road initiative, Shanghai is an important carrier for accomplishing the aforesaid national tasks. Located at the entrance of the Yangtze River, Shanghai is endowed with a strategic traffic location accessing to rivers and seas. It has densest economic activities, highest economic effect and highest degree of openness in the Yangtze River Economic Belt. Carrying dual missions of the "leader" of the Yangtze River Economic Belt and the "bridgehead" in serving the Belt and Road initiative, Shanghai plays a pivotal role in the big pattern of China's opening-up and the "linkage among the eastern, middle and western area" of the Yangtze River Economic Belt.

Prior to the Belt and Road initiative, the golden waterway travels eastwards all the way, in which, Shanghai is undoubtedly the "leader" of intra-domain economy, and the "bridgehead" of export-oriented economy; after the Belt and Road initiative is proposed, the *Outline of Yangtze River Economic Belt Development Plan* clearly pointed out to create three growth poles of the Yangtze River Economic Belt, and promote development and openness at both ends of the Yangtze River Economic Belt

(Shanghai foreign maritime corridor, China-Euro Economic Corridor where Chengdu-Chongqing city clusters going westwards). The leading role remains its position, while the beaten industry has run into trouble. This is bound to weaken Shanghai's radiation to other cities of the Yangtze River Economic Belt and threaten its leading position. This may also diminish Shanghai's role as the outpost of openness and as the bridgehead. Carrying dual roles, how can Shanghai achieve 1+1>2? How to make both roles strong? How to eliminate hedge effect between them and achieve coupling effect? This is an urgent topic to be solved both by decision makers and educational circles.

Based on this, taking "coupling" as the pointcut, this paper analyzes the restriction mechanism of "bridgehead" hedging the "leader", and makes it clear the internal mechanism of the "leader" coupling with the "bridgehead". This paper also proposes the paths and solutions for coupling effect via leading enterprises, "main chain" enterprises and mature financial market.

2. Mechanism of "Bridgehead" Hedging the "Leader"

As the "bridgehead" serving the Belt and Road initiative, Shanghai embodies national strategies and carries strong political responsibility. During decision making, it needs great wisdom for the organic integration of national strategies such as serving the Belt and Road initiative, "four centers" and the construction of the China (Shanghai) pilot Free Trade Zone.

On the one hand, as the outpost of openness, Shanghai shall be adept in making new friends, in addition to building a stronger relationship with "old friends" such as southeast, central and western Asia. At first, we should open markets of the Lancang-Mekong countries, Bay of Bengal and European Union to make Shanghai the bridgehead for eastward openness. Thus, a development pattern in which goods and service trades are synchronous and international and domestic markets mutually integrated will be formed. Shanghai will become the hub and node of connecting hinterland of the Yangtze River and international market for better serving the Yangtze River Economic Belt as the "leader".

On the other hand, after activating overseas market, Shanghai will "consolidate" the overseas market and strengthen the "leader" with "bridgehead". However, without "leading" enterprises comparable to Shanghai's "leader" economic status, Shanghai may just set up the stage while benefits are all for the central and western China. To my mind, as the "bridgehead" in serving the national Belt and Road initiative and the outpost of opening-up, Shanghai's radiation to other cities of the Yangtze River Economic Belt will be weakened to some extent, and its "leader" position will be threatened. What's worse, the "bridgehead" may contradict the "leader".

The mechanism is as follows: the "bridgehead" function in the Belt and Road initiative tends to be stronger→opening-up upgrades→mid- and high-end demands of the central and western cities flow out→Shanghai's radiation to the central and western cities is weakened→Shanghai's "leader" status is declined, which blocks industrial upgrading of the Yangtze River Economic Belt.

3. Mechanism for Reinforcing the "Bridgehead" with the "Leader"

The Yangtze River Economic Belt has a number of clusters and belts, where belts are embedded with blocks, and blocks form belts. Large-, mid- and small- cities along the Yangtze River Economic Belt are reasonably laid out and form an integral part based on differentiated functions and individual services. With high intercity integration and centralized spacial distribution, this area has grown into the six largest community of common destiny for urban development in the world, featuring division of labor, coordination and sharing.

Shanghai is the hub of this global city clusters, and integrates modern industrial function, commercial and financial function, foreign trade portal function and cultural pivot as a whole. Shanghai shall not only highlight its "leader" role in the Yangtze River Economic Belt, and the radiation role of the central city to reinforce the "bridgehead" with the "leader". Leading position is the key, and bridgehead function is the result with bidirectional causal constraint.

The mechanism is as follows: highlight "leader" role of Shanghai in the Yangtze River Economic Belt→focus on the capital and technology—intensive links in the manufacturing industry, and achieve functional upgrading and structural optimization with the chain status of intra-production specialization;→achieve precise location with the central and western cities for benign competition; transform from intra-industry specialization and intra-product specialization to the division of process; realize collaborative promotion and dislocation development based on resource and endowment advantages, and historical and cultural traditional factors→gradually realize echelon upgrade→expand mid- and high-end demands of the mid and west cities on Shanghai→force Shanghai to strengthen its ability to absorb international state-of-art technology by taking advantage of intensified high-end talents scientific research institutions and the policy of "prior to carry and try", and drive innovation of original technology and achievement transformation of Shanghai→reinforce the status of Shanghai's "bridgehead" role in the Belt and Road initiative.

4. Path for "Bridgehead" Coupling with the "Leader"

In terms of economic aggregate, Shanghai is undoubtedly the most important growth pole in the sixth largest urban cluster and the Yangtze River Economic Belt. However, in terms of industry segmentation, Shanghai lacks in industries with extremely strong comparable advantages. According to data, industries with strong comparable advantages include clothing, textile, machinery and transportation equipment manufacturing (RCA of each of these three industries is >1). Obviously, Shanghai's industries with comparative advantages in international trade are mainly labor intensive industry. There is still some gap to expected "four centers". In a word, despite "leader" economic position, Shanghai lacks of leading industries, and "chain leader" enterprises, not to mention hard power such as infrastructures, transportation junction and urban scale. However, Shanghai has a long way to go to truly embody soft power of urban competition. Based on the hedging mechanism and reinforcing mechanism as aforesaid, in my opinion, there are three levels for the "bridgehead" to couple with the "leader":

First, the "leader" city needs "leading" industries. The "leading" enterprise must be a world-level, and is ahead of each industry covered by advanced manufacturing. That means, overall scale index such as output and asset must rank top among world subdivided trade structure, and performance indicators like profit, technology and brand must reach global leading level of same industry. However, it is impractical for Shanghai to cultivate such a lot of "leading" enterprises all on its own. Therefore, we need to spend great efforts in introducing world-class "leading" industries from geographical locations and policy bonuses. At first, we should work on setting up branches of the "leading" enterprise, actively introducing the key functional departments (such as R&D, marketing) of the "leading" enterprises, and finally attract them to settle in Shanghai, which is similar to the headquarters economy.

Secondly, actively cultivate "chain leader" industries. For 40 years after the reform and opening up, Chinese enterprises have got a chance for growth by attending the global value chain dominated by western multinational corporations. Some enterprises have climbed up to the highest end of global value chain and become the "chain leader" enterprises. However, during their rising to high- and mid-end of global value chain, most enterprises have encountered bottlenecks of different degrees. They will not only be "sniped" by western "chain leader" enterprises and even be captured by the later. On this basis, domestic enterprises must give full play of the Yangtze River Economic Belt and huge domestic demand markets, and actively grow self-dominated national value chain, and grow into "chain leader" enterprises. They shall start from domestic markets and gradually expand to overseas markets, and finally grow into brand-new global value chain. We should make the utmost of existing industrial bases of the Yangtze River Economic Belt, and focus on cultivating the 5 world-level manufacturing clusters, including electronic information, high-end equipment, automobile, home appliances and textile.

Lastly, regulate financial market, and practice financial service on substantial economy. An improved financial market will help Chinese industries march towards high- and mid-end of global value chain, and cultivating world-class advanced manufacturing clusters. This boosting function is helpful because of its theoretical support that a perfect financial market can play an irreplaceable role in fast growth process of local "chain leader" enterprises.

The development history of world economy also indicates that a country with advanced manufacturing is bound to have a perfect financial market system, and robust financial market will greatly reduce financial difficulty and cost of enterprises. Only perfect financial market can find these potential "leading" enterprises and "chain leader" enterprises and allocates financial resources for their growth from naive stage to fast-growing phase and mature phase. During cultivation of world-leading manufacturing cluster, on the one hand, a perfect financial market will speed up the development of "chain leader" enterprises and "leading" enterprise, and provide outpouring financial resource supports to the self-dominated national value chain and global value chain; and on the other hand, perfect financial market will directly serve a cluster of supporting enterprises and associated enterprises in the global value chain and promote their growth with the "chain leader" enterprises.

Offshore RMB Business in Free Trade Port to Serve the Belt and Road Initiative

Jianping Ding

Shanghai Institute of International Finance Center of Shanghai

University of Finance and Economics

1. Offshore Financial Business will Bring Larger Innovation Space for the Free Trade Port

Shanghai is working on advancing two national strategies of the pilot free trade zone and the science innovation center, and initially embodies the requirements as the pacesetter and foregoer. Shanghai is the largest financial center in China where all financial markets gather together here. It has accumulated massive data and experience in opening-up and monitoring, and has firstly put forward the direction of "highest openness, finest monitoring, and most accurate service". Shanghai guarantees effective "forceful" release with effective "control", and takes service as priority. System innovation is the key core of free trade zone. Over 100 innovative systems have been promoted in China to cut enterprise costs. The "free trade port", as the extension of the free trade zone, will hold control of logistics links in the global industrial chain and provides financial support.

The report of the 19th National Congress of the CPC proposed to "give more freedom to reform the pilot free trade zone and explore the establishment of a free trade port". Free trade port refers to the port area within the territory of a country or region that is outside the customs control points and allows free access to overseas goods and funds. Apart from the fact that goods trading at the "first line" are exempted from customs taxes and other import and export taxes, the attempt of free flow of capital is the key for improving vitality (See Table 1). Supporting measures must be improved also, such as convenience of foreign exchange and investment management, trade finance related to free trading, shipping finance and foreign exchange settlement. Offshore financial policy innovation brings reform space.

Table 1   Exploration of financial areas of Shanghai free trade port

Field	Shanghai free trade port (currently)	Global free trade port
Open to capital market	Not fully opened. "Shanghai-Hong Kong Stock Connect" is already launched, and "Shanghai-London Stock Connect" is under progress.	Fully opened: Trading at any time is available once the trading account is opened; the bond market liquidity is high.
Degree of freedom of foreign financing	There is line of limit.	No line of limit for debit and credit. Special service is provided.
Currency convertibility	There is line of limit and categorical constraint.	Exchange control is totally canceled.
All-round financial service	Various financial factor markets are under coordination.	Provide all-round insurance, settlement, finance lease, and project financing service.

2. "Efficiency first" is the Characteristic of Offshore RMB Business of Free Trade Port

Currently, RMB is still under strict control under capital accounts. China (Shanghai) Pilot Free Trade Zone needs to be more open in aspects of financing convenience, free exchange, cross-border use of RMB, release of interest rate and exchange control. In addition, financial innovation shall be promoted gradually, and attention shall be paid to the control of financial institutions and prevention of financial risks. "Pilot" of the free trade port in the financial field also involves financing exchange freedom, free access of funds, free trade settlement and developed financing service.

Free trade ports can be the sally ports for offshore RMB businesses, which, through "throat" (logistics link) of global industrial chain, provide a full range of financial services for China's investment in foreign countries such as in the Belt and Road initiative, including buyer's credit, project financing, leveraged buyout and fund settlement (See Fig.1). The effect is that "once the headrope of a fishing net is pulled out, all its meshes open". Harmonious development of the offshore market and onshore market will be developed through innovations of system, product, service and organization. Different from RMB offshore business in the free trade zone, "efficiency

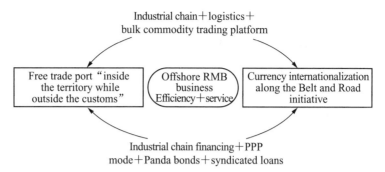

Fig.1　Relationship among free trade port-offshore finance-the Belt and Road

first" is more prominent in RMB offshore business in the free trade port.

"Efficiency" is the main characteristic of the free trade port finance. Here, the term "efficiency" means to meet investment and financing requirements of various institutions and individuals, and provide them with best "customized" structural innovation products. With professional combination of rating agency and various asset management institutions, the Free Trade Port can provide convenience in investment and financing, and one-stop financial services. That is to "pack" financial products with a variety of services (such as tax, insurance)(See Table 2). Non-resident financing business must be highly related to offshore RMB business. In addition, free trade port finance also relates to a number of customer services, such as preparation of budgets, short-term and long-term plans, cash income and payment, debt management, fixed asset, internal and external audit, purchasing, financial reporting, etc. To meet these financial factors and institutional requirements, innovation must be a top priority in the free trade port. "Packed" (bundled) products are inevitably associated with non-resident offshore RMB business. Offshore RMB business is bound to involve synergy of liquidity and derivative. There are many things to be "explored" in the term type of onshore RMB and in the scale of offshore RMB. For the moment, both markets have

Table 2　Links in which offshore finance can "pack" services

Service category	Service details
Tax services	Personal, business, company, payroll, accounting, E-application, country and region, and the like
Personal insurance service	Car, family, life, health, motor home, lessee, moped and vessel, and the like
Business services	Commercial real estate, debt, worker group, group heath, pension, and the like
Senior service	Supplement medical insurance, maintenance, final expense, emergency care, pre-planning, and the like

their "shortcomings".

The above "packed" (bundled) products are inevitably associated with non-resident offshore RMB business. Offshore RMB business is bound to involve synergy of liquidity and derivative. Current situations of liquidity and derivatives of the onshore and offshore RMB markets are as showed in Table 3.

Table 3   Liquidity of RMB offshore deliverable, offshore non-deliverable forwards and onshore deliverable markets

	Offshore RMB market	Offshore NDF market	Onshore RMB market
Foreign exchange spot			
Term	Spot (T+2 deliverable)	None	T+2 value spot
Day trade (USD 1 billion)	2—3	None	20—50
Unit trade scale (USD 1 million)	5—15	None	10—20
Foreign exchange forwards			
Term	O/N-12m, 18m, 24m	T/N-12m	O/N-2y
Day trade (USD 100 million)	3—5	4—5	6—10
Unit trade scale (USD 1 million)	0.1	10—50	7—10
Foreign exchange option			
Term	O/N-2y	O/N-3y	O/N-2y
Day trade (USD 1 million)	70—300	250—300	1400—2000
Unit trade scale (USD 1 million)	10—20	50	20—30

There are many things to be "explored" in the term type of onshore RMB and in the scale of offshore RMB. Both markets have their "shortcomings".

3. Offshore Business of Free Trade Port Contributes to RMB Internationalization of the Belt and Road

How can Shanghai finance support the Belt and Road? Currently, how to realize expansion from "Shanghai-Hong Kong Stock Connect" to "Shanghai-London Stock Connect"? How to expand the scale of "Panda Bonds" in the offshore bond market? How to innovate "syndicated loan" by Shanghai banking industry? Expansion of offshore RMB market is an inevitable link. China is moving towards openness. Will expansion of offshore RMB impact on stable RMB exchange rate? From 2015 to the beginning of 2017, it's true that China avoided impact on onshore RMB exchange rate by adjusting liquidity of offshore RMB. How to avoid their contradiction? On the one hand, expand RMB offshore products, and on the other hand, maintain stability of RMB exchange. However, we will move forwards to openness with greater strides. Expansion of offshore RMB market is inevitable. It is not a durable method for stabilizing RMB exchange rate by controlling offshore RMB liquidity.

The key to resolve this contradiction is accurate positioning of financial control. In this new era, China (Shanghai) pilot free trade zone accounts must be upgraded both in function and scale. Big data and scientific finance innovation bring in "innovative space" for new type of payment and settlement method and account. How to match the account (identity) of each financial product transaction platform in Shanghai with Binary-digits/quartile subdivided trade structure of HS code? Accurately monitor the combination with "inside the territory while outside the customs" (relaxing restrictions on the first-line and strict control over the second line) of China (Shanghai) pilot free trade port. Customs bonded zones and global logistics are links of production and consumption. Logistics finance brings future innovation space for Shanghai. The core of "openness and monitor" of foreign-related free trade ports still lies in the expansion of free trade accounts. However, China (Shanghai) pilot free trade zone accounts cease to advance in each free trade zone of China. The main reason is insufficient scale of capital pool, which poses high implementation costs on enterprises. Yet, efficiency is low. There is long lag time for fund capital. These problems will be solved with innovation of offshore business of the free trade port.

The Belt and Road initiative will further promote economic and commercial intercourse between B&R countries and China. This will construct network externality of currency area of RMB in regions along the Belt and Road, and improve "currency anchor" status of RMB in international transaction and international finance in these areas. This will be a key step for RMB's internationalization. The root function of ideal currency anchor in the international monetary system is to degrade potential power of a country and transaction expense during world trade and financial flow. For the anchor currency country, overseas trading and investment exchange risk will be sharply reduced.

Along the Belt and Road, there are many countries with strict control on exchange rate and under-developed foreign exchange market. If operating or export incomes and expenses of a Chinese enterprise body are dominated by the local currency, the enterprise can hardly make use of the local financial market for hedging foreign exchange risk. Therefore, there is realistic demand for giving full play of RMB as the local currency for the implementation of the Belt and Road initiative. To reduce exchange rate risk of enterprises, China promotes outright monetary transactions in countries along the Belt and Road, and implements regional direct transaction of currency in these countries. The People's Bank of China carries out a series of coordination mechanism arrangements with currency authorities of related countries, including currency swap, and RMB settlement. Advancing offshore RMB businesses in the free trade port will help realization of the above targets. As this paper finds: multinational processing trade and industrial chain reconstruction may bring new characteristic for the regional reference currency (See Table 4). This is reflected in extreme significance of RMB exchange rate reference and non-significance of ASEAN for RMB reference. Therefore, we should analyze from an updated perspective.

Table 4   Samples for study panel of relationship between the currency of B&R countries and regions and RMB

Area	Country	Number of countries
North Asia	Mongolia	
Southeast Asia	Singapore, Malaysia, Indonesia, Myanmar, Thailand, Laos, Cambodia, Vietnam, Brunei and Philippines	11
South Asia	India, Pakistan, Bangladesh, Afghanistan, Sri Lanka, Maldives, Nepal and Bhutan	8
West Asian and North African (WANA)	Iran, Iraq, Turkey, Syria, Jordan, Israel, Egypt, Saudi Arabia, Bahrain, Qatar, Ymen, Oman, The United Arab Emirates, Kuwait, Lebanon and Cyprus	16
Central Asia	Kazakhstan, Uzbekistan, Turkmenistan, Tajikistan, Kyrghyzstan	5
Commonwealth of Independent States (CIS)	Russia, Ukraine, The Republic of Belarus, Georgia, Azerbaijan, Armenia, Moldova	7
Central and Eastern Europe	Estonia, Latvia, Lithuania, Czech Republic, Hungary, Poland, Slovenia, Croatia, Republic of Montenegro, Serbia, Albania, Rumani, Bulgaria, Macedonia, Slovakia, Belgium	16

As to whether the Belt and Road currency would refer to RMB, we conclude the conclusions as follows:

At first, market scale determines currency reference weight. As Chinese economy develops, in general, countries along the Belt and Road increase the fluctuation weight of reference to RMB exchange rate (i.e., relatively reduce ratio of other currencies of SDR). However, this is far from shaking the status of USD and EURO. In particular, all countries' dependence on huge US market is absolute and overwhelming. This is not changed along with geographical distance and political relationship. This phenomenon can hardly be explained by the "gravity model" in international trade.

In addition, the trace of history is hardly erased. The shadow of original colonial currency's reference to the currency of the metropolitan state and the currency groups still remains. This is reflected in 8 South Asia countries (India, Pakistan, Bangladesh, Afghanistan, Sri Lanka, Maldives, Nepal and Bhutan) with great reference weight to Pound. The former Soviet Union (CIS countries such as Ukraine, The Republic of Belarus, Georgia, Azerbaijan, Armenia and Moldova) significantly refers to Rouble according to statistics.

Secondly, we must obtain pricing right for bulk commodity. Countries having their bulk commodities priced in USD (such as Iran, Iraq, Syria, Jordan, Egypt, Saudi Arabia, Bahrain, Qatar, Ymen, Oman, The United Arab Emirates, Kuwait) can hardly get rid of dependence on USD. In addition, their references to currency of major oil consuming countries are also significant.

Lastly, multinational processing trade and industrial chain reconstruction may bring new characteristic for the regional reference currency. This is reflected in extreme significance of RMB exchange rate reference and non-significance of ASEAN for RMB reference. Therefore, we should analyze from an updated perspective.

Research on Building a Risk Management Center for Overseas Investment in the Belt and Road *

Chen Yin

Shanghai Institute for Free Trade Zone Research of Fudan University

1. Preface

When Chinese President Xi Jinping visited Central Asia and Southeast Asia in 2013, he raised the initiative of jointly building the "Silk Road Economic Belt" and the "21st Century Maritime Silk Road", ushering the Belt and Road imitative. In 2015, the *Vision and Actions on Jointly Building Silk Road Economic Belt and 21st Century Maritime Silk Road* was jointly issued by the National Development and Reform Commission, Ministry of Foreign Affairs, and Ministry of Commerce of the People's Republic of China, marking a new stage of overall advancing of the Belt and Road initiative. In May 2017, Chinese President Xi Jinping delivered a keynote speech at The Belt and Road Forum (BRF) for International Cooperation. He pointed out that the Belt and Road initiative achieved great progress in the past 4 years. We should build the Belt and Road into "a road for peace, a road of prosperity, a road of opening up, a road of innovation and a road of civilization" in our future efforts.

Most B&R countries and regions are of relatively low economic level, and have huge investment demands. However, due to backward domestic financial market and relatively low investment and financing capacity, they have huge demands on overseas investments. Under overall background of speeding up "going global", Chinese

---

* This paper is a phased objective of the following projects: "Study on 'Prior to Carry and Try' and Experience Copy and Promotion of China (Shanghai) Free Trade Pilot Zone", the decision-making topic of Shanghai Municipal Government of "Study on Deep Development of Shanghai Free Trade Pilot Zone after America's Exit from TPP"; series topic of Shanghai Social and Science Planning of "Study on Improving Openness of Shanghai Free Trade Pilot Zone" and the connotation construction planning projects of think tank of Shanghai universities and colleges.

enterprises actively participate in the Belt and Road initiative, and increase overseas investments. According to statistics of the Ministry of Commerce of the People's Republic of China, in 2013, direct investment of Chinese enterprises on the countries along the Belt and Road amounted to USD 13.4 billion; this figure was USD 12.5 billion in 2014, and USD 14.8 billion in 2015, with year-on-year growth of 18%. By the end of 2016, Chinese companies have set up 56 economic cooperation zones in over 20 countries along the Belt and Road and invested a total of over USD 18.5 billion, generating near USD 1.1 billion of tax revenues and 180 000 jobs for host countries.[①] Further advances have been made in Belt and Road initiative thanks to Chinese companies' overseas investments on the B&R countries and regions.

However, we must see that after continuous growth, overseas investments in B&R countries and regions fluctuated after 2016. In 2016, direct investment of Chinese enterprises on the countries along the Belt and Road was USD 14.5 billion, down by 2% on year-on-year basis.[②] From January to March 2017, direct investment of Chinese enterprises on the countries along the Belt and Road was USD 2.95 billion, down by 17.8% on year-on-year basis.[③] The reasons are two-fold. On the one hand, with increasing uncertainty of international economic situation, China has stricter control over capital outflow; on the other hand, Chinese enterprises encounter or recognize rising risks during "going global". A growing number of Chinese enterprises have recognized the importance and urgency of risk management of overseas investments.

At the end of March 2017, the *Notice of the State Council on Issuing the Plan for Comprehensively Deepening the Reform and Opening up of China (Shanghai) Pilot Free Trade Zone* (hereinafter referred to as "*Plan for Comprehensively Deepening the Reform and Opening up*") was released, ushering a splendid chapter to Version 3.0 of Shanghai Pilot Free Trade Zone. The Plan clearly required to build Shanghai Pilot Free Trade Zone into a bridgehead for "serving the country's Belt and Road initiative and pushing the main market players to go global". To act as the bridgehead for the Belt and Initiative, Shanghai Pilot Free Trade Zone (SHFTZ) shall give full play of

---

① Data source: website of the Ministry of Commerce.

② Source: *Non-financial Direct Investments from Chinese Enterprises on Countries along the Belt and Road Amounted to USD 14.53 Billion in 2016*, press release of February 15, 2017, China Competition Information.

③ Data source: website of the Ministry of Commerce.

Shanghai's advantages and focus on solving the bottleneck and paint-point problem in implementation of the Belt and Road initiative. Serving the state strategy and relying on Shanghai's advantages, SHFTZ can promote its construction as the bridgehead for the Belt and Road initiative taking risk management center for overseas investments as the breakthrough.

2. Status Analysis of Overseas Investment Risks of the Belt and Road and Management

(1) Status of overseas investment risks of the Belt and Road.

According to the American Enterprise Institute and the Heritage Foundation, there are 33 risk cases of Chinese companies' overseas investments in B&R countries and regions from January 2005 to June 2014 (accounting for 25.4% of the total number of risk cases of overseas investments at the same period), involving amount of USD 56.52 billion (accounting for 24.0% of the total amount of risk cases of all overseas investments at the same period). These cases covered 20 countries, and average amount of money involved in each case was USD 1.71 billion.[1] As above cases shown, Chinese companies' overseas investment risks happened in B&R countries and regions, such as in Southeast Asia, South Asia, West Asia, Central Asia and Central and Eastern Europe. In combination with the "Safety Risk Map of Countries along the Belt and Road" prepared by Li Wei from the China Institutes of Contemporary International Relations, countries and regions in Southeast Asia, South Asia, West Asia, Central Asia and the Commonwealth of Independent States along the Belt and Road have high comprehensive safety risks.

Further, overseas investment risks along the Belt and Road mainly feature intertwined and overlapped risks and high combined risk. Various risks along the Belt and Road are divided into macro risks and micro risks. Macro risks include political, economic, financial, religious, legal, environmental and social risks, as well as traditional and non-traditional safety risks. Micro risks include project operating risks, management risks and financial risks before, during and after the course. Those risks

---

[1] Cited from Li Feng: "FDI Risks in the Countries along the 'Belt and Road' and the Countermeasures", *China Business and Market*, No.2, 2016, pp.115—121.

are often intertwined and overlapped to each other, making them more complex.

B&R countries feature complex political, ethnic and religious environments. In high-risk regions, political, economical and social macro risks co-exist and cross to each other. For example, intertwined risk factors of war, religious conflicts and terrorisms in Middle East evoke a series of macro risks and lead to high overall risk factor.

Moreover, macro risks and micro risks are always mixed and combined. Due to differences in language, religion, culture and custom, as well as restrictions in education, system and market development of host countries, Chinese companies' overseas investment projects encounter teething problems in terms of company governance mode, staff localization, motivation and constraint mechanism; restricted by economic and financial development level, Chinese companies' overseas investment projects lack in options in accommodation of funds and diversification of risk; in addition, facing restricted system, market and information transparency, Chinese companies' overseas investment projects encounter a lot of obstacles in market research and feasibility analysis; and project operating risks and financial risks may overlap with religious, social and political risks due to poor management or error handling, which may be intensified into an irretrievable public event.

Two typical cases are listed below to illustrate combined characteristics of risks of the Belt and Road.

China Overseas Engineering Group Co., Ltd. (COVEC) won the bid for undertaking Sections A and C of Poland A2 Expressway in 2009. However, after bid winning, COVEC faced with combined risks. The first is macro economic risk. During start-up period, international and European economic situations improved, and prices of raw materials (including steel, pitch and sand) soared, leading to high construction costs; the second is management risk. To quickly open European market, COVEC won the bid with a quotation that is half of the governance budget. During project implementation, the work efficiency is low due to language barrier of China-Poland staff; the third is environmental risk. COVEC failed to consider the fact that the Project would go through Poland nature reserve and therefore construction cost must be improved for constructing channels for the convenience of transferring rare animals. In 2011, COVEC had to abandon the Project and bear the compensation of EUR 188.5 million.

WANBAO MINING LTD. (WANBAO) and Myanmar Federal Economic Holding Company jointly developed Letpadaung copper mine in Myanma. However, shortly after commencement, the Project was stopped due to contentious case in March 2012. Then, the project resumed work in January 2015, and was put into operation in March 2016. During project construction, Chinese enterprise faced with a series of risks. Details are listed below: environmental risk: to respond to the charge against environmental damage, the Project Company withheld the fund for mine backfill and ecological restoration; economic risk: to deal with charges from villagers and protesters against land expropriation compensation, job placement and migration relocation, the Project Company raised corresponding standards; religious risk: the Project Company added investment to protect the Buddhism Historic Site within the mine area; political risk: during project construction, Myanmar had political turbulence; the contentious case was initially caused because of villagers' dissatisfaction to land compensation; however, as external political forces introduced in, this event evolved into a stage on which different political forces fought against each other, leading to ever-prolonged shutdown period.

Actually, most overseas investment risks encountered by Chinese enterprises along the Belt and Road are featured by combined risks.

(2) Management status of overseas investment risks of the Belt and Road.

China's risk management of overseas investments along the Belt and Road was in this initial stage.

China is making all-round efforts in the network construction of high-level foreign trade areas (FTA) with countries along the Belt and Road, and providing bi-lateral or multi-lateral policy and rule protections for trade and investment. By August 1, 2017, China signed 4 FTAs with B&R countries and regions, including China—Georgia, China—Pakistan, China—Singapore FTAs and China—ASEAN upgrading FTA. In addition, 7 FTAs (including upgrading FTAs) are under negotiation, and 4 FTAs are under study. China is giving great impetus to negotiations of Regional Comprehensive Economic Partnership (RCEP).

When major overseas investment projects encounter risks, Chinese government takes diplomatic means for intervention, such as Piraeus port project in Greece, Letpadaung copper mine in Myanma, and the like. The Ministry of Commerce, Ministry of Foreign Affairs, embassies and consulates of regions and countries of China along the Belt and Road and think tanks start to regularly issue information of these countries and regions such as national conditions, economic, financial, trading and investment information, as well as risk reports for B&R countries.

Several unilateral or multilateral developmental financial institutions proposed by China have been founded and participated in investment and financing of the Belt and Road, including Asian Infrastructure Development Bank , BRICS New Development Bank, Silk Road Fund, Russia—China Investment Fund, China—CEE Fund and China Development Bank. China Export & Credit Insurance Corporation provides overseas investment insurance businesses, including political risk insurance.

A growing number of Chinese enterprises starts to recognize the importance and urgency of risk management of overseas investments. Increasingly, enterprises begin to take due diligence via consultancy and intermediary services to strengthen risk assessment of their projects; adopt industrial chain of cooperation or participate in the international production capacity cooperation zone to "form closely knit groups when going overseas"; take enterprise governance mode that is more fit for the host country, increase localization proportion and add inputs in risk management such as insurance and legal consultation.

However, there are still large disparities in the risk management of Chinese overseas investments along the Belt and Road when compared to international advancing level, which still lags far behind the enterprises' requirements for "Going Global". Many local governments in China have set up a comprehensive service platform for enterprises to "Go Out", and many research institutions and think tanks provide information of destination countries and regions for enterprises to "Go Out". However, most information is general and highly similar. There is a lack of comprehensive, deep, accurate and customized information required for risk management of overseas investments. Information and resources of service institutions and platforms are not connected and shared. When an enterprise takes risk evaluation, it only sees partial information or information in some modules. Enterprises in different places repeatedly make the same mistake or fall into the same trap. In addition, we are short of international and market-oriented service institutions and talents. For example, existing insurance business of overseas investments are mainly dependent on China Export & Credit Insurance Corporation. There is no international and professional domestic market subject specialized in overseas investment insurance business; existing professional service institutions of domestic marketization mainly target their services at China, and seldom "go overseas along with the enterprises"; universities and colleges mainly provide decision-making consultancy for governments, and seldom provide customized decision-making consultancy for enterprises' "Going Global"; the incentive mechanisms, operating modes and concepts fail to keep up with market requirements; there appears severe shortage of talents proficient in minority language, small nation (race) and laws of small country.

3. Responsibilities and Conditions of Shanghai Pilot Free Trade Zone

The Belt and Road initiative is a master plan for China to expand its opening-up and foreign cooperation in the coming period. As the 19th National Congress of the Communist Party of China points out that, "we should pursue the Belt and Road Initiative as a priority, give equal emphasis to 'Bringing In' and 'Going Global', follow the principle of achieving shared growth through discussion and collaboration, and increase openness and cooperation in building innovation capacity. With these efforts, we hope to make new ground in opening China further through links running eastward and westward, across land and over sea." It is a new requirement proposed by the Party and the Country in a global perspective to build China (Shanghai) Pilot Free Trade Zone into a bridgehead for serving the country's Belt and Road initiative and pushing the main market players to go global.[①]

SHFTZ was initially established to explore new path and accumulate new experience for China's overall deep reform and further expansion of openness. SHFTZ takes a leading role in opening-up, reform and innovation development. To act as the bridgehead for the Belt and Road Initiative, SHFTZ shall bravely take responsibilities in national whole landscape and shall make audacious experiments and adventures, focusing on solving the bottleneck and paint-point problem in implementation of the Belt and Road Initiative. Risk management of overseas investments in the Belt and Road is one of the bottleneck and paint-point problems that affect the whole landscape.

Meanwhile, Shanghai Pilot Free Trade Zone has become one of most important

---

① Cited from the *Action Plan for Shanghai's Bridgehead Role in Serving the National Belt and Road Initiative.*

platforms for Chinese enterprises' "Going Global" (including overseas investments along the Belt and Road) by virtue of convenient investments and trades, open and innovative finance, comprehensive services and good business climate. By the end of 2016, SHFTZ has settled a total of 1 577 overseas investment projects, and Chinese investments have amounted to over USD 54.6 billion. Among them, 108 projects have been invested in 25 countries and regions (including Singapore, Czech Republic, Russia, India, and the like) along the Belt and Road, and Chinese investment amount has been up to USD 2.63 billion.[①] From problem-oriented and enterprise-oriented demands, Shanghai Pilot Free Trade Zone is responsible for exploring system innovation and system integration of policies and measures of risk management of overseas investments for better service for enterprises and protection of overseas investment interests.

Shanghai Pilot Free Trade Zone has its own advantages in prior exploration of overseas risk management along the Belt and Road.

At first, SHFTZ boldly explores institutional innovation system linked with rules for international investment and trade, and makes experimental achievements in investment management cored at negative list management, trading monitoring system focusing on trade facilitation and diversified international commercial dispute settlement mechanism. When these achievements are copied and promoted at different levels across China, conditions for copying and promoting these achievements along the Belt and Road also come into being to some extent.

Secondly, Shanghai Pilot Free Trade Zone and Shanghai International Financial Center are under linked construction to form a perfect financial element market system covering stocks, bonds, currencies, foreign exchange, commodity futures, financial futures, OTC derivatives, golds and insurances. In addition, a global center for innovation, trading, pricing and clearing of RMB products is initially formed. As SHFTZ financial market becomes more global, BRICS New Development Bank and The Global Association of Central Counterparties have settled in Shanghai in successive; Shanghai—Hong Kong Stock Connect and Bond Connect have been put into market, and issuing scale of Panda Bonds has been improved steadily; over 430

---

① Source: Press Office of Shanghai Municipal People's Government, *Press Conference of Shanghai Municipal People's Government on April 1, 2017: Institutional Innovation Achievements and Construction Progress of Shanghai Pilot Free Trade Zone*, April 1, 2017.

foreign financial institutions housed here, accounting for about 30% of total financial institutions in Shanghai;[1] by June 2017, 14 B&R countries and regions have set up 13 branches of foreign banks and 10 offices in Shanghai.[2] In SHFTZ, a diversified insurance market system has been initially established, covering original insurance, reinsurance, insurance asset management and insurance agency. In 2015, a total of USD 4.22 billion buyer's credit line has been provided to over 4 882 customers from 58 B&R countries and regions through export credit insurance (ECI), with underwriting support of USD 7.4 billion.[3]

Thirdly, SHFTZ is located in Shanghai where foreign resources and research and consulting resources are abundant and third-party service institutions gather together. At present, Shanghai has established sister city relationship with 64 overseas cities, in which, 22 cities are along the Belt and Road; among 75 countries who have set their consulates in Shanghai, 34 are along the Belt and Road. Shanghai is home to numerous colleges and universities (including 4 key universities of the 985 Project), various comprehensive and professional think tanks and research institutions. Among the first batch of 25 national high-end pilot think tanks, 2 are set up in Shanghai. An array of domestic and foreign-funded third-party service institutions have settled in Shanghai, covering fields of law, accounting, audit, consultancy and tax. Only in SHFTZ, there are over 40 third-party institutions engaged in law, finance, finance and tax, insurance and investment promotion.

4. Suggestions on Building A National Risk Management Center in SHFTZ

SHFTZ must serve the national strategics, and focus on the paint-point and problem in risk management of overseas investments of the Belt and Road initiative. It should meet the needs of market players by making full use of its advantages and undertake some major national functional carriers to create open cooperation platforms.

---

[1] Source: "Shanghai IFC Sees Smooth Advancing. Where is High 'Gold Content' of Global Cities Comes From?" Xinmin Evening News, April 10, 2017.

[2] Source: "Shanghai Welcomes Increasing Bank Institutions from B&R Countries and Regions", China News, July 21, 2017.

[3] Source: China Insurance Regulatory Commission Shanghai Bureau: A Modernized Insurance Market System is Formed in Shanghai, http://www.cs.com.cn/, March 28, 2016.

Building a national risk management center for overseas investments of the Belt and Road may be a sally port. Specific measure worthy of consideration includes following aspects.

(1) Provide institutional public products, and control rule risks and law risks.

The core of global economic governance is the preparation of rule and system. To a large extent, global economic governance is about the fight for rights of preparing and explaining international rules through peaceful means, and maintaining self-interests to the maximum. In recent years, international investment and trade rules are undergoing major reconstruction. America has dominated the preparation of new investment and trade rules such as TPP, TTIP, TiSA and America-type BIT. The core aim is to maintain and reinforce its dominant right in international rules and protect its trading and investment interests with international rules that are more fit with its own advantages. China has taken an active part in globalization and global economic governance. With the Belt and Road development as the breakthrough, China drives to construct a human destiny community. Therefore, topics, rules and systems are required to embody and practice the development ideas of "making economic globalization open, inclusive, balanced and beneficial to all". Upgrading multilateral trading rules shall be prepared for further protection of international investment benefits and deal with law risks and rule risks of international investments.

Operating for four years, SHFTZ has accumulated experience and made achievements in investment management cored at negative list management, trading monitoring system focusing on trade facilitation and diversified international commercial dispute settlement mechanism. Next, SHFTZ shall not only deepen and expand reform and opening-up pilots and timely integrate, extract, improve these experience, practice and measures (compared to "pearls" of a necklace) to form an institutional achievement of "necklace" type. This will provide topics and texts for bilateral and multi-lateral FTA and even BIT negotiations and promoting RCEP negotiation between China and B&R countries and regions. We will strive for forming a system and rule system with binding fore and power of execution as soon as possible to protect trade and investment interests and to prevent and control rule and legal risks of overseas investments.

(2) Deepen multi-lateral cooperation and enrich multilateral risk control structure.

In addition to strengthening of risk identification, risk early warning and diversification of risk, enrichment of multilateral risk control structure is also an important part of risk management of overseas investments in the Belt and Road. In this aspect, there are some top-level designs at national level. SHFTZ can take advantage of its internationalization and openness to actively create conditions for speeding up practice of related designs.

In 2015, BRICS initially proposed to set up an independent rating mechanism at the Ufa Summit, which was further confirmed in the Goa Declaration.[1] By far, BRICS has convened several conferences to discuss business modes and related algorithms of the rating agency to be established. SHFTZ shall strive for the establishment of the headquarters of BRICS Rating Agency, which is independent from existing Standard & Poor's, Moody and Ftich. With this as the breakthrough, SHFTZ shall promote the credit inquiry, rating and service business of this new rating institution along the Belt and Road. Meanwhile, support eligible enterprises for taking credit rating service of B&R countries and regions and gradually cultivate and build a credit rating agency and system with international influence.

Investment guarantee is an important mechanism in risk diversification of overseas investments. Today, the Multilateral Investment Guarantee Agency (MIGA) of the World Bank is the major multilateral investment guarantee agency in the world.[2] At the national level, a new multilateral investment guarantee agency is under consideration. Some experts recommend to support Asian Infrastructure Investment Bank, and set up Asian Infrastructure Investment Insurance Company or a new type of multilateral investment guarantee agency with similar type. SHFTZ can actively track development of this idea and create opportunities for settlement of this multilateral investment guarantee agency.

Risk management of overseas investments needs international dispute settlement mechanism. At present, it is a general trend to build a specialized and international dispute settlement mechanism and institution for the Belt and Road led by China. SHFTZ can further improve the diversified settlement mechanism for international

---

[1] Goa Declaration pointed out that: "We welcome experts exploring the possibility of setting up an independent BRICS Rating Agency based on market-oriented principles, in order to further strengthen the global governance architecture."

[2] In general, MIGA (Multilateral Investment Guarantee Agency) provides political risk guarantees for investors and loaners or help developing countries to attract personal investment businesses through technical assistance.

disputes, and promote the general international dispute settlement. In addition, SHFTZ can explore diversified cooperation mode between overseas arbitration institutions and Shanghai arbitration institution; build an international arbitration service brand; and strive for the settlement of the international arbitration center for the Belt and Road in Shanghai.

From existing experience, attraction of multilateral financial institution or sovereign wealth fund is an effective way for management and dispersion of overseas investments. SHFTZ shall support development of the BRICS New Development Bank with headquarters housed in Shanghai, and shall, with the help of related national departments, attract multilateral policy or developing financial institutions such as International Finance Corporation (IFC) subordinated under the World Bank, Asian Development Bank (ADB), Asian Infrastructure Investment Bank, Islamic Development Bank, Inter-American Development Bank and European Bank for Reconstruction and Development. In addition, SHFTZ shall attract such major sovereign wealth funds (such as Saudi Sovereign Wealth Fund, Temasek Holdings Limited in Singapore, Abu Dhabi Sovereign Wealth Fund and Dubai Sovereign Wealth Fund) to settle their branches or offices here. In this way, Chinese enterprises can adopt compound investment and financing methods (such as diversified equities, debit and equity combination and syndicated loan) during their overseas investments in the Belt and Road.

(3) Link with Shanghai IFC and strengthen financial comprehensive service.

SHFTZ and Shanghai IFC shall be jointly developed to make contributions to overseas risk management of the Belt and Road in the field of deepening financial service field.

Diversified financing is an important method for effective management of overseas investment risk. SHFTZ can further support enterprises from B&R countries and regions to issue RMB stock products (such as Panda Bonds) in Shanghai Stock Exchange and interbank bond markets, and strive for developing RMB international bond markets of the Belt and Road. SHFTZ can summarize experience of the Bond Connect and Shanghai-Hong Kong Stock Connect. At first, realize connectivity of important stock markets along the Belt and Road and then carry out connectivity of share markets when conditions get mature. SHFTZ can explore to set up a financial asset management company for the Belt and Road and optimize financial asset allocations and disposals along the Belt and Road. In addition, pilots of overseas asset backed security (ABS) can be explored to attract both domestic and overseas financial institutions and institutional investors.

SHFTZ shall encourage and support the construction of Shanghai International Insurance Center. Expand functions of the Shanghai Insurance Exchange, and strive for setting up the "International board" as soon as possible to attract international financial institutions. Innovate international insurance transaction products and improve international risk dispersion function; support Chinese insurance companies to open branches in B&R countries and regions; support all-round cooperation between Chinese insurance companies and local companies and transnational insurance companies; support regional, domestic and foreign insurance institutions to innovate overseas investment insurance products and provide comprehensive insurance services for enterprises' overseas investments, product & technology output and undertaking of major engineerings along the Belt and Road; further encourage the development of re-insurance institutions and services within SHFTZ.

SHFTZ can actively respond to the national concept of networked layout of financial service networks. On the one hand, attract financial institutions of B&R countries and regions for setting up branches in SHFTZ by improving conditions; on the other hand, encourage and support Chinese financial institutions to lay out networks along the Belt and Road or promote service connectivity through agent banks.

SHFTZ shall also impose stricter financial control requirements on financial institutions and enterprises in the Belt and Road initiative, such as pressure test, anti-money laundering, anti-terrorism financing and anti-tax evasion requirements; prepare compulsory requirements to embed quota management, system monitoring, risk early warning, risk evaluation and risk report into the ledger accounting system of the free trade account.

(4) Make bold exploration and promote development of professional service industries.

Professional service industry plays an important role in risk management of overseas investments. As mentioned above, at present, the short of international and professional market-oriented service institutions is the bottleneck.

SHFTZ shall combine innovations of overseas management mode and further expand orderly openness of service industry related to overseas investment risk management, in particular, openness in fields of insurance, credit, lawyer, accounting, tax and consultancy; promote competition with openness; cultivate and train international and professional talents, and encourage and cultivate professional and international market-oriented overseas investment risk management institutions in an open, competitive and learning environment; thus, these institutions are encouraged and supported to "go overseas along with" enterprises "Going Out", and carry out professional services related to investment risk managements in B&R countries and regions.

In addition to better and stronger professions; these professional service institutions are encouraged to actively extend towards both ends of the industrial chain. For example, Jiang Tai Insurance Brokers CO., Ltd. registered in SHFTZ, starting from financial insurances, has integrated such services as domestic and overseas insurances, accounting, lawyers and investment and financing services, and provided extension services (such as local due diligence, risk avoidance) for cross-border investments of mid-and small enterprises. Encouraging policies can be adopted to cultivate an extending industrial chain covering insurance companies, consultancy companies and rating companies to form a comprehensive investment risk management institution.

SHFTZ can actively strive for backbone from related national departments for pilot setting up professional overseas security enterprises; strengthen cooperation with governments and enterprises of B&R countries and regions; seek for opportunities to participate in and even create overseas security businesses along the Belt and Road to realize the initiative of "security is the priority of economic and trading cooperation".

(5) Explorations in other aspects.

SHFTZ can intensify explorations in other aspects.

SHFTZ can make concrete efforts in overseas institutions. Relied on Shanghai Foreign Investment Promotion Center, SHFTZ has set up 6 overseas offices since 2015. In addition to continuing the set up of offices in important B&R countries and regions, SHFTZ shall make concrete efforts in overseas institutions and move forward government services for direct and better services in the front line of overseas investment; intensify connect with local governments, chambers of commerce and overseas Chinese communities and cooperation with embassies and consulates; and strengthen risk control services while boosting investments.

At present, Shanghai has established municipal-level sister city relationship with 64 overseas cities, in which, 22 cities are along the Belt and Road. Backed on existing relationship between Shanghai and its sister city and construction of an international cultural metropolis, SHFTZ can build more communication mechanisms and platforms in culture & art, educational training, health care and tourism and sports; fully improve people-to-people and cultural exchanges of B&R countries and regions, and improve civil friendship and cooperation for winning people's support for overseas investment risk management.

With the principles of problem-oriented and enterprise-oriented, explore more effective incentive mechanisms, and encourage and attract colleges and universities, think tanks and other study institutions for providing targeted and operative decision-making and consultancy services (such as risk early warning, risk evaluation and risk management) for the Belt and Road. Meanwhile, strengthen risk education. SHFTZ can imitate regular issuance of financial opening and innovative cases. To be specific, related departments can unite industrial associations and think tanks for continual collection, classification and processing of successful experiences and typical cases of overseas investment risk management of the Belt and Road. Regularly (as recommended: semi-annual) publish such data for educating and warning related market bodies.

Research on the "Going Out" Strategy of China's Electric Power Equipment *

Shixiang Zhang   Yixuan Lin

College of Economics and Management of Shanghai University of Electric Power

Electric power equipment manufacturing industry is a crucial strategic industry in the Belt and Road initiative and has huge space for coordinated development. From 2006 to 2016, annual output of power generating equipment has been over 100 million KW for successive 10 years, accounting for above 50% of global generating capacity. Amount of exports of key electric power equipment has accounted for over 45% of global value. China has become the largest country for production and manufacturing of electric equipment. B&R countries and regions have rising requirements on electric infrastructure; and Chinese manufacturing enterprises of electric power equipment can take this opportunity for "Going Out" and achieve innovative growth and breakthrough development. Besides, this effectively drives structure upgrading of Chinese manufacturing industry of electric power equipment, and improves overall core capacity of electric power equipment manufacturing enterprises.

1. Background of "Going Out" for Electric Power Equipment Manufacturing Enterprises in China

Under ever-changing and complex situations, China integrates itself into the Eurasian continent through the Belt and Road initiative, and constantly attempts for

* The paper is The Innovation Program of Shanghai Municipal Education Commission(14ZS146); Shanghai Municipal Philosophy and Social Sciences Planning Subject(2013BGL016); Key Research Base Construction Projects of Humanities and Social Sciences of Shanghai Universities and Colleges(WKJD15004); Key Project of Consulting and Research of Chinese Academy of Engineering(2016-XZ-29). The Reception date is November 13, 2017.

innovation to occupy commanding height of economic development. Infrastructure industrial chain is fundamental to the Belt and Road initiative; and countries along the Belt and Road have heavy demands for infrastructure. This demand, in return, directly drives upstream and downstream industries and enterprises to go global. Deepening implementation of the Belt and Road has brought huge export potential for electric equipment in the form of equipment set and EPC.

(1) The Belt and Road initiative brings new opportunity for electric power equipment manufacturing enterprises in China.

First, countries along the Belt and Road have huge market demands on electric construction infrastructure. B&R countries are mainly developing countries and emerging economies. Most countries and regions have poor infrastructure and low economic development level. In consideration of their economic strength, they have insufficient fixed capitals and capacity for building and maintaining infrastructure, and are in urgent need of external capitals. Political turmoil in some of these developing countries could make their infrastructure construction even worse. Therefore, most external funds would not venture to invest in these countries. Electric development is the lifeblood of economic and social development of each region. Without electrification, there would be no industrialization, urbanization and informatization. These countries have constant and quick demands for electric power equipment manufacturing of electric power construction. This brings unique opportunity for electric power equipment manufacturing industry in China to "go out" for overseas development. According to related statistics and forecasts, line loss rate of most countries along the Belt and Road is over 20%, far higher than that of China (6.64%). It is expected to drive overseas market demands of primary and secondary equipment enterprises of the network distribution through transformation and upgrading of power grid. Demands for non-water renewable energy continue to grow, and new demands for overseas wind power, photovoltaic and nuclear power are also strong. "Going out" of electric power equipment manufacturing industry in China will drive electric construction and promote overall infrastructure construction and economic development of these countries for connectivity and mutual benefits. For these reasons, China shall give full play of development advantages of electric equipment manufacturing industry and actively devote in the development of countries along the Belt and Road.

Second, technical output of electric power equipment manufacturing industry has broad development space. The Belt and Road connects the vibrant East Asia economic circle at east end and developed European economic circle at west, and encompasses countries with huge potential for economic development in the middle part. It can be seen that there is great gap in economic development level among countries along the Belt and Road, with significant discrepancy from China. Low economic development level of some countries along the Belt and Road has restricted development and utilization of their power supply. Power shortage, in return, restricts economic development of these countries, resulting in vicious spiral of economic incomes. This also means that countries along the Belt and Road have huge development potential and space. Through years of development, China has established good electric equipment manufacturing system and product system, and produced a batch of new technologies and products for competitive high-end electric equipment manufacturing. Overseas overflow effect of manufacturing industry technology becomes prominent. The fact of multi-sided consistent interest demands and complementary advantages has urged China to cooperate with countries along the Belt and Road in terms of electronic equipment capacity.

(2) Breakthroughs of electric power equipment manufacturing industry.

First, improving technology level of electric equipment. Electric equipment in China, represented by large-size complete equipment for power generation with proprietary intellectual property rights, UHV complete equipment for power transmission and transformation and complete set of equipment for smart grid, has reached world level. Landmark and major technical equipment and products include: power generation equipment: 1 000 megawatt ultra-supercritical thermal power unit, 700 megawatt and above hydroelectric generating set; 1 000 megawatt nuclear power unit; 300 megawatt F-level heavy-duty gas turbine; transformation and transmission equipment: 1 000 kV UHV complete set of AC power transmission equipment; ±800 kV UHV complete set of DC power transmission equipment, and complete set of transformation and transmission equipment for smart grid; key and core parts: safety valves for ultra-supercritical thermal power unit and large nuclear power plant; protective circuit breakers for large-size generator unit, 5-inch 7 200V/3 000A, 6-inch 8 500V/4 000A—4 750A electrically controlled thyristor, and DC transmission converter valve for ±800 kV and below.

Second, improving capacity of electric equipment for supporting Stage major engineering construction. After 30 years of unremitting efforts, a batch of world-leading electric equipment have been developed based on our national conditions. They embody the principles of a combination of "production, learning, study and application" and are result of introduction, absorption and re-innovation of technology. Such equipment has been applied in a wave of major national engineering constructions such as 600 megawatt supercritical thermal power engineering in Qinbei, Henan, 10 000 megawatt ultra-supercritical thermal power project in Yuhuan, Zhejiang Province, 1 000 megawatt ultra-supercritical air-cooled thermal power engineering. in Lingwu, Ningxia, ultra-supercritical circulating fluid bed project in Baima, Sichuan, Three Gorges Hydropower Project, Xiangjiaba Hydropower Project, Phase II Nuclear Power Project in Ling'ao, Sanmen Nuclear Power Project, Guanting—East Lanzhou ±750 kV AC transmission and transformation project, Xiangjiaba—Shanghai ±800 kV UHV DC power transmission project. Such equipment guarantees the implementation of national energy strategy of "West-East Electricity Transmission Project" and becomes a central pillar of strength for supporting national major engineering projects.

Third, China is growing into a manufacturing power of electric equipment. From 2006 to 2016, annual output of power generating equipment has been over 100 million kW for successive 10 years, accounting for above 50% of global generating capacity. By the end of 2016, installed capacity of generating equipment of China has outperformed that of US and reached 1.6 billion KW, ranking first in the world. Since 2008, annual output of transformer has been over 1 billion KVA for successive

Table 1　Scale of electric power equipment manufacturing industry in China from 2010 to 2015

Year	Number of enterprises	Total assets (RMB 100 million)	Year-on-year growth (%)
2010	26 161	27 326.56	24.73
2011	18 301	33 025.24	23.62
2012	19 808	38 544.74	10.69
2013	18 652	39 330.62	9.33
2014	19 079	43 370.73	9.57
2015	19 632	45 125.06	8.39

Source: China Machinery Industry Federation.

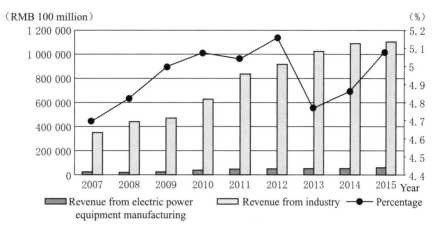

Source: China Machinery Industry Federation.

Fig. 1   Operating incomes of electric power equipment manufacturing
industry in China from 2007 to 2015

8 years. Since 2014, electric power manufacturing industry has made big progress. China has been among the world largest manufacturing countries of electric equipment thanks to a series of advantageous factors, such as great demands from application fields, significant technological innovation capacity, breakthroughs in major equipment and quick adjustment of industrial structure. In the future, electric equipment market demands will be greatly improved as Chinese Government increases construction input on power supply and power grid. In 2015, industrial output of electric equipment manufacturing industry in China was over RMB 5 trillion; main operation income was RMB 5.33 trillion; profit was RMB 311.2 billion; total import and export volume was RMB 164.9 billion; the industry scale has been increased constantly (See Table 1, Fig.1 and Fig.2).

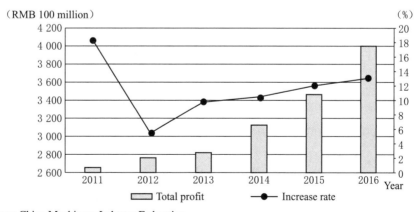

Source: China Machinery Industry Federation.

Fig. 2   Total profits and growth rates of electric power equipment
manufacturing industry in China from 2011 to 2016

(3) Necessity of "Going Out" for electric power equipment manufacturing enterprises.

First, respond to the Belt and Road initiative and seize the opportunities of strategical development. The Belt and Road initiative brings with the electric power equipment manufacturing enterprises in China better political supports and rare opportunities of overseas project investment. The Belt and Road initiative is expected to bring new opportunities for grid construction and investment, speed up the global promotion of domestic electric power equipment, and promote the demand growth from overseas clean and renewable energy market. Under the background of the Belt and Road initiative, manufacturing cooperation for electric power equipment can deepen foreign relations, especially the economic and technical cooperation between China and the countries along the Belt and Road, and strengthen the international influences and the right of speech of China in the high-tech industry.

Second, enhance the capability of independent innovation and technological progress, increase profits and employment, and promote the sustainable development of the industry and related industries. As a key industry in the national economy providing power components to power generation, transmission, transformation, distribution, utilization and other segments, the electric power equipment manufacturing is in urgent pursuit of independent innovation to improve its competitiveness. The key to sustainably develop the industry and related industries lies in its capability of independent innovation and technological progress. The transformation of China's manufacturing industry from "big-scale" to "powerful" industry and from "Made in China" to "Created in China" requires the important driving force from the "Going Out" of electric power equipment manufacturing, which can not only lead to better development of the electric power equipment manufacturing itself, but also drive the development of upstream and downstream industries and the rationalization of foreign trade structure.

2. Main Forms of "Going Out" for Electric Power Equipment Manufacturing Enterprises in China

In general, "Going Out" often crosses geographic boundaries and requires several ways and means of talent introduction, cooperative research and development, trade and investment, cross-border M&A, joint ventures, project contracting, etc. Implementation of the Belt and Road initiative and "Going Out" is an important way for large enterprises to realize "globalization", a major opportunity for private enterprises, and also a key path for upgrade and development of SMEs. The "Going Out" policy of electric power equipment manufacturing emphasizes on the "Going Out" cooperation among electric power enterprises, equipment manufacturing enterprises and power construction enterprises, and at the same time prevents the homogeneous and cut-throat competition among domestic enterprises. In addition, through establishment of international financing platform and international marketing network, the research on international development of products can utilize industrial funds and state-owned capital gains to promote the "Going Out" of competitive industrial capacity of electric power equipment and support overseas investments and M&A. In the initial stage of "Going Out" for electric power equipment enterprises, the geographical advantages of large-scale electric power equipment groups and the western frontier areas have become more prominent. The terminal energy metering equipment also occupies certain market shares. As the Belt and Road initiative contributes to upgrade of power and energy infrastructure and promotion of franchising mode, electric power equipment enterprises are expected to comprehensively realize the "Going Out" policy. The enterprises with sufficient cash flow and completely covered product series are supposed to get involved in overseas projects EPC and current business modes relying on their groups, as well as new demands from the overseas markets of intelligent terminals (meter/charging pile/ energy management system) and new energy power generation. During transformation from single equipment export to franchising of overseas projects, the listed enterprises that have laid out overseas market channels in advance are deemed promising.

In recent years, electric power equipment enterprises mainly go global in the following ways: first, set up factories near the market supply side, such as the coal mining and petrochemical industrial services for explosion-proof products, and some domestic enterprises have set up factories in Iran to better provide direct services to the front-end market; second, set up factories in the front end of raw materials, such as the African factories set up by some special transformer enterprises in areas with lower copper price; third, directly merge overseas enterprises. The business mode is gradually transforming from the traditional single equipment procurement to package solutions, including BOT, BOO, PPP, EPC and other emerging modes. The PPP mode, i.e. "Public-Private-Partnership" mode, basically operates in the form of procurement, in which government departments and the winning bidder specify their rights and obligations by executing

Table 2 PPP Mode in Project Management of Electric Power Enterprises

Type of project	Benefits
Nuclear power projects	It will be conducive to the introduction of advanced foreign technologies and absorption of advanced management concepts in China and also will be able to strengthen the government's control ability. Ensure the advanced technologies of nuclear power projects while maintaining quality and safety of projects.
Hydropower project	It can not only increase financing methods of projects, but also spread financing risks of projects. In the PPP model, the government's dominant role is to provide reasonable assistance to projects and to make the project more financially viable.
Wind power project	It is of great positive significance for optimizing the financing structure of hydropower projects and can promote the sustainable development of power enterprises. The power projects can achieve the benign management of financing sources.

contracts and establish a specific-purpose enterprise to raise funds for further construction and project operation. The PPP mode is in line with basic characteristics of the Belt and Road initiative as the introduction of private enterprises has greatly reduced the financial burden on government departments. Introduction of PPP mode may obtain great application values, especially in the areas of special equipment, electrical machinery, equipment manufacturing products, and other large-scale equipment and major projects, which features possibilities of "Going Out" under the PPP mode (See Table 2, Table 3).

Table 3 Success Cases of PPP Mode Projects Involving Electric Power Equipment Manufacturing Products at Home and Abroad

Case name	Industry (categories)	Time	Region	Result
Domestic				
China Taiping - CGN Nuclear Power Project Claims Plan	Electrical machinery and equipment	Since 2012	China Guangdong	On going
First PV Poverty Alleviation PPP Project in China	Electrical machinery and equipment	Since 2014	China Anhui	Succeeded
Jiuquan Urban CHP Centralized Heating Project	Electrical machinery and equipment	Since 2009 Completed in 2014	China Gansu	Succeeded
Foreign				
Poznan Municipal Waste Heat Treatment Plant Project in Poland	Electrical machinery and equipment	Since 2004 Completed in 2013	Poland and EU	Succeeded
Hinkley Point C Nuclear Power Project in UK	Electrical machinery and equipment	Since 2016	China, UK, France	On going
Jordan Red Sea Project of SINOHYDRO Corporation Limited	Electrical machinery and equipment	Since 2012	China and Jordan	On going

Source: relevant public informationas of September 2017.

Since 2007, SGCC has actively advocated the "Going Out" policy, constantly opened up overseas markets from Philippines, Brazil and other developing countries to the developed countries such as Italy, Portugal and Australia, and shifted its business focus from labor export to technology and management output (See Table 4). Participation in power transmission and distribution network of foreign power enterprises is conducive to promoting the domestic equipment manufacturers to go abroad. It is also an important way to effectively break the monopoly and export equipment, similar to the domestic reform of power management system with incremental distribution network.

Table 4 Technology and Management Output from State Grid Corporation of China

Year	Major events
2007	Formed a consortium with Filipino enterprises to acquire a 25-year concession at the price of USD 3.95 billion
2010	Invested USD 989 million to acquire 7 transmission enterprises in Brazil and a 30-year concession to their transmission assets
2012	Acquired 41% shares of a power supplier in SA, Australia
2012	Invested Euro 387 million to acquire 25% shares of Portugal's national energy company
2014	Acquired Australian equity of Singapore Power Ltd, including 60% SPIAA shares and 19.9% SPAusNet shares
2014	Invested EUR 2 billion to acquire 35% shares of Italy's national power grid company
2016	Executed the contracts for Egypt EETC500KV national grid upgrade and transmission projects
2016	Signed a shareholders' agreement with Russia's power grid corporation to set up a joint venture for grid business
2016	Acquired 24% shares of the transmission network operator of Greek's national power corporation

Source: relevant public informationas of September 2017.

3. Status of "Going Out" for Electric Power Equipment Manufacturing Enterprises in China

(1) Status of "Going Out" for electric power equipment manufacturing enterprises in China.

In 2015, the overseas businesses of major power transmission and distribution equipment enterprises continued to grow, of which the overseas revenue of TBEA and China XD Electric accounted for 21.6% and 10.9%. Due to globalization of smart power grids, exports of smart meters have steadily developed and leading power enterprises such as Hexing Electrical Co., Ltd. have also emerged in the industry. In 2016, in addition to the orders of engineering industries obtained by Shanghai Electric Power Generation Group in Egypt, Indonesia and Bangladesh, the Shanghai electric service industry has also gained certain benefits and executed subcontracting contracts for Philippines projects utilizing domestic utility boilers. In addition, the Stanari project in Bosnia and Herzegovina, which was designed, manufactured and constructed by Dongfang Electric Corporation, was put into commercial operation. It was the first large-scale infrastructure cooperation project since the formal establishment of diplomatic relations between China and Bosnia and Herzegovina, and also the first thermal power EPC project in Europe independently designed and constructed by Chinese enterprises; Harbin Electric Corporation targeted to seize the high-end overseas and new business areas, promote enterprises to go up on the basis of "Going Out" and compete with the advanced enterprises in the world. Its power plant projects have been gradually marching into the high-end power markets in Middle East, South America, Turkey and Eastern Europe from its traditional markets in Vietnam, Pakistan, Philippines, Indonesia, etc. (See Table 5).

From the perspective of foreign trade, the scale of import and export of electric power equipment manufacturing has been reduced (See Fig.3). Specifically, in 2015, the localization rate of China's electric power equipment continued to increase, and the import substitution effect further increased. The growth rate of imports dropped from 1.73% in 2014 to −10.75%. Due to the sluggish global economic recovery and weak overseas market demands, the growth rate of electric power equipment exports dropped sharply to −3.51% from 6.95% in 2014. After 2016, the lack of domestic and foreign demands for electric power equipment and the import substitution effect further continued, while the annual import and export volume continued to grow negatively. However, the sharp decline in growth was eased, with growth rates of −6% and −2% respectively.

(2) Status of "Going Out" for leading enterprises of electric power equipment manufacturing in China.

Taking Shanghai Electric Group as an example, it has continuously taken

Table 5 "Going Out" projects of electric power equipment

Year	Item	Associated enterprises	Equipment	Participation mode
2013	Cambodia Sesan No.2 hydropower station	China Huaneng Group	Hydropower equipment	Project construction and management
2014	Wind power transformers dominating main markets of Ethiopian	Taikai Group	Wind power equipment	Establishing branches + product export
2014	EPC contract of Vinh Tan coal-fired power plant	Energy China	Thermal power equipment	EPC + operation
2015	Belarus wind power generation apparatus	China Huayi Electric Co., Ltd.	Wind power equipment	Product export
2015	Brazil Belo Monte Phase II project	State Grid Corporation of China	Domestic electric power equipment	Investment + contracting + operation
2015	Full-life framework agreement of Cernavoda No. 3 & 4 nuclear power units	China General Nuclear Power Group	Nuclear power equipment	Agreed MOU
2015	Replacement project of Koeberg nuclear power station in South Africa	Shanghai Electric	Main nuclear power equipment	Subcontracted manufacturing
2016	Brazil Jeri hydropower station	DFEM	Hydropower equipment	EPC + operation
2016	Pakistan Matiari-Lahore DC transmission project	State Grid Corporation of China	Power transmission equipment	Project cooperative agreement
2016	Wind power towers exported from Lianyungang to UK	CSWind Corporation	Wind power equipment	Product export
2016	Blyth offshore wind power generation project	MHI Vestas Offshore Wind Co., Ltd.	Wind power equipment	Product export
2016	Montenegro MOZURA wind power project	State Grid Shanghai Municipal Electric Power Company	Wind power equipment	Investment + contracting + operation

Source: relevant public information as of September 2017.

measures to implement the "Going Out" policy. In August 2016, Shanghai Electric and Shanghai Electric (Hong Kong) Co., Ltd., a wholly-owned subsidiary, signed a share purchase agreement with four parties (holding 100% shares of TEC4). The company is committed to expanding the energy and smart manufacturing businesses, and in the future will, through innovative collaboration, product diversification, active market exploration and other ways, promote the common development among the company

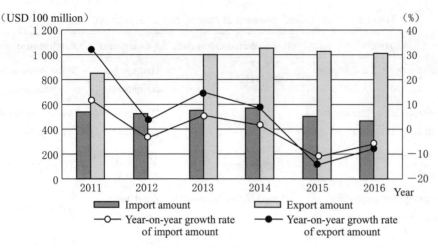

（USD 100 million）　　　　　　　　　　　　　　　　　　（%）

Source: China Machinery Industry Federation.

Fig. 3　2011—2016 Import and Export of electric power equipment manufacturing in China

and acquired parties. In the past seven years, China's electric power equipment has accounted for about 40% shares of the new electric power equipment market in India, and India is now the largest overseas export market for electric power equipment in China. In recent years, along with the rapid economic development, demands for electricity in India has also risen sharply. However, the supply capacity of its local electric power equipment manufacturers is limited. Therefore, China's electric power equipment manufacturing can take advantage of this opportunity to develop the Indian market. According to the statistics of India's Ministry of Power, from 2012 to 2017, India had already started construction of 76 000 MW of installed capacity, of which over 60% of the equipment was provided by Chinese manufacturers. Where Shanghai Electric, Harbin Electric and other major Chinese power generation equipment manufacturers have entered the Indian market. Shanghai Electric has developed India as its largest overseas market. At present, it has 12 power station construction projects and achieves an installed capacity of 20 000 MW, accounting for half of China's exports of electric power equipment to India.

Since the 12th Five-Year Plan, Shanghai has made remarkable achievements in many aspects by consistently serving the national equipment manufacturing development, integrating resources, exerting its advantages and continuously improving the high-end equipment manufacturing. As indicated in data released by Shanghai Customs in January 2017, taking the export of electromechanical products as an example, in 2016, the customs territory of Shanghai Customs exported RMB 850.68

billion of electromechanical products to the countries along the Belt and Road, and the total export value of electromechanical products from January to June in 2017 was RMB 442.321 billion, accounting for a large proportion (70.6%) of total export value, an increase of 1.2 percentage points.

With the construction of smart grids and the advancement and development of energy Internet, the flow of circuit information will shift from one-way to multi-way and from chains to networks, but these objectives must be supported by electric power equipment. In September 2016, Shanghai Municipal Commission of Commerce and Commission of Economy and Information Technology awarded Lingang area as "Shanghai Demonstration Base for Equipment Going Out and International Cooperation of Production Capacity" to actively promote the development of local equipment manufacturing enterprises and key institutions, and facilitate leading enterprises to drive the common development of SMEs. The construction of demonstration bases in other areas will be gradually carried out in the future and the leading role of demonstration bases, including Lingang area, will be actively exerted, making it the benchmark for "Going Out" of equipment from Shanghai and even China.

4. Factors Influencing "Going Out" of Electric Power Equipment Manufacturing in China

(1) Technologies of domestic electric power equipment manufacturing.

Most electric power equipment manufacturing enterprises still features large scale and less competitiveness. Strong reliance on imported core technologies and weak capacity for independent innovation lead to low added value of products, leaving them at the low end of the global value chain. For example, the environmental protection technology of coal-fired units, large-scale pumped storage units, blades of heavy-duty gas turbines, technologies of package equipment for power transmission and transformation, new high-temperature superconducting transmission and transformation equipment, etc. Although the introduction of technologies has made the domestic manufacturing self-fulfilled, most enterprises rely on imitation. In addition, key components, materials and supporting systems also rely heavily on imports. In respect of reliability and energy consumption indicators, certain gaps still exist between major foreign equipment and electric power equipment manufactured by Chinese enterprises.

Therefore, the need to effectively strengthen the macro control and improve the demand structure will force the electric power equipment manufacturing to a high-end and environmental transformation.

(2) Existing development problems of domestic enterprises in electric power equipment manufacturing.

Obscure mergers and acquisitions, quick success, lack of professional experience and lack of knowledge can easily make enterprises in trouble. In Beijing, Shanghai, Guangzhou, Shenzhen and other first-tier and second-tier cities, rising living and business costs have lead to significant loss of skilled workers and compound talents, disproportion of input and output, increased pressure on corporate human costs, and severe shortage of high-end innovative compound talents in some areas. Therefore, retaining talents and cultivating comprehensive talents will allow powerful intellectual enterprises to go out and help build the success of the Belt and Road initiative.

(3) Difficulties in technical application.

Chinese technical standards and norms are often not used in product exports and technical output, mainly because most Chinese standards directly specify parameters based on empirical or experimental data so that they have poor adaptability in different environments abroad. The vicious competition among different domestic and foreign enterprises is also not conducive to the healthy development of enterprises abroad. This means that China has accelerated the construction of a linkage mechanism for domestic standardization technical institutions and promoted more independent innovations and special technical advantages as international standards based on the latest developments in industry and technology both at home and abroad.

(4) Environment of host country.

In the course of "Going Out", it is inevitable to face the pressure from trade frictions and blind competition in the process of technological and market competition with other developed countries. The dangers of terrorism, extremist forces and armed separatism exist in Middle East countries such as Syria, Lebanon, Afghanistan, Pakistan, etc., gathering safety problems and economic risks. In addition, risks of internal control such as project management and construction safety are also potential. Enterprises aiming to achieve localized management and development will inevitably pay attention to the integration of project investment, construction and operation, combination of equipment production and marketing, resource integration, as well as cultural integration, employment, environmental protection and other issues. To strengthen researches on the host country's national security, under the premise of effectively controlling risks, it is imperative to vigorously build a community of responsibility and common destiny, and advocate the concept of sustainable development.

5. Facilitate Domestic Electric Power Equipment Manufacturing Enterprises to "Go Out" under the Belt and Road Initiative

The institutional advantages of concentrating efforts on major issues and advantages of the big power and large-scale market in China have increasingly become the hard core of the development and growth of our enterprises. China's electric power equipment manufacturing enterprises should make full use of these advantages and not be limited to concentrating the manufacturing of high-speed rail and nuclear power equipment on a few state-owned enterprises. Large, medium and small-sized enterprises should establish a syndicate to effectively form an innovation force to prevent them from being beaten by foreign enterprises one by one, and embark on the road of "high-end exploration, key breakthroughs and step-by-step progress" to build their own brands, seize the market shares and form own brand effects. After investigation, I believe that "Going Out" of China's electric power equipment manufacturing enterprises can be implemented as a four-phase strategy.

(1) Upgrade and transformation as brand strategy.

Enterprises should first of all carry out strategic positioning of their own brands while strengthening their international competitiveness with independent intellectual property rights as the core. Establish a R&D system of "Industry, University and Research" with domestic universities, collages and research institutes, strengthen the research and development of solutions for intelligent manufacturing systems in close connection with system integrators, actively carry out international cooperation, introduce and absorb technologies, and continuously promote technological progress so as to maximize internal effects. In the early stage, small and medium electric power equipment manufacturing enterprises can introduce their own brands by establishing and maintaining friendly relations. Join the overseas Chinese Chamber of Commerce and get in touch with Chinese enterprises to find out more opportunities for business cooperation. Then focus on the unity of product labels so that customers and partners can better remember the group's brand. The most important purpose for active participation in bidding is to promote the brand to customers instead of winning bids. While adapting to the environment of different countries, learn from the experiences of successful domestic and overseas enterprises.

At the same time, it should arouse enough attention of relevant government departments to perform their duties and fully cooperate with each other, organize and promote basic scientific research, and integrate resources of all parties to form advantages. Compared with developed countries, China has more small and medium-sized manufacturing enterprises, of which labor-intensive enterprises accounts for a large proportion. At the same time, the information degree of enterprises is generally limited. Therefore, government departments and enterprises should adopt a program that is tailored to local conditions and differentiated, in order to promote the combination of the Internet and manufacturing.

(2) Gain multi-wins based on experiences from key points.

The main context and orientation of the technical equipment differentiation of electric power equipment enterprises are the construction and follow-up operation of power transmission and transformation projects in the future. Therefore, electric power equipment enterprises should expedite the transformation of their role from pure equipment supplier to the EPC contractor of international energy construction projects based on equipment supply. Market competitiveness of enterprises to cultivate products can be realized through continuous industrial upgrading, technological progress, development and transformation, and by improving product quality to serve the brand.

Chinese government may consider using more flexible and market-oriented measures to help the representative offices and offices of countries or cities along the "Belt and Road" to actively play their roles in information and intelligence and transaction services; organize to implement new technologies and new equipment demonstration projects; and then on the basis of pilot demonstration, form and facilitate a new mode integrating digital R&D, design and manufacture of electric power equipment, so as to provide a strong backing for the development of small and medium electric power equipment manufacturing enterprises in overseas markets. Connect with the Asia-Pacific Model E-Port Network and actively promote the information exchange and service sharing between the "Single Window" of international trade and ports along the Belt and Road. Increase policy support and guidance, especially in areas and enterprises with obvious advantages of electric power equipment. To be a manufacturing power, the best external manifestation is to build a group of large enterprises with advantages in brand, corporate culture, scale, technology, capital and quality that can compete with GE and SIEMENS. Shanghai Electric Group also forms its core competitiveness as a "star" enterprise by applying intensive development system framework, in which main businesses, brand culture, core resources and core competencies are highly integrated and unified. The core attraction and radiation of "star" enterprise bring "planetary" and "satellite" enterprises from a variety of industries to turn around it, which is worth learning.

(3) Explore opportunities to maintain profitability.

Under the initial success, the cooperation between the company and host local enterprises (such as power enterprises and electric power equipment enterprises in the countries along the Belt and Road) has been actively consolidated. Main measures are to promote mutual visits of both leadership and strengthen technical exchanges between two sides. Make full use of brand advantages and cost advantages of Chinese manufacturing, actively explore emerging markets such as Brazil and Mexico, and consolidate original market shares.

With the opportunities brought about by the Belt and Road initiative, Chinese government can actively optimize business processes while improving the efficiency of services, and continuously explores and carries out foreign-invested cooperation management mode and related policies and regulations, thus becomes a supporting strength for "Going Out" of enterprises. Electric power equipment manufacturing, power construction industry and associations should strengthen the propaganda and promotion efforts to promote the popularization and application of typical experiences.

(4) Win-Win concept and coordinated development.

In a mature market, only the establishment of wholly-owned foreign affiliates and localization of overseas business operations can lead to better cross-border cooperation and international operations. In the process of "Going Out", enterprises should fully consider economic conditions and actual needs of the host country, adhere to the concept of mutual benefits and common development, and promote the sustainable development of local economic and social ecology as much as possible. In the Belt and Road construction, private-owned enterprises are playing an increasingly prominent role, and the trend of small and medium-sized enterprises entering the developed countries and industrial investment together is more obvious. Large-scale private enterprises such as SANY Heavy Industry, Huawei, Great Wall, Lenovo and Geely have achieved great results in the process of "Going Out".

Deepening of the System Innovation in Shanghai Pilot Free Trade Zone for the Belt and Road Initiative

Jianhua Zhang

International Business School, Shanghai Institute of Foreign Trade

The international financial crisis in 2008 has caused the world economy to maintain a downward trend. Although Chinese economy is developing at a rate higher than the world level, the decline in growth is even greater and there are even signs of convergence with world economic growth, which indicates that both Chinese and global economic growths have entered into a new stage. In order to maintain a medium and high-speed economic growth in the new phase, we must explore the potential growth impetus. Establishing the Shanghai Pilot Free Trade Zone and proposing the Belt and Road initiative are two efforts to explore new impetus for growth through deepening reform and opening up. Since the Belt and Road initiative is an open emphasis of China's opening up and foreign cooperation in new era, ensuring institutional innovations to the Belt and Road initiative has become an inherent requirement for the reform and opening up in Shanghai Pilot Free Trade Zone.

1. Internal Consistency of Two Nation's Plans

We can see the linkage of two plans from the decision-making background, decision-making nature and core requirements of the Shanghai Pilot Free Trade Zone Construction Plan and the "Belt and Road" initiative. For example, both of them are the vision for new national development proposed in the new era. In nature, they are major decisions made by the Party Central Committee and the State Council in 2013.

(1) The Belt and Road initiative becomes a key area of Shanghai Pilot Free Trade Zone.

In September 2013, April 2015 and March 2017, the State Council issued three plans respectively for the Shanghai Pilot Free Trade Zone. The State Council pointed out that the Shanghai Pilot Free Trade Zone is an important measure to explore new ways and accumulate new experiences under the new situation for comprehensively deepening reform and opening up, and put forward the tasks with obvious stage characteristics according to the domestic economic development needs and responding to the new changes in the international economy. Its characteristic terms are "establish", "further deepen" and "all-round deepen", which apparently carry dynamic functions.

The core task of FTA is system innovation, including four aspects: change the functions of the government (deepen the reform of administrative examination and approval system, enhance the ability of in-event and after-event supervision and establishment of a legal business environment), establish a new mode of foreign investment management (explore the national treatment plus negative list management mode before access of foreign investment), expand the service industry opening (including services and finance sector) as well as facilitation of trade investment. These aspects are mutually reinforcing and mutually promoting. Without the transformation of government functions, they will not be able to meet the new requirements of reform and opening up. They will not know the direction of the transformation of government functions without deepening the reform and will also not know how to explore and set up new modes for foreign investment management without expanding opening. Therefore, the successful experiences accumulated by the Shanghai Pilot Free Trade Zone is of utmost importance to the deepening process of China's reform and opening up.

In 2015, the "Plan" proposed that the FTZ should set up a new system of open economy and explore new modes for regional economic cooperation. If the former task is to summarize the system innovations of the above four aspects, then the latter specifically refers to promoting the cooperation and development of the Yangtze River Economic Zone. Although the Plan also proposed that the FTZ should promote the development of the Belt and Road, since the Belt and Road initiative has just been launched (in March 2015), a definite linkage has not yet been established in the top-level design between these two strategies. For example, in the "single window" construction of international trade, we only propose to explore the "single window" for international trade in the Yangtze River Delta and promote the integration of customs clearance in the Yangtze River Economic Zone.

In 2017, the Initiative specifically specified in which aspects the Shanghai Pilot

Free Trade Zone should serve the Belt and Road: "Create cooperative development modes and become a bridgehead to serve the Belt and Road construction and drive the market entities to go out". In response, in October 2017, the Shanghai municipal government issued the "Action Plan for Shanghai's Bridgehead Role in Serving the National Belt and Road Initiative", putting forward that based on the system innovation of the FTZ, the Shanghai municipal government will serve the Belt and Road in respect of economic and trade cooperation, financial services, infrastructure construction, humanities exchange, personnel training, cooperation among sister cities and multinational corporations around the world. As the 19th National Congress of the Communist Party of China pointed out that, "we should pursue the Belt and Road Initiative as a priority, give equal emphasis to 'Bringing In' and 'Going Out', follow the principle of achieving shared growth through discussion and collaboration, and increase openness and cooperation in building innovation capacity. With these efforts, we hope to make new ground in opening China further through links running eastward and westward, across land and over sea; and build the Belt and Road into a new platform for international cooperation." In this way, the two national strategies are not only combined with each other but also serve the Belt and Road, thus becoming a key area for deepening the reform and opening up in an all-round way.

(2) Linkage points of two national strategies.

We have broken down the three parts of Part V in the 2017 Plan into 12 points and matched them with the contents of the Belt and Road initiative to find out the linkage points (i.e. common ground) and differences between the two plans (Table 1). It is easy to see that the task of reform and opening up in Shanghai Pilot Free Trade Zone includes most of the contents in the Belt and Road initiative, especially the facilitation of investment and trade as well as financial services are the common tasks of the two strategic plans. The contents of the Belt and Road initiative were not included in the 2017 Shanghai Pilot Free Trade Zone Plan of the State Council. For example, most of the popular sentiments in the Belt and Road initiative, are echoed in the service plan released by the Shanghai municipal government. In addition, according to the following comparative analysis of economic and trade conditions between China and other countries along the Belt and Road, we think that it should be the task of Shanghai Pilot FTA to reduce bilateral trade imbalances or promote the mutually complementary industries for the purpose of deepening the reform and opening up.

Table 1   Linkage Point between the Shanghai Pilot Free Trade Zone and the Belt and Road Initiative

Part V of 2017 FTZ Plan	Other parts of 2017 FTZ Plan	2015 Belt and Road initiative
Aims and demands: Become a bridgehead, set up a new platform for cooperation in opening up, build a functional hub for resource allocation and give full play to the role of radiation.	Aims and demands: Build an internationally high-level free trade park, and improve investment management, trade regulation, financial services and government management system.	Aims and demands: Upgrade the regional infrastructure; basically establish a high-level free trade area network; and deepen and broaden humanities exchanges.
(XX) Facilitate economic and trade cooperation with high-level facilitation measures		
1. Promote the information exchange and service sharing between the "Single Window" and ports along the Belt and Road.	(VI) Built a "Single Window" at an internationally high level (XIII) Implement new rules for trade facilitation.	Unimpeded trade: Efforts will be made to solve the problem of investment and trade facilitation, and discuss to establish a free trade zone; promote customs and bilateral or multilateral cooperation; accelerate the "Single Window" construction; broaden and optimize trades; expand investment fields; promote new industry cooperation; optimize the distribution of industrial chains; and facilitate opening up in the service industry.
2. Take the lead in exploring a new mode for interconnected regulatory cooperation.	(VII) Establish a new mode for integrated customs supervision. (VIII) Establish a comprehensive evaluation system for classified supervision of inspection and quarantine risks. (IX) Establish a supervision mode for innovative industries with international competitiveness.	
3. Accelerate the construction of complex portal international aviation hub.		Facilities connectivity: Improve the accessibility of roads; establish the transport coordination mechanism; construct ports and aviation infrastructure, etc.
4. Promote port cooperation to form a hub of Asia-Pacific supply chain.		
5. Establish comprehensive foreign investment promotion agencies and a public information service platform for overseas investment.	(XIV) Innovate the management mode for cross-border service trade.	
6. Build the property rights exchange center and technology transfer platform to promote industrial science and technology cooperation.	(X) Optimize the market allocation mechanism for innovative elements. (XI) Improve the system of intellectual property protection and application.	Unimpeded trade: Ibid. People-to-people bond: Enhance scientific and technological innovation through scientific and technological cooperation.
7. Actively promote international capacity and capacity-building cooperation.		Unimpeded trade and facilities connectivity: Ibid.

Part V of 2017 FTZ Plan	Other parts of 2017 FTZ Plan	2015 Belt and Road initiative
(XXI) Enhance financial service function of the Belt and Road initiative 8. Promote cooperation between Shanghai (as a financial center) and financial markets along the Belt and Road. 9. Use domestic and overseas RMB assets to provide financing services for major projects along the Belt and Road. 10. Develop the "Going Out" of integrated insurance services. 11. Support new development banks from BRICS.	(XV) Further deepen financial opening and innovation.	Financial integration: Advance Asian currency stability, and the system construction for investment, financing and credit; expand currency swap and settlement; open up the Asian bond market; set up the Asian Infrastructure Investment Bank, New Development Bank BRICS and Silk Road Fund; support domestic and overseas institutions to issue RMB bonds; implement financial supervision, risk response and credit cooperation.
(XXII) Explore the offshore tax arrangements with international competitiveness 12. Explore tax expansion policies for innovation pilots of service trade.		Unimpeded trade: Ibid.

2. Status and Furtherance of Shanghai Pilot Free Trade Zone Serving the Belt and Road Development

Since the implementation of the Belt and Road initiative, it has become a key task of the reform and opening up of the Shanghai Pilot Free Trade Zone. Nowadays, remarkable achievements have been made in serving the Belt and Road initiative, but in the future, system innovation is still required to deepen linkage.

(1) Status and problem of Shanghai Pilot Free Trade Zone serving the Belt and Road development.

Advances of Shanghai Pilot Free Trade Zone on connecting to and serving the Belt and Road are as follows: first, expand trade and investment with countries along the Belt and Road. Since its establishment four years ago, the FTA has launched over 3 000 projects for "Going Out" and "Bringing In" with the countries along the Belt and Road and the trade growth rate has remained above 22%. 52 countries along the Belt and Road have invested in Pudong with 3 012 investment enterprises and a contractual foreign investment of USD 11.58 billion. The FTA has invested nearly USD 4 billion in 25 countries including the Czech Republic and Indonesia. Second, establish a special promotion mechanism. Establish a national museum for imported goods along the Belt and Road to expand the import of quality goods from countries along the Belt and Road. Third, carry out scientific and technological innovation and cooperation. Establish a transnational incubator jointly with Israel, Russia, Singapore and other countries; introduce activities such as the Pudong-Russia Forum and the Asia-Pacific Science and Technology Innovation Exhibition to build a cross-border project exchange platform. Fourth, set up a service platform for "Going Out" of enterprises. Set up the Belt and Road column in the overseas investment service platform of the FTZ and sign the ASEAN Legal Alliance to promote cooperation between enterprises and professional service providers such as lawyers, accountants, consultants and appraisers, set up the Belt and Road enterprise service center for technology trade measures, and carry out more cooperations and exchanges in respect of certification and accreditation and standard measurement with the countries along the Belt and Road.

These measures of the Shanghai FTZ serving the Belt and Road initiative have well reflected the requirements of the "Plan". When comparing the core tasks of the reform and opening up in Shanghai Pilot FTA and the linkage points between the two national strategies, we think that there is still room for further exploration in the FTA serving the Belt and Road initiative and we cannot be satisfied with the investment trade or economic and trade cooperation within existing rules, it is not the task of the FTZ to be content with existing practices. The core mission of the FTZ is to explore system innovations, which means, based on the construction of the Belt and Road, equal emphasis on "Going Out" and "Bringing in", and the principle of achieving shared growth through discussion and collaboration, we should set up a high-level international platform for trade and investment liberalization and facilitation, through the negotiation with the relevant countries on the investment and trade system and rules, so that this platform will become a powerful starting point for China in developing its high-level open economy and promoting an open world economy.

(2) Shanghai Pilot Free Trade Zone deepens the system innovation framework serving the Belt and Road initiative.

When the domestic and international economic and trade environment changes, or when it is necessary to change the current economic and trade environment in order to break the status quo, system innovation is the first of its kind. The system innovation essentially changes the path dependence on certain systems in the existing system structure so as to form a new structure, thus ensuring that the economic and trade activities will move in the direction conducive to economic structural adjustment and economic growth.

In the plan for deepening the reform and opening up of the Shanghai Pilot Free Trade Zone released by the State Council, the establishment of a free trade zone with the highest international standards and at a highest level is proposed, which is the highest demand for system innovation in the FTZ and also for building an international platform of the Belt and Road. Its essence is to maximize the liberalization and facilitation of trade and investment policies. Meeting these two "highest" requirements will inevitably bring about the following ideal results in system innovation: absorbing current international trade rules with the highest and best standards; establishing higher-level rules that go beyond existing international economic and trade rules; achieving one-to-one rules proposed in economic and trade negotiations with individual countries, including those along the Belt and Road. It can be expected that if the Shanghai Pilot Free Trade Zone succeeds in establishing a free trade zone with the highest and best standards and the Belt and Road cooperation platform in all three areas, then a new open economic system that meets the requirements of new domestic and international economic and trade situations is constructed successfully. It not only can greatly promote the economic development in China, but also can curb the trend of protectionism in international trade and investment, thus bringing the world economy and trade back to the track of open cooperation.

System innovation is the combination of system learning and system creation. It is a combination of "I need" and "he needs", but in the final is "I create". The same is true of system innovation in the field of international trade and economy. The system created by the Belt and Road initiative in Shanghai Pilot FTA includes three aspects: first, bilateral or multilateral negotiations, which are the origin of system creation; second, the horizontal expansion of the system, that is, apply the bilateral or multilateral system achievements in the bilateral or multilateral negotiations with the countries along the Belt and Road; third, the longitudinal system reform, that is, according to the bilateral and multilateral international investment and trade rules as agreed, it will readjust the relevant laws and policies in China so as to promote the reform through opening up.

Under the current international economic and trade background, the system innovation of Shanghai Pilot Free Trade Area based on the Belt and Road initiative has both opportunities and challenges. The opportunities are as follows: Despite the difficult economic growth in the world, the desire of developing countries for opening up and development has not changed or even strengthened. While developed countries and other countries tend to the protectionism of international investment and trade, they still need investments and exports. Specifically, both the governments and enterprises in these countries have seen the potential huge investment and trade opportunities of the Belt and Road initiative. For example, most developed countries are willing to become sponsor members of the Asian Infrastructure Investment Bank and some developing countries hope to learn from the successful experiences of China's economic development. Facing the difficulties in the multilateral investment and trade system, bilateral or regional systems have become the trend. The challenges include: developed countries tend to the protectionism and populism of trade and investment. National conditions of the countries along the Belt and Road determine the different requirements for investment and trade rules in our economic and trade cooperation, which are subject to the constraints of existing international organizations. Some countries have an inherent bias toward China. It is not easy to change the behavior of government and enterprises that are cured in the traditional rules by using the system results featuring openness and innovation.

However, there is no doubt that the successful system innovation based on Belt and Road in Shanghai Pilot FTZ is of epoch-making significance for building a modern economic system and an open world economy. First, strengthen the service function of Shanghai as a bridgehead. The most direct effect of successful system innovation is to further enhance Shanghai's comprehensive urban service functions and develop a higher-level open economy so as to enhance the service level of the bridgehead serving the Belt and Road development. Second, promote the building of a powerful trade country. The system innovation in the FTZ, in particular empowerment for reform autonomy in the FTZ, is conducive to expanding and deepening foreign trade, fostering new trade patterns and new modes of trade, and forming a global trade, investment and financing, production and service network, therefore cultivating new advantages in economic and trade cooperation and competition. Third, promote the construction of a community of human destiny. The practicability, advancement and representativeness of the rules on investment and trade or economic and trade cooperation reached by the FTA and other countries along the Belt and Road not only surpass the obsolete TPP, but also make proper system reserves for future expanding to and connecting with other countries (except for the countries along the Belt and Road) or international organizations. Fourth, form a new impetus for common international development. China's economic and trade cooperation with the countries along the Belt and Road not only has the nature of trade and investment in the usual sense, but also has the potential of boosting the economic growth of these countries, especially the common development of low-income countries and China, through measures such as infrastructure construction, capacity cooperation, scientific and technological innovation and cooperation, and human resources training.

3. Economic Base of Deepening System Innovation in FTA

In spite of many challenges in setting up the Belt and Road international economic and trade activity platform with the highest and best standards, the fundamental challenge of the FTZ lies in the status and requirements for economic development of the country along the Belt and Road. An optimal liberalization and facilitation rules for trade and investment must be consistent with each other's expected maximum benefits. Therefore, this section focuses on the characteristics of economic development of the countries along the Belt and Road.

(1) Economic profiles of the countries along the Belt and Road.

The Belt and Road initiative is an open initiative without clear boundary and number of countries. The prevailing view in academia is that 65 countries, including China, account for one third of the world's countries. According to the classification of the World Bank, there are 16 high-income countries, 21 middle- and high-income countries, 20 low- and middle-income countries and 7 low-income countries. This is a group of countries that is mainly composed of middle-income countries, developing countries and countries in transition, except for the most developed countries. The World Economic Forum divides the impetus driving economic growth into three categories: factor-driven, efficiency-driven and innovation-driven. The stage characteristics for economic growth of the countries along the Belt and Road are shown in Table 2. A comparison of the two subgroups shows that half of the 16 high-income countries are innovation-driven countries, while others are in a state of factor-driven and efficiency-driven or transition to a higher stage. This implies that countries in different stages of development have different requirements on investment, trade or cross-border economic and trade cooperation.

Table 2　National Economic Development Stages

Stage 1: Factor-driven	Transformation from Stage 1 to Stage 2	Stage 2: Efficiency-driven	Transformation from Stage 2 to Stage 3	Stage 3: Innovation-driven development
Bangladesh	Azerbaijan	Albania	Croatia	Bahrain
Cambodia	Bhutan	Armenia	Hungary	Czech
India	Brunei	Bosnia and	Latvia	Estonia
Kyrgyzstan	Kazakhstan	Herzegovina	Lebanon	Israel
Laos	Kuwait	Bulgaria	Lithuania	Qatar
Moldova	Mongolia	China	Malaysia	Singapore
Nepal	Philippines	Egypt	Oman	Slovenia
Pakistan	Russia	Georgia	Poland	United Arab Emirates
Tajikistan	Ukraine	Indonesia	Saudi Arabia	
Yemen	Vietnam	Iran	Slovakia	
		Jordan	Turkey	
		Macedonia		
		Montenegro		
		Romania		
		Serbia		
		Sri Lanka		
		Thailand		

Source: The *Global Competitiveness Report* (2016), the World Economic Forum, p.38. Description: Lack of data from 10 countries.

In 2016, the total population of 64 countries is 4.61 billion, [①]accounting for 62% of the world's population. Among them, 36 countries have a population of no more than 1 million, while Brunei and Maldives are two countries with the least population of 400 000. There are 21 countries with a population of no more than 10 million; 5 countries with a population of no more than 300 million; China and India have more than 2.7 billion people, accounting for 58.6% of total population in 65 countries.

---

① Lack of data from Palestine.

In 2016, the GDP of 63 countries totaled USD 23.3 trillion, [①]accounting for 30.9% of the world's total GDP. The per capita GDP was USD 5 074, which was 50% of the world's per capita GDP. There are 19 countries with per capita income between USD 10 000 and 60 000, 13 countries between USD 5 000 and 10 000, 27 countries between USD 5 000 and 1 000 and only 4 countries with per capita income less than USD 1 000. The per capita income of Qatar (highest) was 104 times more than that of Afghanistan (lowest).

When the rate of economic growth exceeds the rate of population growth, the level of per capita income will surely increase, and it is easy to raise the level of national income under the conditions of a small population. For example, Qatar has a population of 2.6 million. Between 2000 and 2016, its GDP grew at an average annual growth rate of 12.1%, as the highest among the countries along the Belt and Road. In 2016, its per capita income was USD 59 000, also the highest rate in above countries. The populous country does not have such an economic feature. In China, its average annual growth rate was 9.9% over the same period, but its per capita income was only close to 14% of Qatar.

(2) Characteristic of industrial structure.

Within a given period, a country's industrial structure reflects its structural characteristics of factor endowments and the characteristics of economic growth stages. In the long run, under the conditions of open competition, the economic development has responded to the expansion of economic scale (higher per capita income level) and the upgrading of industrial structure. One of the implicit preconditions is that the industries whose output proportion are inclined to decrease will become more and more powerful, and provide a stable basis for the development of other industries. At the same time, such industries must also have corresponding structural upgrading for factor endowment to ensure further supports. However, the evolution of industrial structure in some countries shows obvious heterogeneity due to constraints of development strategy, resources, population and market size, which indicating distorted industrial structure, stagnant industrial structure for a long time, and per capita income level hardly to be improved.

In terms of current industrial structure, in 2016, of the 55 countries with data,

---

① Lack of data from Syria and Palestine.

the agricultural output and industrial output of 38 countries is higher than the world average level, [1]and the manufacturing output of 25 countries is higher than the world average level. Since the service output of only 7 countries exceeds the world average level, the industrial structure of most countries lags behind the world level.

Historically, during the 11 years from 2005 to 2016, there were two salient features of changes in industrial structure of the countries along the Belt and Road: one is the service-oriented development for the industrial structure in most countries and the other is the rapid industrialization of the industrial structure in a few countries(See Table 3). As indicated in the table, the proportion of service output in 44 countries shows an increasing trend while that of only 4 countries shows a slight decrease; the proportion of agricultural and industrial output in 37 countries tends to decrease, among which 35 countries indicate decline in the proportion of manufacturing output, with obvious deindustrialization characteristics. During this period, the industrial output in 15 countries and the manufacturing output in 13 countries increased their proportions in the industrial structure. The fastest-growing countries are Myanmar, Vietnam,[2] Uzbekistan and other countries. The manufacturing achievements of the first two countries are very eye-catching internationally, while the latter have seen rapid growth in the non-manufacturing industries.

Different from the development path of developed countries, the service-oriented industrial structure in some countries along the Belt and Road is not based on developed agriculture or manufacturing industries. In agriculture, from 2000 to 2015, except for the decline of agricultural productivity in 6 countries, the agricultural productivity of the remaining 53 countries has increased by varying degrees(1%—469%), with 39 countries exceeding the world growing rate(39.9%). This leads directly to the fact that the productivity of most countries(41) are higher than the world average level(USD 2 179). However, the agricultural productivity of some high-income countries is very low, such as Poland and Hungary in Central and Eastern Europe. China's agricultural productivity is not only at a low level but also develops slowly, which does not have comparative advantages compared with most of the countries along the Belt and Road.

---

[1] The world average of output structure(%) for agriculture, industry, manufacturing and services in 2016 is 4:27:15:69.

[2] Despite the lack of data from Vietnam in 2005, which cannot be compared with 2016, such judgments can be made based on routine observation.

Table 3   Characteristics of Industrial Structure in the Countries along the Belt and Road (2005—2016)

	Number of countries with no change in output proportion		Number of countries with less proportion of output		Number of countries with more proportion of output	
Agricultural Projects	10	Proportion between 10%—0%	37	The proportion of Myanmar and Kyrgyzstan dropped by 19% and 17% respectively	8	Up to only 4% increase in output, such as Pakistan and Ukraine
Industry	2	Up to 28% to 29% in Bulgaria and Jordan	37	19% decline in Saudi Arabia	15	12% and 12% increase respectively in Myanmar and Uzbekistan
Manufacturing	6	Up to 24% and 24% respectively in Slovenia and Romania	35	8% decline in Malaysia	13	8% increase in Myanmar
Tertiary Industry	7	Proportion between 42%—69%	4	5% decline in Macedonia (highest)	44	Increase rate between 10%—19% in Malaysia, Qatar and Saudi Arabia

Source: The *World Development Indicators*(2017) of the World Bank. Description: The countries listed in the table are the most volatile.

In contrast, China's most competitive advantage is its manufacturing, its manufacturing added value since 2011 has ranked first in the world, and the total size in 2015 was USD 2.87 trillion, accounting for about 1/4 of the world's total(24.6%). The figure of other 64 countries along the Belt and Road only accounts for 63.5% of China's total.

This disparity in the manufacturing between the countries along the Belt and Road and China implies important economic and developmental implications, namely bilateral international capacity cooperation and the promotion of economic development in developing countries. For some countries, the investment and production of some industries in their own countries do not have the advantages of economies of scale or scope, nor comparative advantages, and the introduction of some of China's production capacity may be the best way. At the same time, some industries in these countries want to obtain advantages of economies of scale or scope, they may put production and R&D bases in China and then re-export the products to their own countries, which is a kind of two-way capacity cooperation. The essential significance of capacity cooperation for developing countries lies in making up for the lack of manufacturing or promoting the structural upgrading for the purpose of economic and social development.

(3) Trade characteristics.

In 2016, 65 countries along the Belt and Road achieved a total volume of trade of 13.3 trillion USD, accounting for 31.9% of the total global trade. Their total trade in goods was 10.9 trillion USD and total trade in services was 2.4 trillion USD, equal to 33.7% and 25.3% of respective total global volume of trade. Compared to overall global situation, trades in this area have the following three features: trades of such 65 countries are consistent with the proportion of their total economic scale in the total global trade (30.9%), but significantly inconsistent with the percentage of their populations in the total global population (62%) and their trade in services is less than trade in goods. Thus it can be told that there is still huge potential in trades between those countries and emphasis should be laid on promoting trade in services while increasing the total volume of trade.

In the last decade (2005—2016), countries along the Belt and Road have been active in trade and export & import growth rate of most countries exceeds that of the most developed countries. However, trade growth rate, trade surplus or deficit differs greatly. The most prominent commodities of these countries include manufactured goods and raw materials. Over half of such countries export primarily manufactured goods, 13 countries export mainly raw materials and 5 other countries export foods, which are the main source of their trade surplus. Only two countries (Maldives and Lebanon) have larger trade in services that that in goods and China has the largest trade deficit in services. The most competitive industries in terms of service import & export in countries along the Belt and Road are tourism, computer & IT services and transportation.

It can be seen after comparing trade facilitation of such countries that, with China as the benchmark, 21 countries have higher weighted average duty than China and other 42 countries have lower duty; for most countries, China has very high logistics performance index, similar to that of Israel and Czech Republic. The only countries along the Belt and Road with higher LPI than China are Singapore and UAE.

65 countries along the Belt and Road have obtained annual foreign direct investment (FDI) of 432.94 billion USD during 2011—2016 and direct outbound investment of 282.62 billion USD, accounting for 27.4% and 19.6% of respective total global volume. Meanwhile, foreign investment had greater demand than outbound investment during this period, or in other word, most countries had only limited or

no ability of outbound investment. Among such countries, China is the largest FDI destination and origin, claiming 29.5% and 41.5% in the total FDI volume of these 65 countries respectively.

The following trade characteristics can be concluded by comparing available date of 21 countries in terms of trade situation: China is the largest trade partner for surrounding countries, but not the main trade partner of Central and Eastern Europe countries where China only takes up 1.8%—4.4% of the total trade volume and where trade deficit is the dominant feature in trading with China. Countries along the Belt and Road export a large a variety of goods to China, most commonly minerals, mechanical & electrical products and labor-intensive products, while imports primarily mechanical & electrical products from China.

Since national conditions and economic development in countries along the Belt and Road vary significantly, their investment requirements should be diversified in terms of scale, structure and nature and reflect trends in current international trade investment (such as protectionism). Some countries have relatively stable international trade investment situation, for example, traditionally the largest and most convenient trade partners of Central and Eastern Europe countries are other countries in Europe and obviously, it takes long time and continuous efforts for China to strive to become primary trade partner of such countries. Varied development requirements, unfavorable trends in international trade investment and traditional trade investment situation all pose challenges to establishing Belt and Road trade investment freedom and facilitation rule platform by Shanghai Pilot Free Trade Zone.

4. Ideas of Intensifying Institutional Innovation for the Belt and Road Initiative in Shanghai Pilot Free Trade Zone

In building the best free trade zone with highest standards, Shanghai Pilot Free Trade Zone is actually creating the Belt and Road trade investment freedom and facilitation platform. In such process, focus should be laid on building a framework of international economy & trade rules based on the following requirements and on the principle of "whoever needs it creates it": To enhance China's leading role in restructuring international economy & trade rules and make it favorable for China to build modern economic system and promote creating open world economy and human destiny community.

Firstly, define rules of the best free trade zone with highest standards. Shanghai Pilot Free Trade Zone should not only draws on experience and best practices from countries along the Belt and Road concerning investment trade or economic and trade cooperation, but also actively discuss and define with these countries best bilateral or multilateral economic and trade rules with highest standards. Such rules humble investment trade rules led by developed European and North American countries, making the international community more resolved about developing new rules.

Secondly, control international economic and trade rules to regain leadership. In an era of restructuring of global system of governance and international order, if countries like China have no say in defining new rules, it is certain that they will definitely reduced to second-or third-rate countries in the world with established new governance system and order. Therefore, creation by Shanghai Pilot Free Trade Zone of highest-standard and best free trade zone rules with focus on the Belt and Road initiative should become one of the core contents of new international economic and trade order in order for China to play its leading role.

Thirdly, increase new momentum driving economic development in China. Although reform & opening up has helped China to blend into the global economic system within a short time, China still remains the low end of the global value chain and generates small gains from international trade. To build modern economic system, new international economic relationship should be established to challenge the status quo and the free trade zone should serve the Belt and Road initiative in order to explore and establish new international economic and trade rules, gather and give full play to global innovation resources, accelerate in building new advantages for international competition and cooperation and create China-dominated global value chain to drive economic transformation and upgrading in China.

5. Proposals for Intensifying Institutional Innovation for the Belt and Road Initiative in Shanghai Pilot Free Trade Zone

We can only know where we are heading when we are aware of where we are now. The ideas of Shanghai Pilot Free Trade Zone and the Belt and Road are only in beginning stage and they have a very long and tough way to go towards their expected goals. But a journey of one thousand miles begins with one step. Above analysis helps us to come up with possible policy suggestions.

First, focus on constructing a free port. According to reports of the 19th National Congress of the CPC, greater reforming autonomy will be granted to the free trade zone to explore how to build a free trade port. This is a requirement for construction of the best free trade zone with highest standards. Shanghai Pilot Free Trade Zone should be based on its own advantages and promote its commercial arbitration ability in terms of government functions, trade investment rules, finance and technological innovation to the highest standards and level in order to connect with countries along the Belt and Road in all aspects.

Second, explore sustainable production capacity cooperation rules.Since countries along the Belt and Road differ greatly in geographical area, population, values, income level and resources, it is not wise for enterprises to swarm in for investment and trading. Experience shows that some small countries take unkindness to investment trade of a few Chinese companies without considering consequences and influence. Shanghai Pilot Free Trade Zone should determine proper cooperation methods, scale and rules with countries along the Belt and Road according to local conditions.

Third, promote foreign trade of the service industry. It is a key task for Shanghai Pilot Free Trade Zone to increase degree of openness and enhance export of the service industry because export volume of services is far less than that of goods. Meanwhile, due to underimporting of service, China should minimize trade restrictions on services, open up for cooperation based on transformation and upgrading of traditional manufacturing industry, development of high-tech industry and technological innovation and focus on driving service trade with modern service sector as the core.

Fourth, explore new pattern of cooperation between cities and industrial parks. Cites (including ports) are nodes for cooperation, while parks are carriers of cooperation. Economy of industrial parks is a success in Chinese economic development and also serves as way of going out. However, here we want to underscore that such form of economy is derived from specific national conditions in China and can hardly be copied successfully to other countries without any alterations. What Shanghai Pilot Free Trade Zone needs to do is to explore suitable patterns of industrial parks according to local situation of countries for cooperation. Such economy of industrial parks is bound to be innovation and variation to that in China.

Fifth, intensify infrastructure construction and improve construction efficiency. Shanghai features advantages including location, rules, talents and urban centricity in serving the Belt and Road initiative. But the problem is that, Shanghai has drawbacks compared to cities along the Belt and Road, such as logistic convenience compared to Singapore. Additionally, Shanghai is still far from being capable of competing with top cities such as London, New York and Tokyo in terms of global urban capacity. Hence, Shanghai should continue strengthen infrastructure construction and enhance global urban capacity with focus on improvement of logistic efficiency and cross-border electronic commerce.

Playing Shanghai's Bridgehead Role and Exploring Ways to Build Talent Cultivation System for the Belt and Road Initiative

Ge Xin

Shanghai University of Finance and Economics

Lu Xia

Renmin University of China

In nearly 40 years after reform and opening up, Chinese economy soars with the leadership of the Chinese Communist Party and has made great contribution to world economic development. In 2013, Chinese President Xi Jinping put forward with the initiative to build "Silk Road Economic Belt" and the "21st Century Maritime Silk Road", injecting momentum to global economic and trade development. The Belt and Road initiative means a lot for China to establish tight economic and trade relationship with bordering countries in Central and Southern Asia as well as other European and Asian countries, maintain regional stability and achieve coordinated development. This initiative will also serve as a grand national strategy for the dozens of years to come. In order to implement the initiative, a comprehensive talent cultivation system is required to train many high-caliber talents with cross-cultural understanding and communication skills as well as global perspective.

The problem of talents for implementing the Belt and Road initiative heated up in all walks of life before and after *Vision and Actions on Jointly Building Silk Road Economic Belt and 21st Century Maritime Silk Road* (hereinafter referred to as "*Vision and Actions*") was issued in 2015. And *Several Opinions on Opening up in Contemporary Education* and *Promote Actions for Education Improvement for the Belt and Road Initiative* were issued subsequently, naming top innovative talents, non-common language talents, international organization talents and researchers on nations and regions and outstanding foreign talents working in China as the focus of talent cultivation. In a study session of the Political Bureau of the CCCPC on September 27, 2016, President Xi Jinping again underlined that: a lot of professional talents with good understanding of party and state policies and national conditions in China, global perspective, knowledge of foreign languages, international rules and mastery of international negotiation are required for China's participation in global governance. This shows China's increasing demand for international talents of all kinds as the country develops and grows.

In four years since the implementation of the Belt and Road initiative, policy coordination, facilities connectivity, unimpeded trade, financial integration and people-to-people bond remain the primary goal. Talents are indispensable supports for multi-dimensional connectivity with over 60 countries along the Belt and Road initiative. The initiative can never be implemented without Chinese professionals with knowledge of foreign languages, international rules, global development and regional politics and economics, or foreign talents with good understanding of affairs and demands in China and empathy for China. So talents for the initiative include not only Chinese talents and political, social and economic elites, but also those from countries along the Belt and Road. Cultivation of such talents should be actively explored and addressed by colleges and universities, specialized think tanks and training institutions of top talents. The authors think that Shanghai already has adequate advantages and conditions for building a system for cultivating talents for the Belt and Road initiative and the future work should focus on the following aspects.

1. Major Advantages of Shanghai in Cultivating International Talents and Elites for the Belt and Road Initiative

Successful implementation of the Belt and Road initiative and especially the achievement of "people-to-people bond" are impossible without international talents. As Qu Zhenyuan, Chairman of China Association of Higher Education pointed out, "China requires civilians and cultural ambassadors with excellent international communication competence and strong social influence and reputation to penetrate into social fabric of other countries via NGOs to foster 'people-to-people bond'". Thus, social elites are also essential part of talents cultivation.

Firstly, colleges and universities should make progress and innovate in training professionals for focus fields of trade and finance in the Belt and Road initiative. Colleges and universities in Shanghai can work with domestic and foreign financial, economic and trade organizations and use excellent financial and trade resources in Shanghai to provide students with more opportunities of practice and train them into talents with basic knowledge, practice experience and innovation ability and thus further development of Shanghai Pilot Free Trade Zone following principles of the Belt and Road initiative.

Secondly, historical traditions, languages & characters and manners & customs vary among countries along the Belt and Road. There is no doubt that talents in economics, finance and trade are important, but the importance of professionals in language literature, minority languages, history of nations and international politics cannot be underestimated. The fact is that, China has only limited exchange with countries along the Belt and Road with respect to humanity and social science. Many universities have no such teaching staffs, let alone cultivation of talents. According to statistics of Chinese Ministry of Education, in 20 "silk road" minority languages opened for recruitment in China from 2010 to 2013, 11 of which had less than 100 students. And less than 50 students study Greek, Hebrew, Urdu, Bengali, Nepali, Pushtu, Sinhalese and Filipino. Demands for talents in minority languages will definitely grow as the Belt and Road initiative is implemented. Although Shanghai is rich in resources of colleges and universities, many key comprehensive universities have no relevant teaching resources and education plans in place, except Shanghai International Studies University. This is ill-matched with Shanghai's role of bridgehead in the Belt and Road initiative.

However, mastery of relevant languages and culture is only the first step. In addition to setting up relevant majors in universities, talents can be trained at a higher level, for example, reclassification of current disciplines to train inter-disciplinary talents. Apart from training individuals mastering several languages, "multiple languages+" can also be used as a strategy to combine several languages with different majors, such as "multiple languages+multiple skills" of Shanghai International Studies University. World-class universities in Beijing, including Peking University and Tsinghua University have defined orientations of cultivating international talents with their own characteristics. For example, the objective of training undergraduate talents is "to cultivate high-caliber talents with innovation spirits, practical ability and global perspective who can lead and guide development of various industries." This can be used as reference for comprehensive universities in Shanghai. Universities with abundant resources may apply for setup of Belt and Road graduate and undergraduate programs where students are required to learn such courses as finance, trade, economics, language, history and politics during their stay at school. Meanwhile, students, teachers and researchers from different disciplines can be combined to establish new institutes of Belt and Road. This helps to ensure cultivation of inter-disciplinary talents institutionally and also provide facilities for convergent study by various disciplines in terms of Belt and Road initiative.

2. Introduction: Focus in Helping to Cultivate Talents from Countries along the Belt & Road

In the *Vision and Actions* issued by three central government ministries, it is specified to "increase the number of overseas students, set up jointly-run schools. China should make available government scholarship for 10 000 students from countries along the Belt and Road every year". Building bonds between students & social elites from such countries and China is essential for reinforcing and enhancing strong friendship between China and other countries. Universities and other research & training institutes can train respectively students and public officials from countries along the Belt and Road and working in China.

(1) Cultivation of overseas students.

The first step of institutional cultivation of talents is construction of academic degree programs. How to develop such programs for overseas students from such countries is worth pondering. Now schools including Peking University and Zhejiang University have already set up graduate programs open for students from countries along the Belt and Road. In Shanghai, more universities can set up similar programs for not only overseas Chinese, but also outstanding students from over 60 countries along the Belt and Road and intensify interactions between overseas students and the Chinese society to enhance in-depth understanding between younger generations of different countries. Cultivation plans for overseas students can be targeted based on the following regions: For students from countries along the Silk Road Economic

Belt, identity as a member of the big Asian family should be cultivated by explaining historical exchange and communication between Central Plain Culture of Han Chinese and minority culture in the Western Regions in order to join hands to build a pattern of future development; for students from countries along the 21st Century Maritime Silk Road, interactions between China and them even before the great discoveries of geography should be discussed in order to seek to construct an economic and trade system with higher degree of openness; for students from BRICS, emphasis should be laid on fields and disciplines urgently needed by developing countries by analyzing trends of global economic development and transition.

(2) Training courses for overseas public officials.

The precondition for success of the Belt and Road initiative is recognition and supports from countries along the Belt and Road. Although economy, trade and finance are dominant topics in this initiative, endorsement from government officials is essential. In August 2016, the Second Workshop of Accomplished Foreign Service Officers from Africa was jointly hosted by Shanghai Municipal Foreign Affairs Office and Chinese International Education Center, School of Liberal Arts, Shanghai Jiaotong University. Six African officers gained a comprehensive understanding of China in terms of economy, society, politics, history and culture by attending courses on Chinese culture, China's national conditions and development situations in Shanghai developed specifically for them and visiting new infrastructure, state-owned enterprises, grass-roots governments and agricultural bases. Such workshops for overseas officers should be further promoted. In the past decades, Chinese public officials at all levels went to U.S.A., Europe and developed countries in Asia to learn advanced management techniques and got an insight into local cultural, political, economic and social development conditions. Now China's economy has developed into a higher level and public officials from other countries can be invited to know more about China and learn from China in response to the Belt and Road initiative.

(3) Cultivation of business management talents.

State-owned and private enterprises in China attributes their remarkable success in current Chinese political and economic environment to, in addition to such economic driving forces as product R&D, production and marketing, their unique corporate culture featuring distinctive Chinese characteristics—corporate party organizations. Although it is hardly possible for foreign enterprises to build party organizations as in Chinese companies due to different political and economic system, the role of such organizations in establishing enterprise value system, enhancing cohesive force of staff, strengthening corporate identity and providing organizational benefits is worth promoting. The political nature of the party organizations can be weakened and methods used by such organizations can be highlighted, namely driving mechanism innovation with functions. In order to cultivate talents of business management, reserve talents from foreign enterprises can be invited to China to attend lectures and corporate internship. Moreover, management talents from Chinese-funded organizations founded in foreign countries can go to enterprises with relevant need for on-the-spot teaching and training apprentices. Such practice-and effect-oriented cultivation pattern is sure to win favor of foreign enterprises.

Therefore, the authors believe that, in addition to basic government administration skills when determining training courses, more attention should be paid to enhancing comprehensive understanding of Chinese political, economic and social development by foreign public officials in order to foster stronger empathy for China and make their national decisions more friendly to China.

3. Going Out: Initiative of University Think Tank of Shanghai and Chinese Elites

Sending students and visiting scholars to countries along the Belt and Road is also important for building the Belt and Road talent cultivation system. In the past decades, many Chinese talents went to North America, Europe and Japan for study, but very few went to countries along the Belt and Road. In the future, national funds for study abroad can be made more favorable for students studying in countries along the Belt and Road. Shanghai Municipal Government should also actively cooperate with the Ministry of Education to select and send talents and scholars from various disciplines who are willing to get to know, learn and contribute to construction of the Belt and Road to relevant countries for further study.

Beyond that, long-term site investigations in such countries are equally important. Only those spending a long time studying and working in a foreign country can be able to truly know and understand local social conditions and public opinions. This applies to areas in China where the Belt and Road passes. Solid field investigation should be encouraged rather superficial surface work. This requires that talents to be cultivated should master not only specialty abilities of relevant discipline, but also the ability to acquire information on site and analyze such information in order to meet strategic requirements of the Belt and Road initiative and combine their knowledge with actions. However, some countries along the Belt and Road feature complicated national conditions, unpredictable changes in political situation and great domestic variations in regions, classes and religious sects, rendering it impossible to gain a full picture of their civil demands and prevailing public opinions via official diplomatics. In this case, people-to-people diplomatic talents are required to get an insight of the running mechanism of their whole society through academic researches, NGO volunteer activities and cultural exchanges.

4. Preconditions for Building Platforms of Cooperation in Running Schools or Short-term Cooperative Training Programs in Shanghai

Chunli Bai, President of the Chinese Academy of Sciences indicated in 2015 that: "We are willing to build alliances with scientists in countries and regions along the Belt and Road to discuss our development and support the Belt and Road initiative with science."*Several Opinions on Opening up in Contemporary Education* printed and issued by General Office of the CPC Central Committee and General Office of the State Council in April 2016 underlined the need to "open up the education driven by focus tasks and with the aim of mutual benefits via cooperation"; later the Ministry of Education issued detailed rules of *Promoting Actions for Education Improvement for the Belt and Road Initiative* in July of the same year to call for construction of a community of education by countries along the Belt and Road. In ASEAN Education Week at the end of July 2016, Chen Baosheng, Ministry of Education and leaders from Guizhou Province jointly proposed establishment of "school-enterprise alliance for cultivating talents for the Belt and Road initiative". By now, more than 50 universities and over a hundred Chinese-funded enterprises have joined the alliance. The purpose of this alliance is to build platforms via school-enterprise cooperation to jointly cultivate local specialized talents with global perspective. This shows that governments at national and local levels are taking great efforts to promote cooperation of China and foreign countries in running schools of higher education.

Many researches suggest that China has lost most outstanding students and excellent talents to main developed countries in North America and Europe during education cooperation with them. China is the weak side in such unbalanced cooperation as well as the demand side and the supplied side of good education resources. While the Belt and Road initiative comes at the right moment for Sino-foreign cooperative education since: Firstly, it helps to attract overseas students from countries along the Belt and Road, explore international market of student source and cultivate foreign talents with empathy for China and good understanding of demands by the Belt and Road initiative; secondly, scientific and technological platforms and decision-making think tank created via Sino-foreign cooperation provide intellectual support and consultation services for in-depth implementation of the Belt and Road initiative; thirdly, Chinese talents trained in cooperative education can be sent to work in countries in urgent needs of construction and administration and form tighter partnership.

Shanghai Municipal Government and Shanghai Municipal Commission of Education have abundant experience in education cooperation with foreign universities. For example, Shanghai is home to the first Sino-America university approved by the Ministry of Education—New York University Shanghai, which has cultivated a large amount of talents for development of Shanghai, even of China as a whole. On the basis of such experience, Shanghai Municipal Government should encourage universities in Shanghai to go out, give play to its geographical advantages and cooperate with foreign universities or jointly set up scientific research institutions to cultivate talents to serve the Belt and Road initiative. In addition to universities and education institutes with abilities and resources of cooperative education in foreign countries, other universities can also try short-term exchange student programs or summer/winter camps. Today's students are the foundation of future development in countries along the Belt and Road initiative and their experience at young age will shape the ways of interactions with China in the future.

APPENDIX

附 录

2017 年上海国际智库高峰论坛办会、参会智库简介

1. 主办方

上海市人民政府发展研究中心

上海市人民政府发展研究中心（前身是上海经济研究中心）于 1980 年 12 月 26 日正式成立，于 1995 年 12 月 22 日根据市政府决定，更名为上海市人民政府发展研究中心。上海市人民政府发展研究中心是为市政府决策服务，承担本市决策咨询的研究、组织、协调、管理、服务的市政府决策咨询研究机构。

主要职责：

（1）研究本市经济、社会发展和改革开放中具有全局性、综合性、战略性的问题。

（2）了解动态、分析矛盾、研究对策、预测前景，及时向上海市委、市政府提出决策建议和咨询意见。

（3）负责上海市两年一度的市决策咨询研究成果奖的评奖工作。

（4）组织、协调市政府系统的决策咨询研究工作。

（5）负责上海市决策咨询系统建议库信息管理和维护工作。

（6）受市政府委托，管理有关组织和事业机构。

（7）编辑出版《上海经济年鉴》和《科学发展》杂志。

（8）承办上海市领导交办的其他事项。

2. 承办方

波士顿咨询公司

波士顿咨询公司（BCG）是一家全球性管理咨询公司，是世界领先的商业战略咨询机构，客户遍及所有地区的私人机构、公共机构和非营利机构。BCG 与客户密切合作，帮助他们辨别最具价值的发展机会，应对至关重要的挑战并协助

他们进行企业转型。在为客户度身订制的解决方案中，BCG 融入对公司和市场态势的深刻洞察，并与客户组织的各个层面紧密协作，从而确保客户能够获得可持续的竞争优势，成长为更具能力的组织并保证成果持续有效。波士顿咨询公司成立于 1963 年，目前在全球 50 个国家设有 90 多家办公室。

上海发展研究基金会

上海发展研究基金会成立于 1993 年，是利用自然人、法人或者其他组织捐赠的财产，以从事公益事业为目的，按照国家有关规定的公募基金会、非营利性法人。

上海发展研究基金会以促进对发展问题的研究、推进决策咨询事业为宗旨；以募集、运作资金，研究、交流、资助、奖励经济、社会、城市发展决策咨询项目为业务范围。

二十几年来，基金会大力支持上海市决策咨询研究工作，资助了许多研究项目，并资助开展了上海市决策咨询研究成果奖评奖工作。同时，基金会也组织研究团队，完成了自行设立的或从其他单位承接的一系列研究项目。

近年来，基金会为实现其宗旨而积极探索。基金会每月举办一次"上海发展沙龙"，邀请国内外知名专家、学者就当前的热点或敏感问题作演讲，并与参会者进行互动讨论；每年举办两到三次高层次的研讨会，邀请多位海内外专家与政、商、学界人士共聚一堂，就全球经济和中国经济的形势进行讨论和交流；举办"中国经济未来"系列小型研讨会，针对中国经济发展中一些深层次问题，进行深入的讨论。基金会还通过资助的方式，与大学和研究机构合作举办了各种形式的研讨活动。基金会把各种研讨活动中的精彩内容，不定期地编撰出版内部资料《研讨实录》和《研究简报》，在更大的范围内推广对发展问题的研究和讨论成果。

上海国际智库交流中心

2010 年，按照时任上海市市长韩正关于进一步拓展上海市决策咨询研究工作，汇集国内外专家学者智慧服务上海市委、市政府的科学决策、民主决策，不断扩大中心的国际影响力的指示要求，上海市政府发展研究中心联合埃森哲、凯捷、德勤、博斯、IBM 等 13 家在沪国际智库牵头成立了"上海国际智库交流中心"。2011 年，上海国际智库交流中心召开成立大会并举办首届"上海智慧论坛"。时任市长韩正发来贺信，时任市政府秘书长姜平出席会议，宣读了韩正的贺信，致贺词并揭牌。

自 2014 年起，在原"上海智慧论坛"基础上，上海市发展研究中心将论坛提升为"上海国际智库峰会"，进一步提升了上海市政府发展研究中心整合国际智库的功能，拓展了上海与国际智库间的友好交往。2014 年，围绕上海建设具有全球影响力的科技创新中心战略，上海国际智库交流中心举办了以"问策全球科技创新中心"为主题的第一届上海国际智库峰会，国际智库、委办局和高校学者近 100 人参会，时任上海市政府秘书长李逸平出席会议并致辞。2015 年，召开了以"2050 年的上海：愿景与挑战"为主题的第二届上海国际智库峰会，时任上海市政府常务副市长屠光绍、市政府秘书长李逸平出席会议并致闭幕词。2016年，第三届上海国际智库峰会如期举办，国内外专家学者围绕"如何提升上海投资贸易便利化水平"进行了深入地研讨和交流，为上海投资贸易发展献计献策。

　　上海国际智库交流中心的主要职责是：

　　（1）开展政府决策咨询研究；

　　（2）服务企业发展开展应用研究、企业规划、管理咨询；

　　（3）开展双边和多边国际合作研讨；

　　（4）承担国际合作课题研究；

　　（5）提供专业人才培养、培训与信息服务。

3. 参会单位

世界银行

　　世界银行集团有 189 个成员国，员工来自 170 多个国家，在 130 多个地方设有办事处。世界银行集团是一个独特的全球性合作伙伴，所属五家机构共同致力于寻求在发展中国家减少贫困和建立共享繁荣的可持续之道。

　　IBRD 和 IDA 共同构成世界银行，向发展中国家的政府提供资金、政策咨询和技术援助。IDA 的重点是援助世界最贫困国家，IBRD 援助中等收入国家和资信良好的较贫困国家。IFC、MIGA 和 ICSID 的重点是加强发展中国家的私营部门。世界银行集团通过这三家机构向私营企业，包括金融机构，提供资金、技术援助、政治风险担保和争端调解服务。

　　中国与世界银行的合作开始于 1980 年改革开放之初。中国初期是作为世行面向最贫困国家的国际开发协会的受援国，1999 年中国从国际开发协会"毕业"，2007 年成为国际开发协会的捐款国。2010 年，中国在与世行合作 30 周年之际完成增资，成为世行第三大股东国。

　　30 多年来，为满足中国快速变化的需求，世界银行在华工作的性质也不断作出调整。在早期阶段，世界银行提供技术援助，引进经济改革的基本理念、先进的项目管理方法和新技术。后来，世界银行的工作重点逐渐转向制度建设和知识转让。目前，世界银行主张知识分享，帮助其他国家学习中国的经验。

埃森哲

埃森哲公司注册成立于爱尔兰，是一家全球领先的专业服务公司，为客户提供战略、咨询、数字、技术和运营服务及解决方案。埃森哲立足商业与技术的前沿，业务涵盖40多个行业，以及企业日常运营部门的各个职能。凭借独特的业内经验与专业技能，以及翘楚全球的交付网络，帮助客户提升绩效，并为利益相关方持续创造价值。埃森哲是《财富》全球500强企业之一，目前拥有约38.4万名员工，服务于120多个国家的客户。埃森哲致力驱动创新，从而改善人们工作和生活的方式。

埃森哲在大中华区开展业务已30年，拥有一支逾1.3万人的员工队伍，分布于北京、上海、大连、成都、广州、深圳、香港和台北。作为绩效提升专家，埃森哲将世界领先的商业技术实践于中国市场，帮助中国企业和政府制定战略、优化流程、集成系统、促进创新、提升运营效率、形成整体竞争优势，从而实现基业长青。

麦肯锡

麦肯锡公司是一家全球领先的管理咨询公司，1926年创立于美国，致力于为企业和公共机构提供有关战略、组织、运营和技术方面的咨询。麦肯锡在全球范围内咨询业务的客户包括了最知名的企业及机构，占据《财富》全球500强公司排行榜的80%。在大中华区，麦肯锡的客户遍及15个行业，还包括国家级、地区级及省市级的政府及机构。麦肯锡进入大中华区30余年来，一直致力于帮助本土领先企业改善管理技能和提升全球竞争力，并为寻求在本地区扩大业务的跨国企业提供咨询，同时也积极参与中国公共政策咨询和公共事业建设。目前麦肯锡在大中华地区开设了北京、上海、深圳、香港及台北五家分公司，共有50多位合伙人，300多位咨询师，还有100多位研究员及200多位专业人员。

罗兰贝格

罗兰贝格是一家由合伙人所有的独立机构，合伙人负责掌控公司整体业绩与商业表现。公司成立于1967年，是全球领先的咨询公司中唯一一家德国公司。罗兰贝格起源于德国，秉承欧洲文化，在全球范围内发展壮大，其中包括亚洲和罗兰贝格深切相信能够形成影响力的其他地区。

罗兰贝格力求在咨询与商业领域中与众不同的视角。如今，罗兰贝格仍勇于挑战普遍的思考模式，为客户提供管理商业颠覆性变革与转型的全新解决方案。

公司建立伊始，企业家精神即造就了我们的成长历程，并鼓舞罗兰贝格取得了卓越的成就。简而言之，罗兰贝格的变革精神深植于我们的 DNA 中。近 50 年，罗兰贝格持续发展，2 400 余员工遍布 34 个国家和地区，跻身全球顶级管理咨询公司之列，业务遍及所有主要国际市场。

通过取得与客户的互信，为客户创造可持续的价值增值，罗兰贝格长期为跨国企业、服务型公司以及公共机构提供咨询服务。

普华永道

普华永道是一家世界知名的专业服务机构，企业使命秉承"解决重要问题，营造社会诚信"。其网络遍及 157 个国家和地区，有超过 22.3 万名员工，致力于在审计、咨询及税务领域提供高质量的服务。

普华永道在中国的成员机构根据各地适用的法律协作运营。整体而言，员工总数约 21 000 人，其中包括约 800 多名合伙人。

普华永道被中国注册会计师协会连续 14 年在其下属会计师事务所百强评选中名列第一，在品牌价值及战略咨询公司 Brand Finance 最新公布的"2017 全球品牌价值 500 强榜单"上，名列"全球最强十大品牌"之一。普华永道荣获 2016 年亚太区 The Excellence Award 金奖，是四大会计师事务所及大型咨询机构当中，唯一得奖的机构。2017 年在雇主品牌咨询机构优信（Universum）全球最具吸引力雇主排名中，普华永道获商科学生评为全球五大最具吸引力雇主。作为全球顶尖智库，普华永道会定期发布各种分析和研究报告，帮助中国了解世界，也让世界更准确地了解中国。

德勤

德勤凭借遍布逾 150 个国家的全球网络和近 24 万人才的专业智慧，为 80% 的全球 500 强企业提供服务。2017 财年全球营收 388 亿美元，为全球最大的综合咨询服务提供商（按营收计）。德勤自 1917 年进入中国，已经为大中华区客户服务 100 年，亦是德勤全球网络中发展最快的成员所。德勤一向看重本地市场的实际需求，24 个办公室（中国大陆 19 个，中国台湾 5 个）近 13 500 名员工，按照当地适用法规以协作方式提供综合服务；帮助更多优秀的中国企业、本地企业做大做强；也通过自身全球网络的优势，将更多的外资企业引进来以及为中国企业走出去提供支持，全面协助中国企业实现优质增长并提升国际地位。1/3 香港联交所上市的企业选择德勤的服务，为 800 多家跨国公司及其在中国大陆的关联公司提供专业服务。除向企业提供服务之外，我们也向中央及各级政府、机构提供专业建议，推动国资发展，帮助"引进来，走出去"。自 1993 年以来，德勤一直作为中国政府财政部在国际会计准则和税务系统建设方面的专业顾问。德勤向国务院国资委、地方国资委提供包括国有企业产权代表、董事长绩效考核等多领域的专业管理咨询服务，我们协助一些省市国资委成功建设并推广了风险预警机制。此外，德勤为多个省市政府提供产业规划、招商策略、政府创新转型、电子政务等服务，有很多成功经验。

毕马威

毕马威在中国大陆 16 个城市设有办事机构，合伙人及员工约 10 000 名，分布在北京、成都、重庆、佛山、福州、广州、杭州、南京、青岛、上海、沈阳、深圳、天津、厦门、香港特别行政区和澳门特别行政区。毕马威以统一的经营方式来管理中国的业务，以确保其能够高效和迅速地调动各方面的资源，为客户提供高质量的服务。

毕马威是一个由专业服务成员所组成的全球网络。成员所遍布全球 155 个国家和地区，拥有专业人员 174 000 名，提供审计、税务和咨询等专业服务。毕马威独立成员所网络中的成员与瑞士实体——毕马威国际合作组织（"毕马威国际"）相关联。毕马威各成员所在法律上均属独立及分设的法人。

1992 年，毕马威在中国内地成为首家获准合资开业的国际会计师事务所。2012 年 8 月 1 日，毕马威成为四大会计师事务所之中，首家从中外合作制转为特殊普通合伙的事务所。毕马威香港的成立更早在 1945 年。率先打入中国市场的先机以及对质量的不懈追求，使其积累了丰富的行业经验，中国多家知名企业长期聘请毕马威提供专业服务，也反映了毕马威的领导地位。

安永

安永凭借在全球和当地的专业知识，协助客户保持投资者对客户的信心、管理企业风险、强化控制措施、抓住机遇和发挥企业的潜能。安永向许多大型和快速增长的中国企业，以及在区内经营业务的跨国公司提供审计、税务、财务交易和咨询服务。中国海外投资业务部（China Overseas Investment Network，简称"COIN"）将安永全球的专业人员连接在一起，促进相互协作，为中国企业的国际化发展提供全球一致的高质量服务。安永在美洲、EMEIA、亚太和日本各大区设置了专业的中国商业顾问团队，服务网络覆盖全球约 65 个国家和地区。

安永是大中华区规模最大的专业服务机构之一，在区内提供专业服务已有 45 年。这段期间，安永取得多项具里程碑意义的发展：安永的前身雅特杨会计师事务所（Arthur Young）于 1968 年在香港成立首个办事处；1981 年安永成为首批获准在中国内地开展业务的国际专业服务机构之一。

安永在大中华区设立了共 24 家办事处的网络，分别位于北京、香港、上海、广州、深圳、成都、大连、杭州、澳门、青岛、苏州、天津、武汉、厦门、南京、沈阳、长沙和西安；以及台北、台中、台南、中坜、新竹和高雄。安永在大中华区的员工超过 11 000 名，致力在适当时候，在适当地点配置适当人员，向客户提供所需的无缝衔接及优质服务。

野村综研

野村综合研究所（NRI）作为全球领先的咨询集团，是日本最早和规模最大的智库。NRI 成立于 1965 年，2001 年在东京证券交易所主板上市，拥有 10 000 多名专业人员，年营业额超过 35 亿美元，是目前世界上集智库功能、咨询功能和系统集成功能为一体的最大级咨询集团。

NRI 在大中华地区的上海、北京、大连、香港，和台北设有独立的业务公司，拥有 3 000 多名专业人员。其中野村综研 (上海) 咨询有限公司 (NRI 上海) 是 NRI 在中国大陆的智库及咨询业务总部，业务领域涵盖面向中国各级政府的公共发展战略咨询、面向全球企业及中国企业的管理咨询。

在公共发展战略咨询领域中，NRI 上海已为包括上海、北京、天津、重庆在内的中国近 50 个主要城市的政府提供咨询服务，内容涉及城市中长期发展战略、城市核心功能及功能区域发展战略、产业规划及实施路径等方面。

高风咨询

高风咨询公司是一家顶尖的战略和管理咨询公司，植根于中国，同时拥有全球视野、能力、以及广泛的资源网络。高风咨询公司为客户解决他们最棘手的问题——在当前快速变化、复杂且不确定性的经营环境之中所出现的问题。高风咨询公司不仅为客户"构建"问题解决方案，同时亦是协助方案的执行与落地，与客户携手合作。高风咨询公司的价值观引领着其工作行为——公司致力于将客户的利益放在最根本和最重要的位置；高风咨询公司是客观的，致力于与客户建立长期的合作关系，而不是单独的项目；高风咨询公司将人才视为战略资产，而非纯粹的"人头"；高风咨询公司，从最基层到最高级的顾问，都以帮助客户解决难题和并肩合作提升价值为信条。

凯捷咨询

作为咨询、技术服务和数字化转型领域的全球领先企业，凯捷始终处于创新前沿，在不断发展的云计算、数字化平台领域，助力所有客户把握机遇应对挑战，提升竞争力。依托长达 50 载的丰富行业经验和深厚专业知识，凯捷通过从战略到运营等一系列服务，帮助企业实现商业伟略。凯捷始终坚信的发展理念是：技术的商业价值源于人并由人现出来。凯捷是一家具有深厚多元文化底蕴的公司，拥有来自 40 多个国家和地区的 200 000 名团队成员。2016 年，集团全球营业收入为 125 亿欧元。凯捷是唯一一家在巴黎证券交易所上市，并荣列法指 40 强（CAC40）、欧洲指数（Euronext 100）、道琼斯指数（Dow Jones STOXX）、道琼斯欧盟指数 (Dow Jones Euro STXX indices) 等指数的上市咨询公司。

1997 年凯捷登陆中国。凯捷在中国经历了二十年的发展，成效卓著，已经成为集团重要的战略新兴市场之一。凯捷的大中华区总部设在上海，并在北京、广州、昆山、香港、台北、沈阳、杭州和佛山等地均设有分子公司或运营中心，拥有 2 700 名管理顾问和技术专家团队，业务覆盖了管理咨询、信息技术、金融服务、服务外包、全球研发以及本地化解决方案的实施等。

凯捷中国融合全球技术和服务能力，以客户为中心，以精深的行业和实战经验，运用数字化转型技术，为中国本土以及在中国的跨国企业提供全面和真正具有竞争力的解决方案及服务，与客户共同成长与共同成功。

上海美国商会

上海美国商会成立于 1915 年，是美国本土外成立的第三家美国商会。成立之初，商会仅有 45 名男性美国籍会员，彼时商会以促进美国对华贸易出口为宗旨。经过一个世纪的发展，商会已经成为亚太地区规模最大且最具影响力的美国商会之一，会员结构及宗旨也发生了很大变化。如今商会拥有来自 1 650 多家企业的 3 700 余名会员，其中包括众多知名全球五百强企业，也包括很多中小企业。商会除了致力于推动美中双边贸易以外，也帮助中国投资者赴美投资以及促进美中宏观经济合作。商会的服务覆盖整个中国，并在苏州和南京设立了分支机构。

作为一家非营利性、中立的商业组织，上海美国商会崇尚贸易自由、市场开放、私有企业自由发展和信息自由流通的原则，致力于在中国营造健康良好的商业环境，增进美中商务交往。

中国欧盟商会

中国欧盟商会由 51 家会员企业于 2000 年成立，其目的是代表不同行业和在华欧盟企业的共同声音。中国欧盟商会是一个在会员指导下开展工作的、独立的非营利性机构，其核心结构是代表欧盟在华企业的 25 个工作组和论坛。

欧盟商会目前已拥有约 1 600 家会员公司，并在九个城市设有七个分会，分别是：北京、南京、上海、沈阳、中国华南（广州和深圳）、中国西南（成都与重庆）及天津，每个分会都由当地董事会管理，并且直接向执行委员会汇报。

欧盟商会作为在华欧洲企业的独立官方代言机构得到了欧盟委员会和中国政府的一致认可。它也是民政部认可的外国商会。

欧盟商会是正在成长中的欧洲商业组织的成员之一。该组织将来自全球 20 个非欧盟国家的欧洲商业团体和商会联系在一起。

中国欧盟商会上海分会成立于 2002 年 4 月，如今已拥有近 600 家会员企业，是中国欧盟商会最大的分会。其会员企业构成了 25 个活跃的工作组和论坛，广泛覆盖了各行业和跨行业议题。每年，上海分会和北京及其他分会一起，共同起草年度《欧盟企业在中国建议书》和《商业信心调查》，为会员企业创造更好的在华营商环境提供参考意见。

美中贸易全国委员会

美中贸易全国委员会（USCBC）是非政府、无党派的，非营利的机构，拥有大约 200 家在华经营的美国会员公司。自 1973 年成立以来的四十多年中，我委员会为会员公司提供了大量的信息以及咨询、倡导等服务，并举办了多项活动。通过设在华盛顿的总部以及北京和上海的办事处，美中贸易全国委员会以其独特的定位优势在美、中两地为会员提供服务。

美中贸易全国委员会的使命是扩大美中商务联系，使全体会员从中受益，进而在更广阔的层面上使美国经济获益。我们提倡与中国进行建设性的商务联系——共同致力于消除贸易投资壁垒，并为双方营造一个规范、可预测的、透明的商务环境。

在美中贸易全国委员会的会员公司中，既有诸多知名的大型企业，也有相当比例的小型企业和服务业公司。美中贸易全国委员会董事会是我委员会的管理机构，由杰出的企业领导人组成。本届董事会主席由安达集团（CHUBB）的董事长兼首席执行官埃文·格林伯格先生（Evan G.Greenberg）担任。自 2004 年以来，傅强恩先生（John Frisbie）任美中贸易全国委员会会长。

日本贸易振兴机构

日本贸易振兴机构 (JETRO) 是促进日本与海外国家和地区间贸易与投资的政府机构。前身"日本贸易振兴会"成立于 1958 年，当时以"振兴出口"为工作重心。进入 21 世纪，工作重心已转向吸引海外国家对日本直接投资以及支持中小企业最大限度地开拓全球市场。2003 年由日本经济产业省的下属特殊法人变更成了独立行政法人日本贸易振兴机构。现在，拥有东京和大阪总部，亚洲经济研究所和 43 个国内事务所，在海外 55 个国家和地区拥有 74 个事务所。现在主要的业务有：吸引海外企业对日投资；协助日本农林水产品和食品对外出口；协助日本中小和中坚企业开拓海外市场；通过信息提供及调查研究为企业提供商业活动及通商政策。在中国的上海、北京、广州、成都、武汉、大连、青岛、香港分别设有代表处。

JETRO 特别支援日本的中坚和中小企业开拓海外市场。根据企业的不同需求，向企业提供从出口到向海外投资的"全程支援"的同时，为协助海外企业快速解决所面临的问题，在海外具有现地律师、会计等专家提供咨询服务的体制。此外，还与当地政府协同合作保护知识产权及活用知识产权的商业服务。

深化吸引外国对日本直接投资（FDI）并促进跨境商务合作，FDI 带来先进技术、经验及知识产权，这对于复兴日本经济至关重要。JETRO 作为国外企业投资日本的最初窗口，也致力于研发及雇用能力充足的行业对日本的投资。针对已进入日本市场的外资企业，也向它们提供扩大地区投资的服务。

印度工业联合会

印度工业联合会 (CII) 致力于通过咨询和顾问服务，联合政府部门和工业界的共同力量，创建和维持一个利于印度工业发展的理想环境。

印度工业联合会是一个非政府、非营利性的行业领导机构，由印度工业界自主领导和管理，对于印度经济的繁荣和发展起到了积极的推进作用。印度工业联合会成立于 1895 年，是目前印度最重要的行业协会。它拥有超过 8 500 家的直属成员机构，涵盖国有及私有性质的各大中小型企业和跨国公司。此外，通过 250 个国家和地区部门性协会，联合会更是与 200 000 多家间接会员保持着紧密联系。

长期以来，印度工业联合会始终与政府部门保持紧密协作，共同探讨政策事宜，并通过一系列的专业服务及遍布全球的战略合作网络，帮助印度工业界改善绩效、提升竞争力、拓展商业契机，以此来推进创新与变革。与此同时，它还为印度工业产业界提供了一个利于构建行业共识和拓展业务网络的高效平台。

印度工业联合会始终强调树立企业的正面形象，并积极协助各个工业企业制定和执行企业形象战略规划。它与民间社会机构建立了战略伙伴关系，共同推进印度在平权法案、医疗保健、教育、民生、多元化管理、技能发展、妇女权益和水资源等各项领域的一体化、综合性发展。

印度工业联合会在印度设有 67 个办事处，其中包括 9 家卓越中心（Centers of Excellence）。此外，印度工业联合会还拥有 11 家海外办事处，分别位于澳大利亚、巴林、中国、埃及、法国、德国、伊朗、新加坡、南非、英国和美国，以及遍布 129 个国家的 344 家合作机构。今天，它已成为印度工业产业界和国际商业界之间重要的枢纽机构。

IBM

IBM, 即国际商业机器公司，创立于 1911 年，是一家全球整合的信息技术、咨询服务和业务解决方案公司。**IBM** 公司业务遍及 170 多个国家，运用最先进的信息科技，助力各行各业的客户创造商业价值。同时，**IBM** 吸引并拥有全球最优秀的人才，助力对客户及整个社会至关重要的事业，致力于让世界更美好。

IBM 的业务涵盖技术与商业领域，始终寻求高价值创新，推动持续改造与转型自身的业务。通过从行业领先的大数据、云、社交移动与认知计算技术、企业级系统和软件、咨询和 IT 服务中形成的产品与整合业务解决方案，为客户创造价值。同时，所有这些方案都汲取着全球最领先的 **IBM** 研究机构的创新支持。

目前，**IBM** 致力于推进三大战略——利用大数据推动行业转型、打造竞争优势；利用云计算，重塑企业 IT 架构，推动业务模式变革；以及利用移动和社交技术、并依托安全能力构建企业互动参与体系。**IBM** 正在为现代 IT 骨干创建一个专注于开放创新的全新系统基础架构，以满足新计算时代前所未有、日新月异的需求。**IBM** 员工与客户通力合作，利用公司的业务咨询、技术和研发能力构建稳健的系统，以创造动态高效的组织、更便捷的交通、更安全的空气、食品、更清洁的水源和更健康的生活。

凭借在中国超过 30 年的丰富经验，**IBM** 一直提供领先的技术、卓越的管理和独特的解决方案及服务，帮助推动中国 IT 行业及金融、电信、能源、制造、零售等众多行业的中国企业的创新、转型与发展。

2017 Shanghai International Think Tank Summit Organizers

1. Host

The Development Research Centre of Shanghai Municipal People's Government

The Development Research Centre of Shanghai Municipal People's Government (SDRC) was formerly known as Shanghai Center for Economic Research (SCER) which was founded on Dec. 26th, 1980, and was renamed by SDRC on Dec. 22nd, 1995. SDRC is a decision-making research institution led by Shanghai Municipal People's Government, providing comprehensive consulting services with the functions of organizing, coordinating and managing the government research projects.

Main functions:

(1) Study on the overall and strategic issues concerning Shanghai economy, social development, reform and opening-up.

(2) Trace the dynamic trends, analyze the inconsistency, study the countermeasures and forecast the prospects, submit decision-making proposals and consulting advices to the CPC Shanghai Committee and the Shanghai Municipal People's Government in due course.

(3) Organize the assessment of the decision-making and consulting research results as well as the appraisal of the distinguished research achievements once every two years.

(4) Organize and coordinate the decision-making and consulting research work within the government system.

(5) Conduct the information maintenance work of the Shanghai Decision-making and Consulting Proposals System.

(6) Administrate the related organizations and institutions entrusted by the Shanghai Municipal People's Government.

(7) Compile and publish Shanghai Economy Almanac and Journal of Scientific Development.

(8) Undertake other missions assigned by the leaders of the Shanghai Municipality.

2. Organizers

The Boston Consulting Group(BCG)

The Boston Consulting Group (BCG) is a global management consulting firm and the world's leading advisor on business strategy. BCG partner with clients from the private, public, and not-for-profit sectors in all regions to identify their highest-value opportunities, address their most critical challenges, and transform their enterprises. BCG customized approach combines deep insight into the dynamics of companies and markets with close collaboration at all levels of the client organization. This ensures that our clients achieve sustainable competitive advantage, build more capable organizations, and secure lasting results. Founded in 1963, BCG is a private company with more than 90 offices in 50 countries.

Shanghai Development Research Foundation

SDRF was established in 1993 as a non-profit organization, aiming at development research and decision-making consultations. Over the past decades, BCG have gained high recognitions in academic circles, by establishing high-level platforms for exchanges of views, conducting deep research on development issues and providing constructive decision-making consultations to Chinese governments.

SDRF Newsletter will constantly compile the essential contents of our conferences and research work into brief reports. We wish to further spread the achievements of research and discussion on the development issues, and look forward your feedbacks.

The activities SDRF hold as platforms:

Monthly "Shanghai Development Salon". Well-known experts are invited to make speeches on hotspot topics, and participants from various circles are encouraged to share their opinions. Over the past 10 years from 2005, the salon has obtained great popularity and reputation. Yearly forums on World and Chinese Economy Forums on World and Chinese Economy are held twice a year. They are organized to make a real-time analysis of the economic performances in China and the world in the year, as well as to predict the economic trends of the coming year.

High-level International symposiums. Several high-level symposiums are held every year, which invite honored scholars from home and abroad to present their views around some important macro-economy and international finance, such as global financial governance, international financial architecture, and global economic growth, etc.

The Research work we devote to: SDRF's research focuses on the issues of macro-economy and international finance, such as the reform of international monetary system, RMB internationalization, the regulation of cross-border capital flows, and further enhancing the role of SDR, etc. Several books and pamphlets on these have been published.

Shanghai International Think Tank Exchange Center

Shanghai International Think Tank Exchange Center is one of the open and public decision-making and consulting research platforms, set up by the Development Research Center of Shanghai Municipal People's Government (SDRC). In 2010, SDRC, as required by the then Mayor Han Zheng proactively made contact with thirteen world-renowned think tanks in Shanghai like Accenture, Capgemini, Deloitte and IBM, aiming to further Shanghai's decision making and consulting research by drawing on the wisdom of experts and scholars from home and abroad to enable the CPC Shanghai Committee and Shanghai municipal government to do decision-making in a more democratic and scientific way and constantly expand the influence of SDRC in the world. In January, 2011, the center was established and the first "Smart Shanghai Forum" with the theme "Innovation, Transformation and Development" was also held. Mr. Han Zheng, the then Shanghai Mayor, sent his message of congratulation and Mr. Jiang Ping, the then secretary-general of Shanghai government, attended the forum and delivered an address.

The main responsibilities for the Shanghai International Think Tank Exchanges Center are as follows:

(1) To conduct decision-making research for the government.

(2) To provide application research, business planning, managerial consulting services for enterprises.

(3) To organize international bilateral and multilateral corporation seminar.

(4) To study international cooperation and exchanges subjects.

(5) To provide development, training and information services for professionals.

3. Participants

The World Bank

With 189 member countries, staff from more than 170 countries and offices in over 130 locations, the World Bank Group is a unique global partnership: five institutions working for sustainable solutions that reduce poverty and build shared prosperity in developing countries.

Together, IBRD and IDA from the World Bank, which provides financing, policy advice, and technical assistance to governments of developing countries. IDA focuses on the world's poorest countries, while IBRD assists middle-income and creditworthy poorer countries. IFC, MIGA, and ICSID focus on strengthening the private sector in developing countries. Through these institutions, the World Bank Group provides financing, technical assistance, political risk insurance, and settlement of disputes to private enterprises, including financial institutions.

China began its partnership with the World Bank in 1980, just as it embarked on its reforms. Starting as a recipient of support from the International Development Association (IDA), the World Bank's fund for the poorest, China graduated from IDA in 1999 and became a contributor in 2007. It became the third largest shareholder in the World Bank upon completion of the capital increase approved in 2010, the 30th anniversary year of its partnership.

Throughout this time, the nature of the World Bank's activities in China changed to meet the country's rapidly evolving needs. Initially, the World Bank provided technical assistance to introduce basic economic reforms, modern project management methodologies, and new technologies. Later, the focus shifted to institutional strengthening and knowledge transfer. The World Bank now encourages knowledge sharing to enable the rest of the world to learn from China's experience.

Accenture

Accenture is a leading global professional services company, providing a broad range of services and solutions in strategy, consulting, digital, technology and operations. Combining unmatched experience and specialized skills across more than 40 industries and all business functions—underpinned by the world's largest delivery network—Accenture works at the intersection of business and technology to help clients improve their performance and create sustainable value for their stakeholders. With approximately 384 000 people serving clients in more than 120 countries, Accenture drives innovation to improve the way the world works and lives.

Accenture has been operating in Greater China for 30 years. Today, the Greater China practice has more than 13 000 people serving clients across the region and has offices in Beijing, Shanghai, Dalian, Chengdu, Guangzhou, Shenzhen, Hong Kong and Taipei.

McKinsey & Company

McKinsey & Company is the leading global management consulting firm and by far the largest global management consulting firm in Greater China. Globally, we are the trusted advisor and counselor to many of the most influential businesses and institutions in the world. We serve more than 80 percent of Fortune magazine's list of the Most Admired Companies. In Greater China, we advise clients in over 15 different industry sectors, and work with dozens of government agencies and institutions at the national, regional and municipal levels. Our primary mission is to help our clients achieve substantial and enduring impact by tackling their biggest issues concerning strategy, operations, organization, technology and finance. Today we have more than 350 consultants and over 50 Partners located across four locations in Greater China: Beijing, Shanghai, Hong Kong, and Taipei. They are supported by more than 100 research professionals, and over 200 professional support staff.

Roland Berger

Roland Berger is an independent company, solely owned by our Partners, who are responsible for overall corporate performance and business success. Founded in 1967, Roland Berger remains the only leading global consultancy firm with non-Anglo-Saxon roots. Roland Berger is German by origin, European by nature and global by ambition, including a strong footprint in Asia and other geographies where Roland Berger feels that we can truly make an impact.

Roland Berger has always strived to a different perspective in the field of consulting and business, and today Roland Berger continues to constructively challenge standard patterns of thought and provide clients with new solutions to manage disruption and transformation.

Roland Berger's entrepreneurial spirit has shaped Roland Berger's growth and fueled Roland Berger's outstanding achievements since the early days of the firm. In short, being a game changer is in Roland Berger's DNA. With nearly 50 years of continuous growth behind us and 2 400 employees working in 34 countries, Roland Berger is one of the leading players in global top-management consulting and has successful operations in all major international markets.

Through mutual trust and sustainable value added for clients, Roland Berger has become a longstanding advisor of major international industry and service companies as well as public institutions worldwide.

PwC

At PwC, our purpose is to build trust in society and solve important problems. We're a network of firms in 157 countries with more than 223 000 people who are committed to delivering quality in assurance, advisory and tax services.

PwC China works on a collaborative basis, subjects to local applicable laws. Collectively, PwC has around 800 partners and strength of approximately 21 000 people.

PwC was named strongest B2B brand & one of the world's 10 most powerful brands by Brand Finance 2017, and awarded the Multi-Channel Communications category at the Asia-Pacific Excellence Awards in 2016, which is the only Big Four Consulting firm to win this marketing award. PwC was ranked Top 5 World's Most Attractive Employer for business students. The Chinese Institute of Certified Public Accountants published its Top 100 Accounting Firms in China. PwC China ranked first in the list. This is the 14th consecutive year that PwC won this award.

Deloitte

With over 240 000 people in more than 150 countries, Deloitte serves more than 80 percent of the world's largest 500 companies. One-third of all companies listed on the Stock Exchange of Hong Kong choose Deloitte's service. Based on the reported global revenue of US$38.8 billion for the fiscal year of 2017, Deloitte again takes the lead among the Big Four and is the world's largest professional services provider. Deloitte set up its first rep office in Shanghai, China in 1917 and just celebrated our

100th-year anniversary. Deloitte China is the fastest-growing member firm of Deloitte global network, drawing increasing attention from the management of DTTL.Deloitte Greater China (including 19 in mainland China, 5 in Taiwan) now has near 13 500 people in 24 cities in Greater China. Deloitte China focuses on the real needs of local markets. It adheres to the localization strategy and is transforming to a full-range professional services firm. Deloitte China serves one-third of all companies listed on the Stock Exchange of Hong Kong and more than 800 MNCs and their affiliated companies on the Chinese Mainland. Apart from providing services to enterprises, we also serve the government at all levels. Deloitte constantly supports the central and local governments. Deloitte hopes to leverage its global network to bring more foreign companies into China and bring more local companies abroad, helping promote "a two-way flow of inbound and outbound business activity". Deloitte has been a firm supporter of Chinese government in developing the accounting profession in China. We have proactively participated in the consultation of proposed rules and regulations relating to accounting and tax systems. We'll continue to bring international accounting practices to China and promote the development of local accounting profession.

KPMG

KPMG operates in 16 cities across China Mainland, with around 10 000 partners and staff in Beijing, Chengdu, Chongqing, Foshan, Fuzhou, Guangzhou, Hangzhou, Nanjing, Qingdao, Shanghai, Shenyang, Shenzhen, Tianjin, Xiamen, Hong Kong SAR and Macau SAR. With a single management structure across all these offices, KPMG China Mainland can deploy experienced professionals efficiently, wherever our client is located.

KPMG is a global network of professional services firm providing Audit, Tax and Advisory services. KPMG operates in 155 countries and regions, and has 174 000 people working in member firms around the world. The independent member firms of the KPMG network are affiliated with KPMG International Cooperative ("KPMG International"), a Swiss entity. Each KPMG firm is a legally distinct and separate entity and describes itself as such.

In 1992, KPMG became the first international accounting network to be granted a joint venture licence in mainland China. KPMG China was also the first among the Big Four in mainland China to convert from a joint venture to a special general partnership, as of 1 August 2012. Additionally, the Hong Kong office can trace its origins to 1945. This early commitment to the China market, together with an unwavering focus on quality, has been the foundation for accumulated industry experience, and is reflected in the Chinese member firm's appointment by some of China's most prestigious companies.

EY

At EY, they draw upon their global and local knowledge to help client retain the confidence of investors, manage risk, strengthen controls, grasp opportunities and achieve client's potential. EY offers assurance, tax, transaction and advisory services to many large and fast-growth Chinese companies, and multinationals operating in the region. EY China Overseas Investment Network (COIN) links EY professionals around the globe, facilitates collaboration, and provides consistent and coordinated services to our Chinese clients making outbound investments. Building on the existing China Business Group in the Americas, EMEIA, Asia-Pacific and Japan areas, COIN has expanded our network into 65 countries and territories around the world.

EY is one of the largest professional services organizations in Greater China, having enjoyed a presence in the region for 45 years. EY has reached many milestones, including opening our first Hong Kong office in 1968 as Arthur Young and being one of the first international organizations to establish operations in mainland China in 1981.

EY supports client through EY's network of 24 offices in Greater China. EY is located in Beijing, Chengdu, Dalian, Guangzhou, Hangzhou, Hong Kong, Macau, Nanjing, Qingdao, Shanghai, Shenyang, Shenzhen, Suzhou, Tianjin, Wuhan, Xiamen, Changsha and Xi'an; Chungli, Hsinchu, Kaohsiung, Taichung, Tainan and Taipei. With more than 11 000 employees in Greater China, EY is committed to bring together the right people, at the right time, in the right place to give you the seamless, high-quality service you need.

Nomura Research Institute

As a world leading consulting group, Nomura Research Institute, Ltd. (NRI) is Japan's oldest and largest think tank. NRI was established in 1965 and listed on the Tokyo Stock Exchange in 2001. With over 10 000 professional employees and an annual business turnover exceeding 3.5 billion USD, it is currently the largest consulting group in the world that integrates a think tank, consulting, and system services.

In the greater China region, NRI has independent companies established in Shanghai, Beijing, Dalian, Hong Kong, and Taipei with over 3 000 professional employees. The Nomura Research Institute Shanghai, Ltd. (NRI Shanghai) is mainland China's think tank and consulting headquarters, covering public development strategy consulting services for all levels of Chinese governments and offering management consulting for global and Chinese enterprises.

In the field of public development strategy consulting, NRI Shanghai has already provided consulting services to the city governments of over 50 main cities in China, including Shanghai, Beijing, Tianjin, and Chongqing, which involves aspects such as municipal mid and long-term development strategies, core municipal function and function area development strategy, and industrial planning and execution.

Gao Feng Advisory Company

Gao Feng Advisory Company is a pre-eminent strategy and management consulting firm with roots in China coupled with global vision, capabilities, and a broad resources network. Gao Feng Advisory Company helps clients address and solve their toughest business and management issues—that arise in the current fast-changing, complicated and ambiguous operating environment. Gao Feng Advisory Company commit to putting our clients' interest first and foremost. Gao Feng Advisory Company is objective and view client engagements as long-term relationships rather than one-off projects. Gao Feng Advisory Company not only help clients "formulate" the solutions but also assist in implementation, often hand-in-hand. Gao Feng Advisory Company believe in teaming and working together to add value and contribute to problem solving for our clients, from the most junior to the most senior.

Gao Feng Advisory Company senior team is made up of seasoned consultants previously at leading management consulting firms and/or ex-top executives at large corporations. The Company believe this combination of management theory and operational experience would deliver the most benefit to clients.

Gao Feng is taken from the Song Dynasty Chinese proverb "Gao Feng Liang Jie". "Gao Feng" denotes noble character while "Liang Jie" refers to a sharp sense of integrity. The Company believe that this principle lies at the core of management consulting—a truly trustworthy partner who will help clients tackle their toughest issues.

Capgemini

A global leader in consulting, technology services and digital transformation, Capgemini is at the forefront of innovation to address the entire breadth of clients' opportunities in the evolving world of cloud, digital and platforms. Building on its strong 50-year heritage and deep industry-specific expertise, Capgemini enables organizations to realize their business ambitions through an array of services from strategy to operations. Capgemini is driven by the conviction that the business value of technology comes from and through people. It is a multicultural company of 200 000 team members in over 40 countries. The Group reported 2016 global revenues of EUR 12.5 billion. Capgemini is the only consultant company listed on Paris Bourse, and gloriously ranked CAC 40, Euronext 100, Dow Jones STOXX, Dow Jones Euro STXX indices.

In 1997, Capgemini began operations in China. With the 20-year highly effective development, Capgemini China has become one of the Group's most important and strategic markets. Capgemini China headquarters in Shanghai provides support to its branch offices and operation centers located in Beijing, Guangzhou, Kunshan, Hong Kong, Taipei, Shenyang, Foshan, Hangzhou. With 2 700 professional consultants and technical experts, Capgemini China's business covers consulting, information technology, financial services, outsourcing services, and implementation of localized solutions.

Capgemini China integrates global technology and service capabilities with customer-centric strategy. With intensive industries and best-practical experience, digital transformation technology, Capgemini China provides comprehensive as well as truly competitive solutions and services to companies in China, growing with our clients and achieving success together.

AmCham Shanghai

The American Chamber of Commerce in Shanghai, known as the "Voice of American Business" in China, is one of the largest American Chambers in the Asia Pacific region. As a non-profit, non-partisan business organization, AmCham Shanghai is committed to the principles of free trade, open markets, private enterprise and the unrestricted flow of information. Founded in 1915, AmCham Shanghai was the third American Chamber established outside the United States.

For 100 years, AmCham Shanghai has been at the forefront of American business success in China. Throughout 2015, our centennial year, we have produced a series of events and publications that celebrated our storied history and the opportunities of the coming century. By reflecting on the past, present, and future of the U.S.-China commercial relationship, the centennial program communicated how American business and AmCham Shanghai have contributed to China's development in the past and will do so in the future. The program showcased examples of our impact on China's growth and raised the profile of American business in Shanghai.

European Chamber, Shanghai Chapter

The European Union Chamber of Commerce in China (European Chamber) was founded in 2000 by 51 member companies that shared a goal of establishing a common voice for the various business sectors of the European Union and European businesses operating in China. It is a member-driven, non-profit, fee-based organization with a core structure of 25 working groups and for a representing European business in China.

The European Chamber has nearly 1 600 members in seven chapters operating in nine cities: Beijing, Nanjing, Shanghai, Shenyang, South China (Guangzhou and Shenzhen), Southwest China (Chengdu and Chongqing) and Tianjin. Each chapter is managed at the local level by local boards reporting directly to the Executive Committee.

The European Chamber is recognized by the European Commission and the Chinese authorities as the official voice of European business in China. It is recognized as a foreign chamber of commerce by the Ministry of Civil Affairs.

The European Chamber is part of the growing network of European Business Organizations(EBO). This network connects European business associations and chambers of commerce from 20 non-EU countries around the world.

The Shanghai Chapter was established in April 2002 and currently has over 600 member companies, the largest of all Chamber chapters. It has grown substantially in terms of membership, the number of working groups and fora, as well as its events and lobby activities. The Shanghai Chapter currently has 25 active working groups, desks and fora covering a diverse range of industries and services. Shanghai-based working groups cooperate closely with working groups in Beijing and other chapters to provide input into the annual European Business in China Position Paper, Business Confidence Survey and other advocacy initiatives in order to give recommendations to improve business environment in China.

The US-China Business Council

The US-China Business Council (USCBC) is a private, nonpartisan, nonprofit organization of approximately 200 American companies that do business with China. Founded in 1973, USCBC has provided unmatched information, advisory, advocacy, and program services to its members for four decades. Through its offices in Washington, DC; Beijing; and Shanghai, USCBC is uniquely positioned to serve its members' interests in the United States and China.

USCBC's mission is to expand the US-China commercial relationship to the benefit of its membership and, more broadly, the US economy. It favors constructive, results-oriented engagement with China to eliminate trade and investment barriers and develop a rules-based commercial environment that is predictable and transparent to all parties.

Among USCBC's members are many large and well-known US corporations, but smaller companies and professional services firms make up a substantial portion of the overall membership. USCBC is governed by a board of directors composed of distinguished corporate leaders; the current chair is Evan Greenberg, chairman and CEO of Chubb. John Frisbie has been USCBC's president since 2004.

Japan External Trade Organization

The Japan External Trade Organization (JETRO) is a government-related organization that works to promote mutual trade and investment between Japan and the rest of the world. Originally established in 1958 to promote Japanese exports abroad, JETRO's core focus in the 21st century has shifted toward promoting foreign direct investment into Japan and helping small to medium size Japanese firms maximize their global export potential. JETRO has 74 overseas offices in 55 countries worldwide, as well as 8 offices in China, including our Shanghai, Beijing, Guangzhou, Chengdu, Wuhan, Dalian, Qingdao and Hong Kong, 46 offices in Japan, including Tokyo and

Osaka headquarters.

Helping Japanese firms, especially SMEs, expand business overseas. To help businesses enter or expand into overseas markets, JETRO provides a wealth of support and services, from advice on legal and tax matters to helping firms understand relevant economic partnership agreements (EPAs). JETRO also helps firms with business-related difficulties in these foreign markets, including working with local governments to seek improved intellectual property protection for their products.

Working to further boost foreign direct investment (FDI) in Japan and promote cross-border business tie-ups. FDI, which brings with it advanced technologies, know-how and intellectual assets, has become increasingly important to Japan, helping revitalize the country's economy and keeping Japan at the forefront of the global economy. Facilitating international business and technology partnerships between Japanese and foreign firms in high-tech fields is another important activity for us.

The Confederation of Indian Industry

The Confederation of Indian Industry (CII) works to create and sustain an environment conducive to the development of India, partnering industry, Government, and civil society, through advisory and consultative processes.

CII is a non-government, not-for-profit, industry-led and industry-managed organization, playing a proactive role in India's development process. Founded in 1895, India's premier business association has over 8 500 members, from the private as well as public sectors, including SMEs and MNCs, and an indirect membership of over 200 000 enterprises from around 250 national and regional sectoral industry bodies.

CII charts change by working closely with Government on policy issues, interfacing with thought leaders, and enhancing efficiency, competitiveness and business opportunities for industry through a range of specialized services and strategic global linkages. It also provides a platform for consensus-building and networking on key issues.

Extending its agenda beyond business, CII assists industry to identify and execute corporate citizenship programmes. Partnerships with civil society organizations carry forward corporate initiatives for integrated and inclusive development across diverse domains including affirmative action, healthcare, education, livelihood, diversity management, skill development, empowerment of women, and water, to name a few.

With 67 offices, including 9 Centres of Excellence, in India, and 11 overseas offices in Australia, Bahrain, China, Egypt, France, Germany, Iran, Singapore, South Africa, UK, and USA, as well as institutional partnerships with 344 counterpart organizations in 129 countries, CII serves as a reference point for Indian industry and the international business community.

IBM

IBM is a globally integrated technology and consulting company headquartered in Armonk, New York. With operations in more than 170 countries, IBM attracts and retains some of the world's most talented people to help solve problems and provide an edge for businesses, governments and non-profits.

Innovation is at the core of IBM's strategy. The company develops and sells software and systems hardware and a broad range of infrastructure, cloud and consulting services.

Today, IBM is focused on four growth initiatives—business analytics, cloud computing, growth markets and Smarter Planet. IBMers are working with customers around the world to apply the company's business consulting, technology and R&D expertise to build systems that enable dynamic and efficient organizations, better transportation, safer food, cleaner water and healthier populations.

POSTSCRIPT

后　记

按照 2017 年度市委市政府重点工作安排，经与上海国际智库交流中心成员单位共同商议，上海市人民政府发展研究中心联合本届轮值主席单位波士顿咨询公司共同举办了"2017 年上海国际智库高峰论坛"。

本次论坛由上海市人民政府发展研究中心国合办、波士顿咨询公司和发展基金会组成论坛筹备组，在上海市人民政府发展研究中心的领导下具体开展会务组织和策划工作。为做好会议筹备工作，2017 年 7 月份起，上海市人民政府发展研究中心与波士顿咨询公司开展了多次讨论，商讨高峰论坛初步筹备方案；10 月中旬，筹备组召集 18 家上海国际智库交流中心成员单位召开高峰论坛筹办预备会议，确定了本届论坛主题——"如何发挥上海在'一带一路'中的桥头堡作用"，启动演讲嘉宾邀请、演讲主题角度的选择等工作；11 月上旬，筹备组围绕论坛主题公开征集了本市高校和国际智库关于"一带一路"投资建设方面的相关研究报告，编译整理了经济学人智库《"一带一路"沿线国家风险分析》等相关中英文报告，并将相关研究报告送呈各智库单位参阅。

本次高峰论坛得到了市政府办公厅、市外办等方面的大力支持和指导，尤其是获得了波士顿咨询公司梁瑜女士、世界银行驻华办公室吴晶女士、埃森哲公司黄蕾女士、麦肯锡公司张帆先生、罗兰贝格公司王可佳女士、普华永道张艳女士、德勤杨伟娜女士、毕马威黄锋先生、安永黄武先生、野村综研白英华女士、凯捷咨询靳慧军先生、高风咨询张倩女士、欧盟上海商会倪晓辰先生、上海美国商会张菲霏女士、美中贸易全国委员会上海代表处许子兰女士、日本贸易振兴机构刘元森先生、印度工业联合会杨春兰女士、IBM 蒋晓飞先生等上海国际智库交流中心成员单位联络人员的鼎力支持和积极配合。

本书的出版得到了各位与会国际智库和专家学者以及上海世纪出版股份有限公司格致出版社的大力支持，上海市人民政府发展研究中心国合办承担了大量译校和主要编辑工作，信息处和科研处的同仁也给予了积极协助，在此一并表示感谢！

上海市人民政府发展研究中心国合办

上海国际智库交流中心

2018 年 5 月 4 日

According to the Key Work Arrangements of CPC Shanghai Municipal Committee and Shanghai Government of 2017, the "2017 Shanghai International Think Tank Summit" is co-organized by the Development Research Center of Shanghai Municipal People's Government (SDRC) and the Chairman-in-office Boston Consulting Group (BCG) after discussion with member units of Shanghai International Think Tank Exchange Center.

The Summit Preparatory Group includes International Cooperation & Exchange Office of the SDRC, Boston Consulting Group and Shanghai Development Research Foundation, which is responsible for detailed summit organization and planning under the leadership of the SDRC. For better preparation, the SDRC and Boston Consulting Group has discussed primary preparation plans of the Summit for several times since July 2017; the Preparatory Group convened the Preparatory Meeting with 18 SDRC member units in the mid of October; at the Preparatory Meeting, the theme of this Forum was determined as "How to Play Shanghai's Bridgehead Role in Serving the Belt and Road Initiative", and the invitation for guest speakers and selection of speaking topics were initiated; the Preparatory Group collected related research reports on investment and construction about the Belt and Road initiative from universities and colleges in Shanghai and international think tanks; complied and classified related English and Chinese reports from the Economist Intelligence Unit (EIU) (such as "One Belt, One Road: an economic roadmap"), and presented these reports to each think tank for reference in the beginning of November.

This Summit has received much support and guidance from The General office of Shanghai Municipal People's Government and Foreign Affairs Office of the Shanghai Municipal People's Government. Special thanks are due to all of the contacts of the

SDRC member units who had lent their support and coordination, including Ms. Liang Yu from Boston Consulting Group, Ms. Wu Xiao from China Office of the World Bank, Ms. Huang Lei from Accenture, Mr. Zhang Fan from McKinsey Company, Ms. Wang Kejia from Roland Bergen, Ms. Zhang Yan from PwC, Ms. Yang Weina from Deloitte, Mr. Huang Feng from KPMG, Mr. Huang Wu from Ernst & Young, Ms. Bai Yinghua from NRI, Mr. Jin Huijun from Capgemini Consulting, Ms. Zhang Qian from Gao Feng Advisory Company, Mr. Ni Xiaochen from European Union Chamber of Commerce in Shanghai, Ms. Zhang Feifei from The American Chamber of Commerce in Shanghai, Ms. Xu Zilan from Shanghai Office of the The US-China Business Council, Mr. Liu Yuansen from Japan External Trade Organization, Ms. Yang Chunlan from Confederation of Indian Industry, and Mr. Jiang Xiaofei from IBM.

This book has been published with the generous support from all participating international think tanks, experts and scholars and Truth & Wisdom Press of Shanghai Century Publishing (Group) Co., Ltd. International Cooperation & Exchange of SDRC spent a great amount of time for translation checking and key editing of this book; and colleagues from Information Div. and Research Management Div. also lent active assistance. We therefore would like to take this opportunity to publicly thank all of those involved!

International Cooperation & Exchange

Office of the SDRC

Shanghai International Think Tank Center

4th May, 2018

图书在版编目(CIP)数据

上海在"一带一路"建设中的桥头堡作用:2017 上
海国际智库咨询研究报告/上海市人民政府发展研究中
心编. —上海:格致出版社:上海人民出版社,
2018.9
(上海市人民政府发展研究中心系列报告)
ISBN 978 - 7 - 5432 - 2916 - 7

Ⅰ.①上… Ⅱ.①上… Ⅲ.①"一带一路"-区域经
济合作-经济发展-研究报告-上海 Ⅳ.①F127.51

中国版本图书馆 CIP 数据核字(2018)第 177919 号

责任编辑 程 倩
装帧设计 人马艺术设计·储平

上海在"一带一路"建设中的桥头堡作用
——2017上海国际智库咨询研究报告
上海市人民政府发展研究中心 编

出 版	格致出版社	
	上海 人 & 出版社	
	(200001 上海福建中路 193 号)	
发 行	上海人民出版社发行中心	
印 刷	上海商务联西印刷有限公司	
开 本	787×1092 1/16	
印 张	23.5	
插 页	12	
字 数	428,000	
版 次	2018 年 9 月第 1 版	
印 次	2018 年 9 月第 1 次印刷	
ISBN 978 - 7 - 5432 - 2916 - 7/F · 1154		
定 价	118.00 元